P9-EML-594

CHILD DEVELOPMENT

The Emerging Self

PRENTICE-HALL PSYCHOLOGY SERIES

A. T. Jersild, Editor

PRENTICE-HALL INTERNATIONAL, INC., *London*
PRENTICE-HALL OF AUSTRALIA, PTY., LTD., *Sydney*
PRENTICE-HALL OF CANADA, LTD., *Toronto*
PRENTICE-HALL OF INDIA (PRIVATE) LTD., *New Delhi*
PRENTICE-HALL OF JAPAN, INC., *Tokyo*

CHILD DEVELOPMENT

The Emerging Self

DON C. DINKMEYER

Chairman, Psychology Department
National College of Education
Evanston, Illinois

Prentice-Hall, Inc., *Englewood Cliffs, New Jersey*

PRENTICE-HALL, INC., *Englewood Cliffs, N.J.*

Current printing (last digit):
12 11 10 9 8 7 6 5 4

Library of Congress
Catalog Card No.: 65-21178

PRINTED IN THE UNITED STATES OF AMERICA
13040-C

PREFACE

Child Development: The Emerging Self emphasizes both the internal growth forces and the external adjustment processes related to the "emerging self." At the same time the child is developing internally, he must learn to adjust himself to the problems of self and those about him. While not providing a detailed analysis of all the factors involved in the growth process, this book is instead an overview of the entire field of child development and is accompanied by references to authors who have treated certain of these aspects of development in greater detail.

Various theoretical positions are presented, but the significance of self theory and the specific pattern and style of life in understanding the individual child are stressed throughout the text. Points of view are documented by research in all of the areas. The book aims to provide the reader with the ability to recognize individuality in the child and work with the theory and principles of child development in facilitating the child's total development.

Although the book is organized on a conceptual basis, the emphasis is always on the relationship between these developmental processes. The book first introduces the reader to the general field of child development and its background. This introduction is followed by references to the varied points of view which have had an influence upon research, child study techniques, and theories in the field of child development for our better understanding of the child and the development of human behavior. It is suggested that the student will become most competent in his understanding of the child if he attempts to apply and utilize some of these theories and techniques in the study of an individual.

The chapters are organized to focus on certain pertinent issues which should direct the attention of the reader to some of the major concerns in the area of child development. Within the content of the chapters, the reader will find questions that are partially based on the knowledge of what has been read, but which should also extend the ability of the reader to apply and go beyond the data to the implications of this knowledge for working with children. These questions are placed within the body of the text to cause the reader to stop and ponder the implications of some of the material he is reading. Questions in this form should enable the student to become truly ego-involved in the concepts presented within the book.

A readings list is included beginning on page 394, which has extensively keyed articles from a large variety of readings books to each chapter of the book. This list should enable the interested or advanced student to go into greater detail in each of the areas covered by the text.

Each chapter attempts to present some significant research on the area involved. It also will point out particular articles on the reading list that might be of special interest while directing the reader to books particularly related to the chapter topic. At the conclusion of each chapter there will be a brief discussion of the implications of the material concerned for teachers and parents.

The student is encouraged to become acquainted with several children to the extent that he may see some of the principles of human development in action. Where the book is used in connection with a course, certainly required observation experiences would add considerable depth to the content of the course.

It is the hope of the author that this text will provide a comprehensive survey of the child development area, and specific implications for practical work with the child in school or home. It should enable the individual to apply a human theory of motivation to an understanding of relationships with the child.

Many persons have helped me in the preparation of this book. I am grateful for the opportunity to learn about children through observation of my own children and other children I have had the privilege of knowing as an elementary and high school teacher, camp instructor, athletic coach, and certainly as a psychologist in the schools and in private practice. These children have taught me as much about human development as any experiences in the classroom or in reading.

Certainly one who writes in a field that is as broad as the area of child development must acknowledge a debt to those who have preceded him, both for their theoretical assumptions and their specific research. These people I have named by citing their writings and research. This should serve both to acknowledge their contribution to the broad field and guide the reader to the original sources of much of this material.

I would like to thank Priscilla Cooper for her assistance during the early development of this manuscript. I wish also to acknowledge the contribution of my colleagues in the Psychology Department who have provided me with a regular source of stimulation in this area, especially the help of Sara Ewald and Robert Greising who assisted in the critical analysis of this material in its early stages. In addition, the reviews and constructive suggestions contributed by Dr. Arthur DeLong, Dr. Reuben Rusch, Dr. Weldon Frase, and Dr. Gerald Kowitz were most helpful.

Sincere thanks are in order for the assistance of the people at Prentice-Hall. An important influence on this material has been received in the form of the critical review and evaluation which was conducted by the professional reviewers, Dr. Arthur Jersild and Dr. Don Hamachek. They also helped by providing leads to material which expanded the content of this volume.

I would like to acknowledge the support provided by my family during my prolonged preoccupation with the project. In particular I acknowledge the assistance of my wife who has provided regular typing assistance, patience, and encouragement in the development of this book.

D.D.

CONTENTS

To My Wife JANE

And Our Sons DON *and* JIM

1 INTRODUCTION TO CHILD DEVELOPMENT

Each person comes to the formal study of child development with a unique background and a unique set of expectations. Unlike the approach to many academic disciplines, opinions have already been formulated and points of view developed. For some, reading in fiction has provided a number of insights into the world of the child. Others have been exposed to newspaper columns and popular magazine articles. Still others bring their experiences as members of large families, as parents, siblings, baby-sitters, club leaders, or teachers in a variety of settings. Everyone also brings the experience of his own childhood, which obviously has an influence upon his understanding of the child.

The varied expectations of students influence their ability to profit from the study of the child. Some expect to develop specific competencies in preparation for parenthood or teaching. Others may seek to understand a specific child more adequately. Still others want to relate the material to their specific needs in any one of a large number of professions that require an understanding of child psychology. Thus, one recognizes that child development is frequently studied by students of widely varied experiences, backgrounds, and expectations. Their previous experience may even hinder their ability to understand child development.

THE PURPOSE OF STUDYING CHILDREN

Regardless of individual backgrounds and concerns, it is desirable to examine our purposes in studying child development. We want to acquire the following competencies:

1. The ability to recognize individuality. This implies the ability to recognize the uniqueness of each child's traits and view of life.
2. An understanding of the theories and principles of child development so that one can understand development in terms of

the varied hereditary, environmental, and self influences usually involved.
3. An increased effectiveness in observing and interpreting the pattern of individual behavior.
4. The ability to differentiate and evaluate the effectiveness of varying points of view in child study.
5. The development of a point of view and set of principles basic to guiding children more effectively in the learning and adjustment processes.
6. The ability to locate and utilize a variety of resource material from the vast literature on child development.

Thus, the student of child development should be involved not merely with learning a number of facts, but also with developing skills which can help him both personally and professionally throughout his life. This necessitates the continuing and purposeful observation of children in action, to supplement regular class study. As times goes on, he will be able to apply his knowledge and experience to interact more effectively with children.

ALLIED FIELDS OF STUDY

Child development is a broad behavioral science that draws upon many fields. The child development specialist must truly be multidisciplinary by giving consideration to findings from scientists and students in related fields.

Anthropology

Anthropologists have contributed much to the understanding of children by pointing out cultural influences on the developing personality. Their studies have brought an awareness of the effects of different cultures and even of the effects of regional cultures within single countries. They have shown the importance of socioeconomic status as a factor to consider in understanding the child. Anthropology, by pointing out the effect of culture on values, attitudes, and ideals, clarifies how a culture helps shape development.

The contribution of anthropology to child study can be explored more thoroughly in many books and journals, including:

Benedict, Ruth, *Patterns of Culture*. New York: Houghton Mifflin Company, 1934.

Linton, Ralph, *The Cultural Background of Personality*. New York: Appleton-Century-Crofts, 1945.

Mead, Margaret and F. C. Macgregor, *Growth and Culture*. New York: G. P. Putnam's Sons, 1951.

Biology

Biological research has brought an awareness of the influence of hereditary factors on child development. The study of prenatal functioning and early postnatal development is a specific contribution of the biologist, to whom much of our understanding of genetics and other aspects of physical growth is due. For further study, refer to:

Berelson, Bernard and Gary Steiner. *Human Behavior: An Inventory of Scientific Findings*. New York: Harcourt, Brace & World, Inc., 1964.

Gesell, Arnold, *Infancy and Human Growth*. New York: The Macmillan Company, 1928.

Psychology

Psychology has made a major contribution to the field of child study through its development of (1) various points of view about human behavior and (2) techniques for measuring individual differences. The psychologist has been interested in research and experimentation, and many of the studies presented in this book were developed and presented by psychologists. Also, the child development specialist has been able to draw analogies and formulate hypotheses on the basis of general principles developed from the study of intelligence, motivation, emotion, learning, and other fields of general psychology. The student of child development will want to become familiar with a number of publications in the field of psychology which include:

Annual Review of Psychology. Palo Alto, Calif.: Annual Reviews, Inc.

Carmichael, L., *Manual of Child Psychology,* 2nd ed. New York: John Wiley & Sons, Inc., 1954.

Child Development. Yellow Springs, Ohio: Antioch Press.

Child Development Abstracts. Lafayette, Ind.: Society for Research in Child Development, Inc., Purdue University.

Child Psychology, Yearbook 62, Part I. Chicago: National Society for the Study of Education, 1963.

Hoffman, Martin L. and Lois W. Hoffman, *Review of Child Development Research,* 1. New York: Russell Sage Foundation, 1964.

Psychological Abstracts. Washington, D.C.: The American Psychological Association, Inc.

Sociology

The sociologist has been interested in the study of the behavior of man in the group. He has focused on the importance of the social situation in which behavior develops. Sociology's study of social forces emphasizes the fact that both at home and in school one is dealing with the child within the group. Behavior becomes particularly meaningful when seen in relationship to the social setting. Thus, sociology reflects the total personality as a function of human relationships. Suggested supplementary reading includes:

Bossard, James, *The Sociology of Child Development,* rev. ed. New York: Harper & Row, Publishers, Inc., 1954.

Clausen, John A. and Judith R. Williams, "Sociological Correlates of Child Behavior" in *Child Psychology,* The Sixty-second Yearbook of the National Society for the Study of Education, Part 1. Chicago, Ill.: The University of Chicago Press, 1963, p. 62.

Medicine

Child study has been influenced by many different areas in the field of medicine. Knowledge of the way glands affect general physiological functioning has led to research by medical personnel in some of the child development institutes on the effect of hormones and vitamins on child development. Medical research is also responsible for the increasing use of drugs in treating psychological disturbances of childhood. Pediatricians have emphasized the significance of the developmental history in understanding the individual. They have been particularly interested in such problems as feeding, toilet training, sleeping, and other early developmental habits, and are the source of much information about prenatal factors and nutritional influences.

Pediatricians have also been concerned with the establishment of norms and the assessment of the developmental status of children. The need for longitudinal studies—the continued study of the same children over an extended period of years—was shown by the problems that developed in the establishment of norms. The psychiatric and pediatric literature can be explored further in:

Kanner, Leo, *Child Psychiatry.* Springfield, Ill.: Charles C Thomas, Publisher, 1957.

Watson, E. H. and G. H. Lowrey, *Growth and Development of Children.* Chicago: Year Book Medical Publishers, 1962.

Education and Educational Psychology

The growth of education as a profession has been accompanied by the development of the field of educational psychology, which is devoted specifically to a study of the child in the educational setting. Educational psychologists have been concerned with problems involving the interrelationship of child development and educational practice, the psychology of learning, motivation, guidance within the school, and the assessment and evaluation of school children.

The student of child development will find the work of educational psychologists presented intensively in such materials as:

The Encyclopedia of Educational Research. New York: The Macmillan Company, 1960.

Handbook of Research on Teaching. Washington, D.C.: American Educational Research Association, 1963.

Review of Educational Research. Washington, D.C.: American Educational Research Association.

These publications were all prepared by the American Educational Research Association and provide a wealth of practical material on the child and his experiences in one of the most vital of his developmental tasks, that of functioning within the school and meeting its expectations.

INSTITUTES OF CHILD DEVELOPMENT AND CHILD STUDY

The student of child development should be aware of the large number of research institutions devoted to child study. This section will give a brief overview of some work already done at these institutions. They are constantly producing research of interest to both parents and teachers. The student who desires to do advanced study or who wants to become more familiar with some of the basic research in the field might obtain from these institutes (see list on page 408) information regarding their current research or a bibliography of their publications.

Some of the earliest growth studies were those started by W. Dearborn at Harvard in 1922. The Harvard Growth Study gave both mental and physical tests annually from the time of entrance into first grade until completion of high school to one of the largest school populations studied up to that time.

Bird Baldwin at the Iowa Child Welfare Research Station was one of the first to investigate such factors as the interrelationship of mental and physical development. He was also involved in studies of mental and physical growth curves as early as 1921.

Lewis Terman at Stanford conducted an intensive study of gifted children, which became a classic in the field.[1] These children were studied in detail beginning in 1921–1922. Follow-up studies occurred in 1927–1928, 1939–1940, and 1950–1952, and questionnaire contact was made as recently as 1955 and 1960.

Following is a brief overview of some of the types of research being conducted at child study institutes around the country. The student who is interested in a more extensive review of the institutes should refer to:

Kagan, Jerome, "American Longitudinal Research on Psychological Development," *Child Development,* 35 (1964), 1–32.

The Child Research Council (Denver, Colorado) has been functioning since 1923. Its major focus is on the entire life cycle of growth, with par-

[1] Lewis Terman, *Genetic Studies of Genius* (Stanford, Calif.: Stanford University Press, 1925–59), Vol. I-V.

ticular attention to the adaptations and adjustments of the individuals within the study. One of the objectives has been to search for laws that would make it possible to make predictions on an individual basis. Associated with the School of Medicine at the University of Colorado and under the leadership of a medical doctor, it has kept extensive medical records on all of the children involved, including records of physical growth, X-ray studies, blood samples, and basal metabolisms. There have also been extensive psychological tests of intellectual and affective functions in the attempt to determine the relationships of all aspects of development.

Fels Research Institute for the Study of Human Development (Yellow Springs, Ohio) operates four departments—physiology and neurophysiology, physical growth and biochemistry—a clear indication of its broad multidisciplinary approach. It has produced extensive studies of the autonomic nervous system and the relationship between this system and the behavior of individuals under varying conditions. There has been an attempt to develop a physiological basis for understanding some of the relationships that may exist between temperament and performance. The psychology department at Fels has investigated personality development extensively. Among the major problem areas under study at Fels have been the relationship between changes in IQ and personality; the influence of parental behavior and attitudes on a child's development; the long-term stability of personality traits from childhood throughout adulthood.

Because of the many disciplines involved in research at the Fels Institute, this must be considered one of the most complete longitudinal studies available anywhere. An example of their long-term intensive study of development can be found in a monograph by Sontag, Baker, and Nelson.[2] Second-generation children have been added to the study and promise to provide students of child development with a continuing series of significant information. While the major commitment at Fels has been to longitudinal study, cross-sectional and experimental approaches have also been utilized.

The Institute of Human Development (University of California, Berkeley, California) has been engaged in a longitudinal study of personality and behavior development in a group of normal children. This is essentially a genetic study, and has focused on clinical observation of the development of adjusted and maladjusted behavior. The investigators have charted, by age and sex, the frequency of various behaviors as reported

[2] L. Sontag, C. Baker, and V. Nelson, *Mental Growth and Personality Development: A Longitudinal Study*, Monographs of the Society for Research in Child Development (Yellow Springs, Ohio: Society for Research in Child Development, 1958) XXIII, No. 2.

by mothers over an extensive period of time. This research has been a basis for determining the types of problems which tend to increase with age, those which decline with age, and those which tend to reach a peak and then subside, as well as those which tend to show little or no relationship to age. The study has tended to raise questions about some facets of present personality theory and has given a more clear-cut picture of the development of normal children.[3]

Investigators at the University of California have also engaged in an intensive study of adolescence. Children first seen at eleven to twelve years of age were followed rather intensively for the next six years. Follow-up studies were conducted with this group when they were between thirty-eight and forty years of age.

The Berkeley Growth study under the direction of Nancy Bayley and Dorothy Eichorn began with infants within the first two months of life. Each child was seen at six-month intervals until eighteen years of age. Follow-up was conducted with the subjects at ages twenty-one, and between age twenty-one and twenty-five. Extensive data on the relationship between the development of intelligence, anthropometric data and maternal behavior have been collected.

The University of Minnesota Institute of Child Welfare has also been involved in long-term study of the development of children.

In one study,[4] the extent to which later adjustment can be predicted from earlier psychological measures and other data was examined, with a view to developing a screening instrument to identify children and adolescents with potential psychological difficulties. The institute, under the direction of John Anderson, has also conducted a follow-up study of its nursery school children. Contacted at about the age of twenty-eight years, the subjects were tested and interviewed. Comprehensive data on the adults and the earlier childhood information derived from records of mental tests, parent interviews, and behavioral observations are used to investigate the relationship between adult adjustment and early experience.

The Child Study Center at Yale University is a Department of Study, a Research facility, and a community resource for essential services to children and families. Staff members come from the discipline of psychiatry, psychoanalysis, clinical and educational psychology, pediatrics, psychiatric social work, public health, sociology, and nursing. There are three

[3] Jean MacFarlane, L. Allen, and M. Honzik, *A Developmental Study of the Behavior Problems of Normal Children between Twenty-one Months and Fourteen Years* (Los Angeles: University of California Press, 1954).

[4] Institute of Child Development, *A Survey of Children's Adjustment Over Time: A Report to the People of Nobles County, Minneapolis* (Minneapolis: University of Minnesota Press, 1959).

divisions: Child Psychiatry Unit, Child Development Unit, and the Nursery School Unit. Research interests are diversified and have produced publications such as "Modern Perspectives in Child Development." [5]

The Merrill-Palmer School (Detroit, Michigan) longitudinal studies of individual development are designed to disclose the pattern of each child's growth and his total family constellation and to determine ways in which this fundamental knowledge can contribute to an understanding of the basic processes of growth. The school has developed techniques for appraising developmental status and progress and for utilizing the concept of maturity indicators, which are any clearly defined stage of development either of function or of a structure or body part. Complete records are kept on the children at Merrill-Palmer for use in evaluating their stages of maturity. Measurements are not considered as set points in development, but rather as a range or zone of performance.

The Institute of Child Study (University of Toronto, Toronto, Ontario) bases its research on observation of the many aspects of the normal child's development, including physical, mental, personality, social, perceptual, motor, and physiological factors. Its unique focus has developed from studies related to the Security Theory of the former director, W. Blatz, who believed that a person was secure to the extent that he could make decisions and accept the consequences of his decision. According to Blatz, "independent security," although perhaps never fully obtainable, represented the ideal adjustment.[6]

Gesell Institute of Child Development (New Haven, Connecticut) has concentrated on studies concerning the readiness of children for school. Its clinical services have been available for children from birth through age sixteen, and it also provides lectures for parent groups and syndicated columns on child problems. An interesting study has related to the development of a school placement examination. Research investigators have reported the development of a fairly satisfactory method of determining a child's developmental level, and hence proper school placement. The Gesell Institute has been conducting workshops for developmental guidance coordinators on the use of this examination service within the school.

Iowa Child Welfare Research Station (State University of Iowa, Iowa City, Iowa) has been known for some of the most significant historical studies in the field of child development. One project, the development of a program for education in human behavior, led by Dr. Ralph Ojemann, has focused on preventive psychiatry and the development of materials of a mental health nature for use in the schools.

[5] A. Gesell and F. Ilg, *Child Development* (New York: Harper & Row, Publishers, Inc., 1949).

[6] Institute of Child Study, *Studies of the Growth of Security* (Toronto, Ont.: University of Toronto Press, 1959), and W. Blatz, *Understanding the Young Child* (New York: William Morrow & Co., Inc., 1944).

The Institute for Child Study (University of Maryland, College Park, Maryland) originally developed by Daniel Prescott, is unique in that it has focused primarily on servicing school systems and providing leaders for child study groups. The purpose of this work is to arrive at a better understanding of all children through intensive study of individual children. The workshop and field services of the institute have been utilized in many communities throughout the United States.

This brief presentation should make one aware of the great amount of time, effort, and money involved in child development research by formally organized institutes.

THE WHOLE CHILD AND GROWTH INTERRELATIONSHIPS

To understand the child and his development you must recognize that no one factor can ever be discussed without considering its relationship to the whole. All growth and development are interrelated, whether they be the interaction of the organism with its environment, the effect of intellectual factors upon emotional development, or the influence of social factors in motivating the child. Although individual factors may be separated for academic consideration, interactions with the child will soon make you aware of the importance of interrelationships. As you come to see all growth as part of a pattern, you will more effectively understand the individual. Many facets of growth and development are confusing when viewed in isolation, but they take on meaning when related to the total pattern of physical and psychological growth.

Developmental information helps you to see the child in relationship both to normative expectations and to his own uniqueness and particular style of life. As your awareness of the significance of developmental patterns grows, the child will be seen in relationship to the sequence of development. It will be easier to understand his problems if you try to understand what he is specifically attempting to accomplish as an individual and how his efforts fit his particular pattern. The approach to understanding the child, then, is characterized by recognition that the individual has an indivisible unity. Any attempt to understand his behavior without seeing it in the light of the total pattern will prove ineffectual.

Basic to an understanding of behavior is recognition of the fact that the individual is constantly seeking to maintain or establish equilibrium. This implies that patterned behavior is inevitable. At any given time the individual is obviously making the most effective adjustment he knows how to make from his point of view. Thus, it is imperative to learn how he views the world and how he has come to interpret his environment and experiences.

1. What does the concept of the whole child and growth interrelationships imply for school records? Which types of record might be particularly effective in producing understanding of the child?
2. How might a study of growth interrelationships contribute to an understanding of a child who is having adjustment difficulties in the school or at home?
3. What are the implications for the organization of the schools and for the types of learning experiences in the theory which stresses the interrelationship of all growth?

FUNDAMENTAL NEEDS OF CHILDREN

A major purpose in studying child development is to help you relate to children effectively. In order to accomplish this it is necessary to integrate knowledge of children into a framework that facilitates action. Knowledge of need theory will be of great assistance. In order for the child to maintain the psychological equilibrium previously mentioned, there must be need satisfaction. Needs will be discussed at length in the chapter on emotional development; at this point we will merely indicate the child's fundamental needs.

1. The need to be loved and accepted unconditionally.
2. The need for security—to be safe and relatively free of threat.
3. The need to belong, to be a part of the group, and to feel identification and acceptance.
4. The need to be recognized, to gain approval, to feel significant and accepted for the way in which he functions.
5. The need to be independent, to take responsibility, and to make choices.

There are many needs. Much has already been said about them,[7] yet more could and will be said. Here it is important only to recognize that when these needs are denied or unmet, the development of the child will be affected. Need deprivation must be recognized, and action programs instituted to meet them.

4. How would you go about determining need deprivation in a specific child? Discuss the relationship of the basic needs to problems in a specific group of children you have observed.
5. What kinds of forces would affect needs and their potency for a given individual? Is need theory something we can deal with on a preventive basis, and if so, make specific recommendations?

[7] An interesting discussion of needs appears in James Hymes *Understanding Your Child* (Englewood Cliffs, N.J.: Prentice-Hall, Inc., 1952) in which the author refers to "the hunger inside."

Seeing the Pattern in Development

Growth theory and psychological theory both point to the significance of the pattern in comprehending the uniqueness of the individual. Child development specialists like Willard Olson[8] and Cecil Millard[9] have stressed the organismic point of view. This point of view interprets all aspects of development in relationship to a life pattern. In their longitudinal studies they have collected data which have made it possible to see all growth in relationship to a pattern. When comprehensive longitudinal data are available, more effective decisions can be made relative to the individual's adjustment and learning.

Adlerian theory has placed the greatest emphasis on the individual's style of life and his pattern of interaction. Adlerians believe that there is a basic unity to all behavior and that this can best be understood through an awareness of the child's style of life and the goal-directed nature of behavior. The style of life refers to the child's characteristic way of reacting based on his evaluation of self and society. The point of view is subjective. This theory takes a phenomenological approach similar to that of Carl Rogers,[10] Arthur Combs and Donald Snygg,[11] and Gordon Allport,[12] emphasizing the vital need to determine how the child sees the situation and how he feels about it. Stress here is placed on developing familiarity with the child's concept of self to facilitate empathizing with his view of the world.

The theories of Olson and Adler have dealt basically with different types of data—Olson with the primarily physical and mental, Adler with the psychological—but they are in general agreement in their emphasis on the importance of the pattern. In dealing with the child you must be careful to avoid looking at events and interactions as a series of unrelated events. Knowledge of the individual's style and pattern enables you to make predictions about behavior and growth. This approach requires an analysis of the direction in which the individual is moving in terms of both physical and psychological patterns. The parent or teacher who adheres to this point of view attempts to see all behavior in relationship to the whole. He is concerned with the specific event only in-so-far as it relates to the total behavioral pattern of the child. He avoids dealing with a

[8] Willard C. Olson, *Child Development*, 2nd ed. (Boston: D. C. Heath & Company, 1959).

[9] Cecil V. Millard, *The Elementary School Child: A Book of Cases* (New York: The Dryden Press, 1957).

[10] Carl Rogers, *Client-Centered Therapy* (Boston: Houghton Mifflin Company, 1951).

[11] Arthur Combs and Donald Snygg, *Individual Behavior* (New York: Harper & Row, Publishers, Inc., 1959).

[12] Gordon W. Allport, *Becoming, Basic Considerations for a Psychology of Personality* (New Haven: Yale University Press, 1955).

continual series of discrete events and instead has confidence that his knowledge of the total developmental pattern provides a sounder basis for long-term learning, development, and guidance.

---

6. John, age twelve, is the oldest child with a brother Bill, age ten, and sister Jean, age five. John does very well in school, while Bill excels athletically and in social contacts. Jean is the "queen" of the family and obtains service from both adults and siblings.

   John is very concerned that his answers in school be just right. He has considerable tension when examinations are announced and finds it difficult to concentrate as he would like to during the exams.

   Bill appears little concerned about academic demands and must be "pushed" regularly by both parents and teachers to accomplish work.

   John can always be counted on to use schoolwork as an excuse for not completing jobs at home. Bill often volunteers to help and regularly completes the chores expected of him.

   This description is limited by space. What other types of information would you need about these boys to understand them and assist them to function more effectively, as opposed to one who sees development as a series of discrete events would explain this behavior? How would one's actual approach to the child be affected as one comprehends the total pattern and the direction of psychological movement?

Development should be viewed as a product of hereditary, environmental, and self forces. The continual interaction between heredity and environment, combined with the child's primary reaction pattern and his capacity to choose, are the key factors in understanding development. To function effectively with children, it is necessary to have (1) a broad framework, which helps to set guidelines and interpret both behavior and misbehavior and (2) a knowledge of the child's specific pattern. This prevents the adult from dealing with the child on a haphazard basis dictated by the moods of the moment. Instead, he can operate on the basis of already established principles that have been proved effective in understanding and guiding the child's development.

POINTS OF VIEW IN CHILD STUDY

As one delves into the subject, it soon becomes apparent that there are two major approaches to the study of the child. One school of thought is concerned primarily with the factors in development that can be measured objectively; the other focuses primarily on the subjective aspects of the child's experience. The psychologist who uses the objective point of view in his research is primarily concerned with quantitative measurements of physical growth, the development of ability, and other such data. The psychologist who identifies with the subjective point of view is mainly concerned with the child's perceptions and feelings—in other words, with the aspect of the child referred to as the self.

Psychologists might also be divided on the basis of their allegiance to nomothetic laws—those that are generally applicable to all children—or idiographic laws—those that apply to the child as an individual. A considerable amount of normative information has been derived from nomothetic studies, information about the average child and about typical behavior of children at various stages in life. The proponents of idiographic laws feel that significant research and effective practice must both be based upon intensive study of the individual—as they would put it, upon the law of the case. These psychologists, obviously, are in accord with those who have stressed the significance of understanding the developmental pattern and the life style.

The techniques for child study can also be divided by contrasting the cross-sectional, status study with the longitudinal study. In evaluating reading and research it will always be significant to consider whether the data were obtained from a cross-sectional status study or from a longitudinal study.

The cross-sectional, status study is one in which single testings are applied to a large number of cases at the same point in a chronological sequence, e.g., all sixth graders or all eight year olds. Statistical techniques are used with the data obtained to form conclusions about the average child. A composite picture of the average child's course of development is made by combining the results of many cross-sectional testings at different points in the time sequence.

The longitudinal study generally deals with a smaller number of individuals and follows each of them over a longer period of time, usually through several cycles of development.

It is important to recognize that the longitudinal method and the cross-sectional, status study method provide different types of data. The cross-sectional, status study always deals with a child at a specific time or place in his total developmental sequence; it cannot tell what has happened to him prior to this point, nor does it consider his rate of growth. The longitudinal study takes into account the unique designs of individual children who possess highly individualized rates of development; it is considered vital to appraise all of these factors over a period of time. These long-term investigations are characterized by repeated observations or measurements of the same individual in order to consider the pertinent developmental factors.

A POINT OF VIEW IN UNDERSTANDING BEHAVIOR AND MISBEHAVIOR

Insights gained from the fields of developmental psychology, psychiatry, counseling, and learning theory have provided a framework for understanding and correcting problems in the educational process. They can also help to establish guidelines for the understanding of behavior and misbehavior in a number of other personal and professional relationships with children.

To function effectively with children you need to establish a set of formulations that account for the why of behavior and that permit development of a therapeutic approach to the learning and developmental process. The principles presented here have been found effective in understanding and guiding behavior. They essentially present a type of bias about human behavior. The reader should evaluate critically this opinion and decide what modifications are necessary to adapt these principles to his practice. It will be a good idea to make similar critical appraisals of all points of view presented in this book, as obviously you must integrate new principles and ideas with your own philosophy and with your personality assets and limitations.

The suggested framework proceeds on the assumption that every human being is of value and has a right to optimum development as a person of usefulness to society. It recognizes that every human being is different from all others and possesses a unique set of goals, percepts, liabilities, and assets. Each individual seeks significance in his own manner. Our job is to assist each child, without force or pressure, to grow in relationship to his uniqueness through a process which takes into account his uniqueness and makes him an acceptable and contributing member of society.

We would recognize that developmental rates vary from child to child and that learning will be most effective when the proper stage of maturation or readiness is reached. Readiness is not seen as occurring only at certain periods, such as entrance into elementary school or moving ahead to junior high school, but rather as a factor with which all who interact with the child must be concerned.

Every child brings to the school his family, his culture, his goals, and his percepts. We must recognize how this uniqueness affects all of his interactions. Taking this into account, we believe that the utilization of intrinsic motives will generally be most effective in meeting the goals, purposes, interests, and needs of the varying individuals.

We see the child as proceeding through a series of sequential developmental tasks which must be completed for satisfactory growth in our society. The tasks occur in all of the areas of development. When the challenge of one task has been met successfully, the child has the courage to enter into the following tasks. Failure to accomplish the task, however, creates problems in meeting personal, social responsibilities.

Our framework believes the democratic process to be most effective in promoting growth in the individual. It acknowledges that the democratic process may not always be the most efficient, but if the objective is development, then the focus must be on methods which foster development most effectively.

It is fundamental, then, to begin by recognizing the individuality of each child. This implies an awareness of both the child's assets and his liabilities. In order to deal with him most effectively we will find that a knowledge of the child's assets will be of greatest use in promoting his development. However, we must not come to believe that understanding will develop from any mere quantification of traits. In our cognizance of individuality we must seek to determine how the individual searches for significance. Primarily through informal observation and occasionally through formal techniques we become aware of the ways in which the child views the world. We can thus determine his uniqueness, his purposes, and his style of life, and use this knowledge to maximize his development within society.

Biochemical individuality was demonstrated in the research of Dearborn and Rothney[13] when they found that in over three thousand children no two cases presented exactly the same developmental pattern. This is a surprising finding in the physical realm, and we can be even more certain of this same uniqueness in the psychological realm. We therefore caution against any attempt to type children in groups as gifted, slow-learning, culturally deprived, underachieving, or antisocial, if the intent is to give each member of a group identical treatment. The establishment of groups does not destroy or eliminate individuality. Recognition of the great value and significance of individuality would avert the error of assuming that proper grouping eliminates individual differences.

The child is studied in relationship to his readiness, his rate of development, and his interests. The varying levels of individual development and maturity should be considered whenever educational plans are being made. Proper educational placement frequently necessitates an increase in the individualization of instruction. This approach suggests that we act on research findings which have already demonstrated that the mean, median, or modal scores are not representative of the great range of individuality usually found in the group. The range of differences in almost all of the crucial factors increases as the child matures. Cook's finding of a four-year range in general intelligence among first graders and the increase in

[13] W. Dearborn and J. Rothney, *Predicting the Child's Development* (Cambridge, Mass.: Science-Art, 1941).

this range to almost eight years by the sixth grade demonstrates the increase in variability.[14] As the child matures, variability increases.

UNDERSTANDING OF GOALS

A recognition of the purposive nature of behavior assists in understanding the child's actions. We hold that most behavior is purposive and that actions are directed toward goals. This approach prefers purposivism to mechanism in any attempt to understand and guide behavior. While we would not deny causation, we feel that for most individuals it may be more important to become aware of the purpose than to look pessimistically at the cause, for, as we become aware of the purpose of behavior, we are then in a position to attempt to redirect and re-educate the child. Thus, we take a stand with a type of finalistic causality, believing that for the practitioner comprehending the goal for the future, an awareness of purpose is vital. This implies that students, teachers, and parents must become, in a sense, students of psychological movement. The movement will point to the direction of the purpose. The goal is really a stimulus that motivates and directs the action of the child.

It is important to remember that goals may be conscious or unconscious. The individual is not always aware of his purposes or goals. The child may pursue many goals to achieve satisfaction and security; these goals do not necessarily produce interpersonal conflicts or misbehavior. In the individual's attempts to meet his needs he may, however, resort to some of the goals of misbehavior, which have been listed by Dreikurs as: (1) the attention-getting mechanism, (2) the struggle for power and superiority, (3) the desire to retaliate or revenge his own feelings, (4) the display of inadequacy, inferiority, or assumed disability.[15]

A child may prefer to seek attention in a pleasant manner, but he will act negatively if he has to, because this is better than being ignored. The child for whom attention is a primary goal will sometimes seek to achieve it through positive and successful efforts. Other children may resort to charm or cuteness. Often it will appear that the child's main purpose is keeping people busy with him. The child whose goal is power sets out to show that he can do what he wants and that he will not do what you want him to do. Even when you defeat this child, he is all the more convinced of the value of his goal, power. After all, by subduing him have you not also placed a great value on it? Another time this child may merely attempt to find a more effective method of achieving his goal.

[14] W. Cook, "Individual Differences and Curriculum Practice," *Journal of Educational Psychology*, Vol. XXXIX (1948), 141.

[15] Rudolf Dreikurs, *Psychology in the Classroom* (New York: Harper & Row, Publishers, Inc., 1957).

The child whose goal is revenge believes his place can be won only by being extremely disliked. Antisocial behavior for these children may be rewarding in terms of the place it permits the child to take within the group. For some individuals status may be developed more effectively by going against the group's wishes than by conforming. The term vicious is actually viewed by these children as a symbol of success, for their goal is to retaliate and your response to their provocation of either you or the group is their triumph.

The child who uses a display of inadequacy to attain his goal is frequently so discouraged that he cannot believe in his own worth. He uses or develops his inability as a protection. He does not participate or contribute, hoping to avoid what he anticipates would be even more discouraging experiences. This child will tend to exaggerate his inability so that nothing is required or expected from him.

We can all learn to do a better job of recognizing some of the goals of misbehavior. Observing the individual's movements, checking our own spontaneous reactions to the child's misbehavior, and noting the way in which the child responds to our corrective efforts are all ways in which we can help ourselves. In the section on Motivation we will deal more extensively with ways of diagnosing the child's goals.

All behavior, then, has social meaning and gains relevance in relation to a specific social setting. The child will best be understood when he is seen in terms of his specific social environment and his set of interpersonal relationships. This point of view places social striving in a primary instead of a secondary position in explaining human behavior.

The approach discussed here should make us aware of the role of various defense mechanisms in reducing tension. Understanding them may well provide an explanation of the child's behavior and offer direct clues to the meaning of his conduct. We could also say that the child's feelings serve as indicators of his psychological movement.

MAJOR LIFE TASKS

Each individual is confronted with three major life tasks—work, social, and sexual. As we observe his methods of coping with these major tasks, we can more adequately understand his behavior. The approach is always consistent with the life style, giving a clear picture of his view of life, his concern for others, his cooperativeness, and his courage. Failure to function in school according to expectations is a symptom of lack of courage or fear of cooperating. Primary work tasks frequently appear first in the home, but some children are successful in evading all the duties assigned to them by parents. Here we can see the way in which the child has already chosen to deal with some major life tasks. The school usually does not permit an easy evasion of the work task. When the child comes to school and encounters responsibilities, the characteristic manner in which he accepts the challenges of the school can provide a picture of his adjustment to life.

The social task involves getting along first with other members of the family and eventually with one's peers. The individual's social relationships reflect his attitudes toward society. Observation will help us to determine whether he is moving toward people, against people, or away from people. The child's social interactions give us real insight into his general adjustment to life's expectations.

Every child eventually becomes a man or woman, and he must start in childhood to play a sexual role appropriate to his culture. Some understanding of the child's feelings of adequacy can be obtained by observing the manner in which he undertakes to play an appropriate sexual role. The boy who insists upon demonstrating his virility may really be concerned about his capacity to play an appropriate sexual role.

The major life tasks that we have described so far are those human beings must deal with in different settings throughout life. In attempting to understand the child we must become familiar with developmental tasks and the way in which the child approaches them. This knowledge will assist in determining whether the specific child seems to be achieving an appropriate balance between dependence and independence—namely, an appropriate affectual pattern. Is he achieving a wholesome set of attitudes toward himself? It is important to recognize that the major life tasks arise in varying degrees at various times in the life of the individual and that his response to these tasks and their adequate accomplishment are what enable him to adjust effectively.

INDIVIDUAL PERCEPTIONS

Every individual exists in his own perceptual field. For him, reality is his life space or private world. We then are concerned with the way in which the individual experiences himself and his total environment at the instant of action. The child's behavior makes sense to him because it accords with his view of the world. From the point of view of the behaver, everything he does seems reasonable and necessary at the time he does it. If we are to be successful in changing his behavior, it will be important to comprehend his subjective view and his private logic. It is vital to see through his eyes and hear through his ears. Our listening, then, will be concerned with discerning the message his words and actions convey. It is often helpful as we either listen or observe, to ask how we would behave if his physical make-up, relationships, and experiences were ours. Empathy precedes understanding. It will come when you attempt to put yourself in the other's place.

A simple surface manipulation that achieves the teacher's immediate goal will not fundamentally change the child's view, purposes, or goal. If he feels, "People are against me. I don't belong. I'm the worst student in this group," he will function accordingly regardless of the objective facts. We must, therefore, become familiar with methods of assessing the child's style of life and self concept.

Each individual makes personal interpretations of his experiences and assigns unique meaning to all that goes on about him. He does not really have experiences in common with others; rather he translates each experience into his own terms. This implies that the individual has a freedom of choice and does decide for himself. The individualized interpretation of experiences underscores the importance of assessing the style of life. Certainly it points to the problems in any educational approaches which fail to take into consideration the subjective view of the individual.

Behavior is always consistent with the concept of self, and perception changes under conditions that have relevance to the individual's basic need to enhance this self. The child is always moving toward growth and self-enhancement as he perceives it. Close inspection of his behavior, then, will point to his goals. Rogers has described this as follows: "Behavior is basically the goal-directed attempt of the organism to satisfy its need as experienced, in the field as perceived."[16]

We can come to a better understanding of the individual if we see his behavior in terms of meeting some present need. Johnny's misbehavior may be most distressing to us but at the same time may provide insight into the types of corrective action we will need to take.

We contend, then, that the organism reacts as a whole to the perceptual field. Any stimulus-response explanation of behavior eliminates the all important intervening variable of the organism itself, denying the individuality of responses. We believe that the individual is more than the receiver of stimuli. We would add to the S-R model a S-I-R concept, indicating the capacity of the individual to interpret and perceive as he chooses. This approach cautions against assuming mechanical explanation of cause and effect—the child is what he is because he has been rejected; there was a divorce; he has a physical handicap. This type of automatic and mechanical evaluation of children does not produce insight. We must consider, instead, how the child interprets the parent's feelings, the divorce, or the physical handicap. How does he use the environmental situation?

This suggests that the child will live up to his reputation. If we treat him as "difficult to teach," "incorrigible," or "impossible to discipline," he

[16] Rogers, *Client-Centered Therapy*, p. 491.

will often justify our expectations. His actions are always a reflection of his present values and goals. Corrective efforts will of necessity deal with methods of changing his view of the world.

NEED DEPRIVATION

We believe that there is obviously a hierarchy of needs as Maslow has indicated.[17] The physiological needs, such as food, sleep, and exercise are basic to our understanding of the child's behavior. We need to attend to them but must also recognize that some may be beyond our particular capacity to manage effectively. Our deeper concern is with the psychological needs of feeling secure, belonging, being accepted, being loved, being able to love, and being approved. We know that the individual must develop a feeling of self-esteem and self-actualization—a feeling of worth or worthiness—in order to function effectively within the school or family atmosphere.

A considerable amount of anxiety or insecurity, resulting in lessened effectiveness in the life and developmental tasks, can be closely related to need deprivation and can affect the purposive responses the child chooses as a reaction to a situation. When needs are not met, there is fertile ground for the development of aggression, withdrawal, learning disabilities, and truancy. We would strongly suggest, however, that these may all be looked upon as symptoms. It is our responsibility to seek ways to reduce need deprivation and at the same time to become more perceptive of why the individual uses need deprivation in this manner.

Disturbances in behavior or adjustment and learning should be looked upon as signals or symptoms of psychological disturbance. We would avoid treating the fever and suggest dealings with the infection. These disturbances are interfering with normal development. In order to achieve academic learning most effectively, the child must be able to invest appropriate psychic energy in his school experience.

The psychology of use indicates that it is not the possession of mental capacity, but the use to which the individual puts the capacity that is our concern. We should investigate each type of learning and behavioral disturbance, in light of the total situation and our previous assumptions about the individual's functioning. Frequently, we will find that children do not function because for them the material is unrealistic. It does not fit into their present conception of the world. For other children, the school material may have little intrinsic value. It in no way relates to their goals, purposes, and needs. Still other children may not wish to change

[17] A. Maslow, *Motivation and Personality* (New York: Harper & Row, Publishers, Inc., 1954).

their values or to abandon immaturity and ineffectiveness. They may not wish to compete with either the group or their own capacities. A child may feel that caution is necessary because too much progress on his part may result in certain pressures or demands.

If a child does not learn, is there something he fears? What purpose is served by this behavior? We need to come to grips with a number of factors in understanding any individual's failure to function. For some children, failure to function is caused by the dynamics of discouragement, overambition, inadequacy, and feelings of not being as much as is expected. For example, if a child feels that he does not belong in the group he will obviously be distracted from accomplishing tasks set for the group. Some children lack confidence in their ability and are sure they will not succeed. They assume that they are worthless, inadequate, or failures, and concern with their status hampers their positive movement toward a functioning capacity. They assume that they cannot either compete or function. The overambitious lack the courage to be imperfect; they cannot accept the fact that all of us have certain imperfections and failures. As a result, if they cannot be first, the most, or the best, then they become the last or the worst. These children have a characteristically pessimistic view of life, feeling it really is not worth the trouble. Comparing themselves with their peers and feeling inferior, they do not try to keep up to par.

Symptoms serve to keep the child safe and protect him from having to extend himself and accomplish what he fears he cannot do. This type of distorted perception and concept of self affects the evaluation of all his experience and serves as a continual limitation to functioning in children who do not wish to compete, who are concerned about taking on any additional responsibility. Learning for them is more threatening than the situation where they do not learn.

Fundamental to our approach, then, is the concept of multiple causation in understanding problems in either learning or personal social behavior. We would always encourage child study to consider all the significant factors in child study. What role do basic physical factors play in studying the individual? What clues are provided by his growth rate, level of maturity, health history, general appearance, or motor skills? Certainly, his love relationships with parents, siblings, and other significant persons outside the family are highly influential. Other insights can be derived from the cultural background that the child is internalizing and the type of socialization processes he is experiencing in the home, the community, and the school. Certainly the peer group and the role that he seeks and obtains in it can provide a partial explanation of behavior. In what ways does he achieve status? What is his concept of self; how does he feel about himself; what meaning does he give to all of his experiences? An investigation of the child's capacity to learn and his educational achievement should be conducted. We need to investigate his emotional reactions and to assess the adjustment mechanisms he uses in coping with his problems. Beyond multiple causation, however, is an added dimension —the investigation of purposes, goals, and the style of life.

Research at the University of Michigan by Olson and Hughes has indicated the relevance of physical and psychological developmental patterns to academic achievement. As we learn more about these developmental patterns, we will be better able to understand the relationship of different types of growth to academic success. In the psychological realm, the individual's evaluation of self and society also assists in determining the "law of the case," or style of life, familiarity with which will give real direction to counseling, corrective work, and re-educational efforts. This characteristic pattern of responses is the guideline for the individual's action. A knowledge of this life plan helps us see in a meaningful manner psychological movement. Thus, we can understand not only misbehavior, but the ways in which the individual achieves the healthy goals of satisfaction and security.

2 THEORIES ON CHILD DEVELOPMENT

There are many theories on how the child grows, matures, and develops. One school of thought looks upon development as a continual series of responses to stimuli, apparently without any action or selection on the child's part. Others view development in terms of past experiences and stress the influence of certain types of "traumatic experiences."

Obviously, then, your personal and professional relationships with children will be affected by the point of view you eventually adopt. Let us, therefore, examine some of the theories that have influenced child development research and practice. This knowledge will help you place in perspective some of the issues discussed in subsequent chapters. It will also enable you to recognize the influence of a particular commitment on the design of a research study or some practical recomendations for child management. Although it is not the place of the child development course to cover child development theories extensively, it is pertinent that you be aware of the place of theory in the decisions that others have made and that you will make in working with children. The points of view we will consider have served to explain behavior and influence the practice of parents, teachers, pediatricians, and psychologists.

THE PSYCHOANALYTIC POINT OF VIEW

The theoretical formulations of psychoanalytic theory have provided, perhaps, some of the most pervasive influences on child development theory and child training practices of recent decades. Psychoanalytic theory has attempted to explain both unconscious and conscious development. Sigmund Freud was the father of this school of thought, and his influence on the thinking of psychologists, psychiatrists, and psychoanalysts has been extensive. Although his work was primarily with adults, he paid considerable attention to the recall of childhood experiences and gave initial emphasis to the importance of developmental history in studying the child. His theory stressed the vital role of early childhood experiences in the formulation of certain patterns of behavior.

The psychoanalytic point of view can be viewed as a biological theory of personality, although the biological drives are placed within a social context. The theory maintains that unless the basic drives, i.e., instincts, are gratified during early interactions, the child will leave infancy with some degree of fixation, and will be somewhat impaired in his ability to adapt and adjust to life situations. When gratification during the succeeding stages of development is insufficient, the child will fall back on earlier patterns of behavior for gratification, a process which the psychoanalyst calls regression.

These concepts of fixation and regression are related to a sequence of development. In Freudian theory, the personality progresses from the oral stage to the anal and then the genital. The experiences that occur during each period are believed to affect the character traits manifested throughout life. Freud stressed the decisive role of early infancy and childhood in laying the basic character structure of the individual.

Psychoanalytic theory postulates a psychic economy, a structure made up of three parts—the id, the ego, and the superego. The id is present at birth. It is concerned solely with need satisfaction and is controlled by the pleasure principle, seeking pleasure and avoiding pain. The ego decides between internal needs, manifested by the id, and external demands. The ego plays an executive role, representing the reality principle in-so-far as it limits the pleasure principle of the id. The ego has an important part in the processes of maturing and assuming responsibility. The superego represents the social regulator of the psychic structure—those family values and adult figures of significance in the child's early life. Sometimes referred to as the conscience, the superego serves as a censoring agent. One function of the ego, then, is to serve as the bond between the assumed aggressive nature of man (id) and societal influences (superego) and to keep them in balance.

Freud believed that the developmental process consisted of a series of fixed stages through which every child passed in sequential order unless he became fixated. The individual, Freud postulated, had impulses to use psychic energy and chose to use it to obtain pleasure through different regions of the body as he moved from one stage to another. This energy impulse toward an object was called "cathexis" by Freud.

The first of the four classical periods identified by the Freudian is the oral period, in which the child's most organized source of gratification is sucking. Tension and relaxation revolve around the sucking urge and the relief created by the act of sucking. It is during this period that the child develops his feelings about acceptance and, according to Erikson, his basic sense of trust or distrust in people. This is a period in life of maximum passive dependency.[1] "Oral type" in a psychological report characterizes the individual as primarily passive and dependent.

The second crucial period, according to Freud, is the anal period which occurs when the child is ready to control his excretory functions. During this period of acquiring bowel and bladder control, the child must integrate the impulses of retention and elimination. At this time the anal zone is of greatest importance in the child's development. His rapidly developing abilities come into conflict with adult demands and his continuing needs for love and security. The issue of toilet training frequently places the development of abilities and the need for security into conflict. While the control of urination and defecation can give the child a feeling of increased power and self-respect, he may also become anxious and concerned about his security at this time. The anal stage finds the child striving for mastery of his external world. It is at this time that traits related to orderliness, punctuality, and thrift are believed to develop. Negativism is also a characteristic trait of the "anal" period.

The third period known as the phallic or "oedipal" period, is the stage in which the child becomes aware of genital differences. This is also described by the Freudians as the period in which he is most aware of his love for his parents. This love is originally directed toward both parents, but during the phallic period the Freudians believe that the child develops a gradually increasing affection for the parent of the opposite sex, referred to as the "Oedipus complex." The boy, for example, develops a new form of love for his mother and senses the father as his rival. These mixed feelings about the father can create anxiety, and have been described in detail in terms of the "oedipal" situation. In terms of behavior, the child is alternately very cooperative or exceedingly difficult to live with. Personality is now beginning to take shape, and defense mechanisms, the characteristic method of dealing with adjustment problems, are becoming apparent.

In the fourth or latency period the child diverts some of his primary love interests to people outside the home. Initial repression seems to arise at this stage, which is also described as the time in which the child, more than at any preceding time, extends his concerns to his peers. He is now becoming involved in education, society, and the development of his superego. The analysts have tended to describe this period as the calm before the storm of puberty.

Freud's libido theory was built around the construct that libido is sexual energy with which zones other than the genital are endowed in childhood; associated with it is the pleasure obtained from such functions as

[1] Erik Erikson, *Childhood and Society* (New York: W. W. Norton & Company, Inc., 1950).

eating and regulation of the bowels. Psychoanalysts place a prime importance on the libido in describing all of human motivation.

For the Freudians, then, a child passes through stages characterized by an emphasis on various areas of libidinal localization. If anxieties at any stage become too great, the child may regress to an earlier stage for gratification. The Freudians postulate a definite intrapsychic organization of personality combined with the development of certain defense mechanisms, including fixation, regression, projection, denial, sublimation, repression, and others in which tensions are relieved by redirection. This has been one of the major contributions of Freudian theory.

One of Freud's major contributions was in the recognition of unconscious motivation. He pointed out that we frequently are not aware of why we act as we do. His concern with unconscious motives influenced psychology to deal with the whys of human behavior instead of simply describing what people do.

---

1. According to Freudian theory, some motivational forces are unconscious. What implications does this theory have for the effective functioning of the teacher or the parent; for learning theory and motivation?

Although Freud's contact with children was limited, several of his followers did extensive work with children, two of the better-known child analysts being Melanie Klein and Anna Freud. According to Klein children experience sexual impulses and anxiety even in the earliest years. She developed the play technique as a substitute for free association; she also stressed the symbolic nature of play activity and the therapeutic importance of interpreting it to the child in therapeutic work.

Anna Freud's system of psychoanalytic treatment for children followed definitely defined series of steps. She stressed the importance of developing a cooperative atmosphere and extending support to the child. Her approach places less stress on interpretation and is definitely more indirect than Klein's. She believed in the importance of sessions with parents and teachers in order to strengthen the progress made in psychoanalysis with the child.

The psychoanalytic point of view emphasizes the place of the basic drives. The psychoanalyst believes that chronic failure to gratify these drives results in permanent personality distortions requiring therapy. Freudians emphasize inborn needs and instincts and press awareness of the ego's ceaseless effort to compromise between internal and external demands. This approach leads us then to a recognition of how various defense mechanisms operate to reduce tension. The defense mechanisms may well help us understand the child's behavior and give us direct clues as to the meaning of his conduct.

2. Give examples of how a knowledge of defense mechanisms can be of value to the teacher or other professionals who work with children.
3. What are some of the problems involved in assuming a sequence of psychological stages through which all children must pass?

A multitude of books has been written on and by the Freudians. For purposes of child study, the following are of value:

Erikson, E., *Childhood and Society*. New York: W. W. Norton & Company, Inc., 1950.

Freud, A., *Psychoanalysis for Teachers and Parents*. Boston: Beacon Press, 1960.

Freud, S., *An Outline of Psychoanalysis*. New York: W. W. Norton & Company, Inc., 1949.

Hall, Calvin, *A Primer of Freudian Psychology*. New York: Harcourt, Brace & World, Inc., 1954.

Josselyn, I., *Psychosocial Development of Children*. New York: Family Service Association, 1948.

———, *The Happy Child*. New York: Random House, 1955.

Klein, M., *The Psychoanalysis of Children*. New York: Grove Press, 1960.

Watson, R., *Psychology of the Child*, chap. 5. New York: John Wiley & Sons, Inc., 1959.

THE ADLERIAN POINT OF VIEW

The assumptions of Adlerian psychology are quite different from those of the psychoanalysts. Originally associated with Freud, Alfred Adler developed some basically different theories with which his name is identified. The beginning student might most clearly discern the differences between Freudian and Adlerian theory by contrasting several issues.

Freudian	*Adlerian*
Objectifying psychology, biological causal explanations	Subjectifying psychology, subjective causal explanations
Nomothetic, general laws	Idiographic, laws applying to the individual
Atomistic, analysis by elements	Holistic, organismic conception
Mechanistic description	Phenomenological description
Biological drives	Purposes, social needs

From this list you can see that the Adlerian is concerned with psychological laws that apply to understanding the individual. He looks at behavior in terms of the individual's perception of the situation. Great emphasis has been placed on viewing behavior in relationship to the total situation.

Adlerian theory sees man as relatively free in the determination of his behavior. He is more than a product of external influences or hereditary forces. The child is purposive and striving, involved in making decisions, and engaging in activities that enable him to pursue his goal.

The Adlerians recognize man as being essentially a social being. All behavior has social meaning and can best be understood when seen in the context of the child's social setting, whether it be the family, the class, his peers or some other group.

The Adlerians feel that most behavior is purposive, that actions and movements are directed toward a goal. To see behavior in terms of its purposes is to understand it. The Adlerian takes the teleological approach to the understanding of behavior; as a result, he assumes quite a different posture from the advocate of a direct causal relationship between environment and the behavior that is produced.

---

4. Clarify how the psychologist who takes a causal approach in the explanation of behavior differs from one who takes a purposive approach. How can one explain differences in the behavior of children from a divorced home, a particular school, or the same socioeconomic group based on these two approaches?

According to Adlerian theory, man is understood only in terms of his phenomenological field, the world and self as experienced by the individual at the instant of action. It is more important then to know how the child sees the situation or feels about it than to know what has objectively occurred. It is assumed that the child's behavior makes sense in terms of the way in which he views the world. The child from this point of view is not merely a receiver of stimuli. He has the capacity to interpret and assign meaning to events that occur about him. Adlerian theory recognizes the part that the individual plays in giving meaning to his experiences. It also places a premium on the individual's freedom of choice. Adlerians place a great emphasis on belonging as a basic need; they believe that the need to be a part of the group, to find one's place and belong, explains many types of behavior.

The Adlerians did not develop a scheme with either specific stages or a particular psychic economy. Instead, their stress upon the total set of factors to be considered in studying man brought them to the concept of the life style, i.e., a human being's evaluation of himself, the people about him, his world, and his place in that world. It is his characteristic pattern of responses, his attitudes, values, and basic assumptions.

The Adlerian theory recognizes that the child's actions may be based on faulty assumptions or mistaken views. It seeks recognition of the fact that while the behavior of a child may appear to be inappropriate, the child himself believes that this is probably the most effective way he can behave at the time. The child, from the day of birth, interacts with the people about him and is in the process of learning the rules and limits of his society. His first experiences come from the members of his family; as he observes and accumulates these experiences, he develops certain attitudes and convictions. Adlerians believe it is important to take into consideration such factors as the family atmosphere and the family constellation.

The family atmosphere refers to the relationships in the home in which the child first gets his experiences with social living. The social attitudes within the family influence the attitudes he eventually develops. This is the place in which the varied influences of the community first reach the child. In the simplest form the relationships the child develops reflect the atmosphere within the family. While family atmosphere is not necessarily a direct determinant of behavior, it does present the child with competitive and cooperative atmospheres which he may choose to adopt or reject.

The family constellation refers to the child's place among his siblings. His position plays an important part in the development of his personality. Both competition and alliances among siblings are frequently expressed in fundamental personality differences and similarities. While present Adlerians would not look at the ordinal position of eldest, second, middle, youngest, or only child in terms of certain classical statements about these positions, they would be concerned about what the child's evaluation of his position within the family constellation has been and how he presently sees the world. By taking into consideration the psychological response of the individual to his position, the Adlerians place an emphasis on positional psychology.

In dealing with the difficult or disturbing child, Adlerians feel it is important to recognize the child's goals. Dreikurs believes that the goals may be either active or passive and may utilize either constructive or destructive methods.[2] He feels that this basic pattern of activity is established early in life and is difficult to change. The pattern obviously is a reflection of the child's style of life. The four types of behavior patterns Dreikurs mentions are: (1) active-constructive, (2) active-destructive, (3) passive-constructive, and (4) passive-destructive.

The active-constructive child is extremely ambitious to be the first in the class; his goal orientation is toward success. The active-destructive child is the one who may be impertinent, defiant, clownish, or bullying. The passive-constructive child achieves his goals by being charming and receiving special attention for what he is and not for what he does. The passive-destructive child is characterized as lazy and may manifest his laziness in actions ranging from ineffectual response to total inaction.

[2] Rudolf Dreikurs, *Psychology in the Classroom* (New York: Harper & Row, Publishers, Inc., 1957).

Dreikurs has formulated the four goals of misbehavior: (1) attention getting, (2) power, (3) revenge, or the desire to retaliate, and (4) the display of real or imagined inadequacy and inferiority. These goals will be discussed at greater length in the chapter on Motivation and Discipline in Child Development.

---

5. Carl is usually the last to get out his paper and pencil for assignments. He starts his work after a reminder from the teacher. He rushes to be first in line for recess. The children all laugh at his actions on the playground. If the behavior of the child is purposive and goal-directed as the Adlerians claim, what does this imply for our understanding of Carl? How might the teacher function more effectively with Carl? How is the purposive concept of potential use to the professional person in his interactions with the child?
6. The Adlerian-oriented and the psychoanalytically oriented teacher might function quite differently in the classroom. Give a description of the effect of these theories upon child management either in the home or in the classroom.

The following books are suggested for further reading in this field:

Adler, Alfred, *Understanding Human Nature*. New York: Premier Books, 1957.

Adler, K. and D. Deutsch, *Essays in Individual Psychology*. New York: Grove Press, 1959.

Ansbacher, H., *The Individual Psychology of Alfred Adler*. New York: Basic Books, 1956.

Dinkmeyer, Don and R. Dreikurs, *Encouraging Children to Learn: The Encouragement Process*. Englewood Cliffs, N.J.: Prentice-Hall, Inc., 1963.

Dreikurs, R., *Psychology in the Classroom*. New York: Harper & Row, Publishers, Inc., 1957.

———, *Challenge of Parenthood*, rev. New York: Duell, Sloan & Pearce, Inc., 1958.

Dreikurs, R., *Fundamentals of Adlerian Psychology*. Jamaica, B.W.I.: Knox Educational Services Ltd., 1958.

Dreikurs, R. and V. Soltz, *Children: The Challenge*. New York: Duell, Sloan & Pearce, Inc., 1964.

Way, L., *Adler's Place in Psychology*. New York: Collier Books, The Macmillan Company, 1962.

THE DEVELOPMENTAL MATURATIONAL POINT OF VIEW

The developmentalists, led by Arnold Gesell, emphasize the concept of maturation. They believe that all development occurs in definite, patterned, and internally controlled sequences, which apply not only to the growth of tissues and organs, but also to functions and behavior. Culture and environment are considered to be only secondary influences. Developmentalists hold that environmental factors may modify but not generate the progressions of development. Maturation is achieved through the regulatory mechanisms, which are responsible for determining the direction of all development. Maturation is responsible for those developmental phenomena which seem to develop in an orderly fashion independent of specific practice. Gesell was particularly influential in establishing techniques of developmental diagnosis for pediatricians and other child-growth workers. Norms of behavioral development were established by researchers at the Child Study Center at Yale University. Gesell maintained that the behavior of the child was patterned and to an extent largely predictable.

Gesell also believed, although it is not often acknowledged, that while certain stages in the developmental sequence were inevitable, they were entered at different times owing to differences in rates of growth. The developmentalists describe particular stages, but not when a specific child will enter them. Gesell states his position most clearly when he says that "the reader is warned that the age norms are not set up as standards, and are designed only for orientation and interpretive purposes . . . the prevalence and significance of individual variations are recognized at every turn."[3]

The developmental theory, pointing to the importance of the cyclic nature of all growth and behavior, is perhaps best portrayed in the following table from the Ilg and Ames book *Child Behavior*.[4]

THE CYCLIC SEQUENCE OF BEHAVIOR STAGES

2 years	5 years	10 years	Smooth, consolidated
2½	5½–6	11	Breaking up
3	6½	12	Rounded—balanced
3½	7	13	Inwardized
4	8	14	Vigorous, expansive
4½	9	15	Inwardized-outwardized, troubled, "neurotic"
5	10	16	Smooth, consolidated

This theory, then, makes an excellent basis for combining the concepts of individuality and set stages. Gesell felt that the stages in any given behavior could be outlined in advance. At the same time, he recognized that personality, rate of development, and particular abilities would be indi-

[3] A. Gesell and F. Ilg, *Infant and Child in the Culture of Today* (New York: Harper & Row, Publishers, Inc., 1943).
[4] F. Ilg and L. Ames, *Child Behavior* (New York: Harper & Row, Publishers, Inc., 1955), p. 12.

vidual and unique. The developmentalists urge recognition of each child's individuality, while recognizing that certain types of behavior will occur regardless of external intervention. The approach, then, stresses the importance of recognizing and respecting each child's basic in-born individuality.

Gesell and his co-workers regard development as determined by nature from within the organism and assign environment only a secondary role in the modification of behavior. Thus, both at home and at school Gesell would advocate the policy of letting the child develop at its own pace. Either forcing or limiting the child will only create negativism and a lack of productivity. The developmental plan of the individual is central to this theory.

Gesell's work has had a tremendous impact upon the field of child development. His writings were probably more widely disseminated than any other full-length book on child development until Spock's *Baby and Child Care.*[5] Related books on the developmental theory are:

Gesell, A. and F. Ilg, *Infant and Child in the Culture of Today.* New York: Harper & Row, Publishers, Inc., 1943.

Ilg, F. and L. Ames, *Child Behavior.* New York: Harper & Row, Publishers, Inc., 1955.

———, *Parents Ask.* New York: Harper & Row, Publishers, Inc., 1962.

THE SOCIOCULTURAL POINT OF VIEW

The cultural anthropologists' view of child development places greater emphasis on environmental influences. They believe that the child is a function of the specific sociocultural forces that impinge upon him. They assert that the values and institutions of each culture produce a distinct personality type. To be accepted, a member of a specific society is forced to act in certain ways. Thus, needs are related to specific cultures. The anthropologist does not ignore basic physical or organic needs but holds that the manner in which these needs are met is a function of the culture. Each need is modified to some extent by the culture.

Ashley Montagu exemplifies this point of view when he refers to personality as a product of interplay between the organism, society, and the social interactional effects and the culture. The interaction of these variables yields the functioning child.[6]

Margaret Mead has theorized that cultural trends implement and interfere with natural trends and that out of this we create personality.[7] Ruth

[5] B. Spock, *Baby and Child Care* (New York: Pocket Books Inc., 1957).

[6] A. Montagu, *The Direction of Human Development* (New York: Harper & Row, Publishers, Inc., 1955).

[7] M. Mead, "Age Patterning and Personality Development," *Amer. J. Orthopsychiat.*, 17 (1947), 231–240.

Benedict has maintained that behavior traits are culturally selected. She feels that the customs into which the child is born shape his experience and behavior from birth.[8] These theorists, then, have broadened the base of understanding in child development. They insist that one must look at the biological, cultural, social, and psychological factors in order to come to an understanding of the child.

An effective integration of these various life sciences in our contemporary American culture has been made by Robert Havighurst. His developmental task concept has considerable implications for all professionals working with children. Havighurst has defined the developmental task as follows:

> A developmental task is a task which arises at or about a certain period in the life of the individual, successful achievement of which leads to his happiness and to success with later tasks, while failure leads to unhappiness in the individual, disapproval by society, and difficulty with later tasks.[9]

These tasks are described in terms of specific learning which the individual needs in terms of his specific society. This, then, enables one to see the relationships between needs, maturational processes, and cultural demands.

Inspection of a list of developmental tasks indicates that they are based on psychological, biological, and cultural factors. The concept of developmental tasks is particularly useful because it can help clarify tasks important for school children at different ages. There are also implications for the most effective timing of educational efforts. The continuity of development is outlined as the tasks at various age levels are related to preceding tasks. The set of developmental tasks below will give the reader a clearer picture of Havighurst's conceptual framework.

Developmental Tasks of Infancy and Early Childhood

1. Learning to walk. Between the ages of nine and fifteen months, when the bones, muscles, and nerves have developed to the proper point, the child begins to walk, and during the following years learns to run, jump, and skip.

2. Learning to take solid foods. As the baby's digestive system and ability to chew develop, he gradually becomes able to make the change from liquid to semisolid to solid food. The way in which the child is fed and weaned will affect his personality.

3. Learning to talk. Biologically the child is ready to talk shortly after

[8] R. Benedict, *Patterns of Culture* (New York: Houghton Mifflin Company, 1934).
[9] R. Havighurst, *Human Development and Education* (New York: David McKay Co., Inc., 1953), p. 2.

birth. He begins by making various sounds to which the people in his environment attach meaning. Between the ages of twelve and eighteen months he utters a sound in a particular situation which is a word. He then proceeds rapidly to a single word sentence and from there to multiword sentences. Vocabulary grows faster than knowledge of grammar. Girls mature faster than boys.

4. Learning to control the elimination of body wastes. The nerves and muscles that control urination and defecation are fully developed between the ages of two and four years. The child is considered toilet trained when he has acquired voluntary control of urination and defecation and accepts the responsibility for keeping himself dry and clean. Toilet training is the first moral training the child receives and the methods of training affect his later character.

5. Learning sex differences and sexual modesty. He learns the anatomical differences between the sexes and is taught to behave in ways appropriate to his sex in conformance with his culture.

6. Achieving physiological stability. Most of the homeostatic mechanisms that regulate the adult body are not functioning effectively until the fifth year. This is a purely biological task.

7. Forming simple concepts of social and physical reality. The child gradually makes generalizations from the world around him and learns simple concepts such as man, animal, round. His nervous system must have developed to a certain level, and he must have been provided with various experiences before these concepts can be formed.

8. Learning to relate oneself emotionally to parents, siblings, and other people. Unconsciously the child imitates the people around him and gradually identifies himself with other people, especially his parents. The way this task is accomplished is important in determining his social relations in later life.

9. Learning to distinguish right and wrong and developing a conscience. The child learns the concepts of good and bad from the people around him. Later character is built upon this base.

Developmental Tasks of Middle Childhood

1. Learning physical skills necessary for ordinary games. The skills are acquired as the bones and muscles develop. The peer group rewards the child for success and expects boys to do better than girls.

2. Building wholesome attitudes toward oneself as a growing organism. This task consists of developing habits of cleanliness and safety consistent with the culture and attitudes of adequacy and pleasure in using the body as well as a wholesome attitude toward sex.

3. Learning to get along with age-mates. The child learns to get along

with children outside the family and looks to peers rather than family for social approval.

4. Learning an appropriate masculine or feminine social role. While there is no sex difference in physical activity during this period, there is increasing differentiation in social behavior.

5. Developing fundamental skills in reading, writing, and calculating. The nervous system has matured enough by age six for learning these skills, but in many cases the muscles and eyes have not developed sufficiently until the middle of the period.

6. Developing concepts necessary for everyday living. The child has developed many simple concepts before he reaches school and from concrete experiences develops many more. As he grows he is able to handle concepts at higher levels of abstraction.

7. Developing conscience, morality, and a scale of values. The first rules for behavior are imposed by the family, but later the child learns rules for every activity, develops a set of values, and is able to make choices in accordance with the demands of his culture.

8. Achieving personal independence. The child frees himself from identification with parents and gradually becomes able to make his own plans, choose activities and friends.

9. Developing attitudes toward social groups and institutions. Attitudes are developed by imitation or by pleasant or unpleasant experiences. During this period the child learns attitudes from those outside the family.[10]

The following books are suggested for further reading in this field:

Benedict, Ruth, *Patterns of Culture*. New York: Houghton Mifflin Company, 1934.

Havighurst, R., *Human Development and Education*. New York: David McKay Co. Inc., 1953.

Linton, Ralph, *The Cultural Background of Personality*. New York: Appleton-Century-Crofts, 1945.

Mead, Margaret and F. C. Macgregor, *Growth and Culture*. New York: G. P. Putnam's Sons, 1951.

Montagu, Ashley, *The Direction of Human Development*. New York: Harper & Row, Publishers, Inc., 1955.

JEAN PIAGET'S POINT OF VIEW IN DEVELOPMENTAL PSYCHOLOGY

Jean Piaget, the Swiss developmental psychologist, has concerned himself with theoretical and experimental investigations of the qualitative development of intellectual structure. He has engaged in a long-term study of ontogenetic change and has developed a highly original theory of intel-

[10] R. Havighurst, *Human Development and Education*, chaps. 2, 3. 4.

lectual and perceptual development. Since his formulations tend to be detailed and complicated, only the major constructs which have an influence on a general understanding of human development will be presented here.

Piaget has studied the child's language, reasoning, moral judgment, cognitive structure, and intellectual development through careful and extensive observation of the child's spontaneous behavior. The work has tended to be more descriptive than predictive.

Piaget believes that intellectual operations never exist in isolation from a governing totality, an organizing principle which it is vital to discover. He has studied the structures of developing intelligence as opposed to its function and content. Content is the observable behavior while function is the process by which the new is assimilated and the old is accommodated to the new. Piaget has postulated the existence of cognitive structures between function and content and has gone on to study in detail the developmental changes in these structures, seeking to identify levels of cognitive development. His work is characterized by an interest in the qualitative characteristics of development.

Piaget feels that all adaptive behavior can be understood only in terms of its organization as a total system (holism). He has found it possible to interpret a diverse range of supposedly unrelated behaviors in terms of their underlying structural whole, and has developed a succession of developmental stages for a given behavior, emerging in an unchanging and constant order, each incorporating the structure of the preceding stage and each characterized by an initial period of preparation and a final period of achievement. Two processes are vital for development—assimilation, in which the child incorporates new elements into the existing structure; and accommodation, in which the structure itself adjusts to new elements. In this scheme the child is viewed as an ever organized entity which accommodates itself to external reality. This position clearly is an organism-environment interaction position, accounting for both maturation and learning while placing the emphasis on the interaction.

Cognitive development consists of actions which become progressively internalized. Assimilation and accommodation are complementary processes which bring about adaptation and development. Piaget has divided the ontogenetic span into three periods of invariant sequence, although the chronological age for each may fluctuate considerably. They are:

1. The period of sensory-motor intelligence (0–2 years). This is the period in which the child moves from egocentrism to differentiation of self and object. This is a period for development in perception of space, time, imitation, and causality. Sensory-motor intelligence is only able to link successive perceptual states, one by one.
2. The period of preparation for an organization of concrete operations

(2–11 years). This is the period in which the child's representational thought first emerges, and eventually stabilizes. Representational thought has a symbolic capacity for organizing a set of separate events. It is free from the limits of concrete reality and permits symbolic manipulation.

3. The period of formal operations (11–15 years). In this period the representational thought now becomes oriented toward reality and able to deal with the mastery of an ever widening variety of problems.

Piaget's formulations and the ensuing experimental data have indicated a functional continuity which exists between the emergence of sensory-motor skills and the development of concept formation. This stands in strong contrast to the traditional separation of such spheres of development. Piaget has also emphasized system property in contrast to specific isolated behavior. His theory suggests qualitative observations of development and a consideration of periods of cognitive reorganization in the child.

In addition to Piaget's ideas about developmental stages, he developed a theory of transition, the processes which propel the child through the ontogenetic sequence. This continuous process is one of equilibration. In the interaction of the individual with his environment the processes of assimilation and accommodation get out of balance, forcing the individual into the next stage of development to restore the balance.

Piaget has encouraged an intensive look at the developmental stages in the psychological structure of the child himself, resulting in a conceptualization of the qualitative organizational changes taking place in the growing child's mental processes. While he would not be viewed as an applied scientist, he has contributed a system which provides a detailed normative frame of reference. It provides guidelines and limitations in the area of cognitive development. He has also provided the child development field with a large number of new and interesting dependent variables for research and experimentation. Like some of the other theorists, Piaget has contributed a descriptive approach to development which presents a structure for the type of behavior that develops with age. The great range of Piaget's concern has provided the child development field with an exciting change in its frame of reference. His work is described in detail in the following books:

Bruner, J. S., *The Process of Education*. Cambridge, Mass.: Harvard University Press, 1960.

Flavell, J. H., *The Developmental Psychology of Jean Piaget*. Princeton, N.J.: D. Van Nostrand Co., Inc., 1963.

Inhelder, Barbel and J. Piaget, *The Growth of Logical Thinking from Childhood to Adolescence*. New York: Basic Books, Inc., 1958.

Piaget, J., *The Language and Thought of the Child*. New York: Harcourt, Brace & World, Inc., 1926.

———, *Judgment and Reasoning in the Child.* New York: Harcourt, Brace & World, Inc., 1928.

———, *The Child's Conception of the World.* New York: Harcourt, Brace & World, Inc., 1929.

———, *The Moral Judgment of the Child.* London: Routledge & Kegan Paul, Ltd., 1932.

———, *The Psychology of Intelligence.* New York: Harcourt, Brace & World, Inc., 1950.

———, *The Origins of Intelligence in Children.* New York: International University Press, 1952.

THE BEHAVIORIST POINT OF VIEW

The behaviorist approach, which places primary importance on studying observable types of behavior, has been presented best by B. F. Skinner, F. S. Keller, S. Bijou, and D. Baer. They view the child's development as a series of changes in interaction between the organism and its environment. Behavior is defined as consisting of a series of responses which are dependent upon the previous stimulus. Environment, from this point of view, is a strong force on the child's changing personality; change comes about as a result of the way in which the human organism interacts with a stimulus environment. Their approach is best characterized by an understanding of behavior as a function of or a consequence of stimulus events. Bijou and Baer have abbreviated this as follows: $B = f(S)$.[11]

Stimuli are recognized as those presently functioning during the interaction and those that have functioned in the past. Behavior is a direct function of events in the current situation and in the history of previous interactions. Behaviorists believe that the proper emphasis for developmental psychology is a concentration on the history of the organism's previous interactions.

They see the child as a set of interrelated responses to stimuli. While the behaviorist viewpoint tends to stress almost entirely observable and external events, there is also some recognition that in psychological analysis of behavior we may need to consider other events. Bijou and Baer have best expressed this as follows:

> Some of the stimuli emanate from the external environment, some from the child's own behavior, and some from its biological structure and functioning. The child is therefore not only a source of responses; he is also a source of some stimuli. From this point of view, part of the child's environment is within his own body.[12]

This would indicate that factors other than the external may influence development, but the generally held position of the behaviorist is one of a concern for external observable empirically demonstrated facts.

[11] S. Bijou and D. Baer, *Child Development, volume I, A Systematic and Empirical Theory* (New York: Appleton-Century-Crofts, 1961).

[12] S. Bijou and D. Baer, *Child Development, volume I,* 8.

According to behaviorists the child's behavior consists of two types of responses, respondents and operants. Respondents are responses which are controlled by stimuli that precede them, while operants are responses which are controlled by stimuli that follow them. From this scheme, the behaviorist is able to classify any response into one of two categories which he feels are objective and observable.

Bijou and Baer seem to expand the behaviorist theory to an extent as they discuss the importance of stimuli which the child's own behavior produces and which influence his subsequent behavior. They recognize that stimuli generated by the child elicit certain types of behavior, which may follow a child's responses and hence strengthen or weaken the preceding behavior or serve as a cue for further behavior.

This theory presents a picture of the child as a cluster of interrelated operant and respondent behaviors. It makes few and generally no assumptions about unobservable behavior. It recognizes that the child provides a social stimulant to other people but emphasizes that the most significant stimuli originate outside the body.

Behaviorists would focus on the function of the stimulus in order to note objectively the ways in which it controls behavior. They believe that stimuli produce, strengthen, or weaken behavior, and may generalize behavior to new situations and new problems. Stimuli are divided into three types on the basis of their functions. "Three kinds of stimulus functions are noted, an 'eliciting' function, a 'setting of the occasion' for an appropriate response, and a 'strengthening of that response by its effectiveness in changing the stimulation.' "[13]

The position is deterministic in the sense that behavior is controlled and shaped. A variety of events is seen as having a common stimulus function, and behaviorists believe that the child makes a predictable interpretation of the stimulus based upon past experiences and reinforcements.

---

7. A clear-cut theoretical and conceptual difference occurs between those who view behavior as a completely predictable response to a stimulus or as a self-determined, goal-directed response. What are the implications of these contrasting points of view for parents, teachers, psychologists, and researchers? Give an example of a specific practice in one of these areas which relates to one of these theories.

The behaviorists do not accept any particular personality theory in studying the stages of development. They tend to feel that there is not enough information available to make generalized formulations. Thus,

[13] S. Bijou and D. Baer, *Child Development, volume I*, 18.

their study of stages is based on environmental events, maturational changes, and behavioral manifestations.

The child, then, is largely the result of his environment and stimulus events that occur within the environment. Development is made up of progressive changes in different ways of interacting with the environment. Skinner believes that the purpose of psychology is to predict and control the behavior of individual organisms and that as a science psychology should be concerned only with overt behavior. Operant conditioning, a key construct, involves a learning process whereby a response is made more probable or more frequent through reinforcement or strengthening of the response. He postulates that by sequentially changing the contingencies of reinforcement in the direction of a desired behavior, one establishes learning. The contingency is the sequence in which a response is followed by a reinforcing stimulus.

The implications of the theory are clear in pointing to the teacher as an architect and builder of student behavior. He is to be concerned with analyzing the effect of reinforcement and with designing methods to set up specific reinforcing contingencies so that behavior may be brought under a continuously more precise control. In the operant-learning situation the reinforcement would then tend to produce the subsequent set of stimuli. Teachers and parents in this system are concerned with the shaping of proper responses. Justifiably, Skinner has noted that much of our current educational practice has given only lip service to concepts like immediate knowledge of results and truly sequential series of learning experiences. In his system, reinforcement of the desired behavior would occur frequently and promptly. He maintains that effective teaching is dependent upon immediate feedback.

Skinner does not look inside the organism for any explanation of behavior, and he is not concerned with the study of the internal experience of man. It is his contention that techniques can be designed which will manipulate behavior by dealing with the external, specific, reinforcing contingencies. From this point of view those concerned with the child's development would be involved in bringing behavior under the control of specific predictable operants and respondents.

Further information about the behavioral approach may be found in the following books:

Bijou, S. and D. Baer, *Child Development, A Systematic and Empirical Theory*. New York: Appleton-Century-Crofts, volume one, 1961, volume two, 1965.

Skinner, B. F., *The Behavior of Organisms*. New York: Appleton-Century-Crofts, 1938.

———, *Cumulative Record*. New York: Appleton-Century-Crofts, 1961.

———, *Science and Human Behavior*. New York: The Macmillan Company, 1953.

THE ORGANISMIC POINT OF VIEW

Those who hold the organismic point of view have been chiefly concerned with interrelationships in growth and development. Research directed toward describing growth graphically by master mathematical curves, variability units, and age principles has been a major concern. Many of the facets of growth interrelationships have been explored. Willard Olson describes the organismic approach as a focus on the total organism within the social context.

Stuart Courtis has made both intensive and extensive study of the cycles of growth, and is one of the pioneers in the organismic approach. Courtis defined a cycle of growth as a period of specific maturation during which all the elements and forces at work are constant, within allowable errors of control and measurement. He found that under standard and constant conditions, developmental growth takes place in such a fashion that when expressed in lologs (logarithms of logarithms) equal growth takes place in equal periods of time for the individual. Courtis measures growth in units called isochrons. He defines an isochron as one per cent of the total time from incipiency (onset) to maturity of a cycle. Maturity in this context means the point at which growth stops, whether it be a plateau in the growth curve, when the end of a particular growth cycle is reached, or the point at which the entire organism stops growing. The focus is on the importance of cycles in the development of the child.

In C. V. Millard's interpretation of the organismic point of view, all aspects of an individual's growth follow the same pattern. He believed in the individuality of growth due to differences in rate of growth. The orderly sequence of growth, its cyclic nature, the variance in developmental rate, and the interrelationships of all growth were among his major contentions.

W. Olson and B. Hughes used the age principle extensively in developing their organismic age concept. This construct describes changes in terms of the age at which the average attainment occurs. For example, if the average boy at 9 years of age is 51 inches tall, one speaks of 51 inches as representing 108 months of height age regardless of the chronological age at which 51 inches are attained. Age equivalents for converting measurements to growth ages have been developed in seven areas. The organismic age is the average of the following ages: Height Age, Weight Age, Dental Age, Carpal Age, Grip Age, Mental Age, and Reading Age.

Height and weight ages are obtained by physical measurement. Dental age is determined by the number of permanent teeth. Carpal age is derived from the skeletal development as shown by X-ray of the bones in the wrist to detect number, size, and density. The hand dynamometer is used to measure the grip, which yields a grip age. An intelligence test measures the mental age. From achievement tests a reading age may be obtained.

The best statement of the implications of this philosophy comes from the writings of Olson: "The general philosophy as applied to the growing child is a simple one—each child is to be assisted in growing according to his natural design, without deprivation or forcing, in an environment and by a process which also supply a social direction to his achievement."[14]

The organismic point of view is covered in detail in the following references:

Cornell, E. and C. Armstrong, "Forms of Mental Growth Patterns Revealed by Reanalysis of the Harvard Growth Data," *Child Development*, No. 26 (1955), 169–224.

Dearborn, W. and J. Rothney, *Predicting the Child's Development*. Cambridge, Mass.: Sci-Art Publishers, 1941.

Hymes, J., *A Child Development Point of View*. Englewood Cliffs, N.J.: Prentice-Hall, Inc., 1954.

Millard, C. V. *Child Growth and Development*. Boston: D. C. Heath & Company, 1951.

———, *School and Child*. East Lansing, Mich.: Michigan State University Press, 1954.

Millard, C. V. and J. Rothney, *The Elementary School Child—A Book of Cases*. New York: Holt, Rinehart & Winston, Inc., 1957.

Olson, W. *Child Development*, 2nd ed. Boston: D. C. Heath & Company, 1959.

Tanner, J. M., *Education and Physical Growth*. London: University of London Press, Ltd., 1961.

A SOCIAL LEARNING INTERPERSONAL THEORY OF DEVELOPMENT

Harry Sullivan, a psychiatrist, has made a contribution to child development through his analysis of the developmental stages. He placed an emphasis on the child's method of adapting to problems and his way of perceiving the world. Sullivan was concerned with the development of self in relationship to the significant others in the child's environment.

Sullivan believed that the purposes of human behavior could be divided into two major classes, the pursuit of satisfaction and the pursuit of security. Satisfaction, in his terminology, referred to the biological needs, while security referred to a psychological state of well-being, a feeling of belonging and being accepted. For Sullivan, most psychological problems arise in relationship to the pursuit of security. The early experiences of the infant, in this theory, consist of states of comfort, known as equilibrium, and states of discomfort, known as disequilibrium. In infancy the child is

[14] W. Olson, *Child Development*, 2nd ed. (Boston: D. C. Heath & Company, 1959), p. 449.

still entirely dependent upon the care of others to satisfy his needs. It is from his early experiences in the satisfaction of these needs that the child develops certain basic attitudes of trust or distrust, sometimes referred to as security or insecurity.

Sullivan stressed that some of the attitudes of the individuals responsible for "mothering" the child are conveyed to the child through "empathy." This empathy was a means of emotional communication. If the mother was concerned about feeding or sleeping, for example, this anxiety was somehow communicated to the youngster. This feeling was developed on the basis of subtle cues between the mother and the infant. The basic components of the self concept, according to Sullivan, are produced from the reflected appraisals of significant others in the child's life.

Sullivan believed that experience could be analyzed into three "modes." The prototaxic is the earliest mode in which the infant has undifferentiated types of experiences. In the parataxic mode, the infant is able to differentiate and assign meaning to his experiences. However, many of these meanings are autistic or unique to the individual. Eventually, the child's meanings become common, or shared, meanings, which are said to be consensually validated. This experience was labeled the syntaxic mode, indicative that the child's meanings follow reality and logic as generally accepted.

Sullivan points out that parental management practices will have a different effect on the development of the individual in each of the modes. He also made it clear that while the modes were related in a sense to developmental ages, that they were not mutually exclusive. It was his contention that these modes exist in most individuals throughout life; they are not comparable to Gesell's stages.

He set up a series of developmental stages, running from infancy to adulthood, that were characterized by the appearance of new interpersonal needs and new interpersonal relationships. Sullivan believed it was important to recognize that the beginning of a developmental era, in his terminology, had a considerable effect on the development of appropriate or inappropriate responses in the area of personality.

Sullivan made a significant contribution to the theory of human development by placing his constructs within the social-learning frame of reference. Sullivan's major contribution to child development exists in the development of certain clearly defined "stages" of development which stress the subjective view of the individual and the importance of his social contacts.

Sullivan's point of view is covered in detail in the following references:

Mullahy, P., *Oedipus-Myth and Complex: A Review of Psychoanalytic Theory* (New York: Thomas Nelson & Sons, 1948).

Sullivan, H. S., *Conceptions of Modern Psychiatry* (Washington, D.C.: Wm. Alanson White Psychiatric Foundation, 1947).

———, *The Interpersonal Theory of Psychiatry*. New York: W. W. Norton & Company, Inc., 1953.

———, *The Psychiatric Interview*. New York: W. W. Norton & Company, Inc., 1954.

THE PLACE AND IMPORTANCE OF THEORIES IN CHILD DEVELOPMENT

It is important to recognize that all the theories thus far discussed have had an effect upon decisions made in research, in classrooms, and in parental management. The theories have been accepted in varying degrees by various professions over the years. Some have made their greatest impact upon the pediatrician, others upon the parent, and some upon psychiatric and counseling practitioners. They have served, in a sense, as determinants of parental, professional, and teacher actions and reactions. It seems to be quite clear that a person who believes the child to be the product of a series of instinctual drives will function differently from one who considers him a goal-directed being.

Professional actions reflect a decision in favor of either an objective analysis of specific elements or a phenomenological approach. Some decisions must be made about the relative emphasis on learning or perception. Even within the learning field a choice of emphasis must be made between association, conditioning, and reinforcement on the one hand, and goal direction, reorganization, and insight on the other. Thus, at every step, questions will be raised which will necessitate choosing between mechanistic and organismic concepts.

Certainly, the teacher or school system that subscribes to Skinner's point of view would function quite differently from one that adhered to Gesell or the organismic approach to child development. In a way, then, the ensuing chapters will call for a decision regarding these points of view. Your reaction to some of the material related to learning, emotions, social development, and achievement will reveal your stand on some of these crucial issues.

Even observation of the child and analysis of child studies will be affected by your point of view. It is suggested that the beginning student become well-acquainted with varied points of view in child development early so that he may have enough information to guide him in future decisions either professional or personal, that he makes in working with children.

These theories and points of view are not necessarily contradictory or entirely mutually exclusive. All are concerned with the interaction of the organism and his environment. They do tend to place an emphasis on certain concepts and certain facets of behavior. Undoubtedly they all contain elements of truth. The purpose is not necessarily to decide at this stage which approach to accept but, instead, to become acquainted with many points of view so that you can detect their influence upon the research, observations, and studies that will be examined during the study of child development.

A note of caution to the beginning student is indicated. Do not accept or adopt a particular point of view too early in the game. Frequently the naive acceptance of certain theoretical formulations take the inexperienced student way beyond even the wildest expectations of the mature theorist. As you become more sophisticated in the area of child development, however, you will find it necessary and wise to investigate in greater detail the varied points of view.

Since modern theorists seem to be taking various approaches into greater account, it is possible that in the decades to come we will come to accept an integrated developmental point of view. Obviously there must be a concern for incorporating into a workable system ideas from many points of view. All theoretical formulations eventually come into contact with the reality of the developing child within a given social milieu. Future research will undoubtedly modify some of the present points of view in child development. It is certainly to be hoped that the researcher will increasingly take into account some of the varying factors that certain points of view have stressed. One of the reasons for contrasting theories has been a lack of consideration of all the important variables in the analysis of child growth data. It would seem evident that all lines of research and theorizing would profit if they adopted the concepts and concerns of others and included them within their research design.

---

8. Read several research reports in the field of child development. Analyze which variables have been accounted for and which neglected.

SUGGESTED READINGS

Articles

Gesell, A. "Maturation and Infant Behavior Pattern," in *Readings in Child Behavior and Development,* 2nd ed., ed. C. Stendler, p. 25. New York: Harcourt, Brace & World, Inc., 1964.

Mead, M. "Age Patterning in Personality Development," in *Readings in Child Development,* ed. W. Martin and C. Stendler, p. 170. New York: Harcourt, Brace & World, Inc., 1954.

Books

Adler, A., *Understanding Human Nature.* London: George Allen & Unwin, 1927.

Adler, K., *Essays in Individual Psychology*. New York: Grove Press, 1959.

Axline, V., *Play Therapy—Inner Dynamics of Childhood.* Boston: Houghton Mifflin Company, 1947.

Bijou, S. and D. Baer, *Child Development, A Systematic and Empirical Theory.* New York: Appleton-Century-Crofts, volume one, 1961, volume two, 1965.

Erikson, E., *Childhood and Society,* 2nd ed. New York: W. W. Norton & Company, Inc., 1963.

Flavell, J., *The Developmental Psychology of Jean Piaget.* Princeton, N.J.: D. Van Nostrand Co., Inc., 1963.

Hall, C., *A Primer of Freudian Psychology.* New York: Harcourt, Brace & World, Inc., 1954.

Josselyn I., *The Psychosocial Development of Children.* New York: Family Service Assn., 1948.

Josselyn, I., *The Happy Child.* New York: Random House, 1955.

Mead, M., *Childhood in Contemporary Culture.* Chicago: University of Chicago Press, 1955.

Olson, W., *Child Development,* 2nd ed. Boston: D. C. Heath & Company, 1959.

Rogers, C., *On Becoming a Person.* Boston: Houghton Mifflin Company, 1961.

Skinner, B. F., *Science and Human Behavior.* New York: The Macmillan Company, 1953.

Staats, A. W. and Carolyn Staats, *Complex Human Behavior.* New York: Holt, Rinehart & Winston, Inc., 1963.

Tanner, J., *Discussions on Child Development,* Vol. 1, 2. New York: International University Press, 1957.

Wann, T. W., ed., *Behaviorism and Phenomenology.* Chicago: University of Chicago Press, 1964.

Way, L., *Adler's Place in Psychology.* New York: Collier Books, The Macmillan Company, 1962.

3 CHILD STUDY TECHNIQUES

The purpose of child study is to learn as much as possible about the child as an individual, and to apply that knowledge in predicting future development and so influencing it that the child will attain his greatest potential as a fully functioning individual. To accomplish these objectives, we must learn the reasons the child behaves as he does, the goals he is trying to attain, and the feelings he has about his behavior. Child study should not be focused on the child exclusively; the interaction between the child and the significant persons in his environment is of major importance.

The child develops from a combination of biological and cultural factors which function in a social setting. The techniques of child study are varied in order to consider the different factors significant in human development.

OBSERVATION

Observation is the oldest and most commonly used instrument of research. It becomes scientific when it is objective, when meaning can be attached to what is observed, when relationships are perceived, and when systematic observation is used to find the answer to a question.

Observation can be used for several purposes. Through observation you can become aware of the many individual differences among children. You can, in effect, enter into the child's personal framework. Studying one child in depth will give you a deeper understanding with which you can acquire a broader knowledge of all children. Educators frequently use observation to acquire an understanding of behavior in general; classroom teachers use the technique to produce insights into why particular students behave as they do. Through observation over a period of time, you can determine the child's characteristic pattern of response, his feelings and convictions, and his perception of the world about him. Effective observation is basic to comprehensive child study.

OBSERVATION TECHNIQUES—LIMITATIONS

Almy and Cunningham call attention to three limitations in observation.[1] The first is observer bias: that is, the tendency to allow the observer's personal experiences to affect his interpretation of the behavior he is observing. A particular behavior may recall to the observer a similar situation in which he had participated. He immediately assumes that this child is engaging in the behavior for the same reasons he had as a child. This is seldom true. While children's behavior may appear to be similar in pattern, there is great individuality in causes and goals.

---

1. How might you be biased in observing a child? Give an illustration of a way in which your bias has caused you to misjudge someone. What are some factors which might cause a teacher to be biased in her observations?

The second limitation is labeled "halos, horns, and the average." This is the tendency of the observer to generalize and assign stereotypes to an individual's behavior. It has been defined by English and English as "the tendency, in making an estimate or rating of one characteristic of a person, to be influenced by another characteristic or by one's general impression of that person."[2]

Bill is playing with a group of primary children. The observer notes that there is scuffling and Bill is involved. The last time the children were fighting it was determined that Bill was responsible for the trouble. The observer who generalizes would immediately blame Bill, while close observation might indicate he is not the instigator.

The third limitation in observation is assuming that a tentative hypothesis has been proved. This is the tendency to arrive at conclusions too soon. The observer on two or three mornings in the classroom has seen Jane sitting quietly at her desk applying herself to the work at hand, responding when called upon, and volunteering information when volunteers are requested. He would be inclined to decide that Jane is industrious, cooperative, and responsible. However, he does not observe Jane after recess when she refuses to settle down and spends her time walking around the room talking to one person after another and in general disturbing the group.

In another instance, the observer walks into a classroom when the children are organizing committees and the general atmosphere is one of noise and confusion. Another time he enters the room during a project

[1] Millie Almy and Ruth Cunningham, *Ways of Studying Children* (New York: Bureau of Publications, Teachers College, Columbia University, 1959).

[2] H. B. English and Ava C. English, *A Comprehensive Dictionary of Psychological and Psychoanalytic Terms* (New York: David McKay Co., Inc., 1958), p. 236.

period when, again, the noise level is higher than that generally approved for a classroom. He may conclude that the teacher has little control over the group. Had he entered the room during an arithmetic period when attention was centered on the teacher at the board explaining a problem, he might have concluded that the room was overly structured and had too much teacher control.

OBSERVATION TECHNIQUES—TYPES

When observing children, you take notice of what they say and do in a variety of situations, both formal and informal. There are various types of observational techniques which have been described thoroughly in the Encyclopedia of Educational Research.[3] Informal observation is used daily by the teacher to evaluate student performance in his work, his play, and his relationships with others in the group.

Another type of observation is called time sampling. Behavior is observed for specific short periods of time which have been preplanned. For example, the observer decides to watch Johnny for a period of ten minutes at 9 o'clock each morning, at noon, and at 2:30 in the afternoon. It has been found that many of these short and well-distributed time samples provide a more typical picture of behavior than a few long periods of observation. Under such conditions the observer can record more effectively since there is less information for him to record at one time.

---

2. How might Johnny's behavior be different at noon than at 9 a.m., at 10 a.m. rather than 2:30 p.m.? Why would it be important for a teacher to take some systematic time-sample observations?

The third type of observation is the most objective, and is done with checklists and schedules. The observer has a list of specific types of behavior, such as "plays with members of opposite sex" and "raises hand frequently," and records the number of times such behavior is observed. This technique permits the observer to record quickly and quantify specific acts. However, a poorly prepared checklist will present a distorted picture of the child. The traits listed should include both positive and negative actions, be readily observable, and be clearly differentiated. The list should be short enough to facilitate rapid and accurate tallying each time the behavior occurs.

OBSERVATION TECHNIQUES—WHAT TO OBSERVE

The length of the observation period may extend from several minutes to several hours. Authorities do not agree on the ideal length of time that

[3] *Encyclopedia of Educational Research* (New York: The Macmillan Company, 1960).

one should observe but in general concur on the fact that the shorter the length of the observation, the greater the opportunity to record in detail and with accuracy the events that occur. The ideal amount of time for observation varies with the activity of the child and the ability of the observer.

Observations are for the purpose of obtaining information about the child's development in four general areas, physical, intellectual, social, and emotional. What behavior will yield information in each of these areas?

The observer should make note of the child's general appearance. How is he dressed? Are he and his clothing clean? Does he appear to be healthy? Note his height in relation to his weight and age. Notice his body movements. Is he quick or deliberate? How is he coordinated in running, jumping, and throwing? How does he use his body to express feeling? Does he tire easily? What kind of activity tires him?

Clues to the child's intellectual capacities can be found in his ability to follow directions and in the way he expresses his ideas in the classroom and in other settings as well. What are the things which interest him? How aware is he of detail? How well does he remember? How well is he doing in his school work? Does he keep to the point in answering questions? Is he able to draw inferences?

What are the child's relationships with other children? How and when does he relate to them? Does he contribute to group activity? Does he avoid some children? Do others avoid him? How does the child get along with adults? Is he comfortable with them? Does he need to depend on an adult?

In the area of emotional development the observer should notice the child's control over his feelings. How does he express joy or anger? How easily is he frustrated and how does he react to frustration? How dependent is he on personal approval? What are the things he is amused by? Does he show signs of emotional tension, such as nail biting or thumb sucking?

The beginning observer should limit the range of what he watches. He may watch one child intently for five minutes, then switch to another child, and then to a third engaged in the same activity to see whether the behavior observed is typical or atypical. It is wise to start with a child engaged in a quiet activity with few other people involved. For the second observation the observer might choose one activity and watch the group intensely for fifteen minutes. However, even when watching a group activity, it is wise to make one child the focal point and observe the action around him and his interaction with the others in the group. For the third observation the observer may switch his attention to the whole group during a specific activity and watch the interaction of the children in the group.

While the observer should watch the children in as many different activities as possible, he should remain unobtrusive. Children may approach the observer, ask who he is, request help, or in other ways attempt to initiate a relationship. If that happens, it is wise for the observer to smile in a friendly manner, explain that he is just a visitor, and direct the children back to what they were doing or to the adult in charge for help. This is sufficient to indicate to them that the observer is a friendly spectator and that they can feel free to return to their activity. If a child questions what the observer is writing, he is usually satisfied to be told that the observer is trying to learn more about children.

A child's behavior differs in different situations. If the observer is a person with whom the child has a good relationship he will act differently from the way he acts in the presence of an adult toward whom he is antagonistic. Therefore, the observer must remain objective and passive but still project a feeling of warmth into the situation.

---

3. What types of contact would be permissible between an observer and a child? Why should limitations be set? What are the advantages and disadvantages to the observer in limited contact?

Since the purpose of child study is to become acquainted with the whole child, the child should be observed in his life space. The life space is the child's world, the situations in which he is involved, and the people with whom he comes in contact during his daily life. As the child grows older, his life space expands. Since each and every contact has some bearing on the child's development, it is important to cover through observation as much as possible of the child's life space. An example of extremely intensive observation of the life space is illustrated in "One Boy's Day" by Barker and Wright, a record of one boy's activity from the time he gets out of bed in the morning until he returns to it at night.[4] This particular child was watched unobtrusively every minute of the day. In order to minimize the loss of detail through fatigue or lack of time for recording, observers were changed frequently during the day.

OBSERVATION TECHNIQUES—RECORDING

Observations or judgments may be recorded by two different procedures: (1) systematic recording based on scales of units or values to be awarded to various activities, and (2) anecdotal records.

[4] Roger G. Barker and H. Wright, *One Boy's Day* (New York: Harper & Row, Publishers, Inc., 1951).

Systematic Records

The systematic record is particularly good when trying to pick out children who need special help in some area. One device is the rating scale of which there are many types for the study of common traits. Before a trait can be rated, however, it must be defined with sufficient precision so that a number of observers using the scale in the same situation would yield almost identical results.

On a graphic rating scale a horizontal line under which are descriptive phrases appears beside each trait. The person's possession of each trait is noted by a mark at the appropriate place on the line. One of the better known and more widely used is the Haggerty-Olson-Wickman scale for rating children's behavior.

Sample items from each of the four divisions of Schedule B are:

Division I

1. How intelligent is he?

Feeble-minded	Dull	Equal of average child on street	Bright	Brilliant
(5)	(4)	(3)	(2)	(1)

Division II

8. Is he slovenly or neat in personal appearance?

Unkempt, Very slovenly	Rather negligent	Inconspicuous	Is concerned about dress	Fastidious, Foppish
(5)	(4)	(2)	(1)	(3)

Division III

15. Is he quiet or talkative?

Speaks very rarely	Usually quiet	Upholds his end of talk	Talks more than his share	Jabbers
(3)	(1)	(2)	(4)	(5)

Division IV

26. Is he easily discouraged or is he persistent?

Melts before slight obstacles or objections	Gives up before adequate trial	Gives everything a fair trial	Persists until convinced of mistake	Never gives in, Obstinate
(5)	(3)	(1)	(2)	(4)

Procedures for the systematic recording of observations are more objective than anecdotal recordings, and they allow the observer to measure group as well as individual behavior. Limitations exist in the systematic recordings, however, since some traits are more readily rated than others. Each trait must be clearly defined so that it has nearly identical meaning from observer to observer and the opportunity to observe the trait must occur frequently during the total time of observation. The observation or mere noting of a particular trait or the frequency with which it is observed does not automatically lead to an understanding of the child. Frequently it is necessary to know the total situation which helped bring into play the observed behavior. In contrast, the ancedotal records permit more detailed and intensive study.

Anecdotal Records

Anecdotal records attempt to record the actual situation observed. For teachers interested in helping individual children, anecdotal records written by previous teachers can assist in understanding the role of past experiences in formulating the child's style of life. They also aid in an understanding of current situations in the child's life and the child's personal interpretations of his experiences. Teachers need to see life through the child's eyes, to infer his perception of self through their observations of his behavior. While studying and observing children, the teacher can also begin to develop insight into her own behavior, how the child's behavior affects her, and how she affects the child's behavior.

An anecdote is a word picture of an incident in the life of a child, one significant piece in the jigsaw puzzle which, when assembled, will contribute to a more complete picture of the child.

Dr. Daniel A. Prescott lists seven sources for obtaining anecdotal information.[5]

"1. Observing the child in action in the classroom, on the playground, and elsewhere in and around the school and writing descriptive anecdotes about characteristic and routine bits of behavior, as well as about unusually significant or revealing episodes.
2. Studying the child's accumulating records at school and entering significant data from them into his own written record about the child.
3. Making visits to the child's home, conferring with the parents both at home and at school, and recording descriptions of what he observed in the home and significant portions of the conversations with the parent or parents.
4. Observing the child's life space, recording descriptions of it and of

[5] Daniel A. Prescott, *The Child in the Educative Process* (New York: McGraw-Hill Book Company, 1957), pp. 151–52.

things going on in it, and making notes of the child's references to his own life space in his classroom functioning.
5. Conferring with colleagues who have taught the child in the past or are currently teaching him or who have special opportunities for observing him in action, and recording the facts they can give rather than their evaluations of or opinions about the child.
6. Collecting and examining samples of the child's classroom work, including written work done in each subject of study or unit of work, drawings, paintings, and other products of manual or creative activity, and saving characteristic samples of these for inclusion in the study record.
7. Conversing with the child individually and informally after school, at recess, or during free time and recording significant bits of these conversations."

To understand motivation, the direction and purpose of the child's movements, you must see behavior accurately and report it descriptively. This necessitates avoiding recording your immediate evaluation and personal interpretation of the event. Instead, one must observe precisely and recapture in the anecdote the moment of observation.

Dr. Prescott has developed specific characteristics for a good anecdote.[6]

"1. It gives the date, the place, and the situation in which the action occurred. We call this the setting.
2. It describes the actions of the child, the reactions of the other people involved, and the response of the child to these reactions.
3. It quotes what is said to the child and by the child during the action.
4. It supplies 'mood cues'—posture, gestures, voice qualities, and facial expressions that give cues to how the child felt. It does not provide interpretations of his feelings, but only the cues by which a reader may judge what they were.
5. The description is extensive enough to cover the episode. The action or conversation is not left incomplete and unfinished but is followed through to the point where a little vignette of a behavioral moment in the life of the child is supplied."

Research at the Institute for Child Study in Maryland has revealed that the average amount of time needed to write an anecdote is eight minutes.[7] Many situations do not require this much time, although occasionally the writing may take longer. Frequently, teachers have to write anecdotes after school is over. It is helpful to make a few notes as reminders at the time an incident occurs and to have a special looseleaf indexed notebook in which to collect anecdotes.

[6] Prescott, *The Child in the Educative Process,* pp. 153–54.
[7] Prescott, *The Child in the Educative Process,* p. 154.

Children seem to differ as to the kinds and amount of anecdotal information they supply. As a guide, try to record something about each child monthly. It is important to describe the child in a variety of situations—before school, on the playground, at recess, at lunch, in the hallways, at assembly, in special classes, on trips, at co-curricular activities, in the classroom—related both to the learning and adjustment processes. The anecdotes should reveal characteristic habitual patterns as well as atypical behavior. Include episodes that have special meanings to the child and where he seems to be especially involved. You can visit special classes for observation purposes, but events reported by the special teacher as they occur would be more valuable.

The time-sampling technique described earlier is especially useful for describing the child who does not seem to manifest any recordable behavior. Time-sampling alerts the teacher to how much is actually going on even though the behavior is unobtrusive. Note should be made of behavior which gives a balanced picture of the child—not just characteristic patterns with which the teacher is already familiar. It is essential to obtain knowledge of how the child acts in a variety of circumstances.

Anecdotes yield information which is unobtainable in other ways, for example, the following anecdote from the record of a sixth-grade boy:

Nov. 4, 1963, 3:20 p.m.
Carl seemed to wait around after school today. He said, "Is there anything I could do to help?" I indicated I had to alphabetize the papers in several subjects, and he was welcome to help.
He was quick to start on the spelling papers and soon completed them. When I thanked him, he said, "I guess when there is something important to do, I can be helpful too. I never get a chance during the day because Sue, Sally, and Bill always volunteer first."

The accumulation of anecdotes creates an insight impossible to derive from technical and statistical information. In many instances teachers are so involved with children emotionally that they are unaware of each child's individual characteristics. Anecdotal records, especially those taken by the time-sampling technique, can correct this erroneous impression.

Through anecdotal records of facial expressions, mood cues, and conversations it is possible to learn how the child's world looks to him and to become acquainted with the child's purpose. Anecdotes are one of the more effective methods of ascertaining the child's self concept.

Recurring patterns of behavior as described in anecdotal records help identify the developmental tasks at which the child is working and the ease or difficulty he is experiencing in accomplishing them. Recurring patterns also help to identify adjustment problems or faulty assumptions under which the child is laboring. The following are excerpts from cumulative records of a fifth-grade boy.

Dec. 10, 1962, 9:30.

As Janet walked to the front of the room to give her report, Dick left his seat to get his books from his shelf. Janet waited until Dick was seated and had his books in his desk before beginning the report. *D.Z.*

May 6, 1963, 1:00.

I announced the second section of the achievement tests would begin in five minutes and suggested that people sharpen their pencils now. *D.G.*

1:05.

I passed out the papers and began to read the directions. Dick dashed from his seat to sharpen his pencil, keeping one eye on me while he sharpened the pencil and returned to his seat. *D.G.*

Nov. 5, 1964, 9:50.

The children were standing in line to go to the fall music festival. As I opened the door, Dick dashed from the line calling, "Wait a minute! I forgot my music!" He looked in his notebook, in the desk, and finally found the music on his shelf. *D.J.*

Many techniques for assessing the status of a child in his group do not reveal why he has this status. Through anecdotal records the teacher can learn the behavior patterns in a child's interaction with his peers and thus identify underlying causes.

Through anecdotes, the teacher may be able to identify the regular use of certain adjustment mechanisms. When the current behavior is viewed in the setting of a series of anecdotes, and from the subjective view of the child's life space, it takes on new meaning for the viewer. Inappropriate as these behaviors may be from the point of view of the adult, they can be understood as the best possible adjustment for the child under the circumstances. The adult's new insight into the child's behavior brings about greater acceptance and understanding of the child. This change in adult attitudes may eventually permit the child to revise his convictions and modify his behavior.

By rereading the anecdotal records the teacher often discovers a typical response to the child of which he has been unaware and which may have influenced the child's behavior.

Anecdotes are of value in parent-teacher conferences; furnish a background for pupil placement in school; provide information for a counselor or for a psychological consultant; and serve as the basis for understanding problems that may develop between the school and the home.

---

4. What clues do the anecdotes about Dick in the preceding material give us about style of life? What types of supplementary observations or anecdotes would you want about Dick? Give an illustration of how anecdotes may be of value to the school counselor or psychological con-

sultant. How can anecdotes be utilized in parent-teacher conferences? What limitations would you place on the use of anecdotes in either of these situations?

It is important to look at the anecdotes critically to avoid collecting materials that are not of value in understanding behavior. Following are typical anecdotes that should be avoided, together with critical comments and suggestions for making an anecdote of the same situation more meaningful. These anecdotes about Jack started when he was in fifth grade.

Anecdote:
Cannot be depended upon.

Comment:
This is only a statement of opinion rather than an anecdote.

Better:
Oct. 21, 1964, 2:00 p.m.

We were working on a project involving study of the midwestern states. Jack had volunteered to bring the necessary maps from his father's gas station. He said he had forgotten them, but would pick them up today after school. The class agreed that anyone could forget and deferred this part of the project until tomorrow morning. *W.S.*

Oct. 22, 1964, 11:00 a.m.

Jack did not bring the maps. He said, "The ball game lasted longer than I had thought, and there wasn't time to go to the station." Since we could no longer delay, Bill offered to pick them up over the noon hour. *W.S.*

Anecdote:
Not capable of taking any responsibility.

Comment:
This is too general. Perhaps the fault lay with the teacher in not clarifying Jack's responsibilities and how to assume them. We should know what the responsibilities were and how he failed.

Better:
Jan. 18, 1965.

Jack's job was to see that we were signed up for audiovisual equipment and to bring it to our room for use. Plans for the use of this equipment were always made by class committees three weeks in advance and placed on the bulletin board and on a slip given to Jack.

Jack recognized he had caused the class considerable inconvenience several times in the past and again today by failing to sign up for the equipment. He said, "I always think three weeks is a long time, but it passes very fast." *B.H.*

Anecdote:
Doesn't work well with others.

Comment:
Who were the others? What did Jack fail to do?

Better:
March 15, 1965, 1:30 p.m.

The social studies committees were working on their reports. Doris was chairman of the southern states committee which included Jack, Susan, and Bill. There seemed to be confusion in this group so I decided to investigate. "Jack won't cooperate," complained Susan. "What do you want him to do?" I asked. Jack was frowning. "They say I have to study economic conditions in the states, and I am interested in state capitals," said Jack. "Did you volunteer to take economic conditions?" I asked. "There wasn't a chance to volunteer. We were just told her plans," answered Jack. "Is anyone investigating the state capitals?" I asked. The children indicated this job had not been assigned. "In that case, does the group mind having Jack study the capitals?" No one seemed to care. "What about the rest of you—are you all satisfied with your jobs?" They were. Jack went to the reference shelf and started to read. *B.H.*

The preceding anecdotes imply a need for caution in making statements that are empty and worthless generalizations. Subjective thoughts and feelings of the observer should be avoided, if possible. Anecdote writing should not be confused with interpretation and evaluation. Never think of the child's personality as characterized by a particular trait.

To be avoided are five types of anecdotal entries, too frequently found.

1. Evaluative statement—anecdotes that judge a behavior good or bad.

Sample: Gary was always at my desk during mathematics. When I asked him to go to his seat, he showed a bad attitude.

2. Interpretive statement—anecdotes that explain the child's behavior on the basis of a single fact.

Sample: We are making our Christmas presents, and Carl is most uncoöperative. This is because his parents are divorced.

3. Generalized descriptive statements—anecdotes that call characteristic a behavior described in general terms.

Sample: Larry is always annoying the boys in the milk line.

4. Anecdotes that omit a description of the setting—behavior that is acceptable in one setting may be most inappropriate in another.

Sample: Marvin defended his point of view vigorously for five minutes.

5. Undated and unsigned anecdotes—there should always be an indication of how the event fits into the time sequence. The date and time of an anecdote helps the reader capture some of the setting; access to the initials of the anecdote writer provides the opportunity to clarify details.

Anecdotes enable the teacher to observe and record child behavior in a variety of natural circumstances. This type of information, not readily available to any other professional, offers the opportunity eventually to see patterns and help in understanding the child.

In an anecdotal record, the visual and auditory impressions of the behavior just observed are transcribed into a sequence of events, from beginning to end; if possible, the language of the child is included exactly as heard.

The following form is suggested as a way in which to organize anecdotes:

Date *Setting and Incident* *Interpretation*

The interpretation may be in the form of an hypothesis to be confirmed or refuted at a later date after more observation.

After several months of recording the behavior observed, evaluation of the behavior may be made. Among the accumulated anecdotes, information should be found to aid in answering these questions:

1. What are his major self concepts?
2. How does he feel toward his family, his peers, other significant adults?
3. What are his goals?
4. What are the developmental tasks on which he is working?
5. What are his assets and liabilities?
6. What are his values and how do they affect his interactions?
7. Under what faulty assumptions is he operating?

---

5. Write an anecdote of behavior observed in a classroom. Does it contain all the elements of a good anecdote? What did you find to be your major problems in anecdote writing? How can you solve some of these problems in the future?

Observation is discussed more fully in the following books:

Almy, Millie and Ruth Cunningham, *Ways of Studying Children.* New York: Bureau of Publications, Teachers College, Columbia University, 1959.

Carbonara, Nancy T., *Techniques for Observing Normal Child Behavior.* Pittsburgh: University of Pittsburgh Press, 1961.

Cohen, Dorothy H. and Virginia Stern, *Observing and Recording the Behavior of Young Children.* New York: Bureau of Publications, Teachers College, Columbia University, 1958.

Driscoll, Gertrude, *How to Study the Behavior of Children.* New York: Bureau of Publications, Teachers College, Columbia University, 1941.

Rusch, Reuben, and Richard Clark, *Guide for Studying a Child.* Albany, New York: Delmar Publishers, 1960.

SOCIOMETRIC TECHNIQUES

A number of sociometric techniques can assist in understanding attitudes toward self and others. They are used by teachers concerned with obtaining more than fragmentary data about the child. The validity of these techniques is based on the setting in which they are administered and the relationship between the person administering the technique and the child. There must be an atmosphere of friendliness and mutual trust if the results are to be worthy of study.

Although observation produces the widest range of information about the child, other techniques are used for specific information. Sociometry yields information about the individual's status with his peers and intergroup relationships, as well as group standards and values. Sociometric techniques are easy to use and readily adaptable to most situations.

The first sociometric tests were devised by J. L. Moreno for use with delinquents in an institution organized on the cottage plan.[8] They are readily adaptable to classroom situations. The teacher can ask the children to name, in order of preference, three children to sit near, three with whom to work, and three with whom to play. By picturing the results on a chart as in Fig. 3-1 it is possible to discover the "star," the person chosen most often, the "isolate," one who receives no choices; and "mutual choices," those who chose each other.

Much of the success of the sociometric technique depends upon whether the teacher uses the information in rearranging and planning with the group. If the children do not see the results being used, they may not be interested in giving accurate choices. Some authorities suggest five choices, but three are sufficiently discriminating for most classroom populations and involve less tabulating. Results may be tallied as in Fig. 3-1. The children's names are listed in the wide left-hand column, keeping the boys separate from the girls. Each name is assigned a number corresponding to its position in the list. If No. 1 is Jane, the choices made by her are tallied on the first horizontal line in the appropriately numbered column. The numbers heading the vertical columns correspond to the numbers accompanying the names. The tally mark is the preference she indicated.

In our illustration, Jane's first choice was Mary, #5; second choice was Sally, #2; third choice was Greg, #8. John's first choice was Bob, #7, his second was Greg, #8, and his third was Jim, #10. Mutual choices are circled. Thus, Jane and Sally chose each other, as did Jim and John.

Results are tabulated for choices made by the same and opposite sexes tallied in the vertical columns at the extreme left, and choices received, tallied in the horizontal columns at the bottom of the sheet. Columns are totaled for choices received from each sex, mutual choices by sex, and total choices. Jane received a total of four choices, three from the same sex and one from the opposite sex. She chose two of the girls who chose her.

The names are then listed in the order of number of choices received.

[8] J. L. Moreno, *Who Shall Survive?* (Washington, D.C.: Nervous and Mental Diseases Publishing Co., 1934).

Date ______
Group ______
Soc. Ques. ______

CHOICES GIVEN			PUPILS CHOSEN																						
O.S.	S.S.	NAME	1	2	3	4	5	6	7	8	9	10	11	1	22	23	24	25	26	27	28	29	30	31	32
1	2	1. Jane		(2)			(1)			3															
1	2	2. Sally	(1)				2				3														
1	2	3. Ruth	1				(2)		3																
3		4. Esther								1	2	3													
1	2	5. Mary	(2)		(1)					3															
	3	6. John							(1)	2		(3)													
	3	7. Bob						(1)		2		3													
	3	8. Greg							1		(2)	(3)													
1	2	9. Bill	1						3	(2)															
1	2	10. Jim			3			(2)		(1)															
CHOICES RECEIVED - Same Sex			3	1	1		3	2	3	4	1	3													
CHOICES RECEIVED - Opposite Sex			1	0	1		0	0	1	3	2	1													
MUTUAL CHOICES - Same Sex			2	1	1		2	2	1	2	1	2													
MUTUAL CHOICES - Opposite Sex			0	0	0		0	0	0	0	0	0													
TOTAL			4	1	2	0	3	2	4	7	3	4													

FIG. 3-1 Sociometric Matrix Table Showing Choices

List of all members of the group, girls first, then boys. O.S. means opposite sex; S.S. means same sex. Circled numbers are mutual choices. Choices are numbered though given equivalent weight. For example: Jane chose Mary first, Sally second, a mutual choice, and Greg third, and opposite sex choice.

Greg Butler	7
Jim Castle	4
Bob Davis	4
Jane Ellis	4
Bill Freeman	3
Mary Gordon	3
Ruth Harris	2
John Johnsen	2
Sally Martin	1
Esther Shaw	0

From the list it is apparent that Greg is the "star" with seven choices, while Jane with four choices is the most popular of the girls. Esther, the "isolate" was not chosen, and Sally was chosen only once. When the results are pictured, as in Fig. 3-2, it is easier to see the interaction of the

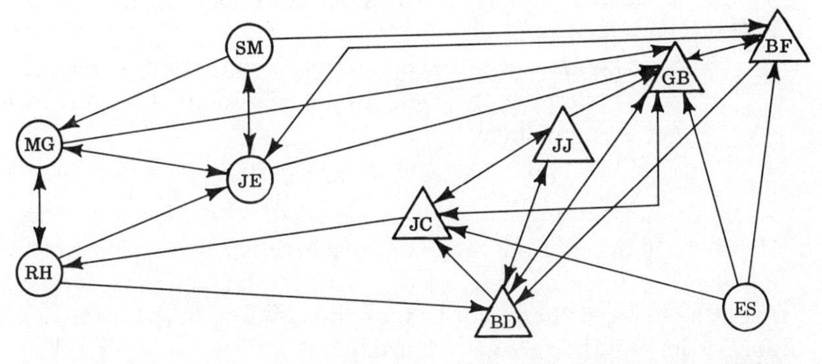

FIG. 3-2 Sociogram of Choices

Girl indicated by circle, boy by triangle.

group. Arrows indicate the direction of choice. Girls are indicated by circles and boys by triangles enclosing the child's initials.

Teachers can use sociometric information as a basis for studying relationships within the class. Children with social power, those chosen frequently, can be selected to give leadership to group enterprises. The isolates can be grouped with the more popular children they choose. The tally can also provide a basis for exploring the values and standards of the class. Group discussion can be used to examine issues.

"Who Are They" is a paper and pencil technique which may help the teacher determine the reasons for the choices made in the sociometric selections. It consists of statements descriptive of children. Each child is asked to write, below the paragraph, the name of a child in the room who would fit the description. Since he is not asked to sign his own name to the paper, it is assumed that the opinions are a true reflection of the child's view of his classmates. There is some question as to the advisability of asking a child to select someone to fit an uncomplimentary description. Certainly, it will not improve the cohesiveness of the group to accentuate a child's liabilities rather than his assets. Forcing a child to name another on the basis of his negative characteristics may immediately widen the space between them. The statement could be adapted to group relationships and should include positive and negative characteristics. A sample of some "Who Are They" items are:

1. Who are the boys and girls that complain about things? Nothing makes them happy. They want to have their own way.
2. Who are the ones that get bothered and upset when they are called on to talk or recite?
3. Who are the ones that are liked by almost everybody in the class?

4. Who are the ones that break rules, rules of the school and rules of the games?
5. Who are the ones who are mean and cruel to other children?
6. Who are the ones who are too shy to make friends easily? It is hard to get to know them.
7. Who are the boys and girls you would like for your best friends?

---

6. If you have access to a classroom teacher, ask permission to assist in making a sociometric study of the room. If the teacher is willing, you might have her first attempt to rank the children in sociometric preference order and then compare her ranking with the actual results.
7. Specifically, how would you use the information on the sociometrics illustrated in Fig. 1 and Fig. 2 to work with this group in a classroom setting?

For more detailed information on the use of sociometrics the student is referred to:

Gronlund, N. E., *Sociometrics in the Classroom.* New York: Harper & Row, Publishers, Inc., 1959.

Jennings, H. H., *Sociometry in Group Relations.* Washington, D.C.: American Council on Education, 1948.

———, "Sociometric Grouping in Relation to Child Development," in *Fostering Mental Health in Our Schools,* Washington, D.C.: National Education Association, Association for Supervision and Curriculum Development, 1950.

DETERMINING THE CHILD'S GOALS AND SELF CONCEPT

Since knowledge of a child's goals and his self concept are important in understanding development, many instruments have been devised to help the teacher get this information, most of them in the form of questionnaires. Because they require a knowledge of reading and writing, they cannot be used successfully below the fourth-grade level unless the teacher has the time and place to talk privately with each child. Some teachers arrange for interview time by assigning the class work at their desks while they interview individuals.

The interest record elicits information about preferred activities in and out of school, favorite radio and television programs, the type of role he would choose to take in a play and why, the kind of animal he would choose to be and why, things the child fears, three wishes, his ambition for adult life, and so on. Answers to these questions frequently reveal conditions at home that worry the child, as well as many misconceptions of what is occurring at school. Knowing why the child makes a particular choice often reveals qualities that appeal to him. If a child says he would like to be an alligator, do not assume it is because the alligator lies in the sun all day. Encouraging the child to give a reason for his choice may reveal that he wants to be an alligator because most people are afraid of alligators. There are many reasons a child may wish to be a bird: a bird flies, a bird is beautiful; a bird sings beautifully; a bird has no one to boss him. Various qualities attributed to every animal, and those which frequently appeal to a child are ones an adult may not even think of. Therefore, it is most important to get the child's reasons for his responses to such questions if the technique is to have any value. A complete copy of the interest inventory is found in the Appendix, p. 410.

---

8. What are some practical ways in which the interest record might facilitate the teaching-learning process? Interview a child with the interest record, and be prepared to discuss and defend what you believe you learned.

A sentence-completion form can produce the same information as the interest inventory and is more successful than direct questions with many children. Children automatically complete a sentence, and the spontaneity with which they respond makes the answers more reliable. Typical sentences are:

Nothing makes me more angry than. . . .
What people like most about me is. . . .
What gets me in trouble is. . . .
My ambition is. . . .
I feel afraid when. . . .

If the teacher has an idea she would like to have confirmed she might include a sentence to elicit the information. Sample forms are included in the Appendix, p. 411.

"I Am a Person Who" is another paper-and-pencil technique to help get a picture of the child's self concept. The child is given a sentence describing a person and is asked to indicate whether this person is very much like him, a little like him, or not like him. Some of the statements are:

I am a person who has many friends.
I am a person who always gets my way.
I am a person who likes to sit and daydream.

A complete copy of the form is found in the Appendix, pp. 412–413.

In addition to yielding a picture of the child's self concept, "I Am a Person Who" may show his contact with reality and any faulty assumptions under which he may be operating. The child who consistently checks the "a little like me" column may be reflecting an overconcern for the opinions of others, a hesitancy to take a positive stand "very much like me" or "not like me" because it might be the wrong answer. The child who is never absent from school yet says that the person who is sick a lot is very much like him is obviously acting under a faulty assumption. The child who sits in a classroom unaware of what is going on around him while he is lost in daydreams yet checks that the person who likes to sit and daydream is not like him is not aware of himself.

By assigning a value of 5 points to the "best" answer (in some cases "very much like me"; in others "not like me"), 1 point to the "worst" answer, and 3 points to the "little like me" answer, it is possible to obtain a total numerical rating. While no norms have been set for the test, ranking the children in one group by their numerical scores enables the teacher to judge the adjustment of the individual as compared with others in the group.

	A Very Much Like Me	*B* A Little Like Me	*C* Not Like Me
I am a person who has many friends.	5	3	1

In the example, which is the first statement in "I Am a Person Who," A is the "best" answer and would receive a score of 5 points. Any answer in the "A Little Like Me" column is always scored 3; so B would receive 3 points. C is the "worst" and would score 1 point. Each question is rated on the same scale. Presumably, the child with the highest numerical rating is the best-adjusted in the group. While no statistical studies have been made with this device, observation would tend to bear out the assumption.

Time is required to think about and interpret the results of both the interest-inventory and the sentence-completion techniques. No completely satisfactory scoring method has been devised for either instrument. However, these techniques can provide valuable clues to explain behavior.

Many teachers obtain essentially the same information from school assignments. An autobiography can be very revealing if the teacher specifies aspects that should be included, such as a description of the child and his place in the family; a description of the family including parents, siblings, and grandparents if they live with the family or are frequent visitors; a description of the home; how the child spends his time; things the family does together; things he likes best to do; his ambitions or dreams for the future. However, it cannot be stressed too strongly that the autobiography must be treated as creative writing rather than an exercise in grammar, if the teacher is using it as a device to learn the child's feelings. The child must know that the teacher is interested only in content and that the work will not be checked for spelling, punctuation, sentence structure, etc.

Some may ask, "Why the autobiography? Can't this information be obtained from the records?"

It is true that facts are contained in school records, but facts are not what the teacher is after. Rather, the child's perception of these facts, the child's view of his place in his environment is sought. The description in the autobiography may not be factual, but rather a description of life as the child would like to live it.[9]

The family constellation presents a picture of sibling interrelationships. The position of the child in the family and the way he views that position influence the way he views his world and himself. Frequently the teacher can learn the family constellation from the school records. If the records do not contain this information, it can easily be obtained from the child. This knowledge furnishes a frame of reference that is invaluable in understanding his behavior. First note the ordinal position of the child in the family. There are exceptions to any generalizations; still you should know the classical descriptions of ordinal positions.

> The eldest child is exposed to a situation where, for a limited period, he is the only child. As an only child it is probable that he receives considerable attention. Then, suddenly, he finds himself dethroned. He must deal with someone who appears to be robbing him of his mother's love. He tries to diminish the disadvantage of being dethroned. He wants to be first, and where he cannot be first he may lose interest. He strives continually to protect his position as the eldest child.
>
> The second child is confronted with a sibling who is always ahead of him. He is not as able as the elder child. He may come to feel that his inferiority is indicated by things that the older can do and he cannot. The second child often acts as if he has extra ground to cover. He has to catch up, to become "more"; more often than not he becomes more of what the eldest is not. He may, for example, become more active or more passive, more independent or more dependent.
>
> The middle child usually has neither the rights of the oldest nor the privileges of the youngest. He has to elbow his way through life. He may feel squeezed out and then tend to feel that life is unfair. Or, the middle child may succeed in pushing both competitors down and thereby gain superiority over both.
>
> The youngest child is the baby. He is the low man in the power structure of the family, but he may well turn this to his advantage. He has a greater chance to be spoiled. He frequently develops characteristics by which he can find a special place for himself, by being the cutest, the most charming, the weakest, the most helpless. Al-

[9] Don Dinkmeyer, "Reconsideration of the Autobiography," *The Vocational Guidance Quarterly*, VI, No. 1 (1957).

> though he may be the most ambitious, it is frequently found that if he cannot surpass all others, he becomes easily discouraged and then gives up in despair.
> The only child spends his formative years among persons who are all bigger and more capable. He soon has to develop skills that assure him the attention and help of adults. He may develop charm and intelligence, or he may become helpless or shy.[10]

With each succeeding birth, the position of each child other than the eldest changes. The child who was once the baby may become the middle child, or he may become the eldest boy and as such assume new importance. The death of a child eliminates one of the competitors, with a consequent change in position and perhaps behavior of the remaining children. There is constant competition among siblings to find a place of importance. Sometimes a child identifies with an older child of the same sex; sometimes he just gives up in discouragement and becomes helpless. In large families there is often an ordinal position by sex, as the oldest, middle, or youngest girl or boy. If there is a large age span between the first and second child, the second child does not have to compete with the first who, in the eyes of the younger, takes his place with the adults in the family, thereby permitting the younger to assume the position of eldest or only child.

The important aspect of the family constellation is not the child's position per se, but how the child views that position. The boy who has three older sisters would probably not view himself as the baby in the family but would assume the position of an only child—the only boy. Knowing the child's position in the family does not predict behavior but supplies hypotheses which can be tested.

In the case of children who are especially difficult to teach, a specialist might ask the child to rate the siblings, including himself, on traits such as intelligence, rebellion, and helpfulness around the house. This technique, which requires special training, can give an interesting picture of interaction within the family and the child's view of the world.

---

9. Johnny is eleven, with brothers twelve and nine who are both good students. The older brother conforms to the expectations of adult society. The youngest boy is very competitive. Make some assumptions about the family values, and describe what you might expect from Johnny.
10. Look at your own family constellation, or one you are familiar with, and explain the behavior of one of the siblings.

---

[10] Don Dinkmeyer and Rudolf Dreikurs, *Encouraging Children to Learn: The Encouragement Process* (Englewood Cliffs, N.J.: Prentice-Hall, Inc., 1963), pp. 21–22.

Early recollections, the earliest specific incidents the child can remember in detail, may be included in the autobiography and can reveal the child's self concept and his attitude toward life. Many psychologists, among them Alfred Adler, believe that perception and memory are both related to the individual's frame of reference. Adler held "that early memories were retained because of a selective factor in memory, and that this selective factor was not repression, but rather consistency with the individual's attitudinal frame of reference, the life style."[11] While detailed interpretation of the recollections can be made only by one trained in projective techniques and analysis of early recollections, the teacher may be able to recognize such attitudes as "I'm special"; "There is danger everywhere"; "I do not do as I should"; "Others must help me," as suggested in Harold Mosak's excellent article on the subject.[11]

Similarly, items usually included in a sentence-completion exercise or the interest inventory may be assigned as topics for creative writing. Wishes are a good topic with which to start, not only because most children would have no trouble with it, but also because it could be most revealing. Reasons for the wish should be included. The quality of information forthcoming would depend to a great extent upon the groundwork laid by the teacher. To stimulate thinking, the teacher might suggest some of the following wishes:

I wish I could help plan things.
I wish I had a brother (or sister).
I wish my teacher liked me.
I wish I were the oldest child.
I wish my family noticed when I did things right.
I wish I did not have so much to do.
I wish I didn't have to grow up.
I wish I were not afraid of mistakes or being criticized.
I wish I were grown up.

Magazine pictures can be used as the bases of stories. The child views the picture and then writes a story about it. Particularly well-suited to this technique are the pictures of Norman Rockwell or advertisement illustrations found in the popular magazines. Younger children enjoy this device, which could provide insight into how the child views the world and his place in that world.

Creative art work is also a clue to the child's self concept, although this is considered more valid before the child has been given instruction in the use of color, line, and form. The child's personality or view of himself may be reflected in the amount of space he uses for the picture and the colors he chooses.

[11] Harold H. Mosak, "Early Recollections as a Projective Technique," *Journal of Projective Techniques,* XXII, No. 3 (1958).

Teachers can develop a better understanding of the child as they become more aware of possible sources of information. Just as you cannot hope to know a child through one period of observation, you cannot hope to learn all about him through any one of the other techniques for child study. You can, however, after focusing on the pattern of behavior revealed by the child's daily work formulate a hypothesis about his self concept which can be proved or disproved through extended observation and the use of other techniques.

PHYSICAL GROWTH ASSESSORS

In addition to knowing how the child views himself and his world, one should know his unique pattern of development. Since the child starts growing from the moment he is conceived, it would be well to have in the school records a developmental history of the child. This should include:

The physical and emotional condition of the mother during pregnancy.
Anything unusual in connection with the birth.
Height and weight at birth.
Was he breast- or bottle-fed? Was he held during feeding?
Age of weaning and any problems.
Age when first tooth appeared.
Age of walking.
Age of talking.
Age when toilet training was begun.
Age when bladder control was achieved. Any regressions? Why?
Age when bowel control was achieved.
Preschool health.
Early habits (finger sucking, nail biting, masturbation).
Age of mother and father at birth of child.
Number and ages of siblings in the family.
Religion of mother and father.
Occupation of mother and father.
Education of mother and father.
Nationality of mother and father.
Any other people who live in the home.

When the child enters school, he often starts a series of regular, consecutive measurements in the physical, mental, and achievement areas. The concern here is not with methods of measurement, but with techniques for recording measurements so that the growth patterns are readily available for the teacher.

One technique for seeing the growth of the child at a glance is a growth-age chart, which is a simple graph. The horizontal axis is the chronological age, and the vertical axis is the growth age.

Willard C. Olson and Bryon O. Hughes, who conceived the idea of growth ages, have recorded in table form growth ages for various measures of height, weight, grip, and number of teeth.[12] The growth-age system is based on the postulate that if the average six year old weighs 43 pounds, then 43 pounds can be expressed as a growth age of 72 months. The growth-age tables are arithmetical averages, computed from actual measurements of large numbers of children at the various chronological ages.

The child's height is measured in inches, with his shoes removed. Weight is measured in pounds with the shoes off and pockets empty. The strength of grip is measured in kilograms on a hand dynamometer. Dental age is determined by the number of permanent teeth. After the physical measurements have been taken, they are expressed in growth ages through the use of the conversion tables, copies of which can be found in the Appendix, pp. 414–419. The growth ages are then plotted on the graph.

The growth graph has a preprinted line for the average child who is growing at the rate of one year of growth age for each twelve months of chronological age. When the growth ages are plotted for the individual child, the teacher can see at a glance the growth pattern for the child in each area of growth as well as how he compares with the hypothetical average child. A separate color is used to graph each of the ages which make up the organismic age: height age, weight age, grip age, dental age, mental age, arithmetic age, and reading age.

While physical measurements must be converted to growth ages, the mental age, arithmetic age, and reading age are obtained from the tables which accompany the intelligence and achievement tests. A convenient method for assembling the data before plotting is the individual growth record card, in the Appendix, p. 420.

The growth data for a girl from first through sixth grade, p. 72, is plotted on the chart in Fig. 3-3.

The Allometric Chart for Mental and Achievement Tests, Fig. 3-4, is a device which may be used to plot mental ages and achievement ages. Since normal growth when graphed produces a curve, the allometric chart has been corrected for the normal growth curve so that the hypothetical average growth of one year of mental age or achievement age for twelve months of chronological age when plotted will result in a diagonal line. Preprinted on the graph are channels of achievement for various IQ levels. Thus, a child with a given IQ should be achieving

[12] Willard C. Olson and Byron O. Hughes, *Manual for the Description of Growth in Age Units* (Ann Arbor, Michigan: University Elementary School, University of Michigan, 1950).

GROWTH DATA FOR A GIRL FROM FIRST THROUGH SIXTH GRADE

	Growth Ages										
Chronological age in months	*Hgt.*	*Hgt. age*	*Wgt.*	*Wgt. age*	*No. of teeth*	*Dental age*	*Grip*	*Grip age*	*Mental age*	*Reading age*	*Arithmetic age*
83									84		
87	46.5	81	50.0	84	0	0	11.7	86			
93									97		
98										87	81
99	48.3	90	54.3	97	8	86	9	67			
105									99		
108										96	94
110	50.8	107	59.3	105	8	86	14	100			
116									123		
120										106	106
122	51.9	112	66.4	116	10	92	13	95			
128									136		
131										118	133
134	55.0	129	74.0	129	14	112	19	124			
140									146		
144										128	149
146	57.0	141	84.5	145	25	141	18	118			

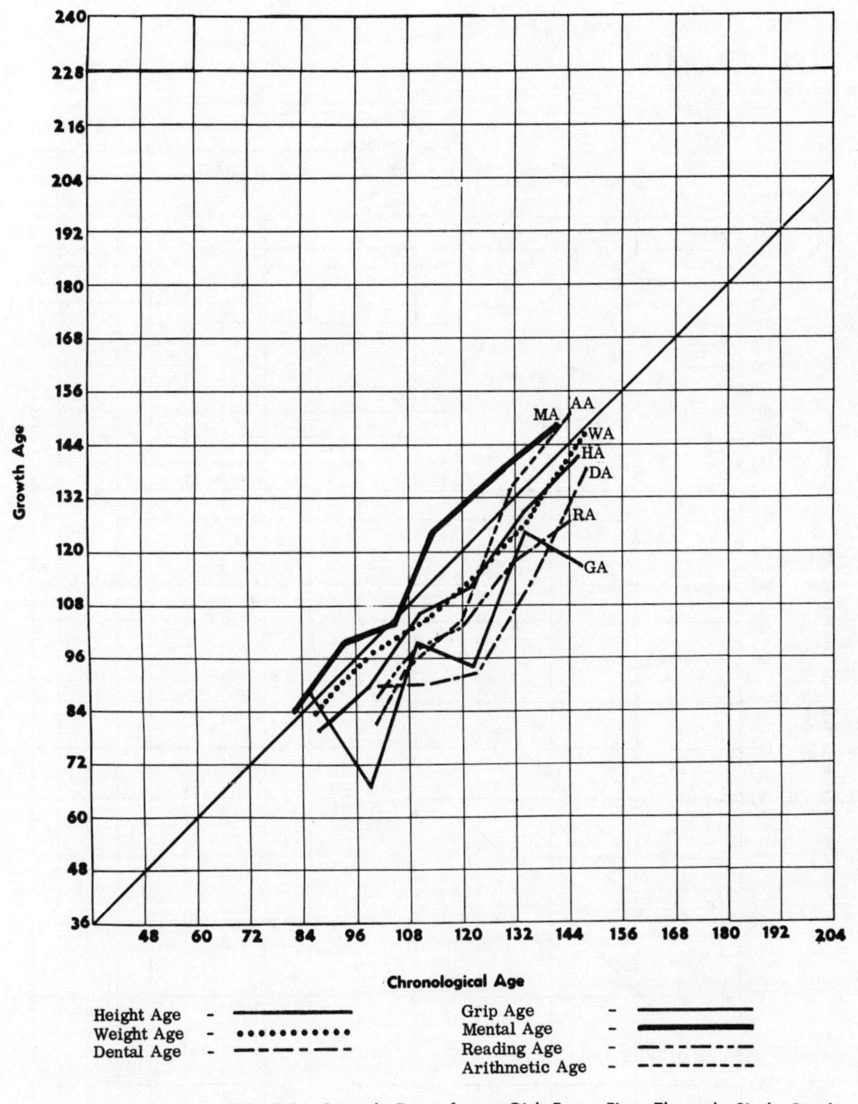

FIG. 3-3 Growth Data for a Girl From First Through Sixth Grade

within the range of the channel shown on the chart. When actual achievement is plotted, one can see at a glance if the child is growing academically within his channel—his normal range—or if he is achieving more or less than would be expected from his IQ.

---

11. What would you, as a teacher, do if you found, by plotting a child's achievement on an allometric chart, that the child was performing above his channel? Below his channel?

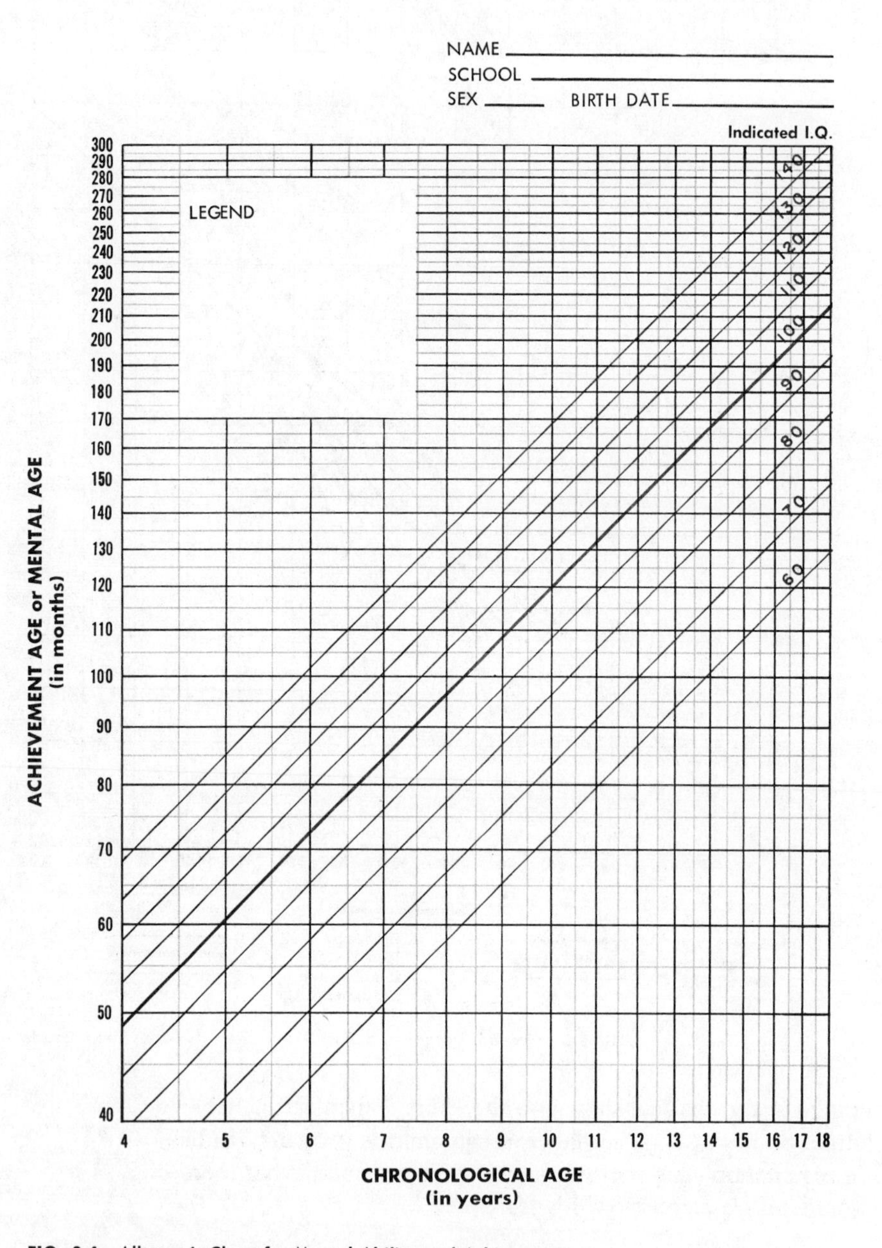

FIG. 3-4 Allometric Chart for Mental Ability and Achievement

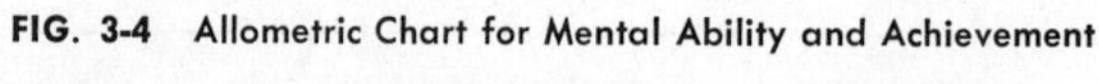

The Wetzel Grid is a graphical technique for judging the physical growth and fitness of a child from data on his weight, height and age. The chart, Fig. 3-5, consists of two main panels: on the left, one plots weight (in Pounds or Kg. on the vertical axis) against height (in Inches or Cm.) on the horizontal axis. Seven Grid Channels running diagonally upwards

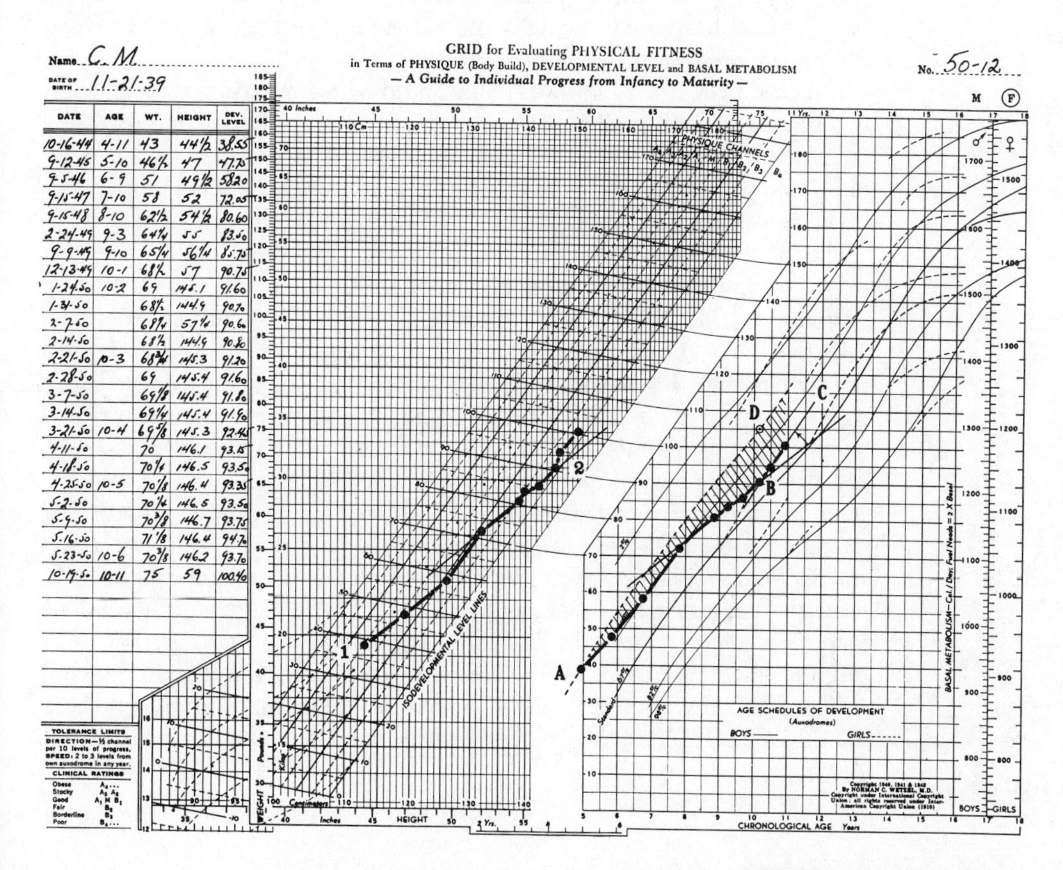

FIG. 3-5 The Wetzel Grid

A typical example of simple growth failure as disclosed by plotting heights and weights on a Grid. The essential signs of growth failure which this girl revealed during her 5-year course of unsatisfactory growth between points 1 and 2 in the channel system, and along her actual auxodrome AB, are: (1) *loss of physique* from channel M to B_3 and (2) *slow-down* in the rate of development which would normally have carried her along the expected auxodrome AD. The vertical distance BD of 14 levels represents growth lag at B and is equivalent to about 1¼ years' development.

Courtesy *The Journal of Clinical Nutrition.*

define types of *physique* ranging from *Stocky* in channel A_3 and A_2, through *Medium* (A_1, M, B_1) to the slender or linear types in B_2 and B_3. On the other hand, Body *Size* is measured in terms of "levels of development" according to the scale at the left of the Channel System. In the right-hand panel, level of development (or Size) is, in turn, plotted against age and thus yields direct visual evidence on the *Speed* or rate of progress. Five calibrated curves show the percentage of children on or ahead of each such standard schedule of growth.

The Grid provides a simple, reliable and direct comparison with a child's own plotted growth progress in terms of body size, physique and direction of growth, as revealed by his course through the channel system, and, additionally, in terms of growth *Speed,* as reflected by his comparative advance along the family of standard auxodromes in the right panel.

The Wetzel Grid appears to be one of the most promising of the tests for appraising the fitness status of school children.

Whatever the technique for studying growth, the concern should be with the gains the child is making in each area over a period of time, rather than with his status at any particular time. In order to gear learning experiences to the individual child, it is necessary to know how he is progressing through his growth cycles in terms of both direction and rate. Tabulations of physical measurements and age or grade levels of achievement are only status statistics. Only as we see the amount of growth that has taken place each year in each area do we have a picture of the progress made. If a child has been growing in height at the rate of nine months in height age for each twelve months of chronological age and then in one year gains nineteen months in height age, the indications are that he is entering another growth cycle. This may be a clue to both parents and teachers to provide a rich environment of experiences from which to choose as he reaches the level of maturation at which he is ready for them.

SUGGESTED READINGS

Articles

Prescott, D., "Basic Assumption in Child Study," p. 45, in *Readings in the Psychology of Human Growth and Development,* ed. W. Baller. New York: Holt, Rinehart & Winston, Inc., 1962.

Stott, L., "Appraising Developmental Status," p. 91, in *Readings in the Psychology of Human Growth and Development,* ed. W. Baller. New York: Holt, Rinehart & Winston, Inc., 1962.

Stendler, C., "How Well Do Elementary School Teachers Understand Child Behavior?" p. 640, in *Readings in the Psychology of Human Growth and Development,* ed. W. Baller. New York: Holt, Rinehart & Winston, Inc., 1962.

Books

Almy, A. and R. Cunningham, *Ways of Studying Children.* New York: Bureau of Publications, Teachers College, Columbia University, 1959.

American Journal of Orthopsychiatry, 33, July 1963, 591–633.

Dearborn, W. F. and J. Rothney, *Predicting the Child's Development.* Cambridge, Mass.: Sci.-Art, 1941.

Garn, S., *Methods for Research in Human Growth.* Springfield, Ill.: Charles C Thomas, Publisher, 1958.

Helping Teachers Understand Children. Washington, D.C.: American Council on Education, 1945.

Millard, C. V., *The Elementary School Child–A Book of Cases.* New York: Holt, Rinehart & Winston, Inc., 1957.

Prescott, D., *The Child in the Educative Process.* New York: McGraw-Hill Book Company, 1957.

———, *The Elementary School Child.* Washington, D.C.: Educational Services, 1961.

Rusch, R. and R. Clark, *Guide for Studying a Child.* Albany, New York: Delmar Publishers, Inc., 1960.

Stott, L., *The Longitudinal Study of Individual Development.* Detroit: Merrill-Palmer, 1955.

4 PRINCIPLES OF DEVELOPMENT

FACTORS OF HEREDITY, ENVIRONMENT, SELF

The student of child development should have a foundation in the principles of human development. These principles explain the basic factors which govern all growth and development. The individual is a product of hereditary, environmental, and self factors.

Hereditary factors are innate characteristics with which the child is equipped at birth. Prime factors in growth, heredity forces control the basic nature of the organism and the rate at which the organism covers the life cycle; they are the basic assets and liabilities, structural and functional, which allow the organism to use both nature and nurture in development. While hereditary factors generally come into play prior to birth, they do influence growth throughout life, just as some environmental forces are operative prior to birth.

The environment is a factor which must be continually studied in connection with hereditary forces. There is an increasing recognition that genes must function within a specific environment. Environmental factors we would consider include the intrauterine environment, the family atmosphere, methods of child training, the family constellation, the total social community and the socioeconomic factors.

Self factors include the child's feelings and conceptions about himself, other persons, society, and his universe of experience, including his convictions, values, goals, and attitudes. The meaning the child inserts into his experiences, his individuality, and the manner in which the child characteristically perceives his experiences are included in the definition of self.

Heredity

Through heredity the child acquires from his parents potentials for development which are inherent in the germ plasm and associated cell structures. The basic agents of development are genes, frequently referred to as determiners of the organism.

Genes are tiny particles, roughly thirty thousand in number, which make up the forty-six chromosomes in human beings. Through a special process of cell division, egg and sperm cells lose half their chromosomes. When the sperm unites with the egg, two halves are joined, providing the new cell with the normal number of chromosomes.

The new individual's life begins, then, at conception, when the sperm penetrates the wall of the ovum releasing twenty-three chromosomes. At almost the identical time the inner core of the ovum breaks to release twenty-three chromosomes of its own. Knowledge of this process enables the student of child development to understand how the chromosomes serve as carriers of the child's heredity.

The immense variety inherent in each individual's genes and the significance of dominant and recessive factors in the study of genes do not concern us here. We need only know that it is the interaction among these genes which predisposes the growth of all the physical structures of the body. What effect genes have on the development of specific nonphysical human traits is not known.

Frequently, individuals are concerned about the influence of heredity on specific traits and ask,

> How tall might our children be? Will they tend to be overweight or thin, well-coordinated or clumsy? How about special talents? Will they inherit mother's talent for music, father's specific skill in sports? Which of these things will develop in a specific offspring?

Each of these factors is dependent upon both hereditary and environmental forces. Certainly, environmental forces can modify or enhance predispositions present in the genes. Even some inherited structural defects can be overcome, as with the use of eyeglasses.

Intelligence is often of much concern to parents. Is intelligence inherited? If we mean only the potential for intelligence present in the genes, then we may speak of intelligence as inherited. If we go one step farther, to define intelligence in terms of its functions or the way in which it is demonstrated, then the proportional influence of heredity drops. Potentialities are inherited. Their optimum development is highly dependent upon the amount of nurture the environment provides and the way in which the individual chooses to utilize this nurture.

Acquired traits are not inherited, nor are character inadequacies, nor the complex behavioral patterns involved in certain types of skills. Certainly the value system of an individual is not inherent. Concepts and assumptions about life are not inherited.

Considerable variance is possible in the development of any individual. In any single mating the possible combinations of chromosomes between the male and the female are statistically enormous; the possibility of any one such combination being repeated more than once has been estimated at about one in three hundred thousand billion. It is apparent that the different combinations possible from roughly thirty thousand genes in the system can assume a figure beyond our capacity to predict or comprehend. When one expands the concept to include all the physiological and chemical factors present in the environment as modifying forces, then the differences possible in human development become, for practical purposes, infinite.

---

1. Sometimes people ask, why are there such great differences in the physical characteristics of children from the same parents? How would you explain these differences?
2. Peter, age thirteen, is an excellent student, tall, with red hair and blue eyes, overweight, argumentative like his father, poorly coordinated in baseball and basketball, but above average in tennis and golf. Socially, he plays with one child but prefers to be alone. How would you explain the above traits in terms of the relative influence of hereditary, environmental, and self factors?
3. If you are observing or studying a child, list some of his traits and discuss them in terms of the hereditary, environmental, and self factors.

Maturation

Closely related to the hereditary factor in our consideration of development is maturation, which is the regulatory mechanism primarily dependent upon physical growth in contrast to experience or training. Maturation directs the biological development of the bodily machinery. It accounts for changes that take place in the absence of specific practice. Basic research in maturation studies points to the fact that behavior patterns of the infant and child are controlled by developmental levels in neuromuscular maturation, and it is futile to try to train a child in some activities before the neural mechanism is ready. The patterns of all behaviors influenced by maturation tend to show evidence of spurts, plateaus, and varying fluctuations. Thus, we can see that maturation and learning are different facets of a fundamental process of growth. In any type of educational planning it is well to look for the cues or signals which reflect a maturity of the neural mechanisms.

The general principle of maturation has certain educational implications. The individual's ability to profit from his experiences is closely related to the level of development he has attained. Practice may accelerate the attainment of a skill when it is introduced at a time the child is ready for it. Imposed before readiness, however, practice may inhibit the individual's potential and carry concomitant discouragement factors which influence his future performance.

Premature practice, it seems evident, is educationally unsound. There are many implications as to its influence on a child's interest, cooperation, and formation of negative attitudes. On the other hand, optimal readiness is a relative factor, and the professional educator must be alert to the possibility that waiting too long may be as harmful as premature forcing or pressuring. Readiness and maturation are concepts which must be applied on an individual basis.

---

4. At present some children are taught to read in prekindergarten and kindergarten while other children do not begin the reading process untill second grade. Relate these varying practices to the concepts of maturation and readiness. Is readiness a concept which should be considered only at the beginning of school or at the onset of a specific developmental cycle? How are the readiness and maturation factors influential throughout all school experiences?

Environment

Parents and teachers are concerned with providing environmental nutrients to maximize development. The most significant factors in the environment appear to be those which promote an atmosphere of security, of basic trust, whether it be between parent and child or teacher and child.

The child needs a secure and happy home life with adequate love relationships. When he is deprived of these love relationships, his capacity to achieve his hereditary potential is limited. Love relationships, in many ways, appear to be as significant as the meeting of physical needs.

There should be wholesome attitudes in the family toward learning and cultural experiences. This implies a family way of life from which the child is able to learn more than from the devices his parents may use to stimulate his interest in reading and participation in cultural events.

The best atmosphere for learning is one in which the child is encouraged. The home or school atmosphere should provide a variety of experiences and opportunities for the recognition of the child's assets. At the same time, it should avoid applying pressure and forcing the learning situation. The potential of an individual is more likely to be reached when the environment offers a wide variety of experiences in an atmosphere in which the individual is accepted as he is.

---

5. Since the environment has been demonstrated to have an effect on the child's development, give examples of how development might be affected by different types of environmental factors, such as family attitudes, position of the child among siblings, socioeconomic position, and other factors you consider pertinent. How can the teacher and the school overcome negative environmental factors?

The Self

An important but often neglected factor in understanding principles of development is the self factor, the person's inner world. It is composed of his feelings, strivings, thoughts, and general view of self and is made up of the evaluations, convictions, attitudes, and assumptions upon which daily decisions are made. When one is in empathy with the self of an individual, then it is possible to understand his pattern of life. Knowledge of a person's life style enables us to look at the purposes and goals which underlie behavior.

The self factor cautions us against interpreting hereditary or environmental influences mechanistically. We must recognize that they interact and are complementary, but the story of development is not complete without including the role that the self plays in dealing with varied influences.

It is probably obvious that it is more important to determine how the individual uses his potentialities and his environmental factors than to determine which ones he possesses. Here is where an understanding of the self or life style facilitates understanding of any given individual. The self is highly influential in the interpretation of hereditary and environmental forces. We have all observed physically handicapped children. Some function quite effectively almost because of the handicap; others utilize the same handicap as an excuse for inadequacy, inferiority, or incapacity.

---

6. How can understanding of the self or the life style be of value to the parent in educating and training the child?
7. What are the implications of the psychology of use—the fact that it is more important to know how the person uses his traits than to know what the traits are—for understanding some of our studies of underachievement and delinquency?

INTERACTION OF HEREDITY AND ENVIRONMENT

Heredity and environment are actually complementary in the total growth process. Heredity must be given an environment in which to function, whereas environmental factors can contribute only to the genetic potentialities of a living and growing organism. Because the factors of heredity and environment are so inextricably interwoven, it is scientifically impossible to separate them and determine the comparative effect of each.

Heredity, through the interaction of genes, sets some limits on our potentialities. Success in attaining the utmost possible development depends upon the interaction of numerous environmental influences, which begin at the onset of life, many months before birth. Montagu[1] has suggested the concept would possibly be clarified if instead of using the word heredity we were to use the word potentialities. A complex of specific potentialities influences the developmental processes and is influenced in turn by the environment. The interaction is so complete that the concepts of heredity and environment are primarily useful as convenient abstractions. Development is constantly being modified by internal and external influences that interact.

The self interacts continually with hereditary and environmental influences and results from the interpretations the individual has made about his experiences. The child's experiences in his primary society, the family, are primary determinants of his conclusions about relationships. His evaluation of self and society and his conclusions, attitudes, convictions, and assumptions make up the life style.

THE ORGANIZATION OF LIFE

Although hereditary, environmental, and self factors may be isolated for analytical purposes, their interaction will never really be understood without comprehension of the dynamic, unified whole—which is more than the sum of its parts.

Edmund Sinnott has attacked the dualistic concept of man's nature, and suggests that

> man's physical life grows out of the basic goal-seeking and purposiveness found in all organic behavior, and that this, in turn, is an aspect of the more general self-regulating and normative character evident in the development and activities of living organisms.[2]

Sinnott contends that human beings are subject to self-regulatory behavior, which seems to be always purposive in that it dictates actions in line with a goal set up in the system. Growth and development, with their increasing differentiations, orderly sequences, and complex interrelated events requiring precise timing are explained in terms of organization, the distinctive character of all life. Thus, the word organism is fortunate in that it emphasizes a significant characteristic of a living thing, its organization.

Sinnott points out,

> A remarkable fact about organic regulation, both developmental and physiological, is that, if the organism is prevented from reach-

[1] A. Montagu, *The Direction of Human Development* (New York: Harper & Row, Publishers, Inc., 1955).

[2] E. Sinnott, *Cell and Psyche: The Biology of Purpose* (New York: Harper & Row, Publishers, Inc., 1961), Preface. Originally published by The University of North Carolina Press.

ing its norm or "goal" in the ordinary way, it is resourceful and will attain this by a different method. The end rather than the means seems to be the important thing.[3]

He goes on to remind us of the basic nature of biological organization.

It is characteristic of living material, as has been shown, that the organisms which it builds grow by orderly progression from one step to the next so that a definite series of bodily structures with specific forms and interrelationships are produced, and that physiological equilibria within them are maintained by constant regulatory adjustments. This progressive, organized, and integrative character of life, its conspicuous and distinctive quality, is most commonly recognized in the development and physiological activity of the body, but it bears a remarkable resemblance to phenomena which are admittedly psychological.[4]

Sinnott quotes biologists extensively as he describes the relationship between the "goal-directed" processes of physiological activity and the concept of purpose, the basis of most psychological activities.

Sinnott has done a monumental job of pointing out the relationship between biological and psychological life. It helps us to understand how all human beings produce activity which tends toward self-actualization. More extensive reading in his *Cell and Psyche: The Biology of Purpose* is recommended.

The developmental processes take on order when viewed in terms of certain principles. The following principles are useful in understanding human development.

DEVELOPMENTAL PRINCIPLES

Growth is patterned

Each child has his own pattern which emerges at his own characteristic rate. Some children mature early, others late. In research or teaching, children should never be compared unless their rate and pattern of growth have been taken into account. We can distinguish readily on a growth chart the children who present early, late, and split growth patterns. The pattern of growth is directly related to the factor of the individuality of growth. The Harvard Growth Study, using one of the largest samples of physical growth available, presented clear evidence of the fact that there are no two identical growth patterns.

Psychological growth also is patterned, and the individual's psychological pattern is also unique. As we become cognizant of these two facts, we

[3] Sinnott, *Cell and Psyche,* p. 33.
[4] Sinnott, *Cell and Psyche,* p. 44.

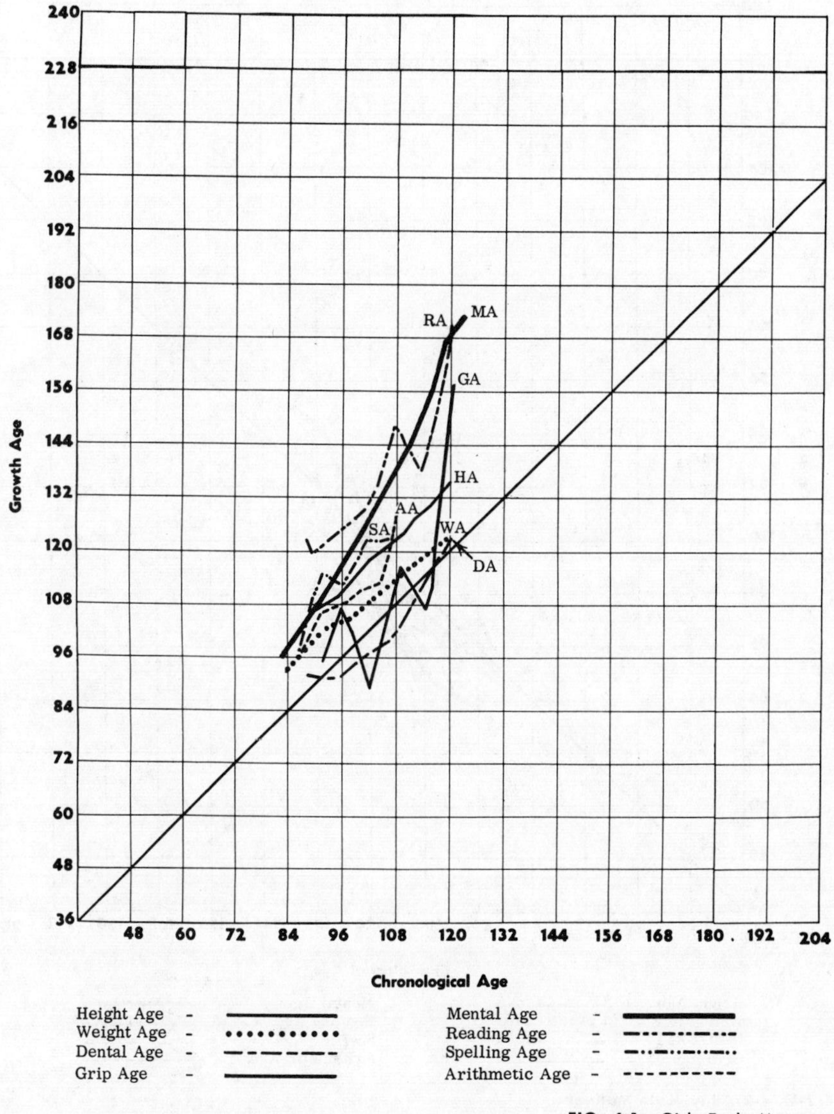

FIG. 4-1 Girl—Early Maturer

are more likely to understand the individual. For example, the psychological interview or developmental history frequently presents us with a picture of a child who was resistive in terms of early feeding functions. At a later stage he may not have assumed responsibility for dressing himself as desired. These facts show the emerging pattern of response, which is psychological as well as physical.

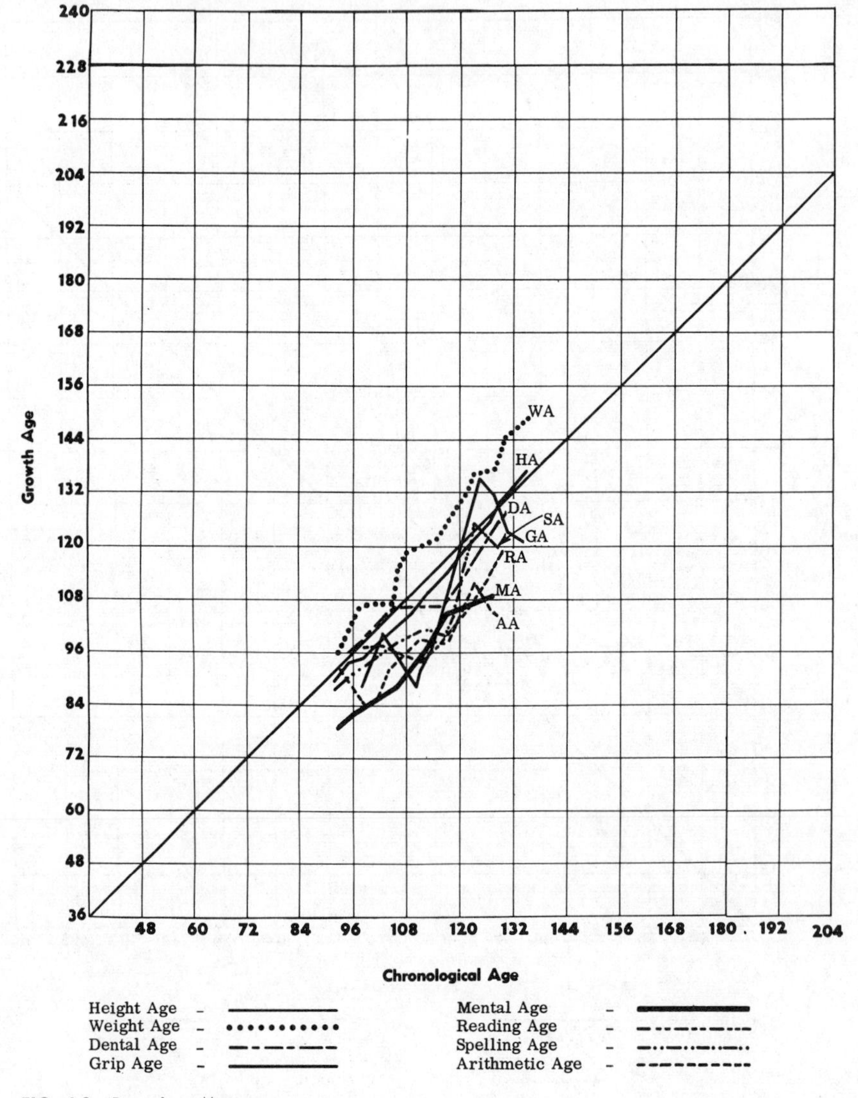

FIG. 4-2 Boy—Late Maturer

Growth is sequential

Growth follows an orderly sequence, which, in general, is the same for all individuals. The work of Gesell and Piaget has been most definitive in establishing the sequential nature of growth. At the simplest level the young child progresses from lifting his hand to sitting up, standing and finally walking. Other facets of skeletal development also occur sequentially, as, for example, the law of cephalocaudal and proximo-distal devel-

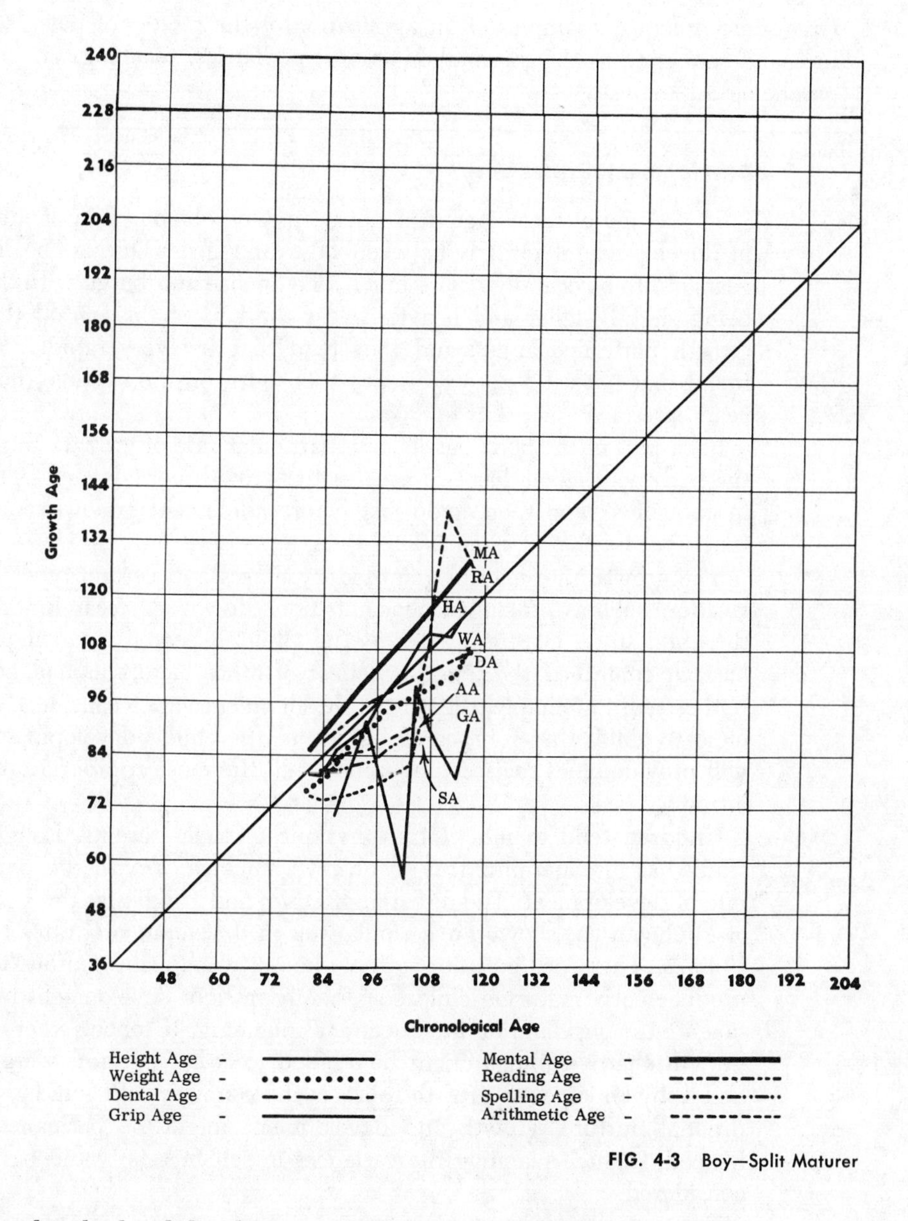

FIG. 4-3 Boy—Split Maturer

opment, whereby head development precedes foot development, and the central parts of the body mature earlier than the peripheral parts of the body. Teeth are acquired in a specific sequence. Individuals vary in terms of time, but the sequence is invariable. Actually, orderly sequence is important in developmental diagnosis for both the pediatrician and the psychologist. Deviations from the sequence provide clues to growth difficulties.

8. Give some practical examples of an application of the factors of pattern and sequence to the parental functions, pediatrics, teaching, or psychological analysis.

Developmental rates vary

The tempo of development is not even. One obvious area of difference in developmental rates is between boys and girls. During the first ten years of life boys and girls are much alike in size and build, with the boys being slightly taller and heavier. Near the end of this period the girls' growth pattern changes, and they tend to grow very rapidly. Bayley[5] found that boys did not experience this spurt, on the average, until two years later.

Each part of the body has its own particular rate of growth. In general, the body as a whole has two accelerated growth periods, one from birth to about five, and then again just before adolescence. However, certain functions develop at a much later time, at a slower rate.

The growth rate may be retarded by illness and certain types of deprivation, such as prolonged poor nutrition. However, research at some of the child study institutes, such as the Child Research Council, Denver, has not confirmed the retarding effect of other factors as had been hypothesized. Put simply, the rate of development varies considerably from child to child; therefore, careful study of the child's developmental rate will provide clues related to readiness and the most appropriate times to introduce tasks.

Children tend to inherit the physique of their parents. Longitudinal study has also permitted us to observe similarities with the parents in rate of development. The research of Olson and Hughes at the University of Michigan has shown great similarities in developmental rates between siblings. There are indications that the early maturing mother tends to produce early maturing children.[6] Family rates of development might be taken into consideration in educational planning. If schools kept detailed growth charts, siblings might be studied to see if patterns were similar and if, by anticipating growth spurts in the younger sibling and giving additional nurture, growth and development might be permanently enhanced. In such planning the variances in self factors would have to be considered.

9. What account do our present educational systems take of rate of development? What are the types of data necessary to make a beginning at-

[5] N. Bayley, "How Children Grow," in *The Encyclopedia of Child Care and Guidance,* rev. ed., S. Gruenberg (New York: Doubleday & Company, Inc., 1963).
[6] W. Olson, *Child Development,* 2nd ed. (Boston: D. C. Heath & Company, 1959).

tempt at assessing rate? Is it necessary to accumulate the data on growth in a specific manner? Show how developmental diagnosis in the schools might be improved by considering the factor of rate. Show how the child's rate of growth may be as much a cause for disturbing behavior as some of the more commonly identified social and emotional causes of misbehavior.

Growth is cyclic

The growth curves that have been studied through periods of change reveal cycles as well as patterns. Courtis[7] has defined the cycle as one or more designs that follow in sequence. In all the major longitudinal studies of development where the same children have been followed over long periods of time, the series of accelerations and decelerations is clearly observable.

Shuttleworth did extensive research on twenty-two kinds of growth and came to the following conclusions:

All twenty-two dimensions exhibit two major growth cycles consisting of accelerating and decelerating phases. The growth phases of the first cycle are initiated at different ages and are of different durations such that the growth trends of the twenty-two dimensions are not synchronized. The growth phases of the second cycle, in respect to a given menarcheal age are initiated at approximately the same ages and are of similar durations such that the growth trends of the twenty-two dimensions are synchronized.[8]

Thus, when certain developmental factors are equated, the cycles appear to be quite similar. The total number of cycles in the life of the individual is still under dispute. Courtis found four cycles in his research, but ensuing research has indicated more. The concept of cyclic growth is characterized by a starting point (sometimes referred to as incipiency) rate, and maximum. Some research tends to show that relationships can be demonstrated between academic and physiological curves by using the cyclic approach to the study of development. Research by Nally was one attempt to establish this type of relationship.[9]

Cycles of growth can be shown as periods of rapid acceleration with an intervening period of slow, steady growth. Scammon identified four types

[7] S. Courtis, "What Is a Growth Cycle?," *Growth,* No. 1 (1937), 155–74.

[8] F. Shuttleworth, *The Physical and Mental Growth of Girls and Boys Age Six to Nineteen in Relation to the Age of Maximum Growth,* Monograph of the Society for Research in Child Development, Vol. IV, Serial 22, No. 3 (Lafayette, Indiana: Child Development Publications, 1939), 446–49.

[9] T. Nally, "The Relationship Between Achieved Growth in Height and the Beginning of Growth in Reading" (Doctoral Dissertation, Michigan State University, College of Education, E. Lansing, Michigan, 1953).

of postnatal growth. The successive periods of acceleration, deceleration, and acceleration are readily apparent in the curve of the growth of the body as a whole. The following chart reflects the curvilinear and cyclic nature of growth.

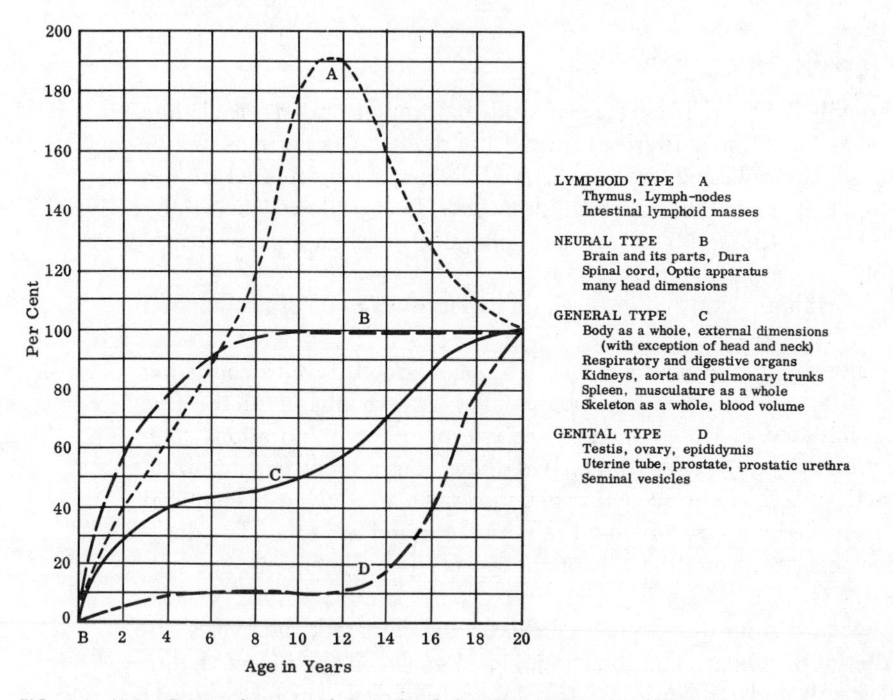

FIG. 4-4 Major Types of Postnatal Growth of the Various Parts and Organs of the Body

From *The Measurement of Man* by J. A. Harris, C. M. Jackson, D. G. Paterson, and R. E. Scammon. Minneapolis: The University of Minnesota Press. Copyright 1930 by the University of Minnesota.

In individual interpretation of a child, single measures are almost useless and must be seen in relationship to the child's unique design. This process is distinctly different from comparing the child with normative data.

Developmental patterns show wide individual differences

We have observed that the pattern of growth is to some extent predictable. However, you should be aware of the great individual differences in developmental patterns which can be seen comparing children or even observing an individual child. Intraindividual variability in rate has been repeatedly demonstrated in longitudinal study, making us aware again of the uniqueness of the individual. This uniqueness can be identified at an early stage of development. Shuttleworth[10] found that the patterns of early maturers and late maturers were similar in many respects if he ignored chronological age and superimposed the curves for the groups in each sex so that maximum growth increments were placed in the same line. The differences in the time at which these increments occurred made the children's actual experiences quite dissimilar.

Individual differences in development are of prime importance to the teacher. General norms give broad indications, but the teacher must expect the individual to differ quite markedly from the norm. While the teacher may be concerned with the cause of the deviation, it is also important to accept and anticipate that there will be deviations from any generally established norm. For example, the age at which various children reach puberty varies quite markedly. The differences are dramatic at this particular phase because it is readily observable, but they are equally significant during all other phases of development. It may actually be more important to compare annual increments in growth for the individual than to compare him with the group. Thus, as we find methods of analyzing each child's own cycles, it will be possible to develop more advanced educational techniques. The implications for the boy in eighth grade who has not begun his growth spurt in contrast to the fully mature eighth grader seems to be self-evident.

The relationship between physical status and psychological characteristics cannot be predicted directly. Mussen and Jones, who did an extensive study in this area, stress that the individual must be understood in terms of his unique factors, and not maturity alone.[11]

---

10. An early-maturing boy and a late-maturing boy are in the same class in school. What effects might their different maturation patterns have upon participation in sports and social activities? Are there any social and emotional problems which may be related to early and late maturation factors? Do the differences in developmental patterns and rates between boys and girls have any effect upon personal-social adjustment and acceptance of school tasks? What might be the advantage of admitting the late-maturing child to elementary school at a later date?

Each phase of development has characteristic traits

Children pass through various developmental stages at different times due to varying developmental rates. However, intensive study of children

[10] F. Shuttleworth, *The Physical and Mental Growth of Girls and Boys.*
[11] P. Mussen and M. Jones, "Self-conceptions, Motivations, and Interpersonal Attitudes of Late and Early Maturing Boys," *Child Development,* 28, June 1957.

has revealed similarities in the developmental stages, which follow relatively stable sequences. Average trends emerge, and certain behaviors follow sequentially.

Gesell felt it was easier to see the cycles of development by establishing norms for various ages and stages. He therefore developed behavioral portraits which delineated characteristics typical of each stage. Gesell himself recognized that development was fluid and continuous and that there were individual differences in rate and timing. The great misuse of his work has been due to the fact that others have not shared his professional caution.

We routinely use chronological age to give us some idea of a child we do not know; in the same way stages of development can indicate what to expect of a child. Even though a child's behavior level and chronological age expectations may not match, the information can still be useful in predicting general developmental patterns. A knowledge of characteristic stages can serve as an introduction to a particular age level; full understanding of a particular child would require analysis of what stage of development the child has reached.

---

11. Acquire a list of normative behavioral traits (see lists developed by Gesell or adapted by other child psychologists or the list included in this chapter under the normative approach). Take this list as a guide for observation in a classroom or on a playground with a given grade level. How many of the children fit the characteristic pattern? Do you note that even at a set grade level or within a definite chronological age grouping some children are behaving like the less mature and others beyond this level of maturity? Give specific examples. Is it true that ten-year-olds as a group may include eights, nines, elevens, and twelves in terms of their behavior characteristics?

Development is a product of the interaction of the organism and its environment

The processes of heredity and environment are interdependent and complementary. Neither appears to be dominant. Obviously, heredity cannot produce its effects without environment, and the environment needs the organism supplied by heredity upon which to produce its effects.

One can never really be separated from the other. Height, while largely determined by heredity, is also affected to an extent by nutrition. Body build, color of hair and eyes, shape of features, and blood type are highly dependent upon hereditary factors, but we could quickly identify a number of other significant factors which are not inherited or which are completely dependent upon interaction between the organism and its environment. Hereditary influences are always affected by the environment, nutrition, temperamental characteristics, primary behavioral patterns, and the individual's style of life.[12]

The body tends to maintain a state of equilibrium called homeostasis

There is a wisdom of the body. The body strives to preserve a constant internal environment despite changing conditions, whether internal or external. When something happens to disturb the body's internal equilibrium, an immediate reaction sets in to restore the state of balance. This equilibrium principle regulates a number of body functions. Body weight and food intake, glandular functions, and the compensation for or healing of injuries supply evidence of the principle of homeostasis. Adolf has estimated that there may be at least a thousand bodily functions simultaneously kept in equilibrium within themselves and with one another.[13]

Much evidence for this principle is found in all kinds of physical development, and there has been some indication that the concept of homeostasis may also be applicable to mental, emotional, and social phases of life as well. The organism in this sense may be thought of as attempting to maintain its pattern in the face of fluctuating conditions. Many stimuli which cause disturbances will bring about a series of reactions directed at restoring the original balance.

---

12. If the principle of homeostasis has application to mental life, what are the implications of this for motivation, classroom methodology, and the curriculum?

There is a unity in growth patterns

When we measure the child by any technique that permits growth equivalents, such as the Olson-Hughes growth ages, the unity in growth patterns becomes evident.[14] This may be related to the fact that each individual develops from a single cell. Children who mature rapidly tend to do so in most facets of growth, although all early maturers do not grow identically. However, it is unusual to find a child in a class who is highest or best in one attribute and then low in most of the rest. When we find this type of child, we might suspect some type of behavior problem. Some

[12] A. Thomas, H. Birch, S. Chess, M. Hertzig, and S. Korn, *Behavioral Individuality in Early Childhood* (New York: New York University Press, 1963).
[13] E. Adolf, "The Self Maintaining Organism," *Scientific Monthly*, 61 (1945), 57–62.
[14] W. Olson and B. Hughes, *Manual for the Description of Growth in Age Units* (Ann Arbor, Michigan: University Elementary School, University of Michigan, 1950).

children develop more slowly, and while their growth curves may not show identical patterns, the similarity of rate in each growth cycle for each child is generally apparent. Exceptions to this rule exist, and these children are sometimes designated as split growers. As one might expect, split growth is frequently accompanied by behavior problems. However, extensive study of various biological correlates shows that, on the average, developmental changes, whether morphological, physiological, histological, or biochemical, tend to occur at similar rates.

Millard's research caused him to feel growth and learning were complementary.

> Organismic drive produces change in the height of an individual. The same drive likewise produces an achievement increase over and beyond learning or teaching efforts. Growth and learning therefore are inseparable, representing a unity which is present throughout the entire period of development.[15]

All growth is related to the developmental rate and the specific maximum development of each child.

Maturation or readiness should precede certain types of learning

We have become increasingly aware that definite degrees of maturity are prerequisite to various kinds of learning. Here maturation may be considered as change in the physical equipment and functioning of the organism—an internal ripening. Practice and experience in the learning process can be effective only if the child is ready. Premature forcing may produce personality disturbances. Pacing, which follows the lead of the individual's maturity indicators, is an effective manner in which to use maturational factors. To make the learning process more efficient, it would be important to consider both premature practice and unnecessary postponement of instruction as violations of the maturational principle.

---

13. Give examples of how education adheres to the readiness principle. Can you think of instances where this principle is completely ignored? Give examples of readiness factors to be considered at all levels of education.

Growth is continuous

Growth tends to proceed quite evenly and smoothly, with developmental continuity, unfolding design, and resistance to displacement. The

[15] C. Millard, *Child Growth and Development* (Boston: D. C. Heath & Company, 1958), p. 21.

unfolding design enables the individual to adhere to an over-all developmental plan and pattern. It has been demonstrated that children frequently return to their patterns after illness or other disturbances. There appears to be a growth impulse that functions continuously during the life of the individual. Old behavior and developmental patterns appear to blend into the new patterns. The child tends to return to his own normal rate of development as soon as external and experimental factors are removed. Olson defines displacement as follows:

> Any organism in a systematic rate of change of growth tends to resist displacement caused by factors involving extra stimulation or deprivation and to restore a projection of the original rate when the factors are removed.[16]

Longitudinal research points to a design for growth and indicates that when the child is exposed to optimal nurture for his design, development proceeds most adequately. At the same time, the child resists attempts to force growth and tends to grow at a faster rate when he is making up for any temporary period of deprivation.

---

14. What are the implications for remedial techniques in connection with the principle of resistance to displacement? If the unfolding design is a gradual process, how should this factor be taken into account in our evaluation of a special method of nurture?

THE NORMATIVE APPROACH

It is sometimes helpful to know some general principles in relation to age-grade expectations. This approach provides a better understanding of cyclic change and illustrates the interrelationship of growth.

You must recognize that wide individual variations are found within any age-grade category to such an extent that the concept of normalcy as a fixed boundary is fictional. The words mode and average generally encompass a considerable range. Norms are generally derived by selecting either (1) the mean, average of all scores added and divided by the number of children in a given chronological age range, or (2) the mode or median score of all scores collected for a given age.

Each grade level encompasses a spread of behavior which overlaps preceding and succeeding grades. Viewing the longitudinal pattern of development, therefore, is most profitable. You must know the individual's pattern and stage of development rather than think of characteristics as occurring at a fixed chronological age.

The order in which developmental stages follow each other is important

[16] W. Olson, *Child Development*, p. 41.

rather than the exact age at which the child reaches one of the stages. Although steps in development are much the same, the way each child goes through the stages is individualized. The common pattern varies according to basic individuality. Ilg and Ames described the alternate stages as equilibrium and disequilibrium.[17] In equilibrium self and society are in balance; in disequilibrium are confusion and cross purposes.

A number of books have been written to present the concepts involved in developmental sequences:

Blair, A. and W. Burton, *Growth and Development of the Pre-Adolescent.* New York: Appleton-Century-Crofts, 1951.

Britton, Edward C. and J. M. Winans, *Growing from Infancy to Adulthood.* New York: Appleton-Century-Crofts, 1958.

Faculty of University School, *How Children Develop,* University School Series No. 3. Columbus, Ohio: Ohio State University, 1946.

Gesell, A. and F. Ilg, "Child Development, Part II," *The Child from Five to Ten.* New York: Harper & Row, Publishers, Inc., 1949.

Ilg, F. and L. Ames, *Child Behavior.* New York: Harper & Row, Publishers, Inc., 1955.

Watson, E. and G. Lowrey, *Growth and Development of Children.* Chicago: Yearbook Publication, 1951.

The following section provides an overview of normative factors pertinent to the elementary school child.

Grade one—the six-year-old child

Many abrupt somatic and psychological changes occur in the child at six. The first baby teeth are lost, and the first permanent molars make their appearance. Glandular and other chemical processes take place that tend to produce a changed child. The child is characterized by instability and organismic refusal to follow a consistent rate of growth. If he is given a series of intelligence tests he is more likely than not to show considerable variation—much more than he would show a year or two later. Growth sequences which are struggling to begin, such as reading, spelling, etc., fail to respond uniformly. Starting points, although often occurring within this grade level, do not all begin at once. Neuromotor responses are not dependable.

Accompanying the somatic and psychological changes are new attitudes and feelings, new moral and ethical developments, and a new concept of self in relation to others. The child shifts from one emotional extreme to another. Consequently, he is confused in evaluating social relationships. His inconsistent health pattern, temperamental vagaries, and

[17] F. Ilg and L. Ames, *Child Behavior* (New York: Harper & Row, Publishers, Inc., 1955).

inadequate social relations are all characteristic of development at a beginning stage of development.

In school affairs he often appears to be regressing. His play is usually harmonious when only one other child is involved. When he becomes a member of a large group he needs direction and guidance. The insights the resourceful teacher includes in her repertoire of understanding is that the six-year-old, in all his confusion, indecision, and "rambunctiousness," is a child going through a growth process which is natural and appropriate for the culture in which he finds himself. Tolerance and understanding should mark her general attitudes. Security, freedom to dramatize, create and explore, and recognition of friendly authority create the proper setting in which first graders can flourish. A nice balance between teacher control and opportunity for developing independence is also desirable.

First graders need room to move in. Motor and muscular movement are common accompaniments of creative and emotional expression. Their actions are more natural than dramatic, although the latter seems to describe them well. The six-year-old's physical and muscular entity is alert and ready to act.

Obviously the kind of learning atmosphere suggested above is superior to formalized instruction in the skill subjects. First, the developmental upswing in various growths is still months away—for some a few months, for others six months, and for a few an entire year. There can be no particular advantage bucking organismic lag, although traditionally this is exactly what is done in many first grades throughout the country.

The six-year-old is ready to accept his teacher as a supplementary mother. Consequently he seeks attention, and is generally pleased by it. When given the opportunity he shows a great deal of affection. He does not want the teacher to take his mother's place, but rather to carry on the kind of atmosphere he enjoys at home. Teacher and parent need early contacts in order to establish a united and coordinated approach.

The first grader's major problem is to adjust to the demands and challenges of home and school. His early years provided him with a single active environment. The school, while providing controls and guides, should broaden his base of activity but not frustrate or incite additional conflict. Not all children of this age show the same maturational readiness.

Grade two—the seven-year-old child

The typical seven-year-old child has stabilized himself in his pattern of development. His various growths are smooth and progressively upward. He presents a picture of a child "quieting down" after his earlier up-and-down irregular progress. Also in contrast to his earlier uncontrolled reactions and spontaneous outbursts, he now can endure extended calm and personal self-absorption.

The average seven-year-old is a good listener. He enjoys having stories read to him and will request repetitions. Radio and television both intrigue him greatly. Seven can be a happy age if parents and teachers allow reasonable freedom.

School and home both need to provide opportunities this age demands for reflection on the happenings in the child's world. He is ready to react to many events which heretofore passed him by. He needs the opportunity to dwell upon the meanings of his various contacts with children and adults. Meanings are primarily in the category of feelings which will form the basis for later emotional and creative reactions.

Significantly, the seven-year-old must be allowed, within reasonable range, periods of reflection. Of all the years regarded as basic for later personal development, this may be one of the most significant and important. He is thinking when his physical counterpart gives the opposite impression. He may explode out of a seeming relaxed or indolent mood into a dynamic, moving child of action.

Between extremes, from isolation to dynamic action, there may be found the beginnings of wholesome, social behavior. Movement away from parent identification includes exaggerated fondness of his teacher. Thus he begins a new guarded relationship with those who are close at hand, indicating the beginnings both of growth in independence and of the trend which, in the later elementary school years, may take him almost entirely away from his parents.

The second-grade teacher should realize that she must maintain person-to-person relationships with the majority of her children. She must be quite free and easily approachable, moving around the room and thereby providing equal opportunity for access to her. These children need expanded contacts, and it is the teacher's responsibility to see that they are provided. In this way she encourages emotional and personal development so necessary to the present and future happiness of the child. A by-product of free, informal, individual contacts is the opportunity for development of speech and narrative skills so essential to the child's personal development.

To already mentioned characteristics of moodiness and helpfulness, let us add independence. The child who occasionally becomes argumentative and disagreeable is displaying a natural desire to express his own thoughts and preferences.

In terms of social contacts on the playground or in the family backyard, his beginning independence is somewhat undisciplined and nongroup-centered. Games that appeal to him are quite informal with a minimum of rule and regulation. His ethical values are forming, and he readily applies standards to others, although he may omit evaluation of his own performance. Again we have here the beginning of a new growth phase in pre-adolescent development. Such behavior is natural and an accompaniment of a growing consciousness of what is good and bad. Often his gripes and criticisms are merely a mechanism for surveying opinions and attitudes of others as to what is right and wrong. Alibis and attempts at scapegoating are particularly common. Parents and teachers frequently attempt to "reason" with the child in order to prove that someone else could not possibly be to blame. Treatment of this kind should be kept to a minimum. He is at the age where he needs an easy out in order not to weaken, as he feels it, his security and sense of belonging.

Grade three—the eight-year-old child

The eight-year-old is embarking upon a consistent growth trend in all phases of development. The sixth year was a year of uncertainty and exploration; seven gave evidence of development but with considerable variation and unreliability. Eight is the time for steady progressive development. It represents a period in which the child is responsive and a time in which teacher and parent can expect good efforts and much gain. It is a receptive period. Character and ethical development, as well as creative and emotional trends, are easily stimulated.

Physically the child is much more mature. Coordination is good, and eyes are sufficiently developed for the more intensive reading activities which are his lot in this grade. He is less susceptible to disease, is ready for rough games, and has the skill for more complex physical activities.

Sex differences both in terms of interests and maturity become noticeable. Girls begin to equal or to show height and weight superiority over boys. They tend to be more proficient in school subjects, definitely show better adjustment to instructional organization and to teacher demands that culturally are more likely than not relevant to the female role.

The eight-year-old is beginning to recognize the conflict between peer and parent requirements and wants status with both. In school he demonstrates some withdrawal from teacher authority. The closeness of his fellows makes him strongly conscious of what they expect of him. He is at the beginning of the stage where he wants their approval more than that of his teacher.

It should not be inferred that these children are all at once social-minded and group-conscious. Eight is only the starting point of a development leading to group stability and organization. The child is attracted by small-group activity, but his attachments are temporary and shifting.

The eight-year-old is ready for creative exploration and experimentation. No one can tell the specific direction a given group of third graders will take when provided with facilities and opportunities for action. Books, working materials of all kinds, laboratories, science equipment, storage space for collections should all be standard equipment for this age and grade. Fundamentals can be learned easily and naturally in a challenging and inviting environment. The teacher for such a group should have broad, diversified interests and be a handyman in every sense of the word.

All in all, the eight-year-old is characterized by beginning independence, diversity of interest, and the start of individual and specific boy and girl interests. Individual differences among children in any particular phase of learning greatly exceed those at an earlier age. Identification with other members of his sex is a dominant need, and its beginning should be assured by the kind of group planning introduced by the teacher.

Grade four—the nine-year-old child

The nine-year-old period has two important characteristics—first, the continuation of that part of the preadolescent growth cycle in which the rate of growth and learning is most accelerated, and second, a noticeable shift toward compelling group relations. This child has not reached the point where there is strong or persistent rebellion against adult suggestion and domination.

Grade four covers just about the middle span of the preadolescent growth cycle. Age nine is not merely the arithmetical mid-point between six and twelve. Growth is not divided equally in terms of the chronological years. It is only coincidental that nine, organismically, represents the mid-point of the total preadolescent developmental sequence.

The upward swing in the developmental sequence elicits the desire for self-direction. The child feels his increasing powers and is self-motivated into a need for directing and guiding his own activities. In school and at home he should have some opportunity to make decisions, to be his own boss, and to exercise considerable direction of his own affairs. He may be disturbed by authoritative interruption which takes him away from his particular project of the moment.

It is believed that the child has fixed potential ceilings. It is also believed that many children have potentialities that lie dormant because of minimum challenges. A nine-year-old may at times be moody, timid, aggressive, or bold.

His sense of fairness gives him a judicial aspect. He evaluates the responsibility of each member of a misbehaving alliance. He would rather participate in adult conversation than have the adult "condescend" to his level. He likes to make out schedules, to plan rules and procedures, and to make lists of one kind and another. A teacher who makes specific assignments and suggests that they be written down will quite generally receive a cordial response.

The fourth grade demonstrates the first real separation of the sexes in their interests. The boys like to roughhouse when they are standing around with nothing specific to do. Girls will giggle and whisper to each other. Withdrawal of the sexes from each other at this time is natural. It seems to be a cultural designation that permits the developing child to orient toward his own sex.

Individual differences among the nine-year-olds are more marked than ever. Girls have caught up with boys in size and are ready to go on to greater growth and maturity differences. Consequently, the modal picture of the nine-year-old must bow to wide individual variation in individual personalities as well as in maturity differences, as is true of any and all modal material.

The work habits of the nine-year-old are pleasing. The eight-year-old showed speed of reaction and prompt application to the task at hand. The nine-year-old combines control and self-discipline along with speed. Because he is cognizant of his growing powers and is able to see the results of his energies he becomes interested in improving himself. He can be kept at practice on mechanical skills—drill in arithmetic and spelling, or practicing a musical instrument. He responds readily to self-evaluation devices, test scores, etc. He will be particularly responsive to drill exercises and studies that enable him to keep records on himself. He learns rapidly, seems to know it, and is intrigued by it. He will repeat drills and exercises which can be timed or scored just for the reward of self-recognized improvement.

Grade five—the ten-year-old child

Ten is generally the age at which preadolescent development nears completion. A corollary to the maturational concept of "final arrival" is that when a maximum (or destination point) is approached, a slowing down in growth increments occurs. Although the unit of growth may show a gradual reduction of gains made, this does not necessarily mean that it diminishes in qualitative values.

The ten-year-old's interests and drives respond to challenges to his skills. In contrast, rote learning and other mechanistic assignments seem to bore him. In the larger project or core assignment area he can easily learn to budget his time, plan with others, and arrive at decisions.

He also takes an interest in the broader social area. Work involving the study of social problems generally is readily accepted. He is sympathetic and open to new understandings. Fifth-grade teachers should be aware of the potential influence they have for providing direction and purpose not only to the child's social thinking but also to his over-all moral and ethical behavior.

In the fifth grade there are children with the maturity of a nine-year-old and others with the maturity of an eleven-year-old. It is altogether possible that these two groups—the one below and the one above—outnumber the modal ten-year-old. Consequently the picture of what really may be expected as fifth-grade behavior is not clear. In terms of maturity, the child we have described is almost at the end of the childhood cycle. The eleven-year-old, as we shall describe later, is beginning a new cycle of growth with its ensuing confusion, instability, expanding group relationships, and increasing disregard of parent and teacher mandate. Since some ten-year-olds have already attained this stage of maturity, it is no wonder that many of them are regarded as disobedient and trying.

The ten-year-old's learning pattern also reflects his approach to the pre-adolescent maximum. When he arrives at his pre-adolescent maximum, he should show gains, but they will be less than those made during the fourth grade.

The end of the preadolescent growth cycle is not a place for extensive remedial work, drill, or pressure to do better.

The typical fifth grader is the executive type. He wants to start at the beginning and proceed to the end. He is an organizer. Unlike the nine-year-old, the ten-year-old will not respond well to monotonous drill assignments, particularly if he has already undergone these experiences in the third and fourth grades.

Maturity difference in the sexes is readily seen at this age. The more rapid development of girls is obvious. Physical growth records document this conclusion. Similar findings are reported in studies of mental development and in comparisons of the achievement curves of boys and girls.

Grade six—the eleven-year-old child

Investigators generally agree that at eleven, particularly, the child comes into real conflict between peer and adult demands. Peer pressures started at ages nine and ten. At eleven it is difficult to maintain equilibrium between peers and adults. The group makes real demands. Although outright rebellion to adult authority may not develop, continuous conflict and aggression always occur.

In school, discipline is always a problem. Some investigators report more behavior problems for fourth- fifth- and sixth-grade children than for any other age group. Conflict with parental desires reaches its peak during the tenth and eleventh years. They often show immature tantrum tendencies occasioned by demands for punctuality, obedience, and submission to family demand and dictate.

The description given cannot be called representative of all sixth graders; it applies only to a minority of roughly one-third, those that are making the transition from preadolescence to adolescence. The two other groups among the eleven-year-olds are, firstly, those who are less mature, whose development is more like that of the ten-year-old, and secondly, those who are precocious, who are started toward their adolescent maturational level. This more mature group has grown out of the earlier period of instability and conflict, has made certain adjustments, has found a new zone of satisfying activity, and is moving closer to a new destination.

Behavior has a strong physiological base. Cyclic changes represent the framework, so to speak, upon which the whole behavior pattern is built. This thesis does not deny the effect of the environment, and self factors. Children with different maturity patterns, equal in every other way, will respond differently to the same environmental motivation. Likewise, the same child at different maturity stages will be more responsive at one time than at another to the same environmental stimulus. Another way of looking at the problem is to point out that behavior at the end of one cycle or at the beginning of another is usually more deviational than during the cyclic upswing or periods of rapid development.

FACTORS INFLUENCING DEVELOPMENT AND BEHAVIOR

The rate and pattern of development can be modified by external and internal conditions of the body. These factors are interdependent and interrelated. Some of the following factors, whose relative importance we shall not attempt to determine, influence development:

Sex. Sex plays an important role in the physical and mental development of the child. Differences in the rate of physical growth are especially apparent. At birth, boys are slightly larger than girls, but girls generally grow more rapidly and mature sooner than boys. Girls, on the average, mature sexually a year before boys, and at this time they are larger than boys. This is definitely apparent at the prepuberty age, from nine to twelve. Girls also attain their full size sooner than boys. The duration of the adolescent spurt for girls averages three years, for boys five years.[18] In mental growth, girls develop earlier than boys and reach their mental maturity slightly sooner. Sex is indirectly influential on development in that the cultural pressures force the child to conform to the culturally approved pattern for his sex.

Glands of Internal Secretion. These glands affect development in both prenatal and postnatal stages of growth. The level of calcium in the blood is regulated by the parathyroid glands, located in the throat, near the thyroid. Deficiency of these glands may result in defective bone growth and hyperexcitability of the muscles. Thyroxin, produced by the thyroid gland, is essential to physical and mental growth. Deficiency in the activity of the sex glands delays the onset of puberty, while hyperactivity brings about a precocious sexual development.

Nutrition. At every age, but especially in the early years of life, feeding is of great importance for the development of the child. Not only is the amount of food eaten important; the quality of the food is vital.

[18] Denver Child Research Council, Denver, Colorado. Personal communication.

Culture. The characteristics of infancy are universal. Culture begins to take its effect during the early training process and overlays or modifies a more basic substratum of behavior.

Position in the Family. The position of the child within the family may influence his development through environmental factors. The second or third child within the family develops more quickly than the first-born, not because of any pronounced intellectual difference, but because of the fact that the younger children may learn from imitating an older brother or sister. On the other hand, the youngest child of the family, especially if he is distinctly younger than the other children, is apt to be slower in his development because he is pampered and given little incentive to develop his latent abilities.

Life Style—Self Concept. The individual's view of life and his evaluation of his world and his place in that world are factors in his development. He may either have the courage to meet varying environmental conditions as a challenge or may use the same environmental factors as an excuse to prevent him from functioning.

IMPLICATIONS OF DEVELOPMENTAL PRINCIPLES

Knowledge of child growth and development principles has implications for those concerned with helping the child reach his optimal development.

1. Intensive child study that takes into account a large amount of developmental information is necessary for adequate diagnosis and school placement.
2. Since there are great differences in rate of growth, it is important that the educator have readily available information that shows rate rather than status. Cumulative records should be designed to this end. Perhaps one of the most pressing and pertinent problems for educational research is that of developing more adequate record systems regarding rate and its influence on the educational process.
3. Growth patterns add meaning and understanding to the totality of growth. They should be utilized in making educational decisions.
4. Since readiness is the capacity that limits and influences the individual's ability to profit from his current experiences, the school should be involved constantly in assessing a child's readiness. The readiness factor also implies that some types of learning may be more difficult if delayed and that practice before readiness is educationally unsound.
5. The importance of determining the difficulty level of some tasks is made clear when we consider it in connection with the concept of optimal readiness. Forcing and pressure are two techniques which tend to ignore design and hence are detrimental. The cyclic and continuous nature of growth will supply us with insight into what we can expect to happen

sequentially. Meaningful tasks should be presented at the appropriate developmental level in an encouraging manner that facilitates the development of self-confidence.

6. Individual differences should be expected, and we should not attempt to eliminate them as though they were a disease. No matter how we go about grouping children, they will learn in accordance with their own abilities, capacities, and purposes.

7. Recognition of the factors of homeostasis and the wisdom of the body implies that in the educational process we might give a more important place to self-selection and pacing.

8. Communication between parents and teachers would be improved if the child's development were presented graphically to show his individual growth pattern.

9. A valuable piece of information would concern the child's self concept and his style of life to explain some of the "why's" of his behavior.

10. Growth is interrelated; when there is a gain in one area we may expect gains in others. We must be ready to anticipate each new stage in a child's growth and development.

We must view growth, then, as something which happens to the whole child. All the principles of development are important and must be related to the individual. We will find most success in dealing with behavior, regardless of our role, when we supply meaningful tasks at appropriate developmental levels in an encouraging manner which facilitates the development of self-confidence.

SUGGESTED READINGS

Articles

Anderson, J., "Child Development and the Growth Process," in *Readings in Educational Psychology,* eds. V. Noll and R. Noll, p. 30. New York: The Macmillan Company, 1962.

Jones, M. and N. Bayley, "Physical Maturity of Boys as Related to Behavior," in *Readings in Child Psychology,* 2nd ed., ed. W. Dennis, p. 407. Englewood Cliffs, N.J.: Prentice-Hall, Inc., 1963.

Mussen, P. and J. Conger, "Hereditary Transmission," in *Readings in Child and Adolescent Psychology,* eds. L. Crow and A. Crow, p. 37. New York: David McKay Co., Inc., 1961.

Mussen, P. and M. Jones, "Self-conceptions, Motivations, and Interpersonal Attitudes of Late- and Early-Maturing Boys," in *Readings in the Psychology of Human Growth and Development,* ed. W. Baller, p. 377. New York: Holt, Rinehart & Winston, Inc., 1962.

Olson, W. and B. Hughes, "Concepts of Growth: Their Significance for Teachers," in *Educational Psychology: A Book of Readings,* ed. A. Coladarci, p. 65. New York: Holt, Rinehart & Winston, Inc., 1955.

Books

Ausubel, D., *Theory and Problems of Child Development.* New York: Grune & Stratton, Inc., 1958.

Blair, A. and W. Burton, *Growth and Development of the Preadolescent.* New York: Appleton-Century-Crofts, 1951.

Havighurst, R., *Human Development and Education.* New York: David McKay Co., Inc., 1953.

Hymes, J., *Understanding Your Child.* Englewood Cliffs, N.J.: Prentice-Hall, Inc., 1952.

Ilg, F. and L. Ames, *Child Behavior.* New York: Harper & Row, Publishers, Inc., 1955.

Montagu, A., *The Direction of Human Development.* New York: Harper & Row, Publishers, Inc., 1955.

Sinnott, E., *Cell and Psyche: The Biology of Purpose.* New York: Harper & Row, Publishers, Inc., 1950.

Thomas, A., H. Birch, S. Chess, M. Hertzig, and S. Korn, *Behavioral Individuality in Early Childhood.* New York: New York University Press, 1963.

5 LEARNING

Mrs. Jones was very upset when she found out that two of her fourth-grade boys had been sent in by another teacher for throwing snowballs. She had also just been informed that a group of her girls had wandered away from the playground at recess and not responded to another teacher's request that they remain on the school grounds. Mrs. Jones did not understand what had happened. She was sure all of her children had *learned* the playground rules. She had lectured to them every day for a week about the rules, and just yesterday everybody had passed a test for which they had to write out ten of the rules. She was sure she had done a good job; but had she?

This exposes us to a crucial area in learning. Did Mrs. Jones' children really "learn" the rules because they were able to memorize and repeat them for her? What does learning actually mean? If the children were able to pass the test, why did they fail to abide by them? How would you explain Mrs. Jones' dilemma?

As we approach the study of learning, a number of questions should be kept in mind. Is there a distinction between intelligence and the child's ability to learn? If so, what is this distinction? How can the parent or the teacher encourage the desire to learn? Are there specific principles which underlie a good teaching-learning situation? How can we reconcile the various theoretical positions in regard to learning? How does the satisfaction of certain needs affect the learning process? If we assume that the child must be at a specific organic level of readiness prior to learning, what, then, is the value of intensive readiness programs? How do grades in school affect the learning process? Do they facilitate or hamper it? These are but a few of the many questions you might ask as you approach a study of the child's learning.

It is through the learning process that the growing child gains competence in using his resources for thinking, doing, and feeling, and eventually establishes his unique selfhood. Because teachers plan for learning every day, many of them recognize that children vary widely in their abilities to learn. They also realize that tremendously varied forms of learning are expected of the child even in the primary grades. In addition to reading, writing, and arithmetic skills, the young child is expected to comprehend concepts, grasp facts, and follow directions. He is expected to develop some understanding about himself, his family, and his community. He is supposed to be able to work and think independently and yet cooperatively. These are only a few of the expectations of parents, teachers, and the child himself in our society.

Although most teachers are aware of the complexities of learning demanded in the school curriculum, not all have a clear idea of the learning process itself. Since the teacher's major function is to direct the learning process, it is important that he acquire a thorough understanding of learning principles.

WHAT IS LEARNING?

Children learn what they live. The teacher and the school are not the only influence upon the child, and learning is not limited to the classroom or to the teacher's objectives. Pupils learn from their total experiences. In the classroom, too, learning is more than simply gathering and memorizing facts, and the child has many learning experiences which are indirect and informal. The teacher is responsible for providing experiences that will contribute to pupil growth. He assists the child to acquire the patterns of behavior necessary for successful living in his society.

Learning, then, involves adaptation of behavior. The emphasis is on behavioral change in the individual, based on his personal and purposeful perception of events, combined with his individual needs and goals. The learner responds to the environment, but behavior is also determined by prior experiences and the way he perceives the situation. To be efficacious, learning must fill needs, meet goals, and make the individual more capable of dealing with his environment. Goal setting by the learner motivates learning. To improve learning, we need to improve the adequacy of guidelines as related to the learning process.

Learning is a change in behavior resulting from the interaction of the organism with its environment. Learning is dependent upon activity or special training and in this sense differs from behavioral change which is solely due to maturation. Learning differs from maturation in that the modification of the behavior pattern in learning is primarily a result of responses to internal and external stimuli whereas maturation occurs in response to forces that are primarily internal.

Learning, then, involves relatively permanent behavioral change which is the result of experience. It must be differentiated from maturation. Learning requires a change in perception, which in this sense is the way in which the individual experiences his universe.

It is important to differentiate teaching and learning. They are far from identical, although many teachers act as if they were. Learning is something accomplished by the learner, for our purposes, the child. Teaching is a function of the adult or teacher. It is quite possible, then, from this point of view to have teaching without learning. Learning is manifested in terms of habits, skills, attitudes, values, insight, knowledge, concepts, and certain memories. It is the process through which all of our experiences exert a modifying force on present and future behavior. As a child learns, you can observe some signs of the learning process. There is a reduction in unnecessary movements. The time required to perform a task is usually reduced. The individual makes a broader range of associations with past experiences. He is able to handle an increasingly difficult set of tasks.

Learning is a personal matter which involves a change in perception. Those involved in directing learning experiences must recognize the importance of ego-involvement. A child cannot readily solve problems that are meaningless to him. A criticism of many learning experiences at school might well be that students are asked to solve problems that do not concern them. The "problem" is the teacher's problem, not one arising out of the everyday experiences, needs, and perceptions of the student.

To evaluate what learning has occurred, the classroom teacher might propose the following questions:

1. Has the information gained been utilized in new situations?
2. Have certain skills been extended or refined?
3. Do I have evidence of new interests and attitudes?
4. How has the experience helped the child to evaluate his own learning?

---

1. Consider your own learning situations in elementary school, high school, and college. How many met the qualifications of a learning situation in terms of the broad definitions proposed? What evidence do you have of behavior change? Try to think of examples of teachers who were most successful in promoting behavioral change and those who seemed more interested in the memorization process. What are the practical implications for evaluation of the pupil's learning if we accept the definition of learning as behavior change based on the purposeful perception of events combined with individual needs and goals?

THEORIES OF LEARNING

The evolution of the educational process has been accompanied by a parallel development in theories of learning. Efforts have been made to test and evaluate many aspects of the learning process. As a result, principles formerly accepted as inviolable have been questioned, and in some instances disproved. New theories help us understand the complexities of the learning process.

Many experiments in the field of learning have involved the study of animals and their reactions in various situations. The validity of this method as it applies to human learning might be questioned. We cannot always assume that what is true of animals is true of people. It is becoming increasingly apparent that the complexities of human personality, self forces, and cultural factors affect human learning in such a way as to invalidate for classroom purposes many analogies with animal learning.

There are many theories of learning and variations of these theories. We shall consider primarily the Stimulus-Response Associationist; the Gestalt Field Theorist, which would include the theorists who see learning as a perceptual problem; and the Developmental Theorist.

A survey of learning theories can be found in:

Bigge, Morris, *Learning Theories for Teachers.* New York: Harper & Row, Publishers, Inc., 1964.

Hilgard, Ernest, *Theories of Learning,* 2nd ed. New York: Appleton-Century-Crofts, 1956.

Hill, Winfred, *Learning: A Survey of Psychological Interpretations.* San Francisco: Chandler Publishing Co., 1963.

Stimulus-Response Theory

Professor E. L. Thorndike of Columbia University, who started his work at the turn of the century, was a primary proponent of the stimulus-response association theory. A biological view which stressed the organism, this theory was dependent to a great extent on data gathered from animal experimentation.

The Thorndike theory was predicated on the establishment of neural bonds between a stimulus and response, and has had a great effect on present school procedures and practices. It claims that every act, physical or mental, involves the setting up of specific pathways in the nervous system. In order for a new act to be learned, pathways between stimuli and responses must first be established. Through repetition, the resistance offered to the nervous energy passing along the pathways is lessened and performance of the act is facilitated. Thorndike believed that the intelligence of an individual depended on the number of inner nervous system pathways or physiological connections in his brain.

This theory, sometimes called "Connectionism" or the "Neural Bond Theory," led to certain laws which were supposed to govern learning. The first of these is the Law of Use or Exercise. According to this law, an individual must have the opportunity to repeat an act correctly and frequently if he is to learn it. This led to the familiar "Practice makes perfect!" and brought about many questionable educational procedures, such as the writing of spelling words and meaningless phrases hundred of times.

It became apparent that practice or repetition facilitated learning but did not insure it. Attitudes and feelings affect the learner's response. Thorndike then developed his primary law of learning, the Law of Effect.

Thorndike's Law of Effect states that if learning is accompanied by pleasure or satisfaction, it is strengthened and the learner's efforts will probably increase also. Conversely, if learning is accompanied by unpleasantness, it is weakened and the learner's efforts will probably decrease. This greatly oversimplified law led to the emphasis on the principles of reward and punishment. Later in Thorndike's writings he modified the Law of Effect to make satisfaction more important than annoyance.

The Law of Readiness is the third law of learning derived from the Thorndike Theory. As the name implies, it states that the learner must be ready to learn. The first two laws, the Law of Use or Exercise and the Law of Effect, are ineffective if the child is not ready. The most effective way to determine readiness, it was felt, was to give the child the opportunity to learn and then observe his behavior. An individual's attitude would show his readiness. Readiness, as a function of maturation, need, and interest, could be promoted by arousing interest in a particular subject before it is introduced. Thorndike believed that if the organism is ready to respond, it is pleasurable to respond.

The Thorndike Theory has stressed the "trial and error" nature of learning. Man's problem solving is basically the same as trial and error. However, man can substitute concepts for behavior, and, therefore, can achieve his goal more readily. The Thorndike Theory tends to oversimplify the complex learning process in which the *whole* individual is involved.

More about Thorndike and his theories can be found in:

Thorndike, E. L., *The Psychology of Learning*. New York: Teachers College, Columbia University, 1913.

———, *Adult Learning*. New York: The Macmillan Company, 1928.

---

2. Thorndike was an early and influential theorist associated with a university which has had considerable influence upon the educational scene. What are some past and present educational practices which show evidence of people's acceptance of his general theoretical principles? In what way do you feel Thorndike may have oversimplified the learning process?

As in the study of any theorist who has written over a considerable period of time, we see that in later writings Thorndike disavowed the Law of Use or Exercise. He also came to put considerably less emphasis on the punishment aspect of learning. It is now generally accepted that learning should occur in a pleasant, secure atmosphere. A mild form of emotional involvement, such as that produced by curiosity, is stimulating to the learning process, but in general, teacher-induced anxiety should be minimized. Whenever the individual is confronted with a large amount of frustration, he tends to focus more on his own inadequacy than on the problem at hand.

Guthrie[1] was another S-R associationist who stressed the concept of contiguity. This meant that a response becomes conditioned to all of the cues present at its original evocation. These associations were formed automatically and instantaneously without either the necessity of repetition or favorable aftereffects. At present, associationists who stress contiguity tend to believe that the new habits form as a result of the contiguous occurrence of stimulus and response. Rewards, then, would influence the performance more than the original learning.

A prominent advocate of the stimulus-response approach to learning is B. F. Skinner. He views teachers as architects and builders of student behavior. Skinner defines learning as a change in the probability of response. Skinner extended the stimulus-response theory to include operant conditioning, a process whereby a response is made more probable or more frequent. An operant is strengthened, or shaped, in Skinner's terms, by reinforcement. Operants are responses which are controlled basically by the rewards that follow them, and then serve as a stimulus. The operant acts are modified through the process of operant conditioning. The contingency of operant conditioning is response, stimulus, and reinforcement in that order. The operant response is followed by a reinforcing stimulus and the probability of recurrence of the operant is increased. Skinner explains all human behavior in terms of respondents and operant reinforcement. Thus, the teacher has to define the task and reinforce or strengthen the child's correct response to increase the probability of its recurrence.

Skinner's animal work has caused him to give serious consideration to the timing and spacing of scheduled reinforcement. Through progressively changing the contingencies of reinforcement in the direction of the desired behavior you can see learning occur. A contingency of reinforcement is a sequence in which a response is followed by a reinforcing stimulus. The operant-conditioning psychologist then deals with the response which becomes the operant, followed by reinforcement and finally stimulus. Successful teaching from this point of view analyzes the effect of reinforcement and sets about to design techniques which set up specific reinforcing contingencies. In this way, it is hoped behavior can be brought under precise control.

[1] E. Guthrie, *The Psychology of Learning*, rev. ed. (New York: Harper & Row, Publishers, Inc., 1952).

Operant learning is a response-stimulus process. The operant learning is under the control of the consequences, the reinforcement stimulus which actually follows the response. The organism first makes the desired response, and then the reward is provided. This reward reinforces the response and makes it more likely to recur. The response is always instrumental in bringing about its reinforcement. From this point of view, then, the essence of learning is not merely stimulus substitution, but response modification and response encouragement via reward. For Skinner, in learning, there is a feedback from the reinforcing stimulus to the previous response. Thus, the emphasis is placed on the reinforcing agent in contrast to the factors that originally elicited the response. The teacher, from this point of view, reinforces the correct response after it is selected. His job is to decide what behavior he wants the student to produce and then to stimulate the student in such a way as to evoke and fix the behavior. Learning objectives are divided into a large number of small tasks and reinforced one by one. In this process it is of prime importance that teachers engineer material in such a way as to time and space properly the schedules of reinforcement.

Adherents to this theory do not try to look inside the organism for any explanation of behavior. Learning is dealt with as an entirely external event. In his writings, Skinner has minimized the importance of group and social forces. A Skinnerian teacher would analyze the effect of reinforcement and design techniques to shape the learning process with precision. Through setting up specific reinforcing contingencies, the behavior of the individual should be brought under precise control. The behaviorist is really convinced that when all the significant variables have been arranged, the organism will respond in a highly predictable manner. Teachers, then, are involved in shaping proper responses.

For more on Skinner's ideas read:

Skinner, B. F., *Science and Human Behavior.* New York: The Macmillan Company, 1953.

Skinner, B. F., *The Cumulative Record.* New York: Appleton-Century-Crofts, 1961.

Skinner's theory obviously has some excellent implications for educational practice. If punishment is unpredictable and does not bring about any permanently reduced tendency to respond, then unpredictable methods in education such as punishment should be seriously questioned. Much teaching has been dominated by an escape type of stimulation. The child has functioned in order to avoid some type of punishment.

Skinner has pointed out that there is too great a lapse of time between behavior and its reinforcement. Teachers should correct papers immediately, correct errors as they occur, and reinforce correct responses. Indicating the right answers on papers rather than the incorrect helps the child to build on his assets instead of discouraging him by pointing out his weaknesses. The child will observe the teacher is concerned about what is right, and will still be able to note his errors. If a test is to be a learning process, it should be returned as close to the time of response as feasible. Skinner would point out that reinforcement of desirable behavior occurs far too infrequently.

The most promising development from the reinforcement theorists has been programed instruction, which leads the student through a carefully arranged sequence of steps to a specific type of behavioral response.

As early as 1926 Sidney Pressey published an article advocating the use of machines for teaching factual information and covering routine drill work. There was little followup until the stimulation of the reinforcement psychologists. Skinner has stressed that teachers do not have the time to reinforce each child adequately, and he claims that mechanical devices could provide this reinforcement. Today's well-designed teaching machine employs many of the Skinner principles. It provides immediate reinforcement for correct answers; it takes small sequential steps; and it trains the student to observe and discriminate.

The classroom of the future will undoubtedly be affected by the appearance of programed learning materials in the form of textbooks and materials for use in machines. They provide the student with immediate reinforcement for every correct response and point to many possibilities for the individualization of instruction and for the wide range of interests, abilities, and capacities in any given classroom. Some of the concepts involved in pacing can be handled effectively through the use of programed materials because the student is permitted to progress at his own rate. Certainly both theorists and teachers will want to utilize in the classroom some of the positive elements of programed learning.

Thelen[2] has pointed out some limitations in the concepts of Skinner and Crowder regarding programed materials. He points out that the only individual difference dealt with is speed in going through the programs. He cites the problems involved in failing to deal with purposes and feelings and makes positive recommendations for improving the materials by including inquiry activities and utilizing discovery by the students.

---

3. What are some implications of behaviorist theory for the teacher? Select a level of education and a specific topic. Give an example of how you might apply some of Skinner's principles to education at the specific level and with this subject. What are some of the limitations of the behaviorist theory?

---

[2] H. Thelen, "Programmed Materials Today: Critique and Proposal," *Elementary School Journal,* No. 64 (1963), 189–96.

Field Theory

The field theory of learning stresses the wholeness of the learning process rather than an analysis of its elements. It is a combination of many psychological points of view, which all stress the important role of the "field" or surroundings in which behavior occurs. In learning, for example, elements of the field would include the self, the family, the classroom atmosphere, etc. Field theory emphasizes the perceptual aspects of learning. One must have a general understanding of the whole before it is possible to understand the parts.

Some of the leading proponents of cognitive field theory include Kurt Lewin, E. Tolman, and J. S. Bruner. For these theorists, motivation is a product of the disequilibrium in a life space. They deal with constructs such as goals and barriers to the achievement of goals. Primary emphasis is placed on the concept that learning is goal-directed. The goals should be self-set and will change in dynamic fashion with the accumulation of new experiences. For these theorists, personal goals are always pertinent. They are concerned with such problems as the indivdual's need to learn and his personal involvement in the situation. For them, insights do not become insights until they are internalized, the students see the meanings for themselves and they affect their behavior.

An example of the way in which the cognitive field theorists approach specific learning tasks lies in the teaching of multiplication tables, where stress would be placed on acquiring a knowledge of the total pattern of the tables. Cognitive theorists stress that it is important for the student to see relationships. For them the tension which motivates is the tension toward a goal.

The process by which a learner acquires new insights is of concern to the field theorists. Perception is defined in terms of the way it exists for an individual at a particular time, and not in objective terms. The child in his environment simultaneously interacts and participates in the perception process. According to field theorists the child gives meaning and order to things in terms of his own needs, abilities, and purposes. Thus, the learning situation is always interpreted in terms of a multiple set of factors which are dynamically interrelated as a whole. Field theorists believe in the purposiveness of behavior and in utilization of the individual's capacity to pursue his self-interests. Considerable attention is given to the psychological setting in which learning occurs. Learning is affected by the relationship with specific persons at a given time. Field theorists hold that processes are affected by the individual's goal, and hence all learning activity is goal-directed. Field theory might be most readily described as a goal-insight theory of learning.

The field theorists, then, see the teacher as leading children to formulate, clarify, evaluate, and solve problems. Promotion of an atmosphere which fosters insight is crucial. Teaching from this standpoint involves developing an understanding of the learner as an individual. As the result of goal directiveness, learning proceeds from a relatively undifferentiated stage to a more elaborate and internally differentiated condition. The child essentially reorganizes his perceptual patterns in relationship to a goal. Some theorists have called this insight. For Lewin, learning was a progressive differentiating of relatively unstructured problem situations.

For further reading, consult:

Bigge, Morris L., *Learning Theories for Teachers.* New York: Harper & Row, Publishers, Inc., 1964.

Bruner, J. S., *The Process of Education.* Cambridge, Mass.: Harvard University Press, 1961.

Hill, Winfred, *Learning: A Survey of Psychological Interpretations.* San Francisco: Chandler Publishing Co., 1963.

Lewin, K., "Field Theory and Learning," *The Psychology of Learning,* National Society for the Study of Education, 41st Yearbook, 1942, Part 2.

Tolman, E., *Purposive Behavior in Animals and Men.* New York: Appleton-Century-Crofts, 1932.

---

4. Describe a specific learning situation which illustrates progressive differentiation or change in perception. This might be in the area of handwriting, number concepts, reading, science, or any other you prefer.

Very close to the field theorists, and for our purposes classified with them, are Don Snygg, Arthur Combs, and Carl Rogers. To them, learning is a process by which the individual changes his behavior. These changes are usually accomplished by differentiation within the perceptual field. Thus, learning is a progressive differentiation from a very general perceptual field.

An important contribution of Combs has been his emphasis on learning as an active process which results from efforts by the individual to satisfy needs.[3] This provides us with an opportunity to include need structure in its relationship to learning. If the child is to learn certain attitudes or skills, the situation should be arranged so that the child furthers his goals by such learning. Little value is placed on repetition and drill in the production of significant learning.

In all of learning and perception, then, the first awareness is of the total situation, and as essential elements come to the fore, the behaver is made aware of his need for each part. All behavior is a type of problem solving related to the individual's ability to perceive new or different aspects of a complex situation.

[3] A. Combs and D. Snygg, *Individual Behavior,* rev. ed. (New York: Harper & Row, Publishers, Inc., 1959).

5. Take a specific grade level and subject and illustrate ways in which the problem-solving approach to learning could be developed.

As one reads the field theorists, it becomes increasingly important to consider in great detail the kind of perceptual field deemed essential for the most effective learning, problem solving, and reasoning. Don Snygg[4] has proposed a number of principles which relate to the learning process. He believes that we should take greater account of the child's need for self-esteem and a feeling of adequacy. Unlike the reinforcement theorists, he would utilize the individual's goals, which are personal, to produce true learning. Activities which diminish self-esteem would be avoided. In terms of the total learning situation, Snygg believes that any attempt to teach children before they are ready is not only an unproductive use of time, but also tends to build up concomitant attitudes and avoidance which will interfere with later learning. He believes that we should re-evaluate teaching in light of the general purposes of the schools. He maintains also that it is more important to produce pupils who actually utilize desirable techniques of living on a regular basis in their daily lives, rather than merely talk about them. The attitudes which are acquired along with the subject matter, he feels, may be even more significant than the subject matter itself. This would caution the teacher to be aware of how the subject matter is taught and what attitudes the pupils are forming toward the subject. On the transfer of training issue he asserts that skills are both better retained and more frequently used when they are learned under conditions very similar to those in which they will be actually used.

There would be little argument with the reinforcement theorists about the importance of pacing the experiences of children in an appropriate manner so that they do not need to be repeated. The perceptual field theorist would stress the desirability of a different experience once a child does not develop a desired attitude or skill. The perceptual approach calls for a close look at the atmosphere for learning as revealed through the interactions between the children and the general climate for learning created by the teacher and student. The student should be free from threat and operating in an atmosphere of acceptance, even though he is aware of his limitations. Teachers with this point of view would accept and stimulate curiosity. They would also encourage exploration. The teacher would truly be more of a guide than an engineer. The teacher, from the perceptual approach, then, is concerned about methods of facilitating the clarification and change of meanings. To complete this theory, they would recognize that effective teaching requires the intelligent use

[4] A. Combs and D. Snygg, *Individual Behavior.*

of the teacher's personality as a tool to assist others to new experiences; hence, teaching in many ways would always be highly individualized.

Carl Rogers is a psychologist primarily associated with counseling and therapy. However, some of his writings have touched upon the significance of his theory for learning. He, too, begins from the perceptual point of view. Rogers is concerned about assisting the person to see himself more accurately and seeks a greater acceptance of self. The learning process he envisions produces an individual who is more self-confident, flexible, self-directed, and less rigid in his perception. It enables him to adopt more realistic goals for himself and eventually to become more accepting of others. Rogers would say that significant learning will occur more readily when the child perceives problems he wishes to resolve. Thus, the teacher's role is one of creating a facilitating classroom climate. This has some obvious implications for planning. The teacher must be aware of the child's problems and willing to deal with them. He must accept the student as he is and understand how certain feelings may affect the child's capacity to learn. Learning, then, is always presented in terms of making resources available to the child as contrasted with forcing. The teacher's task is to promote the natural tendencies of the individual to learn, to develop, explore, and create. The child should not be forced into a mold in which he sacrifices his creativity and lives entirely in terms of the teacher's standards. This type of democratic atmosphere which Rogers advocates has been researched.[5] The evidence appears to indicate that there is more promise of freeing the mind for uniqueness, self-direction, and self-initiated learning, with no concomitant loss in factual or curricular learning as typically experienced in the conventional class.

Rogers, then, would utilize the self-actualizing tendency of the child, believing that students who are in contact with life's real problems function more effectively.[6] Thus, the personal relationships between the teacher and the student and between the individual students become highly significant. The types of problems selected and the provision of resources to explore them are important conditions for this theory. A Rogers-oriented teacher would have available a variety of resources and techniques and many types of educational devices to promote learning. He would recognize that all of the members of the class contribute to the accumulated learning.

---

6. Roger's point of view opens up many opportunities to see the teaching process in a different light. Assuming for the moment that you accept Rogers' point of view, describe some of the ways in which the Rogerian would function in the organization of the learning process.

---

[5] C. Rogers, *On Becoming a Person* (Boston: Houghton Mifflin Company, 1961).
[6] C. Rogers, *Client-Centered Therapy* (Boston: Houghton Mifflin Company, 1951).

Developmental Theory

The developmental view of the learning process, best represented in the works of Daniel Prescott, Cecil Millard, and Willard Olson, suggests that the child is more than a mere mechanism, as many of the stimulus-response associationists seem to imply. Learning occurs as a result of something more than what is done from the outside. Learning is an active process which, in a sense, is originated by the child. Developmentalists encourage us to look at some of the factors that influence learning. They suggest that we take into account the child's health, his growth level, his rate of maturing; also, the climate of love and the amount of emotional security afforded him. The subcultural elements that have been internalized through interaction with parents and other persons in the community have a significant influence on learning. It is important to know how the child internalizes the cultural background in his socialization processes. From an understanding of the roles and status which the child acquires in the peer group and the status to which he aspires, we can become aware of another important factor in connection with any child's learning. Finally, they suggest that it is important to recognize the influence of the child's self concept and his defense mechanisms if we are to understand some of the difficulties he encounters with learning problems.

From their research, developmentalists build a model which encourages us to recognize that all growth and learning are highly individualized, cyclic, and interrelated. They point out that there must be harmony between instruction and the growth pattern of the child if learning is to be effective. Maturation must precede learning; any attempt to teach without cognizance of the maturation concept cannot be effective. Teaching is best when it coincides with the maturational process of the individual. For the developmental theorist, teaching should neither conform to the average growth of children nor to a rigid grade level. Too much growth research has already demonstrated that many classrooms do not contain even a single "average" child as measured by intelligence and achievement tests. Thus, each child must be assisted to maximal development in relationship to his specific developmental pattern.

Millard conducted several longitudinal studies of academic achievement in which test data were collected over a period of time. He found that the progress of each child tended to follow a pattern of development to the extent that it was impossible to relate deviations from the pattern to differences in teaching methods or teachers.[7] It also was not possible to demonstrate the effects of special remedial help. When the individual curves of progress of these children were studied one could not tell when

[7] C. Millard, *Child Growth and Development,* rev. ed. (Boston: D. C. Heath & Company, 1958).

special help had been given. This caused him to believe that learning had certain growth and development connotations which have not been generally recognized. Learning is more than a product of teaching. It is suggested that teachers become involved in directing child growth and in providing guidance in the selection of learning activities. Perhaps one of the most vital functions would be that of improving or enriching the total educational environment.

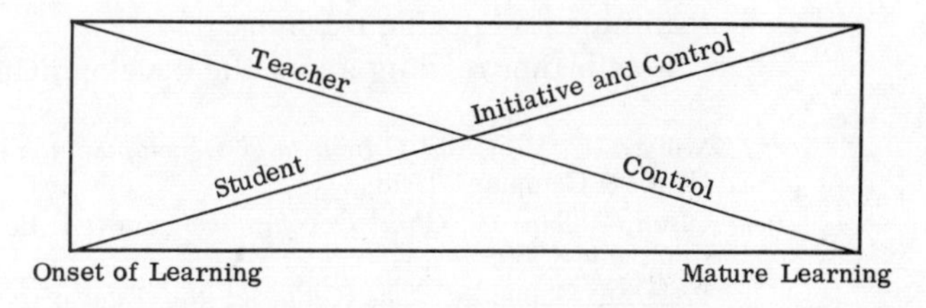

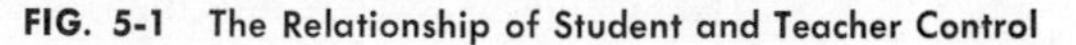
FIG. 5-1 The Relationship of Student and Teacher Control

The simple chart above illustrates that at the start of learning teacher control is high and student initiative low. However, as the learning relationship develops, the relative emphasis and roles are reversed.

Developmental theorists believe that growth and learning are two phases of the same process of change. The process is so complex that no satisfactory distinction can be made between the two. Learning implies modification. The individual is constantly changing. The task of the school is to facilitate desirable change.

Olson suggests that the healthy child will seek from his environment experiences that are consistent with his maturity and needs.[8] Thus, we should study seeking behavior in order to understand readiness. Self-selection suggests that the child will work creatively toward conditions that advance his well-being or his self-actualization. Teaching from this standpoint would not be a matter of setting up assignments, but instead, of serving as an encouraging guide, providing a variety of experiences, and letting the child select according to his level and rate of growth.

Pacing is a concept which is concerned with the acts of the teacher in insuring that the child is provided with materials at the appropriate level and with expectations only in line with his level of maturity. It takes into account the fact that success breeds further success. The teacher, then, is interested in tasks which have an intrinsic value and which cover a wide range of difficulty in order to provide for the great human variability in her room. An increasingly large amount of self-selection materials is available for educators; for example, the Science Research Associates Reading

[8] W. Olson, *Child Development*, 2nd ed. (Boston: D. C. Heath & Company, 1959).

Laboratory and the California Test Bureau Self Instructional Mathematical materials. Beyond this, each teacher can utilize the school and community libraries to provide a variety of resources for the learning situation.

Because all children are not ready to learn the same things at the same age, individual differences become most important in this approach. The school becomes involved in providing experiences which help to broaden the child's concept of his own needs and of the world. However, child study is basic to the learning process, and it is important that each teacher recognize the way in which one child differs from every other child in his readiness for specific learning.

For further reading about the developmental point of view see:

Millard, C. V., *Child Growth and Development,* rev. ed. Boston: D. C. Heath & Company, 1958.

Olson, Willard C., *Child Development,* 2nd ed. Boston: D. C. Heath & Company, 1959.

Prescott, Daniel A., *The Child in the Educative Process.* New York: McGraw-Hill Book Company, 1957.

Educational policy and practice follow certain guidelines if the developmental approach to learning is accepted. Attempts to develop and create homogeneous groups of children would be relatively nonexistent. The school would recognize and accept the problem of great human variability and would seek methods to work with it instead of trying to solve it through an external manipulation factor like grouping. Where grouping was necessary, the basis would never be a single characteristic, but rather a study that included all of the important developmental factors for each child. The teaching task, then, is complicated by the varied tasks undertaken by different children within the class in any particular year.

If each child takes the proper next step in his development, the teacher truly becomes a guide to learning. To be an effective guide, he must know each child in terms of all of the factors which have already been described as influences on learning. Obviously, too, the teacher should be supplied with carefully compiled developmental information at the beginning of each school year. Teachers, then, must become experts in recognizing and accepting individual differences. They must keep cumulative personnel records which are objective and descriptive and which will eventually help to explain the dynamics of behavior, for records are kept in order to reveal the pattern of development. This suggests also that school administrators provide the teacher with time to keep up to date developmental information related to the individuals in their classes.

Learning as Acquisition versus Learning as Growth

For a long time learning has been considered as an acquisitional activity. For some, learning and acquisition were practically synonymous. Learning in the conventional sense required giving evidence of memorized material.

In contrasting learning as acquisition and learning as growth, Millard has presented most concisely the developmental theorist's point of view. Some characteristics of learning as acquisition, as applied in the classroom, have emerged with considerable clarity. The following outline includes most of them:

> First: Learning is classified as acquisition when
> a. There is subject matter set out in advance of teaching as material to be learned.
> b. The teacher's efforts are directed toward bringing children to a predetermined goal.
> c. The emphasis is upon an outcome of possession, achievement, conformity.
>
> Second: Learning is to be classified as acquisition when the activities of the teacher consist of
> a. Setting tasks
> b. Giving reasons for the tasks set
> c. Offering rewards for effort, and setting and administering penalties for lack of effort.
>
> Third: Other activities of the "acquisitional teacher" may be
> a. Expressing sympathy or interest
> b. Controlling order by issuing rules and disciplining offenders
> c. Directing activity by commands or questions
> d. Explaining points not understood
> e. Setting models to be copied or followed
> f. Doing things for pupils they cannot do for themselves
> g. Hearing recitations based on repetitions of memorized materials
> h. Drilling, reviewing, inspecting, and perfecting for no other obvious purpose than for perfection
> i. Making and recording judgments of performance in relation to predetermined standards.[9]

In this situation the control by the teacher is rather complete. Responsibility for what is learned, how it is learned, and when it is acquired resides in the teacher primarily. All teaching and its results from this point of view are able to be measured by subject-matter tests of knowledge and skill.

Teaching in relation to learning as growth takes on a new aspect. It aims not at forcing but at providing the conditions favorable for growth. Learning in the conventional sense is not disregarded but becomes a means to an end rather than an end in itself. Learning is acquired through multiple experiences that have meaning and value for the child, and not through a single passive or isolated activity. Teaching from this point of view is evaluated not by what the child knows but by what he becomes. The following points are characteristic of learning as growth.

[9] C. Millard, *Child Growth and Development*, p. 282.

First: Learning of academic facts is not a major outcome. The accumulation of knowledge is incidental to experience. This means that learning itself is a by-product of experience, something growing "out of" rather than something "added to."

Second: Learning is given a growth emphasis when the teacher's efforts are directed toward helping children either to have experiences or to profit from their experiences.

Third: Subject matter is determined by the needs of the child as brought out and made clear through experience.

Fourth: The teacher stimulates realization of purposes by presentation of objects, situations, or opportunities.

Fifth: The activity of the teacher includes guiding purposes to higher levels which will result in action and changed behavior.

Sixth: Other activities of the teacher are those which:

a. Provide restimulation and guidance
b. Overcome fears and inhibitions
c. Express sympathy and interest
d. Point out successes
e. Explain difficulties
f. Aid in solving conflicts, disputes, etc.
g. Call attention to unnoticed problems, supply materials, references, etc.[10]

The distinct contrast between the two approaches to learning may imply that a teacher must adhere only to one in his conduct of the learning situation. Millard's analysis leads to a recognition that almost all teaching includes both learning as acquisition and learning as growth.

---

7. Your own learning experiences have exposed you to teachers with differing emphasis upon learning as a growth or as an acquisitional activity. What do you think is the difference in terms of the student's reaction to learning? Take either the learning as acquisition or learning as growth point of view and defend it as the most desirable approach to learning.

FACTORS CLOSELY RELATED TO LEARNING

A number of factors have a significant effect on the learning process. You should particularly be aware of the influence of maturation, parents, the social climate, and motivation on the effectiveness of the learning process.

Maturation

The child's maturity has been shown to have a significant influence on the efficiency of his learning. In a number of investigations concerned

[10] C. Millard, *Child Growth and Development*, pp. 283–84.

with the maturation-learning relationship it has been demonstrated learning is most effective in certain periods of the developmental cycle of a specific growth.[11, 12, 13] Adequate maturity reduces the period required for learning. Learning is generally more efficient when the proper stage of maturation has been reached. Thus, instruction and the growth pattern should be synchronized. If the opportunity to learn is withheld when the proper stage of maturation has been reached, other factors may enter to hinder the learning process. Each child has a period of optimal readiness. Instruction before or after that period may reduce the effectiveness of learning or limit the child's potential.

The Child and the Parents

The child's first teachers are the parents, who have a greater influence on him than any other single agency. Many of his habits, attitudes, and values are established by the time he reaches school. Certainly the parents provide the child with his first social interaction. Their attitudes toward learning and the academic discipline serve as a model for him to accept or reject. They should, at every opportunity, encourage and reinforce the child's learning. The school should pay close attention to the development of parent education programs if the work of the school is to be facilitated. The relationship between the parent and school should be a cooperative one.

Parents should not be expected to teach what professionals cannot get across. While parents can provide varied experiences and support the values of the school, they cannot be given the full responsibility for developing interest in the work tasks of school. For example, the teacher should not assume that homework must be regularly checked by parents. Instead, the parents might play the role of supplying certain nutrients to the learning process. The parents might make available materials in the home which promote learning, and also provide opportunities to engage in learning experiences not immediately available in the school setting.

Parents should teach by example. The way they relate to each other is a significant learning experience for the child, who can observe the way in which people act toward each other. His ideas about cooperation and achieving one's purposes are frequently stimulated first in the home. Parents should understand the growth and development pattern of the child. The schools might well utilize parent-teacher contacts to provide parents with child development information and opportunities to discuss difficulties in dealing with developmental problems.

[11] C. Millard, *Child Growth and Development.*
[12] C. Millard and J. Rothney, *The Elementary School Child: A Book of Cases* (New York: Holt, Rinehart & Winston, Inc., 1957).
[13] W. Olson, *Child Development,* 2nd ed. (Boston: D. C. Heath & Company, 1959).

Because of the importance of the parents' role in learning, it should be clear that certain attitudes only hamper the learning process. The demanding parent who expects the child continually to accomplish "more" hinders the child. Pressure at the home has no greater validity than at school. Instead, parents might serve to inspire the child, to encourage appropriate self-expression, and to introduce him to new concepts and ideas. They can both stimulate and utilize his curiosity. Simply answering questions and indicating methods of solving problems can be a very important role for the parent.

Frequently, when psychiatrists and psychologists investigate learning difficulties, they find that the difficulty relates to some problem in the parent-child relationship. Some children refuse to learn in order to show their parents who is boss. Others, get even through the embarrassment of poor report cards or admonitory telephone calls from the school. On the other hand, some children, according to some psychoanalysts, may not wish to do better than their parents because they do not want to make the parent look inferior. The child who makes a lot of progress in school may then be expected to take on additional responsibility at home and give up being babied. In some instances learning and the lessons and values of the school may differ from the values of the parents. This can be threatening to the child and cause him to withdraw from learning. The variance in standards between the school and the home and the resultant inconsistencies may bring about failure to perform.

Parental involvement in the learning process may be considerable and may be both positive and negative. The school administration and professional staff should investigate effective ways to establish adequate communication between teachers and parents, and should seek to assist parents in encouraging their children to enter into the learning process.

The Social Climate

Much that has been said about the principles of development and individual differences has seemed to indicate that all learning is an individual process. It is important to recognize that learning occurs in a social setting. Teachers must learn that the classroom atmosphere is basic to the learning situation. The emotional tone of the classroom, the amount of acceptance and approval, the development of an attitude that fosters creativity are all vital to a good classroom learning atmosphere. We frequently think of emotion as being a hindrance to learning. We should recognize that mild emotion, strong feelings of interest and belonging, can elicit sufficient tension and effort to develop personal involvement in the learning process. In the proper learning climate the child is accepted and hence free to learn.

It is important, then, for teachers to recognize at least two facets of the social climate in learning. First, we cannot teach a child effectively unless we know something about the family situation, community, and social background which helped shape his habits and actions. Also, teachers must be aware of their role as directors of a group and the effect of group interaction on the learning process.

The school is a social institution which is influential in the education of the individual. Society has set up the school to allow the child a period of experimental social functioning. Hence, it is the duty of education to preserve the social heritage and to assist the child not only in mastering facts and gaining understandings, but also in acquiring social techniques, mores, and attitudes. Education should give him skills that enable him to evaluate society and to work toward change that benefits society.

There has been a considerable amount of experimentation on teacher leadership and its influence on the group climate. Classical studies compare autocratic, laissez-faire, and democratic social settings.[14] In an autocratic atmosphere, the leader determines policy, makes work assignments, and determines working companions. In the democratic group, policies are determined by group discussion with assistance from the leader. In the laissez-faire group, the leader supplies the materials but rarely participates in decisions. The autocratic person, it has been shown, gives more orders and more personal praise and approval. The democratic leader acts as a guide who stimulates self-direction and uses recognition as a token of success.

Children in the democratic groups were not as aggressive as pupils of the autocratic teachers, and were motivated to engage in self-sustaining types of activities toward individual and group goals, in contrast to the laissez-faire children, who were dissatisfied with their own lack of accomplishment. The democratic climate, then, has been considered as the best for developing and achieving both the individual and group goals.

---

8. Obviously the type of leadership pattern that the teacher develops in the classroom has an effect upon the outcomes of education. Give some evidence of classroom atmospheres that you have experienced which appeared to be democratic, autocratic, or laissez-faire. Do you feel that certain types of subject matter limit the teacher's ability to use the democratic approach? If you feel that there is a limit, indicate which types of subjects you believe would not lend themselves to the democratic approach and why.

---

[14] K. Lewin, R. Lippitt, and R. White, "Patterns of Aggressive Behavior in Experimentally Created 'Social Climates.' " *Journal of Social Psychology,* 10 (1939), 271–99.

Motivation

An important factor in working with learning in children is motivation. We are here referring to the art of stimulating interest or utilizing interest that is already present. Regardless of the quality of the curriculum, the child can be exposed to knowledge, but obviously he does not always learn. Specifically, he does not always learn what the teacher desires. Many learning situations in the school result mainly in the child's learning negativistic attitudes about certain kinds of subject matter. It is probably fundamental to recognize that the teacher must try to stimulate interest in pupils where it is lacking. The incentive approach to education involves different ways of making a subject palatable. However, the teacher should more than sugarcoat the subject matter; he should be able to take advantage of the interests that the student already possesses.

All students come to school with varying interests. Determining the interests of the individual and working with them to add vitality to the learning process are basic to successful teaching. Interests may be determined in a number of ways. Some are as simple as just listening. However, the Pupil Interest Inventory mentioned in Chapter III will provide the inexperienced teacher with many insights into the child's interests. Permitting compositions to be written spontaneously will offer further insight into the natural interests of the child. You must, however, consider motivation as an intrinsic process, not merely the manipulation of extrinsic factors by the teacher.

---

9. There is a fundamental difference between stimulating interests and developing interests. The effective teacher will probably do both. Give examples of ways that you might utilize and develop already present interests at different grade levels and in various subjects.

It seems clear that we need to work with the child's goals and purposes in mind. For the child, the more clearly the goal is perceived, the more strongly his acts will be motivated. Thus, our efforts should be directed toward making the goal more vital and vivid through assisting in goal selection and clarification.

Rewards and punishment play very important roles in the motivation of school learning. Reward or positive reinforcement, whether it be something material or a teacher's word of encouragement, becomes a form of motivation. The motive of the learner will determine what is interpreted as a reward. If the child's goal is to gain the approval of his peers, a good grade in arithmetic will not be interpreted as a reward unless it is so regarded by the group to which he wants to belong. The teacher might utilize the desire of most children for social approval in the learning process. Once social factors in learning are recognized, then grouping practices can assist learning. Children might be grouped together for mutual encouragement. The teacher also will be forced to focus on constructive ways to assist the child to gain recognition from the group.

Sometimes a child is rewarded by discovering meaning in something he has been working to comprehend. A similar feeling may come from the knowledge that he is making progress and doing well. The motives of curiosity and mastery are effective in the production of learning. Utilizing curiosity enables us to work with the child's natural inquisitiveness about his world. The mastery motive activates the child's desire to be competent and accepted for his accomplishments.

---

10. Give an example of the utilization of the motives of curiosity and mastery in the learning process.

The self-selection principle permits use of the factors of interest, enthusiasm, persistence, and satisfaction in the learning process. Knowledge of results, the giving of immediate information about success or failure, is, of course, pertinent to the learning and motivational situation. Teachers should be aware that generally schools are set up so that fast learners are rewarded over and over again, while slow learners rarely have opportunities to experience feelings of accomplishment.

Punishment is based on fear, the fear of physical pain, embarrassment, or loss of status. It may also completely inhibit the individual so that he does not respond at all. It is not unusual to come into contact with adults who have had so many inhibiting experiences at school that they are unable to engage in an open discussion of their opinions regarding intellectual questions. Punishment is a negative motive at best, and being inhibitory, it does not encourage creative activity. Nevertheless, in the schools we frequently see many examples of actions which are punishments, for example, sarcasm, ridicule, lowering of grades, giving of extra assignments, increasing homework, detentions, dismissal to administrative offices, sending for parents, and withholding recommendations and responsibilities. All of these actions should be seriously questioned as motivational devices. They frequently produce the very opposite of the behavior desired. The basic evaluation systems in the schools, beginning with the awarding of stars and moving on to more formal marks, can easily degenerate into serving as motivation for working toward grades rather than actual educational objectives. Grades within our school systems have encouraged the pupil to work for superficial instead of basic values.

If we accept the purposive nature of behavior, we should recognize that some children endure punishment to get the reward of achieving their particular goal or purpose. For some children, punishment may even serve as a reward in that it gives them the attention they seek or permits them to engage in a power contest or to get even. The results of punishment, then, can be unpredictable and confusing. It is advisable, educationally, to use natural, logical consequences rather than punishment that is unrelated to the act.

A number of studies have investigated the relative valence of factors like praise and reproof.[15] Generally, praise has been demonstrated to be superior to reproof, and rewards more effective than punishment. For some children, development of skill and competence and success are motives in themselves for the continuation of activity. This points to the importance of varying school work sufficiently so that every pupil has a chance to succeed at his developmental level. Success will build self-confidence, which in turn enables children to go about setting realistic goals for themselves.

This approach in motivation stresses the importance of aligning the goals of the teacher and the students. Frequently, in education, the student has one objective and the teacher another; mutual alignment of goals is necessary before progress can be made. Whenever possible, personally meaningful material, related to both present and future needs of the students, should be included. All attempts to utilize mass production methods in education might well be discouraged.

---

11. Give an example of the utilization of personally meaningful material. Taking a specific grade level, indicate how you would utilize personally meaningful material that would be related to present concerns of the children.

Ego involvement, the attempt to involve the whole personality, is quite fundamental to the motivational process. Equally important is recognition by the teacher that learning through experience is more effective than learning through lecture.

Every child needs a curriculum in which he can succeed. This is basic to both efficient learning and healthy personality development. If the curriculum is wisely adjusted to the child's capacities, and is consistent with his growth and development, purposive striving may be achieved through proper motivation. Teachers can do much to adjust the curriculum so that the child can succeed at his developmental level. Obviously, this necessitates knowing more about the developmental level of specific individuals.

Failure makes a person think less of himself, and this lowering of self-esteem generates anxiety. For example, threatening to fail students who

[15] H. W. Stevenson and L. C. Snyder, "Performance as a Function of the Interaction of Incentive Conditions," *J. Pers.*, XXVIII (1960), 1–11.

do not produce in a classroom situation may make those who have had some success work harder, but those who have not experienced success have a tendency to give up. There is considerable evidence that failure results in an impairment of learning which persists throughout the learning task. We might consider if the threat of a failing grade is actually a motivational force.

Opportunity for success and satisfaction can be achieved most readily as teachers become more effective in utilizing the encouragement process, which has been described in detail in another publication.[16] Our purpose here shall be to present a review of the rationale behind the process.

Many children do not learn because they are discouraged. Discouragement stems from a lack of confidence in one's capacity to cope with problems. The individual assumes that he cannot succeed; he anticipates failure, feels inadequate or inferior. Some of his problems stem from early competition within the family. Other problems develop from his own overambition or pressure by significant adults in his life space.

To assist such a child, we must change his concepts and expectations of self. We must seek a way to help him overcome his inertia. Encouragement communicates a faith in the child as he is. It begins by valuing the child, not just the child's attributes. It sets about to build the child's self-respect. This approach gives recognition for effort, not just for accomplishment and achievement. Teachers with an encouragement approach focus on the child's strengths and assets rather than his weaknesses and limitations. Instruction is based on the building of skills fitted to the child's development and paced to permit more success than failure. The book *Encouraging Children to Learn* by Dinkmeyer and Dreikurs gives many examples of the process in actual classroom situations.

---

12. Give an example of how discouragement might affect a specific learning area with a given child. How would you specifically utilize the encouragement process to help a child with a learning problem?

A summary of motivation's function in learning would be helpful.

1. Material should be personally meaningful and individualized to as great an extent as possible. Whenever possible, it should relate to the learner's present life as well as his future life. The material's utility should be shown and practical applications presented. Facts and skills presented should be closely related to immediate concerns, as it is difficult for the individual to solve problems he does not have.

2. Interests and needs are basic factors in motivation. The teacher

[16] D. Dinkmeyer and R. Dreikurs, *Encouraging Children to Learn: The Encouragement Process* (Englewood Cliffs, N.J.: Prentice-Hall, Inc., 1963).

should take advantage of the interests the individual already has and relate them to the subject matter. Too often we seek only to stimulate interest where none is present, instead of attempting to utilize interest factors already inherent in the situation. This suggests that the teacher permit option, choice, and self-selection and encourage participation.

3. In motivating the child, it is important to consider his growth and maturation. Every child has his own natural rate of development. If you try to hurry him or force him beyond his capacity, you are likely to retard instead of hasten development. Material should always be fitted to the child's readiness and maturation factors.

4. To guide learning, you must always take into account the goals and purposes of the individual. The more clearly the goal is perceived by the child, the more strongly the act will be motivated. Those responsible for guiding learning experiences should work for the alignment of teacher and pupil goals.

5. Incentives, such as desire to secure attention and social approval from the child's group, may be used when managed intelligently. The skillful teacher can utilize the group to facilitate learning. The child's behavior can be shifted from the useless to the useful side of the continuum if he is guided into activities where he can get attention by functioning rather than by being a nuisance.

6. An effort should be made to base a learner's attitude toward work on his own intrinsic motives whenever possible. This indicates that the child would be working at serving his purposes, goals, and needs. The teacher who guides the learning process prefers that the child learn for his own sake and out of his own need, not for the sake of the teacher or for grades. Much effort is still needed to focus the child on a meaningful basis for acquiring learning and changing behavior.

7. Each and every child has a unique personality developed through unique experiences. Mass production methods may be effective in manufacturing, but are doomed to failure in the educational process. Adapt the educational method to pertinent personality factors of the child.

8. Some extrinsic motives, such as rewards, may be used in educational programs, but care should always be taken that this is not overdone. It is easy to detect when extrinsic motivations have been overused, when the only reason for exerting effort is winning a grade, a letter, a bar, a pin, or a star.

9. Sincere praise and encouragement should be utilized. The individual's need to think well of himself should be met.

10. Success and satisfaction should be experienced by the learner. This requires the teacher to present materials appropriate to developmental levels and related to pertinent developmental tasks.

11. Teacher-pupil planning should be explored. This permits the learner to become involved in the learning process.

12. Encouragement should be given to projects, field trips, group work, and learning through experience whenever this is feasible and meaningful.

13. The attitude of the teacher toward the learner should include trust, cooperation, recognition of individual differences, and a growth of empathy and faith. Self-evaluation will help facilitate this type of relationship and attitude.

14. The fragmentation of knowledge should be avoided and interrelationships built upon. Many of the subjects in school are interrelated, but teachers frequently treat them as though they were unrelated. The obvious relationship between science and health, for example, could be only a start to the eventual recognition of the interrelationships in all knowledge.

15. Learning should seek to change the phenomenal field of the learner and, consequently his behavior, if it is to be truly effective. Evaluation then would look beyond grades and marks to analyze at least in part the behavioral goals that have been achieved.

PROBLEMS IN LEARNING

The learning process, complex and closely interrelated with the growth process, presents a number of problems, such as transfer, perception, distributed learning, retention, and knowledge of results. In dealing with these as separate problems, always keep in mind the interrelationship of growth and learning.

Transfer of Learning

Educators and psychologists for a long time have been concerned about the applicability of one subject field to another. For example, does learning Latin help or hinder the learning of English? This type of relationship is considered in the transfer of learning. We want to know how much of what we learn can be used and applied in other situations. This should obviously be the long-run goal of any educational process. For a time, the training of the mind and formal discipline were educational ends in themselves, and subjects were frequently taught because they were difficult and supposedly conditioned the mind. Research now points to the fact that training the mind in one difficult task in no way trains the mind for an unrelated situation.[17] Early experiments by Ebbinghaus[18] pointed to the fact that training in the repetition of nonsense syllables or meaningless

[17] J. McGeoch and A. Irion, *The Psychology of Human Learning,* rev. ed. (New York: David McKay Co., Inc., 1952).

[18] H. Ebbinghaus, "Memory: A Contribution to Experimental Psychology," trans. H. A. Ruger and C. E. Bussenius, TC, 1913.

rote memory did not train the mind to do well in a similar task on other meaningless material.

A student really needs insight into a generalization which he can use repeatedly in different situations or problems if the transfer is to occur. When transfer does take place it is usually closely attributable to similarities in the tasks performed. In planning learning situations for children, you should provide experiences that relate as directly as possible to the experience in which they will eventually perform, since there appears to be little transfer between unrelated activities. In other words, we tend to learn what we practice, and educators should set up experiences which relate as directly as possible to educational goals.

We might not expect transfer to occur by having children memorize good conduct rules for when the teacher is out of the room. On the other hand, developing self-control and student government even when the teacher is in the room could be expected to transfer. Teachers with democratically disciplined classrooms have demonstrated that children can run their interpersonal relations well even if the teacher is out of the room. However, this type of cooperation appears to be highly dependent upon having assignments that have been mutually determined by the teacher and the student.

Andrews and Cronbach have done an excellent job of summarizing the research on transfer.[19] They indicate that there are negligible gains in intelligence as the result of studying particular subjects. However, there is much evidence that transfer does occur. To enhance the occurrence of transfer, the teacher needs to point out the possibility of transfer, use varied teaching materials comparable to those to which the learning is expected to transfer, assist in the development of meaningful generalizations, provide practice in applying generalizations, and evaluate the experience by determining how the pupil's behavior in new situations is changed.

Perception

We need to be aware that people perceive situations differently. Many problems in learning occur because of differentiated perception of the task. The teacher has one expectation, the pupil another. No two children perceive in exactly the same way the teacher's expectations for a learning task. Failure to acknowledge these perceptual differences will only create unnecessary difficulties.

It has been demonstrated that perception is highly influenced by our

[19] T. Andrews and L. Cronbach, "Transfer of Training," in *Encyclopedia of Educational Research*, rev. ed., ed. W. S. Monroe (New York: The Macmillan Company, 1950), pp. 1483–89.

subculture, immediate social influences, and goals. The teacher who asks the students to list a balanced diet when their subculture values a diet heavy in carbohydrates is running into subculture problems. How can he deal with the difference in values between the parents and the school?

Sometimes the teacher's limited perception serves as a hindrance to the learning situation. The teacher's understanding of certain human relations, for example, may be limited to textbook descriptions, while some of his students may have been exposed to intensive reading and personal experiences that have taken them beyond his view of this field.

Fifteen children are going on a picnic. The problem is to decide how many sandwiches will be needed if each child is to have two sandwiches. John perceives this as a problem in addition and adds $2 + 2 + 2$, etc. Henry perceives it as a multiplication problem, 15×2. Both arrive at the same answer, but by different methods. However, differences in perception may yield different results. The teacher asks someone to collect the volumes of the encyclopedia that are in use and put them away. Mary collects the books and lays them on the table where they are kept. Joan would collect the books and stand them, in alphabetical order, between the book ends on the table.

---

13. Give an illustration of how teacher's expectations in a learning task may differ from that of a pupil. Illustrate how perceptions of the task may differ among the pupils.

Distributed Learning

Many experiments have been conducted to discover the relative value in mastering a task in one concentrated learning period or many short sessions separated by rest periods.[20] While results vary with the individual, evidence is conclusive that distributed learning results in a shorter time for mastery and greater retention. For the most efficient learning the length of the learning session and of the rest interval depend not only on the learner, but also on the material to be learned.

Closely related to distributed learning is whole or part learning. Should a task be learned as a whole or broken down into various elements? Results of these experiments have not always been conclusive, since individual differences come into greater play. A task that might seem simple to one person will appear complex to another, depending upon his previous experience. Obviously, readiness factors in children and the type of subject matter will affect the ability to comprehend a whole task. Many areas of learning lend themselves well to permitting an over-all presentation in

[20] W. K. Estes, "Learning," *Annual Rev. of Psychology,* 7 (1956), 1–38.

which the whole will lend meaning to the parts. A story is better understood when the plot can be grasped; many constructs in social science clarify certain incidents and periods of history. The whole and then part approach add the feature of meaningfulness.

Retention

Retention refers to the amount of learning present after an interval of time. Although this is difficult to measure accurately, recall and recognition are the methods used in the school situation. Much experimentation in this area has provided the basis for broad generalizations, although no clear-cut conclusions have been reached.[21] Usually, meaningful material is retained longer than material without meaning. Overlearning, practice beyond the point of immediate complete recall, will lengthen the period of retention and increase the amount retained. Subsequent learning of similar material will decrease the retention of the original material. An individual's emotional problems can also interfere with retention.

Knowledge of Results

The importance of the child's being reinforced through immediate knowledge of results in a learning situation is receiving increasing recognition. This has been one of the aims of programed instruction. It can also be done in any personal teacher-pupil contact. The teacher is merely required to give the results of a learning situation to the child as quickly as possible. Teachers might well work at devising methods to give immediate reinforcement to correct responses.

One of the techniques devised toward this end in a testing situation is the Rapid Rater punchboard from Syosset, Long Island, New York. The punchboard can be used with multiple-choice and true-false items. A peg is used to punch the answers on a sheet inserted in the board. The board is devised so that when the correct answer is selected the punch will go all the way through the paper while it does not penetrate for the incorrect response. Thus, one can tell immediately, through the sense of touch, when the correct response has been made.

Morrill, in a comprehensive review of the work on teaching machines, indicates that learning is significantly enhanced by the type of immediate results available from the punchboard.[22] However, research has indicated immediate knowledge of results plus explanation of incorrect responses produces superior results than if the explanation is not given.

[21] E. Hilgard, *Theories of Learning*, 2nd ed. (New York: Appleton-Century-Crofts, 1956).

[22] C. Morrill, "Teaching Machines: A Review," *Psychological Bulletin*, No. 58 (1961), 363–75.

Another reinforcement device has been used in children's games. Selection of the correct answer to a question by either moving a lever or pressing a button will close an electric circuit and cause a bulb to light or a bell to ring. Regardless of the method selected, "psychological feedback" is vital to the learning process.

---

14. Develop a list of ways in which the teacher, without programed learning, can provide for immediate knowledge of results.

The Effect of Pressure Teaching

A vital problem to be investigated is the effects of pressure teaching. We seem to see more and more evidence of attempts to force the learning situation. Many people actually function with children in the belief that better learning will result when a certain amount of "pressure" is applied.

There seems to be some evidence that learning curves will temporarily respond to "pressure." An interesting attempt to test the effects of pressure teaching was a study of fifth-grade spelling. The available data provided

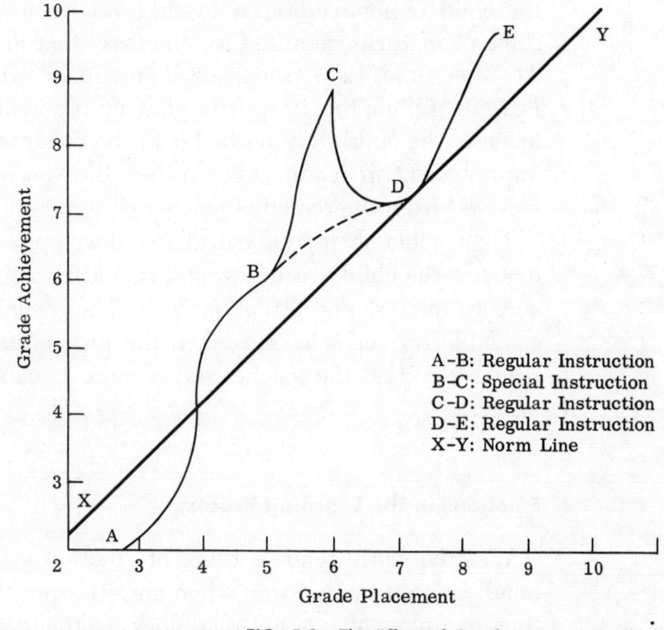

FIG. 5-2 The Effect of Overlearning in Spelling

This figure shows: 1. The loss following special instruction (C-D); 2. No carry-over of special instructional effects; 3. Resumption of initial pattern of growth (D-E).

From C. Millard, *Child Growth and Development*. Boston: D. C. Heath and Co., 1958, p. 270.

group learning curves covering grades one, two, three, and four, and data were collected in the years following the experiment. This experiment lasted for about four months during the winter. In this period of time contests, games, and rewards were utilized, and the children's scores continued to rise until they reached the ninth-grade level. No child was punished, and each child was assured that he contributed his share if his score was better than his preceding score. Improvement was the basis upon which the teacher gave rewards. After the time allotted for the experiment had passed, these children were placed in their regular spelling periods. Fifth-grade work was resumed, and the spelling program went on as it had before the experiment. The nature of the curve following this experiment is highly significant. Within two months' time much of the success gained from the forced learning had been lost, and in the year following, the pattern of emerging growth was almost exactly an extension of the pattern established before the experiment.

This, of course, relates closely to the previous principle of resistance to displacement. The child's growth pattern seems to be highly resistant to extra pressure and rewards.

Remedial reading can be another form of pressure teaching. Frequently the child is not reading at grade level because he has not reached the stage of maturity required for the tasks that are being presented to him. At other times, a personal-social-emotional problem may interfere with learning. Often, too, in spite of glowing reports from the remedial reading teacher, the child does no better in the classroom because his goal is not improvement in reading, but rather, the special attention which he has received from the remedial teacher.

The teacher should have available developmental information adequate to assess the child's readiness and should also observe the child closely for cues to interest and attention span. There should be abundant material available for self-selection when the proper stage of readiness has been reached, so that the teacher serves more as catalyst and guide than taskmaster.

Emotions in the Learning Process

We frequently tend to think of emotion as a disorganizing factor. A mind cannot function well when anxieties prey heavily upon it, and emotions can serve as types of roadblocks to the learning process. However, it is important to recognize also that mild emotions serve as a tonic to the body. They pep up the individual's feelings, whether they are pleasant or unpleasant. The obvious implication is that teachers must live and deal with emotions because emotions can serve to energize the instructional process. There should be enjoyment in the classroom. So, acknowledge the disadvantages of disorganizing emotions, but do not overlook the factor of emotions as a stimulant within the learning process.

We believe that emotions are more than the result of stimuli; they derive from meanings that come through the process of perception. The individual sees by successive approximations what the people he loves believe, and he internalizes the value systems of these people. Thus, emotions can serve in many ways to facilitate the way in which the child feels about the meaning of the classroom situation for himself. When education becomes in this sense an "emotional process" it will function at a significantly higher level.

Providing Optimum Conditions for Learning

When a curriculum is rich and well-selected with the children's interests and needs in mind, motivation for learning can be comparatively easy. Experiences which interest and challenge boys and girls should form the heart of the school program. Opportunities must be provided for first-hand experiences through which knowledge may be related to action. Living and learning at school should relate to all of life. School experiences should be consistent with the physical, emotional, intellectual, and social needs of the child. The aim of the school program must be to give each child the opportunity to grow and develop toward his optimum. He must feel that he belongs and can achieve. Individual differences must be recognized and provided for. The criterion of achievement should be growth in desirable behavior characteristics. Opportunity must be provided for evaluation by both the teacher and the pupil.

The child must see meaning in what he is doing and must have a clear understanding of what is expected of him. Ideas should be presented in as vivid a manner as possible. The use of visual aids is important. There should be frequent and strategic review of material, and overlearning should be encouraged, but not to the point of boredom. Competition with others should be minimized. The child should be encouraged to compete with himself.

A learning environment, then, consists of the inextricable weaving together of the teacher, the children, and the materials. Learning results from the creative act of an effective teacher, and is reflected in the attitude of the children. A good school atmosphere is free of pressure and strain and radiates involvement, excitement, and purposeful activity. An effective learning environment would lead the individual to search constantly for broader horizons and new understandings, to be curious, and to ask questions in eager expectation. A checklist of what constitutes a good atmosphere for learning follows:

"1. Children are given opportunities in both individual and group situations.

2. The child is expected to do that which is in harmony with his ability and growth.
3. Each child has freedom within the limits of a learning situation.
4. The learning experience has importance for the learner.
5. Opportunity is provided for activities varied in type and content, wide in range and challenging in nature.
6. Opportunities are provided for children to recognize that there is more than one way of doing things.
7. There is constructive interaction between teacher and children.
8. The child may practice the behaviors indicated by the objectives of the learning experience.
9. Opportunities are provided for children to appraise their achievements.
10. Provision is made for an atmosphere that fosters self-respect, self-reliance, respect for others, and a cooperative attitude.
11. Children are given equal opportunities with adults to plan and carry out many ideas and activities."[23]

IMPLICATIONS

1. The developmental approach to education strongly stresses the importance of developing a harmony between the instruction presented and the growth pattern of the child.

2. Teaching should not attempt to follow an average growth. All concepts based upon the average child or a particular grade level are perhaps more of a hindrance than an aid to the teaching process.

3. Growth research indicates that it is difficult to relate deviations from academic growth patterns with specific teaching methods. We must spend more time in attempting to recognize clearly the developmental pattern of the child.

4. Maturation must precede learning. The developmental sequence of the learner and the material should be synchronized.

5. An important role of the teacher is as a guide, helping children to explore, experience, and draw conclusions, enriching the total educational milieu.

6. When ideas are organized by the pupil, they are learned more permanently than ideas presented by the teacher and memorized by the child.

7. School work should be varied so that each child in a given grade or "attendance center" has a chance to succeed at his developmental level.

[23] Reprinted by permission of Association for Childhood Education International, Washington, D. C., from *Helping Children Live and Learn*, Bulletin No. 89 (1952), 12–14 (out of print).

If, instead of thinking of specific grade levels, we come to see grades as attendance centers, where teachers are geared to work with learning problems of varied individuals, the learning process may be enhanced.

8. The learning atmosphere is obviously crucial. There should be a constant working toward development of a democratic, accepting climate for learning. This would embrace teacher-pupil planning and group work involving interaction.

9. Fundamental to any real learning is the utilization of self-evaluation techniques which remove external pressures and threats.

10. Techniques for knowing the individual learner become increasingly important. We must work through his interests, knowing his level of readiness and developing ways to individualize instruction.

11. Learning by experience suggests that the teacher work continually to facilitate creative group and individual projects.

12. Ego involvement, an attempt to involve the whole personality in dealing with personally meaningful material, should always be attempted. The teacher should be concerned with improving not only the quantity but also the quality of learning. This implies that we provide opportunities for choice.

13. Since learning is usually based on the development of a relationship, learning difficulties will always involve an understanding of the relationship between the parents and the child, and the teacher and the child. Some of the resistance to learning may be resistance to a significant adult in the atmosphere.

14. The developmental approach to learning places an important focus on individual differences. In any significant educational decisions, it recognizes a variable learner who is developing at a unique rate.

15. Since learning is based on the child's personal and purposeful perception of events, it is important to have access to information about the pupil which identifies his specific needs, values, and goals. Plans for the learning experience must go beyond a mere cataloging of cognitive traits and include purposes and feelings.

16. The adults' role in motivation should utilize not only extrinsic motives but the natural inquisitiveness and curiosity of the child.

17. The teacher should be concerned with the specific reinforcing contingencies which are important in the learning process.

SUGGESTED READINGS

Articles

Bruner, J., "Learning and Thinking," in *The Causes of Behavior: Readings in Child Development and Educational Psychology,* eds. J. Rosenblith and W. Allinsmith, p. 446. Boston: Allyn and Bacon, Inc., 1962.

Burton, W., "Basic Principles in a Good Teaching-Learning Situation," in *Readings in Human Learning*, eds. L. Crow and A. Crow, p. 7. New York: David McKay Co., Inc., 1963.

Frandsen, A., "Learning: An Integration of Theories," in *Readings for Educational Psychology*, ed. E. Page, p. 50. New York: Harcourt, Brace & World, Inc., 1964.

Trow, W., "The Problem of Transfer–Then and Now" in *Readings in Educational Psychology*, eds. W. Morse and G. Wingo, p. 222. Chicago: Scott, Foresman & Company, 1962.

Tyler, R., "Conditions for Effective Learning," in *Readings in Human Learning*, eds. L. Crow and A. Crow, p. 66. New York: David McKay Co., Inc., 1963.

Books

Bigge, M., *Learning Theories for Teachers.* New York: Harper & Row, Publishers, Inc., 1964.

Hilgard, E., *Theories of Learning*, 2nd ed. New York: Appleton-Century-Crofts, 1956.

Hill, W. F., *Learning: A Survey of Psychological Interpretations.* San Francisco: Chandler Publishing Co., 1963.

Kelley, E., *Education for What Is Real.* New York: Harper & Row, Publishers, Inc., 1947.

Pratt, C., *I Learn from Children.* New York: Simon and Schuster, Inc., 1948.

Prescott, D., *Factors That Influence Learning.* Pittsburgh: University of Pittsburgh Press, 1958.

Rasey, M., *What We Learn from Children.* New York: Harper & Row, Publishers, Inc., 1956.

Schmuller, A., *The Mechanics of Learning.* Laurel, Md.: Arthur Cook Supply Corporation, 1962.

Skinner, B. F., *Cumulative Record.* New York: Appleton-Century-Crofts, 1961.

Townsend, E. and P. Burke. *Learning for Teachers.* New York: The Macmillan Company, 1962.

6 SOCIAL DEVELOPMENT

A look at children in their first month of kindergarten offers an interesting study in social development. Susie is always one of the first to arrive. She has many questions for the teacher and participates wholeheartedly in the activities of the class. Susie's mother reports that their relationship has always been spontaneous and that Susie has had an interest in school since last spring, when she realized she was going to be old enough to attend. Susie was able to dress herself completely by age four, and is of considerable help at home with routine homemaking chores.

In a corner of the room is Billy, who appears unhappy and unwilling to join in activities with the other children. The teacher says that it has been most difficult to get Billy to come to kindergarten and that this is the first week his mother has not had to bring him to the door. Billy's mother indicates that she has been very involved with Billy since infancy. He does not dress himself alone, although he can when he wants to. Billy has few friends in the neighborhood to play with, and seems to have spent most of his early childhood in relationships with adults.

This brief description of two children in the kindergarten gives some idea of early social attitudes and values. The way a child relates socially is learned first in the family, with his parents and siblings, and eventually with his peers and other significant adults. If he is denied early experiences which permit him to engage in the give and take of social relationships, his development is hindered by the time he enters the school setting.

Each child develops within a specific social setting. The nature of the specific life space has an influence upon his learning experiences and how he feels about them. Each culture, and to an extent, each group to which the individual belongs, furnish a set of expectations and relationships which influence the eventual development of social skills, behaviors, and attitudes.

Social contact is necessary for normal development. The child develops through the stimulation which he receives from other people. Human behavior is learned in the daily interactions with parents, siblings, and eventually significant others. The child, unlike an animal, cannot fall back upon instincts to survive but, instead, is dependent upon the significant adults in his life. When children are isolated and raised with a minimum of human contact for a period of up to six years, they will show few, if any, human capabilities or responses. Davis presents the interesting case of Anna, who, when she was discovered, did not walk, talk, or in any way show human capabilities.[1]

NATURE OF THE SOCIALIZATION PROCESS

Socialization is the process by which the child learns to interact with the expectations and obligations of various groups. Essentially, it is learning and living the culture of the group to which one belongs. Man is a social being. His interactions with people are what make him distinctly human; therefore, analogies cannot be easily drawn from animal research. The basic needs of all children are the same. The differences between societies can be observed in the way in which children are taught to manage their needs. Children are expected to learn behaviors consistent with the standards of a particular society.

---

1. Speculate on the various factors and purposes which may be operating in producing the behavior of Susie and Billy as they have been described. Specifically, how can the teacher aid Billy's development?
2. What are some specific cultures and subcultures on the United States scene? How can the teacher become alert to these subculture differences in her group? How do you propose to help children understand these subculture differences?

One of the most significant tasks that each human being must face is that of adjusting to others. The child must learn ways of developing effective social relationships with a variety of individuals within his environment.

The biological maturation of the child undergirds his social development. Maturation is basic to the development of certain motor skills and some nerves and muscles used in language. These skills, both motor and language, are basic to a number of relationships. The child must also develop some capacity to differentiate, to empathize, and to understand, before he can function effectively in the social world.

[1] Kingsley Davis, *Human Society* (New York: The Macmillan Company, 1949).

Piaget has illustrated, in a most interesting manner, a way in which the child's early language development is "egocentric," i.e., does not take into consideration the opinions of others.[2] Eventually, as the child matures, he is able to understand the views of others and adjust his speech. In Piaget's terms, his speech becomes "socialized."

Stendler describes the way in which the child meets his dependency needs.[3] Viewing the parent as the socializing agent, she stipulates aspects that have a reward value for the child—physical contact or closeness of the parent. The parent also becomes rewarding to the child by paying attention and expressing approval. This socialization process is concluded in what Stendler refers to as the "helping aspect," the point at which the parent no longer does everything for the child, but helps the child complete a task with which he is having difficulty.

Dependence and independence are interrelated. Originally the child learns to depend upon his mother for acceptance and approval. When he performs, independently, a specific act that wins her approval he is using his dependence to take a first step toward independence. The approval upon which he is dependent frees him to repeat the independent behavior.

Both independence and dependence must be culturally trained, but the period of encouraging dependence is limited. Movement toward independence must begin before the child becomes overdependent. Resistance and what has been termed "negativism" appear in the transition period. Some believe that negativism may arise because the child's understanding of independent behavior does not accord with the parents'. The child may want to make independent decisions which the parent is not ready to permit; the parent may attempt to have the child give up dependence in areas where the child is not ready.

Two critical periods in the formation of overdependency are suggested by Stendler. The first period is when the child begins to test the parents and makes a variety of attempts to control the mother. In the process, he is building a set of expectations in regard to how needs are met; he is learning dependency; he is learning that he can count on other people. It appears to be important, then, that the infant have his dependency needs met during this period. The next critical period in the formation of overdependency comes at the age of two to three. It is at this time that the child must simultaneously give up his control of the mother, accept his dependence upon her, and learn to be independent in culturally approved ways.

[2] J. Piaget, *The Language and Thought of the Child* (New York: Harcourt, Brace & World, Inc., 1926).

[3] Celia Stendler, "Critical Periods in Socialization and Overdependency," *Child Development*, XXIII (1952), 3–12.

3. What are some specific areas in which the child and mother must deal with dependency problems? Describe some effective methods of dealing with problems in feeding or dressing?

Obviously, during both of these periods, a considerable amount of anxiety is produced in all children, because the periods involve interference with goal responses. If the disturbances which occur during these periods arouse excessive anxiety, they may so strengthen the dependency that overdependency results. Overdependent children tend to have low levels of aspiration and a low capacity to tolerate frustration.

Dependency behaviors are directed toward satisfactions derived from contact with or nurture by other people. Actions are considered dependent when they are directed toward obtaining social rewards.

The only longitudinal study of dependence is by Kagan and Moss.[4] Ratings of passivity and dependence, based upon observations when the children were between the ages of six and ten, were compared with ratings of dependence based on interviews conducted when the subjects were between the ages of twenty and thirty. This study indicates that females, who were dependent as children tended to be dependent as young adults. This continuity was not established for males. Kagan and Moss suggest that the difference between the sexes may be a reflection of a cultural "double standard." While dependency in females is generally acceptable in the United States, dependency in boys is increasingly punished following the preschool period.

The studies of Goldfarb,[5] Spitz,[6] and Bowlby[7] indicate that children who were institutionalized in infancy and who did not experience consistent "mothering," became apathetic and socially unresponsive. The studies tend to imply that dependency fails to develop unless the child experiences consistent gratification from some person.

The relation of adult dependency to children's popularity with peers was examined by Marshall and McCandless,[8] who found consistently negative correlations between their measure of popularity and their measures of dependence. In this group high dependency was associated with

[4] J. Kagan and H. Moss, "The Stability of Passive and Dependent Behavior from Childhood through Adulthood," *Child Development,* XXXI (1960), 577–91.

[5] W. Goldfarb, "Psychological Deprivation in Infancy and Subsequent Adjustment," *American Journal of Orthopsychiatry,* XV (1945), 247–55.

[6] R. Spitz, "Hospitalism: An Inquiry into the Genesis of Psychiatric Conditions in Early Childhood," *Psychoanalytic Study of the Child,* I (New York: International University Press, 1945), 53–74.

[7] J. Bowlby, "Some Pathological Processes Set in Train by Early Mother-Child Separation," *Journal of Mental Science* XCIX (1953), 265–72.

[8] H. Marshall and B. McCandless, "Relationships between Dependence on Adults and Social Acceptance by Peers," *Child Development,* XXVIII (1957), 413–19.

low popularity with peers. This suggests that emotional dependence may interfere with some of the child's adjustments to his schoolmates.

Investigators have also been interested in the development of aggression in the child. There seems to be considerable evidence that societies which provide approved aggressive models are likely to produce aggressive children. Anthropologists who have studied the transmission of behavior problems in cultures different from our own tend to find that where an aggressive model or aggressive behavior patterns are lacking, a lesser amount of aggression develops in the child. Observations both in our society and in anthropological and sociological studies indicate that influential adults often provide a model for an aggressive role and encourage aggressive behavior when it occurs.

Several studies have indicated that the parents of aggressive preadolescents and adolescents use physical punishment more frequently and reasoning less frequently than the parents of nonaggressive children.[9]

Sex differences in aggressive behavior have been observed by a variety of investigators. These differences are generally attributed to the forces of modeling and social reinforcement. Anger outbursts by both sexes in early childhood increase to the age of about eighteen months; from then on the frequency declines for both sexes. During the third year of life sex differences become quite marked, with boys consistently showing more anger outbursts than girls.[10]

---

4. How would you explain the increase in anger outbursts in boys during the third year of life? How might this pattern of behavior be modified?

The more severe the punishment that is received for aggression in infancy and in childhood, the more we tend to find direct or indirect expressions of aggression and a considerable increase in anxiety about aggressive acts later on. It has also been demonstrated that the more inconsistency the child experiences the more marked are his aggressive tendencies. Children who are raised in a less authoritarian atmosphere in which there is consistency and acceptance tend to be more open to others. They are friendlier and able to respond in their relationships with peers.

Glueck and Glueck found that the less use of physical punishment in childhood and the more reasoning, resulted in a child or adolescent who was less likely to engage in delinquent behavior.[11]

[9] A. Bandura and R. Walters, *Adolescent Aggression* (New York: Ronald Press, 1959); and A. Bandura, *The Social Learning of Deviant Behavior: A Behavioristic Approach to Socialization* (New York: Holt, Rinehart & Winston, Inc., 1963).

[10] F. Goodenough, "Anger in Young Children." Institute Child Welfare Monograph, Series No. 9, Minneapolis: University of Minnesota Press, 1931.

[11] S. Glueck and E. Glueck, *Unraveling Juvenile Delinquency* (Cambridge: Harvard University Press, 1950).

STAGES IN THE SOCIALIZATION PROCESS

A number of the schools of psychological thought have formulated stages in the process of socialization. Psychoanalysts have described a system in which the child is striving to reduce biologically based drives and adjust to the world about him to achieve pleasure and avoid pain. In their model, the child's interest is focused on himself, and he is well-adjusted to the extent that he finds release from his internal tensions without causing conflict with others in the environment.

Erikson's Stages in the Development of Socialization

Erikson has developed a concept of eight stages through which man progresses in his development.[12] His premise is that the individual is well-adjusted to the extent that he possesses the positive rather than the negative characteristics of each stage.

The first stage is one of trust as contrasted with mistrust. If the child is well-nurtured he develops trust and security. If the infant can endure the mother's absence without becoming anxious because he can depend upon his mother's satisfying his needs, he has passed through this stage successfully. If the child is inadequately handled, he becomes insecure and mistrustful.

The second stage, autonomy versus shame and doubt, is reached during the Freudian's anal stage. The child is being toilet trained. If he is well managed, he comes out of this stage certain, rather than ashamed. This is the period in which the child learns to assert his will.

The next stage, initiative versus guilt, is when the healthy child learns to broaden his skills, to cooperate, and to lead as well as follow. If he is fearful, he will continue to be dependent on adults and be restricted in the development of social skills and imagination.

Entrance into school coincides with the stage labeled industry versus inferiority. It is at this time that the child learns to win recognition by being productive. Work becomes pleasurable, and he learns to persevere. If the child does not feel competent in his skills or satisfied with his status among his peers in work skills, then he may develop a sense of inadequacy and inferiority.

The stage of identity versus role diffusion is reached at the time of puberty when childhood is left behind and the transition to adulthood begins. The individual has to find a place for himself, an identity, a self concept, that corresponds with others' ideas of him. He is seeking answers to the question "Who am I?" Role diffusion implies an uncertainty of one's

[12] E. Erikson, *Childhood and Society*, 2nd ed. (New York: W. W. Norton & Company, Inc., 1963).

place in his world, with an accompanying uncertainty of appropriate behavior.

When the individual has ascertained his identity, he is ready for the sixth stage, intimacy versus isolation. He is now capable of experiencing the intimacy of an enduring friendship or marriage. He is sure of his own identity so that he can completely abandon himself in situations that call for it, without being afraid of losing that identity. Fear of self-abandonment results in a feeling of isolation.

The seventh stage in which a conflict occurs is an outgrowth of the sixth. It is generativity versus stagnation, in which generativity has been defined as parental responsibility, the interest in producing as well as guiding the next generation. The individual is able to work productively and creatively. When this interest is lacking, the individual stagnates and may regress.

The last stage of development which Erikson calls ego integrity versus despair is the culmination of successful completion of the preceding seven stages. Integrity, as he uses the word, means facing reality, recognizing it, and accepting it. The mature individual has developed a self concept he can accept, and he is pleased with his role in life and what he produces.

A Social Interpersonal Theory of Development

Sullivan developed a description of the stages of development which did not relate directly to Freud's emergent biological needs. Sullivan's system was based on the interpersonal relationships which the individual experiences as he pursues security. These stages were infancy, childhood, juvenile era, preadolescence, early adolescence, and late adolescence.

Infancy. The infant organism enters the world helpless and unable to deal with its needs directly. In this stage the infant reacts to the significant adults about him with what Sullivan called empathy—a direct reflection of the mood of the parent.[13] For example, if the parent is anxious, the infant also is uncomfortable. The anxious mother, then, is very likely to have an anxious, crying infant, even though needs are cared for and she is indulgent. The child's states of equilibrium win approval from the parents. Because the infant is unable to make fine discriminations as to what he specifically does to bring about parental responses, he cannot evaluate the approval and disapproval he receives. He seems to be continuously between equilibrium or distress, which, for the child, results in the concept of "good" or "bad" mother. According to Sullivan, this emerges in a self system known as either the "good me" or the "bad me."

[13] H. S. Sullivan, *The Interpersonal Theory of Psychiatry* (New York: W. W. Norton & Company, Inc., 1953).

As the infant becomes capable of differentiating between others and his own bodily limitations, he also develops the need for security. At this time the child first experiences "anxiety" as a consequence of his relationship with significant adults. Anxiety is an interpersonal phenomenon which develops as the infant learns that his comfort is based primarily on the actions of the mother. The child's opinion of self comes out of this early "empathic" relationship with "mothering" individuals.

Childhood. As the child develops motor and language skills which enable him to go about and interact more freely, he becomes the target for education and training. In this period the child learns the dimensions of his culture. As he matures, language becomes a means of communication. He also learns ways of manipulating people to help him achieve security. The child now becomes able to determine certain impulses which provoke anxiety and those which can be discharged without anxiety.

Juvenile Era. The juvenile stage is usually closely associated with entry into school. The child is beginning to see himself as distinct from other entities, to identify the self. He is surrounded by peers, and is now first coming into contact with significant adults other than his parents. In this period the child begins to look at himself objectively and to develop an internal critic who tests his impulses. This internal critic, which might be compared to the superego, is really a reflection of the appraisals of significant adults. Attitudes of competition, rivalry, and eventually more or less realistic compromise begin to appear. The child is engaged in defining his own status and his own self in relationship to the broader culture with which he is daily interacting.

Preadolescence. If the individual is to mature psychologically in preadolescence he must move from egocentric achievements and take his first steps toward believing that satisfactions experienced by others are as significant to him as his own. At this stage he is capable of a more mature love that goes beyond the pursuit of his own security. In preadolescence concern for others is usually expressed toward a friend of the same sex, whose pattern of behavior may be similar to his own. The child's consensual validation is developed as he becomes free to express his thoughts and feelings to this friend. This more expansive concern is similar to the development of social interest in the Adlerian theory. The child is familiar with the tasks and responsibilities of home and school; as he comes to accept them, he is moving toward the basic attitudes necessary for mature psychological development.

Adolescence. There is a shift in interest from a person of the same sex to one of the opposite sex. This is the time when the child must come to terms with the sex drive. Due to the attitudes toward sex in our culture, the adolescent is frequently faced with new problems in integrating his personality.

5. What is the relationship between Erikson's and Sullivan's descriptions of the stages of development? Indicate which of these models is more acceptable to you, and defend your choice.

CHARACTERISTICS OF SOCIAL MATURITY IN THE AMERICAN CULTURE

It is difficult to determine definitely the goals and characteristics of American society because of the multitude of subcultures, which can be defined in various ways, such as geographical areas, ethnic backgrounds, and religious beliefs. Frequently, subcultures conflict, forcing the individual to choose the group with which he can most readily identify. Certain characteristics, however, are considered typical of American society.

One characteristic is success and security as measured by material possessions and job status. American society's emphasis upon material values closely allies success with financial rewards. Cooperativeness, the ability to get along with others, is highly valued in all facets of American life, regardless of age. Regardless of your feelings about another individual, you are expected to learn how to get along with him and to work with him. A premium is placed upon sociability, a seeking out of friendship in contrast to drawing on one's own resources for amusement.

Another characteristic of the American culture is independence. Many children are taught to be self-reliant and to make their own decisions. Children are taught to look out for their possessions and to stand up for their rights.

All these traits are understandable to those of us raised in the American culture, but anthropological studies have proved that they are specific to our culture.

These concepts of American culture are transmitted to the child first by the mother, then the total family atmosphere, and eventually the siblings. The child's view of self develops in this original family unit. As the child expands his contacts with the world, his sources for learning the culture are eventually extended to significant others outside the family, then to the peer group, and finally to a large number of people of all ages.

Socialization, then, is a leveling process. During the preschool years the child learns how to interact by observing, imitating, and relating with those about him. When he enters school, a whole new set of expectations, both from a new significant adult and his peers, is presented to him.

The child's social needs must be considered in understanding his total development. Because of the social nature of the human being, it is important to see him in terms of his interpersonal relationships. The child needs both to give and receive affection. He must be able to count on others. He must also be able to contribute to a group and have the opportunity to do things for others. To be part of a group and participate in planning for it represent other important social needs.

---

6. What are some practical ways to afford the child opportunities to show affection in the school setting? How do these social needs change the direction of the teacher's expectancies?

SOCIAL AND CULTURAL BACKGROUNDS

Each social class appears to have distinct values, characteristic patterns of behavioral expectations, and differences in child-rearing methods.

It is interesting to note, however, that regardless of the child's social class, the community's major socializing institutions, the school, the church, and the social agencies, all reflect middle-class outlooks and aspirations. Children of every social class attend functions of these agencies and are frequently expected to conform to standards considerably different from the expectations of their cultural group. This situation can create conflict, confusion, and hostility. Traditionally, we have believed that working-class parents are more concerned with the immediate consequences of a child's actions. They tend to be concerned about the misbehavior and its correction. For the working-class, stress is placed on the development of qualities that will assure respectability, obedience, and cleanliness. Middle-class parents place a greater premium on internalized standards of conduct. They are concerned about honesty and self-control. It is important for the middle-class boy to be curious, and for the middle-class girl to be considerate. The middle-class parent more frequently responds to misbehavior by attempting to take into account the child's motives and feelings. The classes obviously differ in what is punished and what is ignored.

Some of the differences between the classes have become less marked according to later studies. Kohn found that in dealing with children, age ten or eleven, both working- and middle-class parents seldom used physical punishment, reserving it primarily for extreme situations.[14] However, there seem to be definite differences between the classes. Bayley has demonstrated greater permissiveness among middle-class parents toward the infant and young child, particularly in respect to needs and impulses.[15] As the child matures, however, the working-class generally permits greater freedom from parental control and supervision. Differences between the

[14] Melvin Kohn, "Social Class and Parental Values," *American Journal of Sociology,* LXIV, January 1959, 337–51.

[15] N. Bayley and E. Schaeffer, "Relationships between Socioeconomic Variables and Behavior of Mothers toward Young Children," *Journal of Genetic Psychology,* XCVI, March 1960, 61–77.

classes seem to lie in the method of child training and not in the amount of concern. There seems to be little definitive evidence to justify a stand on the enduring effects of social class on personality and social development. One large-scale correlational study of socioeconomic level and personality favored the middle-class child in "adjustment."[16]

Evidence has accumulated of considerable discrepancy between the values and expectations of middle-class teachers in the urban schools and the values of lower-class students.[17] These studies have tended to point out that children from economically and socially deprived parts of the population are disadvantaged in school because they have not been motivated toward educational opportunities and are not acquainted with materials presented to the child in the classroom. The children frequently lack a vocabulary to compete effectively with other children. On the other hand, the children of the middle class are better prepared to accept the values of the school and are more likely to find these values supported, accepted, and encouraged in the home.

---

7. Give some specific examples of ways in which children from certain social classes may be educationally disadvantaged. How would you specifically propose to deal with these students?

SOCIALIZATION FORCES

Important social forces affecting the child's development include the family, the family constellation, the peer group, and the significant others.

The Family

Every individual has a basic need for security which is satisfied through belonging. He needs to know where and how he fits in. This belonging in one group or setting enables him to develop the skills by which he can enter new groups and find a place for himself there, too.

The family is the first and most important socializing agency. Its emotional attachments are crucial in the development of all relationships in life. In this setting the child first begins to understand how human beings relate to each other. We must be aware that the child, as he first observes human relationships in the home, has no basis for comparison. He be-

[16] L. Burchinal, B. Gardner, and G. Hawkes, "Children's Personality Adjustment and the Socio-economic Status in Their Families," *Journal of Genetic Psychology,* XCII, June 1958, 149–59.

[17] W. Warner, R. Havighurst, and M. Loeb, *Who Shall Be Educated?* (New York: Harper & Row, Publishers, Inc., 1944).

lieves, at least for a time, that all human beings relate to each other in this way. The family should be the place in which the child can feel unqualified acceptance. When members of the family are always after him to change or to improve, some of his feelings of security are affected.

The family represents an ethnic background, a religion, and a social status. The child is even affected by the father's occupation, in that it tends to place him within a certain cultural context. Certainly the religion, ethnic group, and educational attitude all dictate certain rituals, habits, and attitudes. While the child may eventually be freed to choose which attitudes he will accept and adopt for himself, he is originally influenced by his early exposure at home.

Others in the community also have expectations of the child based upon his background. He soon realizes that in a sense the successes or failures of older members of the family influence his development and behavior. The neighbors remember Johnny's older brother, and may be suspicious or especially accepting because of their previous experience. Frequently, when the child goes to school, the comment is made "One of the Smith children, what could you expect?" or "He's one of the Browns; naturally he'll do well."

The family is also influential through the decisions it makes for the child. He lives in a certain part of town; he goes with the family on vacation; certain people are invited to the house; frequently even the choice of a television program is supervised by parents. In this manner, the family is the original interpreter of the community to the child and sets the standards for evaluating various institutions, neighbors, and programs.

The child's experiences within the family eventually develop for him a sense of acceptance or rejection by the primary group. This rejection may have various effects on the child's personality. Symonds states that when either or both parents reject a child the child is likely to be aggressive, attention-getting, hostile, hyperactive, jealous, or rebellious. The child develops a variety of attention-getting mechanisms.[18]

Parents can also hinder the development of their children by giving the child more attention than is necessary for healthy development. This "smother" love prevents the child from assuming responsibility. Such parents sometimes choose the child's friends or hinder him from making any social contacts outside of the family. Parents sometimes hinder the social development of the child in subtle ways. The mother may dominate the child by being the victim, the martyr, the weak or self-sacrificing individual, who keeps the child in service to her and does not permit him to step out into the world. The father may develop a faulty relationship with the child by demanding excessive obedience.

[18] P. Symonds, *A Psychology of Parent-Child Relationships* (New York: Appleton-Century-Crofts, 1939).

Conflicts between the parents may give the child a feeling of insecurity. Differences in religious or ethnic backgrounds frequently introduce conflicting customs which confuse the child early in life. He is not really able to choose, but at the same time he cannot sort out the consensual pattern.

The size of the family also has an effect on socialization opportunities for each child. In the small family with a smaller number of contacts, each person's influence on the child's development becomes more significant.

Studies conducted at Fels Institute by Baldwin, Kalhorn, and Breese studied the relationship between parent behavior and the behavior and personality of their children.[19] Their research suggests that democratic living practiced in the home has a great effect on children's behavior in the school. Children from democratic homes were more active, more socially outgoing, and higher in intellectual curiosity, originality, and constructiveness. They found that children of highly intelligent parents were less confident, were rated lower in large- and small-muscle skills, and displayed a relatively greater amount of physical apprehensiveness.

There is mounting evidence that discipline in the home affects the child's social development. Children from autocratic homes are more frequently rated as unpopular with classmates, more quarrelsome, more sensitive to praise and blame, and less considerate than children from democratic homes. Authoritarian and extreme parental controls are detrimental to the social development of the child.

The family, through the parents, serves the child and society best when it provides an atmosphere of acceptance, when the child receives love, and encouragement. The parents provide the child with a set of standards and security. The child should have an opportunity to take on responsibilities and make choices at an early stage in life. He should also be permitted to experience the natural consequences of inappropriate choices, while the parent still provides support. The child should be permitted to profit from his mistakes. This indicates that there should be minimal interference from adults. If the child is less dependent upon adults and able to experience the consequences of his behavior, he is eventually better able to cope with the realities of living.

---

8. In observing a child, make some tentative hypotheses about the specific family situation which may bring about his behavior. If possible, interview a parent of the child's or observe interaction between the child and parent. What do you feel can be done in a specific child training situation you know about to prevent certain deterrents to social development?

---

[19] A. Baldwin, J. Kalhorn, and F. Breese, "The Appraisal of Parent Behavior," *Psychological Monographs,* 63, No. 4 (1949), 313.

The Family Constellation

A significant factor in the social development of the child is the opportunity for social interaction among siblings. A study of the family constellation reveals the characteristic relationship of each member of the siblingship to each other. Each family provides a unique set of circumstances for the development of social attitudes, values, and convictions.

Each family has a distinct configuration, and the role of each child is influenced by the atmosphere at home and the personality of each child. Being parents of a first child is a new experience for the adults, whose attention is focused on this single child. Their affection is directed to the one child, and relationships are established within the family. When the second child arrives, the group immediately shifts positions. The new baby usurps the position of the older child, and the older child feels dethroned. Each succeeding baby brings about new interactions and new interrelationships and provides the opportunity for new meanings and interpretations by each member of the constellation.

If we look closely at the relationships among members of the family constellation, we are likely to find alliances and rivalries. Due to continual interaction within a family constellation, children present a constant threat to each other's positions. Therefore, we cannot make categoric statements to fit a set ordinal position. All first-born children are not by virtue of their position in a constant fight to stay ahead. The middle child is not always squeezed between the other siblings. These relationships are always dependent upon the meanings and interpretations which the child brings to the situation. However, sibling relationships are the first the child has with the people who are not in authority over him. This, then, can become the first method of coping with people at the peer level. It is important to avoid developing unnecessary rivalry between siblings under the guise that it stimulates each to further effort. The possibility is just as great that it will bring on unnecessary discouragement.

Each child within the family constellation makes decisions for coping with this situation. These decisions have an obvious influence on the behavior of each of the other children. A child who is aggressive in demanding his rights could stimulate aggression or withdrawal in the other siblings. Some children cope most effectively with their siblings by being the "good" child, by defeating them at every turn, by being "better," and by making certain that the parents note the difference. This form of cooperation with parental mandates, which is really based upon the premise of making the other siblings "look bad," is a faulty manner of developing social relationships. Parents should learn to recognize this tactic early in the game and not reward it.

In observing the social relationships that various members of the constellation form, we note two general types of relationship, which might be termed the allies and the competitors. Competition between children is frequently expressed in fundamental differences in interest and personality. If one child is extremely athletic or vitally interested in science and the other children feel they cannot compete, they may withdraw or devote themselves to the arts or mechanical skills. However, similarity among siblings is an expression of the general family atmosphere. If parents and children all value good grades in school, the scholastic activities of the children may be quite similar.

In addition to the mother's important role in the social development of the child the constellation obviously has a telling effect upon the development of social behavior. The family constellation is the first place in which the child is forced to interact with people who are at his approximate age level. In attempting to understand social behavior, you would do well to look at the early formation of attitudes in the constellation.

---

9. Tom is the oldest of three boys ages 15, 13, and 11, in a family that values good scholarship. He is a "B" student, excels in athletics, and is helpful around the house. Hypothesize about the other boys' behavior and explain in terms of alliances and competition. How may competition between the siblings bring on unnecessary discouragement? Illustrate either theoretically or from a specific situation.

The Peer Group

The child eventually moves from the family circle to relationships with his peers. In American society the peers seem to assume an increasingly important role in the formation of social behavior. Peer groups are really the distinct society of the child. This is the area in which the child is able to make the transition from his family role to the status of an adult. Supervision occurs among equals. Belonging is a basic need, which once more asserts itself within the peer relationships.

Peer groups are an important corrective agent. Peers serve to keep the child conforming to the social expectations of the group. They actually provide for the child a workshop in human relationships. It is here that he first comes into contact with children of varied religions, social classes, and ethnic backgrounds. This is the area in which he learns to accept, work with, and cooperate with people who hold different opinions and convictions. They also provide the child with a new form of security and belonging. The group will have similar interests and accept him on the basis of the role that he plays. Peers promote the transfer of loyalties from the family unit to the group, serving as a stepping stone in the development of loyalty to a wider group in society. Peers also have an important effect on the child's self concept by giving him a feedback about the kind of person he is and the kinds of behavior for which he will be accepted or rejected by his peers.

The original peer group may be children in the immediate neighborhood, but eventually a larger variety of peer groups becomes available. Then the child may choose on the basis of his interests and social status needs. The educative influence of the peer group is important in that it provides the child with a unique set of give-and-take relationships. To belong, the child must live within the code of the specific peer group, keep its secrets, and be willing to meet its expectations.

The child's readiness to interact effectively with peer groups has been conditioned to an extent by the experiences of the family within the family constellation. The child who has been valued and accepted by the family and who has learned how to interact with his siblings is better able to choose a peer group in which he can find his place without sacrificing his values. Each group provides the child with a unique role. Children, therefore, will select a peer group on the basis of roles which they feel they can play effectively.

While the effect of nursery school experience on academic development has not been thoroughly explored, progress in the social area seems to be clearly indicated. Schools report that children who have nursery school experience are, at least at the start, more socially active than children without this experience. However, children who do not have experience tend to catch up very rapidly in social development. Studies point to differences in social adjustment and social poise between children who attend nursery school and those who do not. Children who attend are usually more highly socialized and self-reliant, show more initiative, and are more spontaneous.[20]

Since peer relationships are a vital developmental task, it might be important to look at the traits which seem to relate to high sociometric status within a peer group. Children who have high acceptance generally are outgoing, reflect emotional stability and dependability, and are physically attractive, usually athletically skilled, cooperative, socially adaptable, and friendly.

Children generally rejected by their peer group tend to be demanding, arrogant, or apathetic, and have few outgoing interests. These children sometimes reflect a considerable amount of egocentricity and introversion, which interfere with their participation in the activities of the group. They are considered to be shy and withdrawn. This group also includes

[20] A. Jersild and M. Fite, *The Influence of Nursery School Experience on Children's Social Adjustments,* Child Development Monograph, No. 25, 1939.

the child who finds group experiences unrewarding because he feels socially incompetent and the child who is willing to accept his position outside of the group in order to meet other needs which have a higher value to him.

---

10. What are some of the varied roles a child might play in peer groups? How would various groups meet different status needs? Give a specific example of how a child might be willing to function outside the group because of other needs of greater value to him.

The Significant Others

Sullivan was the first to impress us with the important role of significant others in the development of the child. People with whom the child comes into contact and with whom he identifies become significant others for him. They vary in accordance with the range of the child's activities. It might be a parent, sibling, older child in the neighborhood, milkman, delivery boy, policeman on the corner, teacher, neighbor, or leader of a child group.

The child's first examples for social learning through imitation occur in the family constellation. However, as his life space expands, he has a whole new series of models. If we observe young children at play, we can note the unique meanings which they attach to their experiences. Through the child's contacts with individuals by whom he is approved and accepted, he comes to identify and learn a variety of social roles. He may engage in random and exploratory activity at times, but much of his activity is centered upon gaining attention and approval. As the child matures, he may tend to identify with and imitate those who seem to be approved, and who he feels approve of him. This is another method by which values and social attitudes are formulated.

The significant socializing forces, then, are the family, family constellation, peer group, and all of the significant others. In these relationships, the child develops his ability to give or receive attention and affection. He learns the give and take of life. If the relationship between the expectancies of the family and the family constellation are similar to the expectancies of the peer group and the significant others, the child's socialization takes place more rapidly. If there is considerable conflict in values and standards among these various agents, his social progress is less certain.

Regardless of the attitudes that the child encounters whether of parents, siblings, or peers, the important consideration is how the child perceives the attitude of others, rather than the attitude itself. The child functions on the basis of his beliefs and convictions, more than on some abstract concept the parent is trying to teach without conveying through example.

THE DEVELOPMENT OF SOCIAL BEHAVIOR

Growing up entails a series of group memberships which begin in the family and continuously expand. A secure early home environment is helpful to the development of social skills. When values in the home are not taught consistently and the child discovers a disparity between what the parents teach and how they behave, the development of internal controls and conscience is established more slowly. It has actually been demonstrated that parents who are accepting during infancy tend to make it easier for the child to relate effectively with his peers.

The Preschool Child

From birth each child has individual characteristics and a unique rate of growth. Each child interprets social events about him in accordance with his developing style of life and thus experiences his environment uniquely. Although the characteristics of age groups may be described, this is merely normative behavior. Developmental sequences may be anticipated, but the rate at which they are experienced varies among children.

Maturation is basic to the socialization process. The child's development of motor skills must precede some social skills. A considerable amount of play is based upon the child's mobility. Choice may be a factor in his proceeding socially at a slower pace, but his over-all social development is limited by certain maturational factors.

From Havighurst's developmental tasks of infancy and early childhood the following three tasks appear to have significance in social development:[21]

1. Forming simple concepts of social and physical reality.
2. Learning to relate oneself emotionally to parents, siblings, and other people.
3. Learning to distinguish right and wrong; developing a conscience.

The new-born infant is aware only of his needs and makes them known by his increased activity level. As he grows physically, he grows in awareness of the environment around him. This physical growth is accompanied by increased social awareness and a developing capacity for social interaction.

The interaction of the mother with the child during these early weeks does not affect the developing infant's physical needs only; adequate mothering means satisfying the child's social and emotional needs as well. Joyce Robertson, in a study of twenty-five infant-mother pairs at a Child-

[21] R. Havighurst, *Human Development in Education* (New York: David McKay Co., Inc., 1953).

Therapy Clinic in London, observed the development of the babies in bodily tonus, muscular activity and achievements, quality and quantity of responsiveness to both the mother and the wider environment, communication, and expression of feeling.[22] Robertson found that the twenty babies who were adequately mothered were satisfactorily developed at the age of twelve months, while none of the five inadequately mothered babies was. This study is another indication of the signficance of developmental interrelationships physically, socially, and emotionally. The developing infant who is cared for physically but otherwise ignored may at first show signs of distress and later become apathetic and autistic.

Gradually the developing child takes more interest in the people around him. He enjoys watching other children. If his family has been responsive to him, he anticipates friendly relationships. He comes to enjoy social interaction.

By two years of age the child usually plays well with older children. He is happy to watch others, but has not yet learned to play with children his own age. This is a period of parallel play. Children of this age like to be together, but each plays with his own toys. They may exchange toys, but they do not play together.

The child moves from parallel play to playing with one other child and then to group play for short periods of time. He adjusts to children outside the family. Play is the fundamental arena in which children experiment with their social relations. In periods of neighborhood free play, the child acquires a new idea of his place in the world. He must adapt to group requirements or be excluded.

Thus, the family is the first step in the socialization process for the young child. Within the confines of the family the child gets his first experience in living with other people and making adjustments to them. The family selects what shall be passed on to the child; it also evaluates many of the experiences to which the child is exposed. However, the child's primary reaction pattern and his capacity for selective response are also influential upon the course of his early social development.

---

11. How, specifically, can a child's motor skills affect his social development? Can advanced motor development occasionally serve as a deterrent to social development?

Middle Childhood

The importance of the peers increases in the period of middle childhood. While deference is still paid adults, parental domination is resented

[22] J. Robertson, "Mothering as an Influence on Early Development," *Psychoanalytic Study of the Child* (New York: International University Press, 1962).

when peers are present. By the time the child enters school, a number of the developmental tasks should be accomplished. The child's interests and activities broaden in number and complexity, and he learns to adjust to a number of formal and informal groups.

School becomes a laboratory for expanded experiences in social living. In the school setting the child is for the first time intensively introduced to gaining recognition on his own merits outside the family circle.

When children enter kindergarten, many attitudes and beliefs have already been formed, some of which may have to be unlearned. In the new setting, opportunities are present to help shape the child's social attitudes. The child can benefit greatly from being in a social group. The presence of all kinds of children may be quite upsetting at first, but it creates exactly the kind of situation in which he can come to understand social relationships. It is here that mutual respect, rights, and obligations can be taught most effectively. The child is helped to develop self-control and is encouraged and guided to make desirable emotional responses and to express his feelings through manipulation, language, or rhythmic expression.

The social developmental tasks of middle childhood are:

1. Learning to get along with age-mates.
2. Learning an appropriate sex role.
3. Developing concepts necessary for everyday living.
4. Developing conscience, morality, and a scale of values.
5. Developing attitudes toward social groups and institutions.

When the child goes to school, he encounters a world vastly different from that to which he has been accustomed. He enters a new environment containing many more people than previously. Freedom has to be curtailed; contacts are multiplied, more adjustments to other persons are necessary. In addition to encountering more rivals, the child learns that competition may take one form in the schoolroom, another on the playground, and still another on the way to and from school.

Throughout the elementary school years, the child's behavior is increasingly affected by what other children think and do. Their habits, interests, likes, and dislikes become most influential. Beginning with the middle elementary school grades, many children develop what appears to be a behavior pattern quite dominated by the peers. Peer identification is wholesome for the child's development and indicative of normal personal-social development. Although peer influence may be disturbing to adults at this period, it is a sign of social growth.

Acceptance by the peer group is important to the child, as lowered social status may cause him to feel inferior. Not being accepted by a group is the greatest hardship a human being can endure. Inferiority feelings may result in the inadequate development of a feeling of belonging to a group which is expressed through a voluntary desire to participate and contribute. The child at this time is getting his first extensive exposure to subcultures other than his own.

An important learning derived from the peer group is the discipline of the group. The discipline acquired at home or at school is frequently one of respect for authority. The same children who at home and at school will not take any part in establishing or enforcing rules often voluntarily develop in their peer groups a rigorous code of conduct and methods of enforcing them.

Teachers often overlook the significance to children of peer acceptance and peer group pressure. These relationships can be disruptive and disturbing, or they may make positive contributions to good learning situations. With increasing maturity the child becomes less egocentric and learns to subordinate his own desires so that group goals may be reached. The relationships a child has with his peers determine to a great extent how he views the world around him and how he views himself.

---

12. Mr. Carvon, seventh-grade teacher, is especially impressed with Robert's work in science. He frequently calls the attention of the class to how well Robert does the work and suggests that other students might profit from his example. He notices that Robert is not accepted socially by the other boys and decides to intervene and point out Robert's fine qualities to the group. Evaluate the teacher's effect on Robert's total development. What suggestions would you have for Mr. Carvon?
13. Give examples of inappropriate parental domination when peers are present. How can the parent deal effectively with the child's relationship to the peer group? What are the ways in which peer influence can be beneficial to development?

Preadolescence

Preadolescence, as the name implies, is the period immediately preceding adolescence. For girls, typically, it comes between the eleventh and thirteenth year, for boys between the ages of twelve and fourteen. In the American school program it corresponds with the seventh, eighth, and ninth grades.

The developmental tasks of the preadolescents are concerned with preparation for adult life. Among them are:

1. Achieving new and more mature relations with age-mates of both sexes.
2. Achieving a masculine or feminine social role.
3. Accepting one's physique and using the body effectively.
4. Achieving emotional independence of parents and other adults.

5. Developing intellectual skills and concepts necessary for civic competence.
6. Achieving socially responsible behavior.

In the American culture, preadolescence is the period when children are expected to learn appropriate sex roles. Tomboy activities of girls are now less acceptable in the eyes of both child and adult society. Effeminate behavior patterns of boys are viewed with disapproval by both peers and adults. The sex differentiation results in an apparent antagonism between the sexes, and is characterized by the formation of age-sex groups. Both boys and girls tend to reject standards set by adults—standards which had been largely accepted by the children prior to this time.

The preadolescent school group is the most heterogeneous of all the elementary groupings, so heterogeneous that it can hardly be considered a social group. The chronological age span may be from eleven to fourteen in grade seven, while the social-maturity age span may be even greater. Because of laws which keep many children in school until they reach their sixteenth birthday, the span of intellectual ability in the seventh grade may be from fourth to twelfth grade.

Preadolescents tend to choose friends and form groups on the basis of common interests, but with a distinct separation of boys and girls, even though their interests may be the same. They wonder about many things, but have not always reached the point of discussing their problems even with their peers. In his contacts with others of various backgrounds, the child is exposed to ideas that are different from his family's. He discovers that parents are not all alike, and, noting differences in parental requirements, he begins to question the policies of his own parents.

The preadolescent is beginning to learn that he has different roles to play in different groups and must find his place in each of the groups of which he is a member. He now has increased opportunity to choose the groups to which he wishes to belong.

---

14. How is failure in the developmental tasks of preadolescence related to the developmental tasks of middle childhood? Take one of the preadolescent developmental tasks, and from your observations illustrate its importance at this stage.

Friendships

The highest level of social development lies in the child's ability to satisfy his social needs by selecting certain individuals for more intense social contacts. These individuals are usually children whose qualities furnish the basis for mutual satisfaction of interpersonal needs. In some instances, the child may be similar in personality make-up; in other instances the traits of the friend will serve to complement the traits of the child.

Most evidence indicates that friends have similar traits. The similarity is probably basic to adequate interaction. Friends tend to be from approximately the same chronological age, socioeconomic status, grade in school, and IQ. During childhood a preference for children of the same age level is usually strong. It is interesting to note that friends usually have a similar level of skill in interpersonal relationships.

Horrocks and Buker did an intensive study of friendship patterns and friendship fluctuations during childhood.[23] Their study indicates that the capacity for lasting friendships gradually increases during childhood and adolescence. They did indicate that some children did not seem to learn how to maintain friendships as adequately as others. However, it was their opinion that the skills necessary for forming adequate friendships were teachable. Their data reveal a trend toward greater stability of friendship with increasing chronological age and corresponding higher grade placement in school. Data analysis of the average of friendship fluctuation indices for the various chronological age groups form a continuous downward trend in friendship fluctuation from the year five to year eighteen. This is evidence of the average increase in stability of friendships in children as they grow older.

Girls are more socially active than boys throughout the entire elementary school period, and they tend to establish more intimate and confidential relationships with each other. The capacity of the child to form friendships and to maintain them on the basis of meeting others' needs as well as his own is a strong indication of the development of social maturity.

The Need for Achievement

A characteristic of the child which plays an important role in his social development is the relative amount of achievement motivation he evidences. For our purposes, achievement motivation is evidenced when a child has strong feelings about the process of evaluation and is concerned with approval and disapproval, whether it be of self or others. The child who is achievement-motivated produces behavior which receives the approval of others.

Adler suggested the satisfaction of achievement needs is one of the significant goals of human behavior. Certainly feelings of inferiority and the striving for superiority point to the significance of achievement as basic to satisfactory and secure human experiences. The person who cannot achieve, or who does not feel accepted on the basis of his achievements, is not secure in his interpersonal relationships.

Kurt Lewin also emphasized the importance of achievement motiva-

[23] J. Horrocks and M. Buker, "A Study of the Friendship Fluctuation of Pre-Adolescents," *Journal of Genetic Psychology,* LXXVIII, (1951), 131–44.

tion.[24] He was one of the first to investigate the concepts of human achievement and level of aspiration. Lewin found that successful goal attainment often produced renewed and increased goal striving.

Research studies consistently indicate that achievement is more often stressed in the training of American boys than American girls.[25] Achievement motivation is also influenced by the child's social class. Some studies have indicated that while the father's occupation is not important and has little effect on school performance in the early grades, it seems to have a significant effect on achievement after the fourth-grade level.

One of the most interesting longitudinal studies with implications for achievement was done by Sontag and his colleagues at the Fels Research Institute.[26] This study showed that children with increasing IQ were more emotionally independent of their parents. For the children in this study, childhood achievement behaviors were sometimes, though not always, predictive of adult achievement performances. Almost twice as many boys as girls in the Fels Group increased their IQ.

Mounting evidence indicates that girls who are especially competent in reading and arithmetic achievement have mothers who are less affectionate and less nurturant.[27] One might hypothesize that the girls were really put on their own to meet certain needs.

Crandall's research indicates that the motivation for achievement in boys and girls is quite different.[28] Girls appear to be more motivated by the approval and affection of others, boys by internal demands and a need for self-approval.

The Fels Institute has produced an interesting longitudinal study which indicates that by early elementary school age the achievement behavior of both girls and boys is predictive of adult behavior.[29]

---

15. The classroom setting frequently does not provide equal opportunities for achievement. How can the teacher meet achievement needs of

[24] K. Lewin, *A Dynamic Theory of Personality* (New York: McGraw-Hill Book Company, 1935).

[25] R. Sears, E. Maccoby, and H. Levin, *Patterns of Child Rearing* (Evanston, Ill.: Row Peterson & Co., 1957).

[26] L. Sontag, C. Baker, and V. Nelson, *Mental Growth and Personality Development: A Longitudinal Study*, Monographs of the Society for Research in Child Development, XXIII, No. 2 (1958).

[27] V. Crandall, R. Dewey, W. Katkovsky, and A. Preston, "Parents' Attitudes and Behaviors and Grade School Children's Academic Achievements," *Journal of Genetic Psychology* (in press).

[28] V. Crandall, "Motivational and Ability Determinants of Young Children's Intellectual Achievement Behaviors," *Child Development*, 33 (1962), 643–61.

[29] H. Moss and J. Kagan, "Stability of Achievement and Recognition Seeking Behaviors from Early Childhood through Adulthood," *Journal of Abnormal and Social Psychology*, LXII (1961), 504–13.

children who are not able academically? What are the types of activities which would meet the boys' need for self-approval?

DETERRENTS TO SOCIAL DEVELOPMENT

Social development is hampered by overprotection and pampering by the parent, which produces in the child a desire to be noticed, even if negatively. Too many controls make the child dependent upon the parents for his social satisfaction. An autocratic atmosphere in the home, characterized by parental domination, does not permit the child to recognize the choices in social behavior that are available to him. Children from an autocratic atmosphere tend to be more quarrelsome, unstable, and inhibited. These children are literally afraid to try. They are overimpressed with the dangers in life. The child has much to learn from firmness and must experience limits, but the atmosphere must be kind as well as firm.

Social development is hampered by mistake-centered training; which emphasizes what is wrong. If a child is too frequently confronted with a continual series of negative commands, he comes to believe that there is something wrong with him and that he dare not try, because things do not work out. In this connection, physical punishment tends to retard social development, in the sense that it moves the child away from reality and makes him more dependent on adult affection. The child who is a recipient of physical punishment tends to set the standards for conduct external to the self and hence is extremely handicapped in interaction with peers where no adult is available to set limitations.

A child's social maturity can also be hampered by unrealistic expectations on the part of the parent. Too high expectations that he adhere to the model of the "well-adjusted child" or that he become socialized more rapidly than his readiness dictates, discourage the child. When parents force and punish a child in a social direction the message the child receives is, "You are not what you should be." This attack on the child's self concept inhibits functioning in a social area.

Considerable conflicts between the various socialization forces and expectations will deter social growth also. The family, the peers, the significant adults, and the school should try to reinforce each others' values as much as possible. In order for social standards to be set, the other social institutions of the community should be supported by the home.

HELPING THE CHILD BECOME SOCIALLY ADEQUATE

The child's style of life, which includes his basic attitudes toward others, is formulated early in life. The early interaction between parent and child is most significant in setting up the child's self image. The child gets his picture of self from the appraisal of others.

With the very young child, undesirable behavior can be eliminated by distracting the child from antisocial activities. If, instead, the adults become excited and overly absorbed in the "bad behavior," the child's tendency to respond in this manner may only be strengthened.

It is important to avoid giving a reward to socially undesirable behavior. At the same time, the parent can support the child's attempts to engage in social relationships. They should avoid experiences which make the child fearful or skeptical about his ability to be accepted socially.

Social adequacy is fostered as exploration is stimulated. The child who is interested in visiting children or participating in social activities should be supported. For the child who does not readily find social experiences, it may be necessary to analyze his interests and try to put him in contact with children of similar interests.

However, it is important to recognize that the concept of readiness is as relevant to social growth as it is to reading. Recognize the individual differences in the primary reaction patterns and the social maturity of children. Avoid forcing children into social experiences, because of parental concern. The child can easily interpret this concern as a belief that he is socially inadequate; the result is more inadequate social behavior. Instead, try to develop experiences that provide social success by giving the child access to children with similar social skills or children who may complement each other's social needs.

A child's social adequacy is also influenced by people's beliefs in his sense of social responsibility. A variety of leadership opportunities enabling the child to take on responsibility should be made available both within the home and the school. The assumption by both parents and teachers that the child must first be responsible in order to be given responsibility is faulty. We must not require a sense of responsibility as a prerequisite for permitting or selecting a child to function. Often the child who most needs to find a new social place within the group is denied it, because an adult does not feel that he is responsible.

Parents and teachers, to an extent, should avoid projecting their goals and expectations on the child. If we recognize individual differences, we will certainly accept that not all children are outgoing, friendly, and eager for social contact. While focusing on an atmosphere designed to foster the growth and development of such traits, our acceptance of their lack lends support which may eventually make the child feel more adequate socially.

Valuing and accepting the child as he is, even without the skills that you hold to be important, is vital for social development. The child who cannot immediately relate to other adults, who appears shy, who tends to hang on the edge of crowds, cannot change if he is rejected because of these traits.

The child's social development will best be promoted through encouragement of his social contacts. We should look for the positive elements in the way in which he relates to others and point them out to him. We should be concerned about building his self-respect and self-image in social areas. If he is not immediately ready to function socially, our faith that he is operating in the way which makes most sense to him at this time, enables him to develop socially.

---

16. Give examples of specific ways in which forcing the child socially may actually produce more inadequate behavior. How would you deal with the shy, socially withdrawn child?

THE FORMATION OF SOCIAL ATTITUDES

It is increasingly evident that both parents and schools need to be concerned about the social perceptions and attitudes of children. In a culture that is increasingly diverse, we must understand one another and be able to accept differences.

Research indicates that children acquire a considerable amount of their social prejudices toward other racial and religious groups, not through direct experience, but through contact with prejudiced peers, parents, and socially biased adults. Yarrow, Trager, and Davis made a study of children in kindergarten, first, and second grade, which reveals that attitudes toward racial and religious groups are learned early in childhood.[30] Children are instructed in such a way that attitudes are formed toward a group; seldom is differentiation made among members of the group.

The social learning of the child is most frequently a reflection of his subcultures and the social relationships which exist in his neighborhood. In acquiring their values, children reflect their own interpersonal experiences with members of other groups, and not the adult values which exist about them. As the child's chronological age increased, Yarrow found evidence that he became more aware of group conflicts, patterns of exclusion in society, and the forms of stereotyping of attitudes became more set. This study also revealed that at an early age children develop negative self feelings based on their group membership. Thus, membership in the group tends either to abase or enhance the child's image of self.

This study indicates a definite need for information and for the acquisition of social techniques for adjusting in a society that is becoming more

[30] M. Yarrow, H. Trager, and H. Davis, *Social Perceptions and Attitudes of Children,* Genetic Psychology Monographs (1949), Vol. XL, 327–447.

socially diverse all the time. Human relations groups in a number of the large cities have been taking direct steps to provide information and techniques that can have an effect on the development of attitudes.

THE SCHOOL AND SOCIAL DEVELOPMENT

The school represents one of the first major challenges to the child in the social area. He must engage in new relationships with an adult figure, the teacher, and with a large group of peers who are not of his choosing. There are new expectations about getting along with others, and school offers the first intensive contact with children who represent a variety of subcultures.

The school, for the child, becomes an important source of status, some of which derives from the child's ability and willingness to deal with the work tasks. Children who are not readily successful in this area may find other methods of attracting the teacher's attention. The cute, charming, and even the socially withdrawn child may find that their behavior gives them a special place with the teacher.

The child also has to meet with the expectations of the peers in a new setting. While the children are in academic competition, with one another, they are also involved in just as significant a search for a place within the group. They must understand the various points of view that exist within the group and must learn to consider the rights of others as well as their own. Social acceptability is frequently related to the capacity of the child to understand the needs of others.

Schools are becoming increasingly aware that children develop at various rates in academic and intellectual areas, but this same recognition has not been granted to differences in social development. It is fundamental that a child's social development proceeds at a faster or slower pace according to his experiences with significant others in the group.

Developmental psychology has made us aware of some of the "ages and stages," but it is interesting to contemplate whether these stages would be so apparent in children if their social needs were met more adequately. When the child is understood and his social needs are provided for, some "stages" may not necessarily develop.

There is considerable evidence that the social climate of the group has a significant effect on the attitudes developed by members of the group. Perhaps the most significant studies in this area were conducted by Ronald Lippett and Ralph White.[31] In a classic study that is often quoted and that should be examined in detail by serious students, Lippitt and White in-

[31] R. Lippitt and R. White, "An Experimental Study of Leadership and Group Life," in *Human Development: Selected Readings*, ed. M. Haimowitz and N. Haimowitz (New York: Thomas Y. Crowell Company, 1960).

vestigated the effects on group and individual behavior of providing three pure styles of leadership—"democratic," "authoritarian," and "laissez-faire" for clubs of eleven-year-old children.

The authoritarian leaders decided practically all policies and procedures. They took responsibility for assigning tasks and companions in any group activities. They remained aloof from group participation. The democratic leader was interested in developing policies through group decision. He encouraged discussion and frequently provided alternative procedures so that the group might make a choice. The group made decisions about partners in projects and the division of responsibility. The laissez-faire leader played a comparatively passive role and allowed complete freedom to the group for individual decisions on group procedures. He made no attempt to evaluate and merely supplied information and help when asked.

The groups organized on a democratic basis were motivated to engage in self- and group-sustained activities. They participated whether the leader was present or not. The groups which experienced authoritarian leadership either tended to become aggressive or apathetic. The children in the laissez-faire situation were generally the least efficient and became increasingly confused and unhappy with their growing lack of accomplishment.[32] There is significant evidence that the group atmosphere has a considerable effect on the convictions, attitudes, and progress of the individuals and the group. Evidence indicates that the democratic style of leadership, as defined by Lewin and his co-workers, is most productive.[33]

In considering these studies it is important to recognize that the leaders played distinct roles which resulted in individuals who were as completely democratic or authoritarian in their leadership as it is humanly possible to be. The typical teacher will not be a pure type but more frequently a blend of these behaviors. It is probably quite important that the teacher have some flexibility in roles so that she can meet various personality needs.

The teacher in training is frequently impressed with the importance of recognizing individual differences and meeting these individual needs in the instructional process. However, it is just as important that she recognize her role in working with a group. The school is a social setting. This is an opportunity for children, under the supervision of a group leader, to develop socially.

The goals of group work in the classroom center around the develop-

[32] R. Lippitt, "Studies in Topological and Vector Psychology I, An Experimental Study of Effects of Democratic and Authoritarian Group Atmospheres." University of Iowa Studies in Child Welfare, XVI, No. 3, 1940.

[33] K. Lewin, "Behavior and Development as a Function of the Total Situation," chap. 15 in *Manual of Child Psychology,* ed. L. Carmichael (New York: John Wiley & Sons, Inc., 1954); and K. Lewin, *Principles of Topological Psychology* (New York: McGraw-Hill Book Company, 1936).

ment of cooperation among students. It is important that they develop an interest in the needs of others and a willingness to participate in give-and-take relationships. The group also provides an opportunity for identification, and here the teacher must strive to encourage each child to identify with the group. The group also can fill each child's need to belong.

One technique available to all teachers is group discussion. There should be a regular opportunity in the classroom for the child to express himself and to listen to others. This can only come about in an atmosphere in which individuals feel free to express their opinions and make suggestions. This implies that the teacher is socially mature and able to accept criticism of procedure. When the teacher helps the group to participate in developing group plans, and eventually to evaluate group progress, he is helping the children to mature.

Group discussion is based upon mutual acceptance, and the leader shares in the positive interpersonal relationship that develops within the group. To be effective in the classroom, group discussions should not be used to lecture or to get over a point. The goal is not to get the class to confirm the leader's opinion. At the same time, group leaders need to be careful to set limits for the discussion, so that members of the group can take responsibility for the nature of their comments and contributions.

Teachers soon learn that the group can either be an obstacle to the instructional process or a help in the children's development. However, the child's behavior must always be viewed as part of his social interaction with other children. Group discussion time can be used to deal with emergencies, but it definitely should not be construed only as an emergency measure. Group discussion should be planned on a regular basis, and the discussion should relate to topics that are pertinent to the concerns, interests, and goals of the students. Every teacher works in relationship to strong peer-group loyalties. One job is to help integrate the group so that a group cohesiveness develops. Jennings established experimentally that an improved social climate resulted in higher achievement.[34] A considerable portion of classroom work can be organized on a group basis, and a teacher conserves energy when he assists children to acquire the social skills necessary for group cooperation.

---

17. Observe a classroom where group discussion takes place. Is the teacher merely devising methods for the children to confirm her point of view? How can the group be an obstacle to educational progress?

Co-curricular activities are an important part of the school experience and are basic to the socialization process. These activities must be man-

[34] H. Jennings, *Sociometry in Group Relations* (Washington, D.C.: American Council on Education, 1951).

aged in such a manner that they permit maximal social adjustment. Supervision of co-curricular activities is needed to implement the long-range purposes and goals of this program.

Belonging to the group, then, meets certain specific needs of the child. It gives the individual support which frees him to act. It also helps him to face reality and test his abilities with his peers.

Supervised group experience helps him to appreciate and develop the social skills fundamental for human relationships. It is in this setting that he can comprehend tasks of leading and following. The effective group leader can help point out to the group, and at times to individuals in the group, their purposes in certain kinds of social interactions.

Improved social relations have an effect on the learning of the individual. As the child becomes more secure, he is able to concentrate on the tasks at hand. The importance of group acceptance can increase a child's motivation to learn. In a well-knit class, group loyalty can be a strong motive for success. The general morale of the group also provides opportunity for the development of favorable attitudes toward learning experiences. Finally, the exchange of ideas in group discussion provides the opportunity for clarification.

The teacher should be involved in the utilization of sociometric results in the classroom. Sociometrics can help promote group solidarity, and committee work can be assigned in such a manner as to promote social growth. The teacher needs to be aware of the interpersonal relationships which exist in the group and the ways in which new relationships can be used to promote social growth.

The child who is rejected by the peer group requires special understanding. The behavior of rejected pupils is frequently designed to gain the attention of peers, rather than to antagonize the teacher. This does not mean that the teacher must accept a pupil's antisocial behavior, but it does indicate that the behavior should be handled without a display of personal feelings or possible resentment toward the pupil.

The rejected child usually does not feel secure or adequate. He is frightened by new learning situations, and resists change. Any possibility of failure is usually avoided. This child reacts strongly to teacher criticism, and his self-esteem is injured as his sense of inadequacy increases. While it is important that the teacher provide an accepting atmosphere for these children, certain specifics can develop out of sociometric evaluation. For example, in the arrangement of seating in the classroom and the development of committees, it is important that children who are isolated or rejected by the group be given their first choices. These children require the greatest opportunity to establish satisfying social relationships. Students who do not accept the isolated or rejected student should not be placed in the same work groups.

In working with the isolate, the child who is not chosen by others, the teacher should note whether this child attempts to make social contacts or whether he regularly withdraws from social interaction. This will give some measure of the extent of feelings of discouragement and inferiority. These children can be nurtured back into the group as certain assets which they have are made apparent to other children. A good device is to conduct an inventory of some of the strengths of children who are isolates and place them in positions within the group which permit them to contribute to group life.

---

18. Give specific examples of how you would deal with the social isolate who is strong in science, music, art, or any other field. How would you deal with the social isolate who appears to be satisfied with his role in the group?

STABILITY OF SOCIAL DEVELOPMENT

Considerable research has been directed at investigating the long-term stability of personal and social behavior. Martin did a study to investigate the stability, individuality, and continuity of psychological development.[35] The study was done with children of nursery school age. Over a two-year period of observation, he found that children tended to demonstrate the same relative amount of aggression, dominance, dependency, autonomy, achievement, and friendship-affiliation traits.

The study demonstrated both constancy and change, while the frequency of behavior increased with age; constancy occurred in such a way that the child tended to maintain his position in the group in regard to frequency of behavior. There is adequate evidence of unique social behavior patterns of the children studied. These individual behavior profiles were unique both in content and form. Martin concluded that 80 per cent of the children's behavior profiles were stable over a two-year period at the nursery school level. In referring to the unchanged and emerging individualized pattern, Martin states, "It is as if each child has his own 'behavioral economy,' which persists through time. Admittedly, he modifies his behavior but only in search of enduring goals."[36]

Anderson also reported findings of consistency in personality traits.[37] However, the fact that behavior at the nursery school level was predictable over a two-year period of time does not mean that behavior could be

[35] W. Martin, "Singularity and Stability of Profiles of Social Behavior," in *Readings in Child Behavior and Development,* 2nd ed., ed. C. Stendler (New York: Harcourt, Brace & World, Inc., 1964), pp. 448–66.
[36] W. Martin, "Singularity and Stability of Profiles of Social Behavior," p. 465.
[37] J. Anderson, "Personality Organization in Children," *American Psychologist,* No. 3 (1948), 409–16.

predicted from this level to adulthood. The Kagan and Moss studies indicate that very few of the behaviors observed between ages three and six were predictive of related behaviors in early adulthood.[38] Kagan and Moss did stress that all behavior is patterned and underscored the importance of comprehending the patterns.

IMPLICATIONS

1. The child learns methods of appropriate social interactions in the family, with his peers, and from significant others. The quality and quantity of these contacts should stimulate social development. The child can learn social behavior only by participating in the give and take of interpersonal relations. Responsible adults need to be as aware of this area as of mental development.

2. Children are taught to manage their needs in line with specific cultural expectations. The teacher must be aware of the cultural and subcultural expectations of each child in order to understand behavior adequately. The school can assist children in understanding variances in cultural expectations.

3. Dependency upon mother is a prerequisite for the development of the child's independence. Mother must realize that it is an important developmental step to have the child become dependent upon her for acceptance and approval.

4. Acceptance and forcing are important concepts as the child moves from dependence to independence. The parent must be willing to permit the child increasing participation in decision making and avoid pushing him to take on only those responsibilities the parent wants to give up.

5. Dependency is a consistent trait in females from childhood to adulthood. This trait in the member of the family primarily responsible for child training has implications for the type of security the young child experiences. The girl child is rewarded for dependent behavior, which is less acceptable in the boy and may influence his self-acceptance.

6. Dependency fails to develop without experiencing consistent gratification from some person. The early management of children has long-range effects.

7. Physical punishment tends to produce aggressive children. Parents who provide frequent physical punishment would appear to be engaging in a self-perpetuating series of interactions.

8. The specific traits valued by the society and the subculture influence development of the child's traits. Society's institutions must deal realistically with these varying value systems.

[38] J. Kagan and H. Moss, *Birth to Maturity* (New York: John Wiley & Sons, Inc., 1962).

9. Some children come to school educationally disadvantaged owing to membership in certain social classes. Educational planning by the teacher must recognize these differences and attempt to provide appropriate experiences.

10. The learning of human relationships occurs first in the family setting. More education in understanding these relationships should be provided for future parents while they are in school. The school frequently requires an understanding of everything but self, and self in relationship to others. This educational experience could be of great value in a preventive sense.

11. Democratic living practiced in the home has been shown to enable the child to participate more effectively in the school experience. The home should provide the opportunity to operate in an atmosphere that permits choice and accepting the responsibility for one's choice.

12. The peer group affords the child contact with varied religious, socioeconomic, and ethnic backgrounds in a setting devoid of authoritarian relationships. Peers make concrete some of the lessons alluded to within the family setting. Due to the significance of peer relationships, the teacher must take them into account in planning learning experiences.

13. The expectancies of the family and family constellation should be similar to the peer groups and significant others if socialization is to take place rapidly. When there is great divergency between these forces—when the family, for example, values certain customs and rituals which are ridiculed by the other groups—the child may tend to fluctuate his values in line with the social setting of the moment.

14. Children vary in their readiness for social contacts, their need for social contacts, and in the rate that they enter or leave some relationships. Adult acceptance of the child's attitudes instead of forcing promotes social development.

15. Entrance to school demands increased social contacts from the child. Organization of the learning experience so that it facilitates these contacts is a responsibility of educators.

16. The discipline of the group is frequently more effective than discipline by adults. Educators must observe the discipline of the group, permit it to function when wholesome, and provide guidance when it is detrimental to the objectives of education.

17. The skills necessary for forming adequate friendships are teachable. While these skills might be best acquired in the family at an early age, guidance activities in the classroom, discussion groups, and in some instances individual counseling can serve to provide reorientation in this area.

18. Social maturity is evidenced in the capacity of the child to maintain friendships that meet the needs of others as well as his own. This type of activity by the child should be encouraged.

19. Successful goal attainment often produces renewed and increased striving for the goal. It is important to provide goals which, while adequate in their challenge, also provide opportunities for success.

20. The motivation for achievement in boys and girls is significantly different. Girls may be motivated by teacher approval, but boys are more likely to be motivated by activities that permit self approval.

21. A continual series of negative commands serves as a deterrent to the child's courage and social development. It is important to seek adequate elements of the child's functioning and encourage these. Focus on the child's unacceptable behavior may only guarantee the establishment of such behavior.

22. It is important to avoid giving a social reward to "bad behavior." The adult's concern and involvement in the elimination of a trait frequently provide the reward that sustains the trait.

23. Children become responsible as we provide opportunities for assuming responsibility. If responsible behavior is a prerequisite for assuming responsibility, many children can never develop in this area. Responsibilities are frequently given to children who need them least.

24. Attitudes related to racial and religious groups are learned early in childhood, and are a reflection of parental values and the subculture. Attitude formation must be an early school concern if changes are expected.

25. The social climate of the group has a significant effect on the attitudes developed by members of the group. The teacher who wants to develop self- and group-sustained activities organizes the class on a democratic basis.

26. Group discussion is effective in promoting social development. It must give the child a genuine chance to participate and to express himself. While this discussion can occur on an impromptu basis, there should be regular planned periods for group discussion.

27. Sociometric evaluations should lead to action on the part of the teacher. Seating arrangements and committee work should foster development. Some children can develop most adequately by being permitted to encourage the socially discouraged.

28. Social behavior tends to become constant and persist. We are cautioned against assuming that social traits are all related to stages that will pass.

SUGGESTED READINGS

Articles

Dreikurs, R., "Group Discussion as Educational Process" in *Readings in Educational Psychology,* eds. W. Morse and G. M. Wingo, p. 336. Chicago: Scott, Foresman & Company, 1962.

Horrocks, J. and M. Buker, "Friendship Fluctuations during Childhood" in *Psychological Studies of Human Development*, 2nd ed., eds. R. Kuhlen and G. Thompson, p. 447. New York: Appleton-Century-Crofts, 1963.

Lewin, K., "The Effects of Social Climates" in *Readings in Child Psychology*, 2nd ed., ed. W. Dennis, p. 468. Englewood Cliffs, N.J.: Prentice-Hall, Inc., 1963.

Books

Blatz, W., *Understanding the Young Child.* New York: William Morrow & Co., Inc., 1944.

Bossard, J., *The Sociology of Child Development, rev. ed.,* New York: Harper & Row, Publishers, Inc., 1954.

Cunningham, R., *Understanding Group Behavior of Boys and Girls.* New York: Bureau of Publications, Teachers College, Columbia University, 1951.

Erikson, E., *Childhood and Society.* New York: W. W. Norton & Company, Inc., 1950.

Gronlund, N., *Sociometry in the Classroom.* New York: Harper & Row, Publishers, Inc., 1959.

Lifton, W., *Working with Groups.* New York: John Wiley & Sons, Inc., 1961.

Northway, M., *A Primer of Sociometry.* Toronto: University of Toronto Press, 1952.

7 DEVELOPMENT OF THE SELF CONCEPT

To arrive at a better idea of the role played by the self concept, let us examine part of the day of a boy age twelve, in grade six, who is of average intellectual capacity. He awakes in the morning to be told by his mother, "Now Larry, don't forget to brush your teeth, hang up your clothes, and take out the dog." His dad notices that some of these tasks are not being performed as rapidly as expected and gives Larry a second reminder. He eats breakfast in an atmosphere in which the members of the family are concerned with their own problems, and the newspaper. As he leaves for school, he is reminded, "Now be good today, Larry."

During the first period at school, arithmetic, Larry is assigned a problem at the board in which he is not certain of the fundamental processes. The teacher reminds him, "I told you you would need to learn the multiplication tables in order to do these problems." He is dismissed to his seat.

At recess on the playground, he seeks out some boy friends. Soon there is some jostling and fighting with Larry at the top of the pile. His physical prowess in this instance results in more challenges, each of which he handles to his advantage.

During the next period the discussion is about different parts of the United States. Since Larry has traveled frequently with his parents, he is able to contribute much to the discussion. The teacher notes his contributions, and Larry volunteers to do some additional research about one of the states and its products.

We could continue to describe typical incidents in Larry's day but we have enough now to illustrate the role of the self concept. If the self concept is thought of as a set of expectations and anticipations plus evaluations, we can readily see how the incidents described have confirmed Larry's expectancies. His parents' reminders convince Larry that they do not expect him to function, even though he is twelve years old, or why must they remind him continually about his teeth, his clothes, and the dog? Experiencing little acceptance by his parents he, perhaps, leaves the home feeling less than a success.

The arithmetic period in school presents him with the teacher's expectation and evaluation of those who do not memorize the multiplication tables. His dismissal to his seat again leaves him feeling inadequate. On the playground, his strength and vigor serve him in good stead and provide him with an area where he can feel adequate and successful. He anticipates that other children are not as strong, and he attacks and masters these physical tasks exceptionally well. Larry enters the discussion of the United States with confidence. He has performed well in the past, having practical experience in the geography of the country. The teacher's mild acceptance and encouragement assist him to volunteer for extra work in the area.

In this simple example we can see the relationship between the child's experiences and the formation and establishment of the self concept. Larry anticipates a number of areas in which he will not do well and will not gain acceptance, and daily anticipation is confirmed. In other areas Larry expects to do well, and his performance permits him to feel adequate and accepted. As Larry has a continuing number of similar experiences, he will develop a relatively fixed view of his capacities and expectations in both academic and interpersonal situations. In a sense we have a preview of the adult Larry who may give up easily in some activities and persist in others. The teacher and the parents should examine incidents such as these to see how their interactions with Larry are affecting his self concept.

We have already discussed the two broad frames of reference in psychology—the objective or mechanistic approach and the subjective or perceptual approach (Chapter I). When we use the objective approach, sometimes also referred to as stimulus-response psychology, we attempt to explain behaviors in terms of set stimuli to which the individual appears to be reacting. This has been a fairly useful means of obtaining information about "average" or "normal" behavior and many significant statistical studies have been built upon this approach. However, most of us are forced to deal with individuals, and normative data frequently are not useful in explaining a particular individual's motives and behavior.

The subjective approach has been useful in arriving at a better understanding of the individual. This approach starts with the assumption that behavior is purposeful and caused and that people behave as they do because of the way things seem to them, and not solely because of set external stimuli. A person's behavior at any given time makes sense to him in terms of how he perceives the situation. Meanings are personalized; therefore each human being views life in a unique manner. Man's uniqueness rests on the fact that he is a social being able to have attitudes, to interpret, and to give meanings to all the stimuli about him.

It is important to live with other people happily and with minimum stress; but for effective functioning it is also imperative to learn to live with oneself without too great a loss of emotional energy. The individual who is continually in conflict and dissatisfied with self cannot mature and fulfill his potentials satisfactorily. As the child grows, he must learn to understand his assets and use them in a socially acceptable way; he must also recognize his liabilities and learn to correct those which can be remedied and accept those which cannot be changed. This sense of personal worth combined with responsibility to others helps the individual to adjust effectively in his world.

We recognize the effect of two forces that influence the child—his heredity and his environment. Debate about the relative effect on the child's development of either of these two forces is pointless. The child is not merely a product of hereditary forces, nor is he a result of the environmental stimuli about him. This is one case where the sum is greater than the parts.

EARLY INDIVIDUALITY

Thomas and his associates conducted an interesting study of the temperamental characteristics of infants in relation to the development of psychological individuality.[1] Their investigations point to personality development as the result of the interaction of the infant, endowed with definable characteristics of initial reactivity, and a broad environmental complex of factors. They contend that individual differences in responsiveness exist in young infants. In an intensive study of the first two years of life they were able to identify initial characteristics of reactivity.

Thomas adopted the following nine categories for the assessment of individuality in behavioral functioning:

1. Activity level, the motor component, related to motility.
2. Rhythmicity, the predictability and unpredictability in time of any function.
3. Approach or withdrawal, the nature of response to a new stimulus.
4. Adaptability, frequency with which responses are successfully modified in desired directions.
5. Intensity of reaction, the energy level of the response.
6. Threshold of responsiveness, the intensity level of stimulation necessary to evoke a discernible response.
7. Quality of mood, amount of pleasant in contrast to unpleasant behavior.
8. Distractibility, the effectiveness of extraneous environment stimuli in interfering with, or in altering the direction of, the ongoing behavior.
9. Attention span and persistence, the length of time, and the continuation of an activity in the face of obstacles.

[1] A. Thomas, H. Birch, S. Chess, M. Hertzig, and S. Korn, *Behavioral Individuality in Early Childhood* (New York: New York University Press, 1963).

Analysis of the data reveals a predominantly stable set of longitudinal data. The child's characteristic behavior persists relatively unchanged in a significantly large number of children. "All in all, 78 of the 80 children maintained a statistically reliable rank pattern over the first two years in four or more of the nine categories."[2]

Data analysis was treated in three distinct manners to investigate the initial pattern in relationship to its stability. Thomas reports, "In summary, each of the three methods of data analysis—preponderance, rank, and percent-rank index—has contributed evidence that initially identifiable characteristics of reactivity are persistent features of the child's behavior throughout the first two years of life."[3]

This study demonstrates that children can be identified in terms of styles of functioning. Furthermore, it implies that "all the infants will not respond in the same fashion to a given environmental influence."[4]

Child-training practices have different behavioral results depending on the nature of the child. The child's behavior is influenced by his primary reaction pattern as well as by his environment. This approach does not hold that environmental influences are direct determinants. In fact, it questions any attempt to apply to children rules that are universally valid.

Children are apparently able to adjust to a variety of child-care techniques. "Most of the children were regular rather than irregular, highly adaptable rather than unadaptable, and preponderantly positive in mood."[5] There are indications in the study that the primary reactive characteristics of the child, and not the attitude of the mother, determined the course of events. The study suggests that we need to become skilled in identifying the primary reactivity pattern of the child. The interaction of parents and children can become more effective when parents recognize their true roles instead of feeling that their practices always directly shape the child.

The child perceives and conceptualizes. He has within himself the creative force that enables him to give meaning and to interpret. Past experience and his value system assist him to evaluate all of his experiences continually.

The self is one's inner world. It results from evaluational interaction with others, becoming the consistent personal perception of "I" and "me." The child's perception of the reflected attitudes and judgments of those who compromise his world serves as the foundation for the formulation of self. The self concept really is the individual's anticipation of his general acceptance or rejection in a given situation. As the self concept is formulated, it tends to shape new experiences to conform to established patterns. Be-

[2] Thomas, *et al.*, *Behavioral Individuality*, p. 68.
[3] Thomas, *et al.*, *Behavioral Individuality*, p. 71.
[4] Thomas, *et al.*, *Behavioral Individuality*, p. 84.
[5] Thomas, *et al.*, *Behavioral Individuality*, p. 87.

havior then becomes an attempt to maintain the consistency of the self concept, a homeostasis at the psychological level.

The real challenge in psychology comes in the attempt to predict individual behavior, to understand an individual beyond the normative sense, to know not only how he is like others, but also in which ways he is unique, and why. The self concept and the life style, then, are the keys to personality. Raimy, who first defined the self concept in 1943, said of it:

> The self concept is the more or less organized perceptual object resulting from present and past self observation . . . (it is) what a person believes about himself. The self concept is the map which each person consults in order to understand himself, especially during moments of crises or choice.[6]

Raimy showed how the self concept serves as an executive in that it represents for the individual a way to make a variety of decisions with some consistency. Margaret Mead[7] considers the self as a social structure deriving from a social experience. For her, the individual child experiences himself from the reflected views of the group. Ausubel indicates that development of the ego comes from the continual interaction of social experience and the already existent personality structure, mediated by perceptual responses.[8]

The self concept serves to integrate and differentiate a variety of learning experiences. Much of the individual's behavior is an attempt to maintain the consistency of his self concept. The self, then, is developed through the child's interaction with people and his total environment. To a great extent, it is shaped during infancy and early childhood. As the child experiences life situations, his continual evaluation facilitates adjustment. The self permits the child to act, to adjust, to do more than merely respond to a specific stimulus. The self permits the child to make decisions and to personalize his reactions. Jersild has best explained it as follows: "It is a composite of a person's thoughts and feelings, strivings and hopes, fears and fantasies, his views of what he is, what he has been, what he might become, and his attitudes pertaining to his worth."[9]

The self is essentially a social product arising out of experiences with people—parents, siblings, relatives, peers, and the general community. Self awareness does not happen all at once but is a growth process which be-

[6] V. C. Raimy, "The Self Concept as a Factor in Counseling and Personality Organization" (Unpublished Doctoral Dissertation, Ohio State University, 1943).

[7] M. Mead and M. Wolfenstein, eds., *Childhood in Contemporary Cultures* (Chicago: University of Chicago Press, 1955).

[8] D. Ausubel, *Theory and Problems of Child Development* (New York: Grune & Stratton, Inc., 1957).

[9] A. Jersild, *Child Psychology*, 5th ed. (Englewood Cliffs, N.J.: Prentice-Hall, Inc., 1960), p. 116.

gins during infancy and early childhood. As all the sensations about the child are interpreted by him, the process of selfhood begins.

POINTS OF VIEW ON SELF CONCEPT

Approaches to understanding the self concept, its development and role in behavior, have been varied.

Freud

Freud structured the total personality around three major systems, the id, the ego, and the superego. Freud felt that the self, or in his terms, ego, was that which modifies the psychic energy of the id. The ego determines modes of expression and facilitates reaction. In Freud's theory, the id, the ego, and the superego in the mentally healthy individual form a unified and harmonious organization. Working together cooperatively, they enable the individual to carry on effective transactions with his environment. If the three systems are at odds with one another, the person is said to be maladjusted.

The id functions on the pleasure principle to reduce or free the person from tension. The child's impulsive behavior and actions are associated with the strong id.

The ego is governed by the reality principle, the aim of which is to postpone the release of energy until the object that will satisfy the need has been discovered or produced. Eventually, the reality principle leads to pleasure, although the child may have to endure some discomfort while he searches for reality.

The superego is the moral branch representing the ideal rather than the real, and it strives for perfection instead of reality or pleasure. Freud felt that effective disciplining of the child takes place not through instruction, but through the child's unconscious incorporation of the parent image which became the superego. The superego was made up of two subsystems, the ego ideal and the conscience. Ego ideal corresponds to the child's conception of what his parents consider to be right. The parents convey their standards to the child when they reward him for conduct that conforms to their standards. The superego is the representative in the personality of the traditional values and ideals of society as they are handed down from adults to children. It should be recognized that the child's superego is not a reflection of parents' conduct, but rather of the parents' superego. The child has many models for the superego in teachers, ministers, policemen, and anyone whom the child admires or considers an authority figure.

Thus, the id might be regarded as the product of one's biological endowment, the ego as the result of interaction with objective reality in the higher mental processes, and the superego as the product of socialization and the vehicle of cultural tradition. The term in Freudian psychology, then, which is closest to self concept, is the construct of the ego.

Adler

The Adlerian term covering the same area as that of ego psychology or self concept is the life style. The child is born into a total community where he is confronted with carrying out the tasks of life and learning effective methods of coping with them. The child first learns to interact with the people in his family. In this primary society of parents and siblings, the first views of life are formulated. The child relates to this total family atmosphere and comes to conclusions about how to live effectively within it. Here attitudes are formed that make up the life style. Understanding the child's purposes and goals, offers an insight into the style of life or self concept. Adlerians believe that all of the child's actions are a result of this general life style, which is based upon an evaluation of self and society.

The child's evaluation of self and his position gives unity to his personality. Then, all of his actions and attitudes become expressions of this life style. From the early formative years the style of life works through experiences that eventually develop into a characteristic pattern of reactions and evaluations. The subjective interpretation of his experiences eventually forms the guidelines for all of his psychological movement. This self-consistent unity, which Adlerians have also referred to as biased apperception or private logic, then serves as a measuring stick for all the decisions of life.

Thus, the life style does not come out of any specific experience, but, instead, from the continual repetition of the approach used to cope with the tasks of life. Each child adopts certain means which facilitate his life plan; as his experiences confirm his anticipations, the style of life becomes set. We must remember that when people appear to be behaving inappropriately their behavior is always consistent with their approach or style of life. They "make" their experiences.

The Adlerians recognize that behavior is the result of more than hereditary or environmental forces and that the self and the individual's creative power to evaluate his experiences are crucial in understanding the why of behavior. The child's perception determines his behavior more than the so-called reality of the situation. Each child's style of life guides all his actions and accords with his goals and purposes. A knowledge of the style of life provides insight into the behavioral theme. The child is asking, "Who am I?" and "How can I achieve my goals?" The continual interaction between the environment and the child's evaluation of it produces the style of life.

Adlerians prefer to refer to the self area as the life style. The unity in the individual's thinking, feeling, and expressions of personality is the life style. What Freud called the ego, Adler termed the life style of an individual.

Phenomenological Psychologists

Arthur Combs and Don Snygg have made a major contribution to understanding the self concept in their theoretical formulations regarding the perceptual view of behavior. They feel that one must observe behavior from the point of view of the individual himself. They state that people are not behaving according to facts as observed by others, but according to facts as they view them; therefore, the unique perceptions of the individual child assist him in the formulation of his decisions. An object may be heavy or light, large or small, as judged by the individual, who always operates on the basis of how things seem and not in terms of some external objective criterion. If a social situation seems difficult to a child, he functions as if it were, regardless of adult efforts to cajole him about the "reality" of the situation. David is asked to show a special skill or talent to the guests. He is not sure of himself and, despite the urging of the parents, does not feel his demonstration will turn out well. No amount of talking will change his view of the situation; only a new experience and concomitant new personal meanings enable him to function.

From the point of view of the behaver, then, behavior is always reasonable and purposeful. It has meaning for him and is the best way he knows how to behave at the time. Combs and Snygg point out that if the individual knew more effective ways to behave, he would select them. We must know how each individual perceives his present situation subjectively, not objectively. The concern here is to understand the field of operation and all of its interrelationships. We should use Snygg and Combs' definition of the perceptual or phenomenal field, "By the perceptual field, we mean the entire universe, including himself as it is experienced by the individual at the instant of action."[10]

The child judges that an experience is threatening or will put him in an inadequate or inferior position. Regardless of the objective facts, he will still function as if his view were reality. Thus, from this point of view, referred to as phenomenological psychology, all behavior is determined by the perceptual field. The private world or life space in which the individual uniquely experiences an event becomes the determinant. Phenomenological psychology is also associated with some of the work of Carl Rogers and Kurt Lewin.

[10] A. Combs and D. Snygg, *Individual Behavior,* rev. ed. (New York: Harper & Row, Publishers, Inc., 1959), p. 20.

Man's basic need is for adequacy. His driving force is the desire to enhance himself within his phenomenal field. Rogers and Maslow have referred to this as movement toward self-actualization and growth.

Since people behave in terms of how things seem to be, it is essential to determine the individual's perceptual view. For the phenomenological psychologist the problem of changing behavior is really one of assisting the child to perceive things differently, of enabling him to see the possibility of more effective relationships.

Sullivan

Harry Stack Sullivan was a psychiatrist who emphasized the importance of the child's way of perceiving the world and adapting to it. He believed that the infant learns to make differentiations based on anxiety and that these differentiations later become the self concept. For Sullivan the self concept developed from reflected appraisals of significant others in the child's life.

Sullivan analyzed experience into three "modes." First was the prototaxic, which was the earliest way of experiencing the world. In this stage the infant distinguishes dimly between his body and the external. This type of experience is undifferentiated. Sullivan referred to the next mode of experience as the parataxic, where the infant begins to differentiate his experiences and gives meanings to them. However, these meanings are not logically related, and many are individualized, almost autistic. Eventually, the child's meanings are common or shared; a word means the same to him as it does to all those with whom he comes into contact. At that point the meanings are considered to be in the syntaxic mode. These meanings are considered to be consensually validated in accordance with reality and logic as they are generally observed. Although Sullivan considered these modes of perception to be related somewhat to age, he also recognized that they were not mutually exclusive nor were they necessarily ever outgrown altogether.

---

1. In which way are the various points of view on the self concept similar? How is your understanding of misbehavior affected by acceptance of the Freudian view in contrast to the subjective or phenomenological view? Give an example of variance in either diagnosis, understanding, or treatment of a misbehavior problem.

FACTORS IN THE DEVELOPMENT OF SELF

Every individual has to find a place for himself in society. This is probably his most basic and persistent need. Observing the infant in his struggles to establish social contact, creates an awareness of how basic this need is at all levels. The child brings primary behavior reaction patterns to his interactions with the varied environmental influences.[11]

Mother is obviously important, and her training procedures will have an effect on how the child both perceives society and fits into it. Siblings and other relatives provide him with experiences, and all of these he both absorbs and interprets. Certainly the varied child-raising procedures advocated in the past half century and the various types of individuals resulting from these "schools of thought" testify to the creative power of the individual to give personal meaning to numerous external, objective acts. Psychiatrists, psychologists, and social workers in child guidance frequently hear parents tell of almost identical child-raising procedures which nonetheless brought about extremely divergent results in their children. It has been common to assign the cause for these varied reactions to specific external variables. We must come instead to recognize that the child does more than merely react. His behavior is not directly predictable solely on the basis of external stimuli. We must account for patterns of reactivity observable in early infancy and for the capacity of the child to choose and personalize meanings.

To understand the child requires being more than a good observer, vital as that skill may be. There is a distinct difference between the views of the observer and the behaver, and the perception of the behaver holds the significant cues to developing an understanding of individuals. The child's present feelings and meanings play a part in determining his behavior.

Man's uniqueness rests on his being more than a product of all that has happened about him in the past and present. He has distinct traits such as cooperativeness, decision-making ability, and cognitive powers, which assist him in organizing experiences in a personally meaningful manner. Man operates toward goals and moves with a purpose. His creativity, which enables him to interpret, provides us with a challenge. We regularly observe children whose behavior is dissimilar, even though they have similar traits. Each has the capacity to use these traits for different purposes.

Man's security comes from having a place in society, and the child's self concept arises out of his need to belong and find his place. All of his traits —physical, mental, social, intellectual, moral, and personal—and their unique interrelationships interact to give him his view of the world. These traits in continual interaction with the significant others provide the basis for the development of the self concept.

Security is an important ingredient in the child's concept of self. We must strive to develop situations with children that promote feelings of

[11] Thomas, *et al.*, *Behavioral Individuality.*

satisfaction. This means an emphasis on both the recognition of individual differences and the development of methods to deal with them. Regular encouragement of the individual will assist in building adequacy and security.

The 1950 Mid-Century White House Conference Report on Children and Youth pointed to some simple fundamentals: The child's chief needs from adults are love, encouragement, and guidance.[12] All three of these are essential to develop feelings of adequacy. The self concept has greater opportunity to incorporate social interest and the desire to cooperate in a milieu containing these elements. The individual has the power to translate objective actions of love into acts of selfishness, but generally repeated dosages of love and concern will enable adequacy and security to grow.

Guidance can bring about resistance when it is interpreted as the desire to analyze, plan, and predict for an individual. When it takes on the aspect of mutual concern and becomes a collaborative relationship to assist the individual toward achievement of socially acceptable goals, it can be more readily accepted.

The child's misbehavior frequently results from a mistaken opinion of self. Feeling inadequate and inferior to others, he may give up and concentrate his actions on the useless side of life. In other instances his difficulty may stem from mistaken feelings of superiority to the group and its abilities. Either of these attitudes can result in a discouraged child. Overtly his actions may be exactly the opposite, but in fact the symptoms result from a confused picture of self in society.

Children need the regular application of encouragement just as much as they must have their physical needs met. Encouragement consists of a faith in the individual that gives the individual the freedom either to fail or succeed and still be loved, valued, and accepted. Encouragement implies that your focus is on the positive attributes of the individual and not on his deficiencies; it permits you to let the individual experiment. It allows you to support tasks which do not meet your standards but are indicators of positive movement in the individual.

Encouragement removes your concern from a mistake-centered emphasis and shows your faith in the individual's development. It does not consist of such words as, "My, that was good, and I know you can do better." This basically discourages the child. It makes him feel you expect more than he can perhaps produce at this time. Encouragement instead is based on respect for the individual and his tendency to preserve a steady state internally despite external change—homeostasis. It believes in the wisdom of the body. It recognizes the efficacy of self-selection and pacing.

Research by Olson and his colleagues of the University of Michigan

[12] H. Witmer and R. Kotinsky, *Personality in the Making,* The Fact-Finding Report of the Mid-Century White House Conference on Children and Youth (New York: Harper & Row, Publishers, Inc., 1952).

illustrates the importance of being able to accept individual variability. In a section titled, "Children Who Surprise Us," in Olson's *Child Development* textbook he shows the records of a boy who was extremely delayed in reading until age ten and who then showed steady rises in mental and reading ages up to age sixteen, the end of the period of data collection.[13] This boy was graduated with honors from a leading university. One might wonder whether other children are denied this opportunity because of early discouragement and failure to accept variability.

Johnny was finding school a difficult chore. The children could not respect his halting attempts to participate in the class. The teacher searched to find a way to include Johnny effectively.

One day the topic turned to a social science project involving considerable construction work. Johnny volunteered as chairman of the committee making materials for the project. Soon his facility with his hands drew the admiration of both the children and the teacher. Faced with a different concept of self as an achiever, Johnny was free to use his abilities in other areas. In a relatively short period of time progress was noted in academic areas too.

Johnny made progress as his self concept changed. It is our duty to encourage every child most sincerely. If the emphasis were to shift from a diagnosis of errors to a centering on strengths, both better relationships and accelerated progress could be expected.

The self concept is formulated through the relationships the child has with the people about him and his perception of these relationships. He comes to learn his place. He strives to answer the following questions: "Who am I?" "What am I?" "How can I manage the environment to meet my needs?" "What makes me acceptable?" "What makes me unacceptable?"

There are no set answers to the questions the child proposes, guidelines perhaps, but nothing specific, geared to fit the individual and his particular situation. The who and what questions demand answers about personal identity related to sex, race, religion, age, and socioeconomic status, to mention but a few broad categories. Factual replies are not the solution either, because in each instance a unique set of factors is being formed in relationship to a distinct family atmosphere and a specific constellation of family members. Truly there are never identical creatures, because of the tremendous variety of experiences, meanings, and interpretations which must be associated and interrelated within the individual.

Environmental management varies for each child because of the unique self concepts he meets in those about him. In every relationship new meanings develop for all concerned. Frequently one observes children performing what appear to be identical acts for the teacher and receiving

[13] W. Olson, *Child Development*, 2nd ed. (Boston: D. C. Heath & Company, 1959).

varied recognition. The teacher, justifiably, has a different set of expectations for each child in her room. However, each child must come to know the things that will bring him acceptance, security, and a feeling of belonging.

Thus, you can see the importance of the interpersonal relationships that occur continually. The child needs an atmosphere of mutual trust and cooperation, one that permits him to feel loved, valued, and respected. As his feelings of personal worth develop, his ability to develop adequate relationships with others will increase.

This approach recognizes that in democratic living there are both privileges and duties. It does not give the child feelings of either inferiority or superiority but assists him to see his place as a contributing member of society. It insists that adults and children both have interrelated responsibilities and that the relationship should not be one of master and servant. In our culture, incidentally, the role of master is as often played by the child as by the adult.

The mature adult has the responsibility to develop in an interpersonal relationship an atmosphere of firmness and kindness—the firmness showing respect for the self, the kindness showing love and concern for others. This needs to be done in a consistent manner that permits the child to predict the results of his actions. Lack of consistency obviously hampers the development of the self concept. The child is placed in a situation where he must continually reinterpret his actions and those of others. It is well to be continually aware of the freedom of choice that is operating within us all. The child has the creative power to interpret. This interpretation can lead him to accept or reject adult actions, not a single one of which will necessarily bring about a specific response. Adults are quite dependent upon the meaning which the self concept imparts.

The child quickly comes into contact with the ambitions of his parents, siblings, and peers. From this varied group he formulates his phenomenal field and his concept of how best to achieve his goals. His picture of self, his ethics, and his values form a pattern. When we know an individual well enough, we say, "I could have expected that." This testifies to the predictability of behavior when the pertinent information is available.

---

2. Set up a plan to determine the styles of life of two difficult children in your acquaintance or observation range. What type of information would you need to have available?

BEGINNINGS OF SELF DEVELOPMENT

The development of the self is a process of increasing differentiation from the general to the specific. At first, the child does not have a clear perception of self or the world. However, the child has a growing awareness of self as he begins his interaction with the significant people in his environment. The early roots of the self begin as the child first distinguishes between his sensations and the factors bringing them about. Self-awareness emerges as the child begins to manipulate his body and develop a "body image." This exploration of self and differentiation of self from environment form the first step in development of the self.

Eventually, the child is able to differentiate things of special meaning to him; he can differentiate mother's face from other women. Some of the development can be seen, for example, in the "negativistic" stage, which frequently occurs around the age of two, when the child appears to be testing his self-assertion in opposition to others. The child's opposition to the standards of peers and the group is another way in which feedback about self is developed. The self is also influenced by the child's particular religious, social, and socioeconomic group. It seems evident that we learn to perceive as our culture requires.

Jersild portrays for us most clearly the beginnings of this process:

> The development of self awareness does not occur in an all-or-none fashion which would enable us to assume that up to this point the child does not possess it, but beyond this point he does. It is more likely that a child perceives different aspects of what he eventually calls himself, with varying degrees of clarity at different times.[14]

Self-discovery, then, is a continuing process, not appearing at a specific time but continuing throughout all developmental stages and phases.

As each child develops he is exposed to three broad sets of experiences in the home, the school, and the community. To understand the child one must see the roles that these agencies play in developing the self concept.

The home, of course, offers the first set of experiences, providing the child with many firsts in the acquisition of values. Here is where the child has his first opportunity to assign meaning to the roles of parent, grandparent, child, brother, and sister. From the home arise the child's feelings of adequacy and security.

Perhaps Overstreet has best expressed the influence of the home:

> The unique power of the home stems from the fact that it gets the new human being first—before any other institution has had a chance to make an impression upon him—and it remains his chief environment for so long a time that its "design for living" tends to move into him (in psychiatric terms, to become internalized) and becomes inextricably part of himself before the world outside has any consistent chance to exert a modifying influence. Thus, what life is experienced to be in the home becomes, in large measure, for each individual, what life is interpreted to be in the wider human sense.[15]

[14] A. Jersild, *Child Psychology,* p. 117.
[15] B. Overstreet, "The Role of the Home in Mental Health," in *Mental Health in Modern Education,* 54th Yearbook of the National Society for the Study of Education (Chicago: University of Chicago Press, 1955), p. 88.

The changing self is interpersonal and involves the child and his world. The self is changed by the active contact of the child's personality with the environment. Let us consider some of the things which stimulate change in the child and his personality.

Sullivan believes the changing self to be influenced primarily by other people.[16] He expresses the idea that children's self concepts are influenced by "significant" people. The mother, in his theory, has the first place of significance. The child's self concept changes in reference to the qualities of the mother he is able to internalize.

The self does not continue along a smooth path toward greater self-realization and self-actualization. Each change carries with it the impulse to resist change as the individual tries to maintain his self concept. Thus, the self must be looked upon in a process of continuous change although directed by a central core of stability.

The child may attempt to be like his image, as perceived by others, or his self concept may be changed in an effort to be like his "ideal self." For most children there is often a great discrepancy between their self concepts and what they would ideally like to be. It is important that the teacher and parents be aware that the child tends to judge himself as he feels judged. To be adequate it is important that the real self and ideal self are similar.[17]

The self concept also changes as the child compares himself with his peers and engages in competition. In this measuring of self versus others new standards in self-evaluation are set. Changes in the self concept occur at any time in the child's developmental cycle; however, they are most likely to occur at the beginning of developmental phases. For this reason it is important to be alert to the onset of a new cycle or phase and the special opportunities available for influencing the self concept.

From all of the possible human interactions it is to be expected that interpretations of some situations would be incorrect. However, if a child operates on the basis of faulty assumptions, the response he gets from others will tend to reinforce them. In this way, the faulty assumptions of the individual frequently become stabilized and set.

John does not get along well in school. He complains about the teacher and his classmates and expresses discouragement with the school in general. Only as John has the opportunity to have experiences which will alter his concept about the work, the teacher, and his peers can his anticipations be changed. Sometimes if the child is shown why he feels as he does, a realistic self concept may develop. Many of the faulty assumptions

[16] H. S. Sullivan, *The Interpersonal Theory of Psychiatry* (New York: W. W. Norton & Company, Inc., 1953).
[17] R. Brandt, "Self: Missing Link for Understanding Behavior," *Mental Hygiene*, XLI (1957), 24–33.

of children are devices to protect themselves from change and new experiences. The child feels compelled to maintain his stability and preserve the attitudes and ideas which comply with his present self-image. New events are generally colored by past experiences and already established views. If he did not do well in arithmetic last year, he does not anticipate doing well now. It is therefore important to provide opportunities for a re-evaluation of the individual's experiences. The self concept will change as the child develops courage and confidence combined with a feeling of assertion.

---

3. Give an example of a way in which an individual's faulty assumption eventually becomes established as a method of interpersonal operation. The faulty assumption can be about work tasks or social tasks, but illustrate its effect on the self concept and life style.

The importance of commending a task well done is vital, the satisfaction having a positive developmental influence. A healthy self concept must include some degree of self confidence.

Billy was a fairly good swimmer; yet he had not been able to pass the swimming test at summer camp. Each time he neared the raft, which was the destination for the test, he hesitated, turned, took hold of the accompanying boat. Billy felt inadequate; he did not think he was able to reach the raft. Eventually he gained self-confidence through his instructor's encouragement and later passed the test with the remark, "It's really simple."

Billy's self concept now included new self-confidence and courage. These specific traits had not been part of his previous inner world and self-evaluation. Changes in the self concept, then, depend on the experiences the child is exposed to and the relative amount of opportunity for success and failure. As the child has his anticipations confirmed, the self concept is established.

---

4. Jack, a fourth grader, does average work in school except in arithmetic. Here he starts a few problems, appears to be quickly distracted, and never completes the task. What other information would you need about Jack to help him in arithmetic? Assuming there is no organic defect, how would you help him?
5. One of the most vital functions to be performed by teachers is changing faulty assumptions in relation to academic achievement. Take a specific area of study and grade level, and show how you would work toward this change. Give an example of a way in which the teacher or parent can change or can improve the child's judgment of himself in a specific capacity or ability.

RESEARCH IN THE DEVELOPMENT OF PERCEPTION

There is a growing body of research related to the nature of perceptual development. Pastore, in a review of research, concluded that early perceptual development is primarily a function of maturational change and the increasing capacity to differentiate stimuli.[18]

Page replicated an earlier study of Piaget and found preschool children more successful in recognition, by feeling without seeing, of topological forms than of geometric forms.[19] He indicated this was due to familiarity with these forms. Discrimination of forms appears to be related to early exposure to specific stimulus forms. This research has important implications for readiness for learning.

Cohen, Hershkowitz, and Chodack found younger children less certain than older subjects in their judgments regarding the comparative size of two stimuli.[20] There was evidence that the central processes play an increasingly important role with increasing age; this is particularly true when data are ambiguous, inadequate, or judgments are contaminated by interference.

London studied normal and maladjusted boys between the ages of four and fifteen, presenting them with a series of picture cards which gradually transformed an initial figure into a markedly different figure.[21] He found that in the group of normal boys the older boys made more appropriate discriminations of the changes. The maladjusted boys generalized more than the normals so that the effect of age on discrimination was not so clear. The maladjusted made both earlier and later generalizations than the normal boys did. He concluded that in the development of normal generalizing there was a balance between much abstraction from little data and little abstraction from much data and that the mechanism which maintained this balance was related to socioemotional adjustment.

Another indication of the increasing subordination of external stimuli to the control of central processes in the formulation of meaningful perception is found in the work of Ames.[22] In a longitudinal study of Rorschach protocols for subjects ages two to ten there was a steady decline with age in the objective use of form and detail as organizing stimuli, in contrast to steadily increasing scores on every other major variable.

[18] N. Pastore, "Perceiving as Innately Determined," *Journal of Genetic Psychology,* 96, March 1960, 93–99.

[19] E. I. Page, "Haptic Perception: A Consideration of One of the Investigations of Piaget and Inhelder," *Educational Review,* XI, February 1959, 115–24.

[20] W. Cohen, A. Hershkowitz, and M. Chodack, "Size Judgment at Different Distances as a Function of Age Level," *Child Development,* XXIX, December 1958, 473–79.

[21] P. London, "Developmental Aspects of Discrimination in Relation to Adjustment," *Genetic Psychology Monographs,* No. 57, May 1958, 295–336.

[22] L. Ames, "Longitudinal Survey of Child Rorschach Responses: Younger Subjects Two to Ten Years," *Genetic Psychology Monographs,* 61, May 1960, 229–89.

THE FAMILY'S ROLE IN THE CHILD'S SELF CONCEPT

Studies of children in hospital nurseries shortly after birth reveal great differences in temperament. Some of these differences are due to variances in physical constitution and others to the recently discovered primary reactivity characteristics.[23] However, the differences are variable enough to suggest that the child is a distinct personality from the very onset of life.

The relationship of the parents to each other will have an effect on the child as he grows. The child has need for love, acceptance, limits, and consistency. When they are not supplied in adequate amounts, adequacy being determined individually, the results of faulty training and faulty atmosphere are apparent.

The child is always part of a family constellation. He is influenced by the interpersonal relationships he observes, even if they are only among the adult relatives. If he has siblings, his position in the family becomes another factor in the developing concept of self. His status as the oldest, middle, youngest, or only child can affect his behavior. The difference in age between siblings can be a factor in their assuming traits that might typically be assigned to a different position in the constellation. Certainly the sex of the children in the relationship will affect their interrelationships and the traits they develop. Parental preferences as to both sex and traits also must be considered. It is vital to recognize that in each instance the variables are different enough to bring about a unique individual. There is no set way of interpreting the significance of a particular atmosphere or constellation without observing the behavior the child has produced as a result of these factors.

The home plays a major part in providing the atmosphere within which the child forms his style of life. Patterns of behavior which eventually become habitual and predictable are first practiced in this setting. It becomes evident, then, that those who have the first contact with the developing personality of the child are at the frontiers of mental health. All techniques of child training, whether they relate to dependency, aggression, feeling, or toilet training, play a part in this unfolding experience. Parents need not become overconcerned about all their parental acts. The dangers of smother love have been well described in the literature. However, parents should be aware that whether they intend to train the child or not, the parent and child interaction has a training effect.

The child is exposed to a variety of methods. Parents soon recognize that what worked with Johnny is not so effective with Billy. The parents' contacts with friends, the papers, books, and relatives bring changes in their methods. It is probably most vital for the formation of the self con-

[23] Thomas, *et al.*, *Behavioral Individuality.*

cept that the child be exposed to relatively consistent behavior from the parents. Dreikurs has said: "The child must be clearly aware of what is expected of him before he can adjust himself properly. The more generally applicable laws exist, the more quickly will he grasp their meaning."[24]

Security within the family gives a child a sense of worth and belonging and permits many problems encountered outside to be handled more effectively. This is necessary for developing a feeling of adequacy. Children may suffer from the inconsistency of the parent. One day it may be acceptable for Jimmy to get into the cookie jar because it was done in such a clever manner, but the next time he may be severely reprimanded for the same behavior. These two experiences confuse him about the way to interact with his parents. Some inconsistency is valuable to enable him to handle the flux and change of the world outside the home, but it is essential that the child generally encounters consistent behavioral expectations.

There is evidence that a considerable amount of acting out and delinquent behavior is a form of testing by the child. For some children the parents' control is an indication of love and concern. When there is little control, they feel unloved and uncherished by the parents. Haimowitz, in his article "Criminals Are Made, Not Born," points out that delinquency frequently is a reaction to parental neglect.[25] The child appears to be responding to a feeling that his parents hate him or do not accept him. Haimowitz quotes research that shows delinquency is more closely related to this factor than to income, religion, or broken homes. In reacting to parental neglect, many children are really seeking a more adequate type of control system from the parents.

At present, much of the disciplinary relationship between the parent and the child is clouded by the issues of superiority-inferiority and autocracy-democracy. As long as we deal with our children feeling that we are superior and can make autocratic decisions, the child cannot develop feelings of adequacy, nor can the relationship promote growth and interpersonal satisfaction. Instead, the relationship should be built on the basis of mutual respect.

Parental love is a vital factor in self-development, a core element in the structure of self. The child is always free to choose his response, but certain adult attitudes tend to bring about certain responses from the child. Rejection usually makes the child devaluate himself and produces hostility and rebellion. Overprotection may develop irresponsibility and excessively strong needs for approval. Inconsistent discipline may lead to a lack of self-control.

[24] R. Dreikurs, *The Challenge of Parenthood* (New York: Duell, Sloan and Pearce, 1958), p. 63.

[25] M. Haimowitz, "Criminals Are Made, Not Born," in *Human Development Selected Readings,* eds. M. and N. Haimowitz (New York: Thomas Y. Crowell Company, 1960), pp. 359–75.

Love and warmth are essential, but there must be a balance. In a faulty relationship, Johnny may be so preoccupied with his self-enhancement that he cannot understand why another child does not give him the book he wants or why the teacher does not pay attention to him just when he wants her to. His relationship with his peers and the teacher will be faulty because of early overprotection.

Too much praise and overindulgence by the parents can be just as harmful as the lack of it. Susie is a physically attractive child, and this is her basis for social position in the family. She therefore relies on her prettiness for acceptance and prestige instead of seeking to be accepted on the basis of the way in which she functions. Parents must be realistic in their evaluation of the child's ability so that the child is able to meet the expectations of other segments of society. Overprotection which creates dependency in the child can hinder adjustment. When the child starts to school, he soon discovers that his every demand and wish are not granted. He must know how to handle this conflict, or he will be confused when the teacher does not act like mother in meeting all of his expectations and needs.

Family expectations also affect the development of the self concept. If the parents have achieved a place of distinction, they may push their child to attain a similar goal. If they did not have the opportunity for education or the acquisition of a specific goal, they may try to force the child to reach goals they themselves were unable to achieve. The result may be to make the child feel inferior and inadequate, and the attainment of any goal becomes hopeless. The same self concept may result from the child's attempts to compete with an older or younger sibling who is much more adequate or skilled in certain areas. No one is content to be inferior; therefore, the urge for superiority may move the child to strive for recognition and acceptance in other ways.

Threats to the self concept may be handled in many ways. When a certain pattern is formed, it is difficult to change the individual's concept. However, a single threat will be less disturbing when many successes have been achieved. The feeling of adequacy once established is not easily disrupted. The child is more likely to feel adequate as he approximates what he believes he should be ideally. Marked difference between the self concept and the ideal self may result in feelings of inferiority and inadequacy.

The parent should handle the child's relationship to responsibility effectively. As the child attempts to help and assist the mother and, eventually, both parents, their attitudes should be accepting. Responsibility is a trait which develops through exercise. It does not appear automatically in a developmental sequence as an age-related trait. Responsibility can mature the child's self concept and evaluation of self, and should be utilized regularly for this purpose.

The parents' most important role arises out of making the child feel genuinely loved and accepted as he is. The family introduces the child to life and provides him with his early and most permanent self-definitions. It is in this setting that the early guidelines are formulated. Clinical studies point to a close relationship between parents' attitudes toward their children and the adequacy of a child's social and emotional adjustment.

---

6. Janet, age eleven, is an only child. Her parents have high expectations. They provide her with every opportunity to take special lessons and visit places of interest. However, the relationship between Janet and her parents is poor. There is continual protest against her habits of personal cleanliness and her homework. How do you explain Janet's behavior? Give some suggestions for improving the situation.
7. How does the parents' consistency or inconsistency affect development of the self concept? Give some illustrations of ways in which feelings of adequacy might be built through commendation and encouragement. Delineate clearly how you as a parent would utilize responsibility to facilitate the child's total growth.

THE TEACHER'S ROLE IN THE CHILD'S CONCEPT OF SELF

When the child moves from home to school, he is introduced to a whole new world where his parents are not available for support. School provides the opportunity for a reformulation of the self concept. His first dependency move may be to the teacher whose relationship with him will be most significant in terms of his evaluation of self as an achiever. Gradually, his dependency shifts to the peer group. During the early school years the child sees himself through the eyes of his peers, and his self concept is very directly affected by their attitudes. It is essentially from this group that he achieves his identity.

---

8. If the peers play an important part in the formulation of the self concept, how can the teacher and the parent utilize the child's experiences with them for the development of a healthy self concept? What types of peer experiences would tend to produce feelings of inadequacy?

Insofar as the teacher follows the pattern of the home, the child has no reason to question the universality of the feelings and prejudices he has already learned. However, when the teacher differs from the home, the child must face decisions and a growing need for self-judgment. He is confronted with the fact that patterns may be different from those at home, and he must make decisions which might cause him to lose esteem with one significant person or another.

The school provides the child with a new world that operates under new conditions and requires him to observe limits set by a new series of authority figures. This both expands the child's experiences and requires him to cope with new demands and restrictions. Schools serve to provide considerably more than routine academic stimulation. Since the school is concerned with the child's social adjustment, the teacher is active in shaping the child's goals, concepts, convictions, and attitudes. He provides the experiences and environment within which concepts, convictions, and assumptions are formulated. Olson provides us with a concise summary of research in this area:

> Recent studies of the classroom emphasize the group climate as the most important factor in the child's socialization at school, the teacher as a principal agent in establishing this climate, and the interpersonal relationships as the method for establishing the process. Thus the class, in addition to being a place for the provision of content of instruction in the formal sense, is also a laboratory for social learning.[26]

The child recognizes the change in his psychological status soon after he enters school. He cannot be as important in the eyes of his teacher as he is in the eyes of his mother. The love relationship is different. His typical methods of obtaining attention must be changed. Some of the things which were effective with the mother no longer work, but he may be amazed to find that other attention-getting devices are once more applicable. At any rate, he is certain to recognize that his significance in the larger school circle, in contrast to the family circle, is diminished.

The preparation that the child receives for school attendance plays an important part in his feelings about the experience. The parent who uses school as a threat by saying "Teachers will take care of that kind of behavior" is giving the child certain expectations about the schooling experience. The child who comes from a home which sets limits and provides an intellectually challenging environment is more likely to feel that school is an opportunity, not a punishment.

The self concept develops continually out of new relationships. When starting with the child, the teacher is not completely free of preconceived notions about his function. He may have had encounters with the mother that lead him to expect certain responses by the child to his actions. A teacher who has the opportunity to know well the mother of a pupil can often account for many of the child's reactions. Obviously, then, each ensuing teacher has to work in the shadow of her pupils' previous experiences. It is well to recall that the teacher of thirty pupils who were in the same class the year before can still expect thirty different sets of interpretations about the role of teachers.

[26] Olson, *Child Development,* p. 228.

9. How might the teacher get access to the differentiation between the child's concept of self and his ideal self? Which instruments in Chapter III would provide information on this problem?

The child in school has to meet with peer relationships in a distinctly different setting from any he has previously experienced. In certain instances and at certain age levels it is more desirable to act in accordance with the teacher's wishes to gain peer acceptance. Other situations demand that the child act in a nonconforming manner in order to obtain peer acceptance.

The child's sense of belonging in the classroom group can be facilitated by the teacher. A good understanding of group dynamics contributes to his efforts to increase the child's feelings of belonging. Many group techniques are available to assist the child in fulfilling his social and psychological needs. Teachers should be aware that frequently the most annoying children need the most help in formulating the self concept. Annoying behavior is really an expression of psychological needs. If we observe the interpersonal behaviors in the child's psychological movement, we can be alerted to his needs. It is the aggressive show-off defending himself against his inferiority who most needs help and at the same time is most unbearable to the teacher. Suppressing the annoying behavior accomplishes little. Interpreting it correctly as an expression of a need for guidance enables the teacher to plan to meet the individual's specific needs and attempt to switch him to active-constructive patterns of behavior. The way in which the teacher manages the demands of the child certainly influences his self concept.

10. Give some examples of behavior which might be indicative of specific needs. Make a classroom or playground observation with the specific goal in mind of observing behavior which might be indicative of specific needs. Make a classroom or playground observation with the specific goal in mind of observing behavior and relating it to the expression of psychological needs. Can you determine some clues to the child's self concept through observation?

A study of the child's performance in specific subject-matter areas may produce clues to the self concept. Difficulties in spelling may indicate a resentment of order as represented in a very orderly subject. Difficulties in mathematics sometimes are found in children who doubt their ability to solve their problems. These are only generalizations and must be considered in terms of a specific individual.

Many children are discouraged about their ability to perform satisfactorily in school work. This discouragement is usually reflected in accompanying misbehavior. The teacher should be continually aware of his role in helping to shape the child's concept of self as an achiever, and particularly as an academic achiever. The continual series of interactions between teacher and student sets up certain anticipations, and eventually the child operates on these assumptions as though they were fact. Thus, it behooves the teacher to utilize all available techniques to assist each child to feel adequate at appropriate levels in academic achievement. A worthwhile task for every teaching staff early in the school year might be a study of each child's assets. If nothing else, this would shift their diagnostic focus from an overconcern about what is wrong with the child. Also, the teacher who requires himself to seek the strengths in each child acquires the base for a good relationship and a strong motivational tool.

---

11. School psychology has often been accused of taking a primarily diagnostic point of view and affording little treatment. If you look at many typical psychological reports, you often cannot determine the psychological strengths of the child. Through analysis of a classroom group, try to make a list of assets—strengths and adequacies—for each of the children you are observing.

Many of our dropouts and underachievers are children who have developed feelings of inadequacy about academic tasks as a result of their early contacts with teachers.

Two major conditions in school hinder children from acquiring healthy attitudes of self-regard. First, the schools, by the nature of their present setup, continually impress upon large numbers of children the idea that they are not adequate. Children who lack the intellectual aptitudes which are typically rewarded in school meet failure and rejection on a large scale. The schools tend to reward children who perform well and to expose those who may not be able to compete equally to situations in which they are destined for failure. Also, general school policy encourages children to learn different types of academic material, but little about themselves and their important interpersonal relations.

Davidson and Lang found that children's perceptions of their teachers' feelings toward them correlated positively and significantly with their self perception.[27] In other words, the child with the most favorable self image was usually the one who perceived his teacher's feelings toward him as being favorable. Also, the more positive the child's perception of

[27] H. Davidson and G. Lang, "Children's Perceptions of Their Teachers' Feelings toward Them Related to Self Perception, School Achievement, and Behavior," *Journal of Experimental Education,* XXIX, December 1960, 107–18.

his teacher's feelings, the better was his academic achievement and the more desirable his classroom behavior as rated by the teacher. Thus, we can see a continuum of interaction set up by the teacher's evaluation of the child's work and behavior.

Brandt and Perkins, in a study related to the work of the Institute of Child Study at the University of Maryland, also found that teachers who had completed several years of child study and who were actively engaged in an intensive study of child development were able to promote healthier personality growth in children as defined by congruency between the self and the ideal self.[28] It appears evident, then, that the basic incentive which the teacher can furnish is her acceptance and approval of the child as he is; as the teacher communicates this feeling to the child, the positive appraisal serves as a catalyst for growth in all of the child's capacities.

As the child develops, he is exposed to cultures and subcultures. He is identified in terms of his socioeconomic status, religious beliefs, physical characteristics, abilities, talents, character traits, social relationships, and attitudes. In each situation he comes into contact with people who have preconceived opinions about people with either some or all of his characteristics. Frequently their judgments may be faulty and their past experiences narrow rather than broad, but this will not deter them from arriving at a decision about him. The effect of their actions will bring some changes in his self concept. Each individual continually has experiences which cause him to reformulate the self concept. His creative self causes him not only to be selective in his perceptions, but also to use his experiences in a unique manner.

Trager and Yarrow in *They Learn What They Live* show clearly the effect that teachers have on the development of prejudice.[29] Prejudices are developed at a very early age, and Trager and Yarrow point to the importance of acquainting teachers with the prejudices that they communicate to children without awareness. It would be important also that teachers uncover their students' prejudices and seek ways to alter them. Trager and Yarrow report an interesting experiment which demonstrated how prejudice could be lowered through teacher action. The techniques involved developing an understanding of human relations problems, children's needs, democratic values, and a concomitant willingness to accept responsibility for intercultural education.

It becomes increasingly evident that the child must be encouraged to make the most important discovery of all, himself, and that the school

[28] R. M. Brandt and H. V. Perkins, "Research Evaluating a Child Study Program," Monographs of the Society for Research in Child Development, 1956, p. 21.
[29] H. Trager and M. Yarrow, *They Learn What They Live* (New York: Harper & Row, Publishers, Inc., 1952).

must participate in the development of self-understanding. Facilitating the child's ability to draw upon his feelings, to face his feelings, to experience and live comfortably with them, should be part of the educational experience. Jersild has regularly pointed to the importance of developing courses in human behavior and self-understanding of motives.[30] Materials developed by Dr. Ralph Ojemann at the University of Iowa help to provide resource materials for the teaching of self-understanding in the elementary school.[31] It is important to recognize that by the time the child matures into adulthood, learning about the self becomes an extremely complicated process. He has already learned to compensate, repress, project, displace, rationalize, and defend in order to maintain the self. Early education in self-understanding might make it possible for the individual to live more comfortably without the continuous utilization of defense mechanisms.

---

12. Investigate thoroughly some of the materials on self understanding as adapted for childhood education. You might read some of the material by Jersild on education in self-understanding, perhaps beginning with the article "Self-Understanding in Childhood and Adolescence," (see Selected Readings at end of chapter) or you might secure pamphlets from the University of Iowa on basic mental health approaches. Evaluate this material, and give some indication of its potential value in the classroom. What are some other ways in which self-understanding might be facilitated through the facilities of the school?

SIGNIFICANT OTHERS IN THE CHILD'S SELF CONCEPT

As previously mentioned, Sullivan has stressed the role of significant others in the formation of the self concept. He begins by placing an emphasis on the child's mother, but the theory is broad enough to expand to other significant people with whom the child comes into contact. As the child moves away from the home, he develops a growing attraction to peers combined with less dependence upon parents. The peers available in the community set certain models for behavior. They provide a contrast to the values and standards of the home. They afford another opportunity for choice and decision. Some research has indicated that the self concept of the child is often most like that of his best friend.

Children get ideas of what is expected of them from others. The self

[30] A. Jersild, "Self Understanding in Childhood and Adolescence," *American Psychologist,* No. 6 (1951), 122–26.
[31] R. Ojemann, *A Teaching Program in Human Behavior and Mental Health* (Iowa City, Ia.: State University of Iowa, 1960).

concept is really determined by the way in which the child perceives certain crucial experiences. Originally these experiences are with mother, family constellation, and the school. Eventually they are expanded to other experiences within the neighborhood with both peers and adults. Contacts with official public servants, the police, and religious leaders provide feedback for the self concept. The general community attitude toward children can either enhance or restrict development. It would probably be highly advisable for communities to work toward the development of community councils which include children. It is in this type of atmosphere that feelings of adequacy can be most readily developed.

The community and its citizens have a real role to play in the formulation of self concept. The child becomes increasingly aware of the role of his parents and siblings in community life. The respect and status awarded them, or withheld from them, he experiences, and this has its effect on the development of self. Father's position in the community or Mother's concern for the total community life can affect the child's status. Equally important, though, is the way the family feels about community life. The child is not forced to accept the views of his parents, but the opinions they hold about the community and the way in which those opinions are presented provide him with material to interpret and to internalize.

Among the varied forces in the community with whom the child comes into contact are group or recreational leaders, ministers, religious instructors, social workers, doctors, nurses, the police, and other public servants. All of these people have their own concepts about children and how to relate to them, and the quality of these relationships has a major influence on how the child feels about the community. He learns from what people say about various people in the community, but he internalizes much more as a result of his personal experiences with these people and the meanings he assigns to them.

The immediate neighborhood in which the child resides brings him into contact with neighbors who value children in various ways. The neighborhood which accepts child life as it is and subscribes in practice to the view that children are not miniature adults provides a healthy atmosphere for the self concept. This does not imply child-centered communities, but rather mutual respect and a recognition that both adults and children have responsibilities and rights. The child who can learn the true meaning of cooperation in his community is afforded a greater opportunity to develop social interest and social concern.

The effect of the community and its many agencies on the child's experiences are inextricably interwoven with his experiences at home and in school. The whole milieu for child training is set in the community, which establishes the schools and awards stipulated values to its professional school staff. The community makes decisions about the types and amounts of services the school can provide and assigns the teacher a socioeconomic status. All of these acts have a subtle effect on the experiences which the child interprets.

THE SELF CONCEPT IN BEHAVIOR

To guide the child's personal development, begin by seeking to understand the reasons for his behavior. This process can be expedited if you proceed from a frame of reference.

Billy is a seventh-grade boy whom all of the teachers label a troublemaker. He is big, agile, and resistant to teacher demands. He has a long record of unsatisfactory pupil-teacher relationships. However, Mr. Benson at the Y.M.C.A. considers Billy an outstanding leader and a most cooperative boy. Here is the same child exhibiting different behavior.

Why the difference? There are many possibilities. One obvious difference is in the nature of the tasks—recreational at the Y and academic in school. Another is the variance in disciplinary procedures in the two settings. The difference between Mr. Benson and Billy's female teachers could produce some of the variability in behavior. Instead of mechanistically assigning causal relationships to external factors, however, let us consider another possibility.

We know from experience that many big, agile boys match Billy's description generally, except that they fit well into the school situation. Other boys at the Y.M.C.A. also have many of Billy's physical attributes but are not accorded the same kind of recognition as Billy.

You must recognize the distinct, unique set of experiences that causes Billy to act in such apparent contradiction. He brings to each situation his own unique pattern of behavior, his characteristic approach or style of life. His past experiences plus the meaning he has given to them cause him to react differently at school and at the Y. His self concept, which includes his values and his interpretation of his past experiences, can account for the seeming inconsistency.

Joan is a second grader, who is both well-behaved and popular with her peers. However, her academic work falls below the expectations of all diagnostic testing. Although successful in many areas, production in school is a problem. Here again it is interesting to contemplate what causes Joan to fail to live up to expectation. It is vital to know how Joan conceives of school and its tasks. What have been her past experiences, and what interpretation has she given to them? The key to Joan's lack of success may lie in her concept of self as an achiever. What is not logical to the observer may be very logical from the point of view of the behaver.

It seems to be a truism that the child can succeed even if all others have lost confidence in him, but never if he has lost confidence in himself. His self concept is built upon the treatment he receives from others. Respect and love build a worthwhile concept; criticism and contempt suggest to the child that he is of little worth. Frequently a child develops a strong feeling of inferiority or inadequacy because of well-intentioned but poorly received criticism. It is important to design processes that further the growth of children without lowering the child's self-respect. An effective learning situation is one that succeeds in increasing the child's respect for his own worth. A concept of real worth leads to humility whereas lack of a sense of worth leads to contempt for others and bragging.

Because of the potency of the desire to be accepted as a participating member of the group, it is a painful experience for any child to feel inferior or unacceptable. Such feelings restrict the development of social interest and have a negative effect on the formulation of the self concept. The child will experience some feelings of social inferiority in the process of growing up in a world of adults, but he should not continually be made unsure of his social position. Feelings of social inferiority and inadequacy elicit two possible responses. The child tries to compensate, or he withdraws. His compensation may be direct or devious. It may be through useful means or on the less constructive side. It is difficult to predict the direction in which the child will proceed, and we should be alert to the fact that the process of maturation does not automatically bring about a positive change in the self concept. In some instances it merely increases the child's ability to utilize ineffective psychological attitudes; for example, he may become more competent at rationalizing.

A number of factors contribute to the devaluation of self—inferiorities of an organic or physical nature; feelings about strength, coordination, and skill; physical unattractiveness; and the like. We should remember, however, that the child's heredity is not as important as what he chooses to do with his potentialities.

Any situation in which the child senses that he is "less than others" promotes development of the negative self concept. Inferiority feelings are faulty self-evaluations, and it is the role of the significant adult to build the child's strengths in contrast to stressing his weaknesses. Perhaps an attitude of patience and solid faith in the child's capacity to function are most important in child training. The child must have an opportunity to contribute to his society and then be commended because of the manner in which he has functioned instead of being disparaged for a failure to function. In commending children, the stress should be on how they function rather than a cute, attractive, or handsome appearance.

Children see and perceive the world differently from adults. Much of the conflict between parents and children is based upon this variance in perception. Obviously this is also true of the teacher and the classroom. It is important, therefore, to permit the child to express himself and reveal his concepts of the world. These concepts cannot be changed through force or demand; instead the child should be led to experiences which allow him to learn from the consequences of his faulty perceptions. The adult can help develop experiences that permit a new view of life instead of strengthening faulty assumptions.

Frequently, in attempting to supply group motivation, we fail to recognize the importance of understanding a group's frame of reference. For example, a school was concerned about the dirt and litter on classroom floors and desks. To alleviate the situation, the teachers and administrators decided to give awards at each grade level for the neatest room. They soon found fairly intensive competition for the awards in the lower grades, and, conversely, an increasing amount of clutter in the upper-grade rooms. Obviously, the awards had value for the younger children, but were viewed as badges of dishonor by the older children.

This illustrates clearly the importance of seeing the motive and the value system from the point of view of the behaver and not just from an external frame of reference. In considering many of the topics and research studies reported in this book, always ask, "What was the self concept of the individual or individuals under study?" Too frequently research is designed in such a way that it neglects this subjective aspect and deals with children at particular age levels, heights, weights, and mental ages. Sufficient evidence is now available to make us question research efforts which do not also involve a study of a child's subjective approach to the task.

---

13. From the readings list or research journals select several articles which consider the self-concept factor as a variable and several others which do not. How does failure to account for the self-concept factor affect specific research?

In the development of the human being, basic mistakes and faulty views tend to emerge in the child's logic. If we get to know a child well, some are revealed in feelings of being helpless, hopeless, very special, no good, etc. As we become aware of the faulty assumptions and conclusions of the individual, we can predict more adequately the ways in which he will function, eventually identifying a type of life style. The individual, for example, may feel, "I only function when I am approved," or, "I belong if I am the boss." Others may feel, "My place is being intellectually superior, or physically superior." Some operate on the assumption, "Others should take care of me." Obviously these faulty styles of life hinder the individual's capacity to function.

The style of life can be understood more adequately as we permit the child to express himself, as we observe closely, and as we use some of the techniques described in Chapter III.

THE ADEQUATE AND THE INADEQUATE SELF CONCEPT

Merely noting the way in which the child responds to the varied experiences provided in the modern school can produce many insights in a person who is trained to look below the surface. Predictions that influence future behavior, as well as retrospective analysis of causes, can be made when the purpose is understanding the individual and effort is concentrated toward seeing meaningfulness in the totality of psychological movement.

With this approach the individual's purposes can be brought into focus. His self concept can become apparent. It requires seeing the child as part of society and interpreting his actions instead of merely reacting to them. Attempting to understand the why behind behavior is challenging, like the person with defective eyesight who gets his first pair of glasses, you encounter an entire new world.

Some distorted views may become a part of the developing self concept, although bearing no relationship to the objective situation. However, the reality of the self concept requires the individual to act as if they were fact and not fiction. If, for example, he feels inadequate to the task, his behavior will reflect that conviction.

Larry is observed in a reading lesson. His progress appears to be good. He has not been differentiated from the group as being less than adequate. His parents have high ambitions, and he has an older brother, Charles, who has accelerated development and has made superior progress in the development of his reading skills. The parents have commended Larry's successes, but they have also compared him to the accelerated brother. Larry has interpreted his situation as a failure to achieve the expectations of his parents and his brother. He cannot be satisfied with being second best. His school performance is good, but not good enough in his eyes. His private logic interprets his skills as being inadequate, and he does not function to full capacity.

Here objective scores and skills lose meaning. You must know what the scores mean to the individual here and now. Feeling inadequacy is a distorted view, and Larry will operate in reading situations just as if he were inadequate.

The Smiths had three girls before Bobby was born. Mrs. Smith had not been well, and this was their last child. The arrival of a boy drew adoration from parents, siblings, and grandparents. Attention was showered on Bobby for any accomplishment. His every move was watched closely, and all of his needs were supplied almost instantaneously. His most minute request was their command. Showered with attention and able to keep everyone in the family busy meeting his requests, Bobby soon came to feel he was something special, a feeling which worked to his disadvantage outside the home. As he came into contact with children and other adults who did not bestow special attention, he either had to adjust or meet with continual disappointment. Bobby had some freedom to choose his behavior response, especially while he was young, but as he grew older it became increasingly difficult to modify his concept that he was something special.

Some children receive so much that they develop a pattern of expectation and feel they are entitled to this type of treatment. Freudians refer to this as the oral personality, Adlerians as the getting type. The person who feels he is entitled can never get enough. No matter what is done for him, he expected it, and now what will be done next? This distorted view develops in a variety of ways and is a great hindrance to the development of concern for others, cooperation, and social living.

Janet was raised carefully to do what was just right. Emphasis was placed on being good, nice, and right. Avoiding what was bad, naughty, and wrong was regularly stressed. Janet's mother used encouragement extensively but mainly associated it with being proper. All rewards were related to this type of behavior, and the girl developed a strong aversion to anything that did not receive parental approval.

As Janet came into contact with other children, she readily pointed out their errors and did not hesitate to identify ways in which she was superior. This child's view was distorted in that she failed to value and respect people who did not meet her standards. Some children are raised in situations in which they hear about or experience the hostility of people closely associated with them. The human mind has a great capacity to generalize and can shortly transfer these feelings to all with whom it comes in contact. This kind of person can ascribe evil purposes to the best intentions.

No matter how distorted a person's views, for the individual who holds them they are as efficacious as a creed, and his interpersonal relationships and daily decisions are based on them. It is often difficult to understand the religious or political ideas of those who hold opposite views. In one sense distortions in the self concept place people in a world of their own. They play the game by their own rules, running from home to third base rather than first, and criticize those who function in what we consider to be a more orthodox manner.

It has been established that the individual is continually striving to find and maintain his place in society. Distorted views make it most difficult for an individual to relate to others. Each distortion serves to raise barriers and keeps him from his goal of being accepted. Nevertheless, those with experience in counseling attest that it is frequently difficult to get the individual to recognize these attitudes as mistaken perceptions.

In order to help a child having difficulty in adjustment, you must first change his self concept and convictions. Studies have demonstrated that anxiety is lessened when the person can maintain his self image and function according to anticipation.[32] This illustrates why the delinquent or misbehaving child may actually be less anxious when he is functioning in antisocial ways.

Poor self concepts, with their accompanying lack of confidence in mastery of the environment, usually accompany deficiency in the child's school performances. Coopersmith found in a study of fifth- and sixth-grade children that a correlation as high as .36 could be found between a positive self concept and school achievement.[33] A considerable body of evidence indicates that a child with a poor self concept tends to be more anxious and less adjusted, less effective in groups and in the tasks of life, whether they be work, social, or sexual, than a child with a more adequate self concept.

In studying self concept it is important to assess the role of defense mechanisms, which play an important part in the development of distorted views. Defense mechanisms are means of adjusting to reduce tension. They permit the individual to protect his self-esteem and faulty view of life, and at the same time they defend the individual against tension or anxiety. Some of the more common mechanisms include: rationalization, giving good logical reasons instead of the real reason; projection, protecting the self from recognizing its own undesirable qualities by assigning these qualities to others; identification, taking other people's qualities as their own and empathizing their successes particularly and possibly their failures; repression, the unconscious denial of impulses; compensation, making up for weakness in one area by excelling in another.

Defense mechanisms enable a person to change the meaning in a situation or to arrive at distorted meanings. The child soon learns that defense mechanisms enable him temporarily to live more effectively in his social world. For a time they solve problems.

If the mechanisms are viewed as assisting the self in its quest for a place, they take on new meaning. Rationalization is geared to make purposes more acceptable to society. In projection, blame is placed on people who are not as socially acceptable as those with whom one seeks status. Identification is obviously made with people who are held in high esteem by the group with whom the individual hopes to find a place. Impulses and acts which would endanger a person's position are repressed. Finally, compensation may indicate, "Although I cannot do well in one situation, I do strive to become proficient in something that will win me my place."

Seeing the purpose in behavior enables you to see the interrelatedness

[32] A. M. Walsh, "Self Concepts of Bright Boys with Learning Difficulties" (New York: Bureau of Publications, Teachers College, Columbia University, 1956), and L. Lipsitt, "A Self Concept Scale for Children and Its Relationship to the Children's Form of the Manifest Anxiety Scale," *Child Development*, XXIX (1958), 463–72.

[33] S. Coopersmith, "A Method for Determining Types of Self Esteem," *Journal of Educational Psychology*, LIX, 1959, 87–94.

of the defense mechanisms. The goal of the individual is twofold. He seeks his position in society, but in this striving he is always influenced by his self concept. In seeking understanding, we need to ask specific questions about the specific child. Why does he need to rationalize? Why did he choose to compensate in this particular manner? Why does he choose to identify with these particular people? Given a specific child, you can see the direction of his movement and analyze his goals. Remember that behavior is not incidental or disjointed for the individual. Just as the puzzle frequently appears unsolvable until a piece is turned in a different direction and a new relationship seen, so do children's actions seem unexplainable until the meaning that the child assigns to our actions and his is understood.

Learn to recognize the characteristics of the child who is developing an adequate self system and the child who is not. The traits discussed here are not always present in every adequate personality, but they will serve as guidelines. If we bear in mind that behavior is always a function of the total field at the time of action, it will enable us to use these constructs in the widest sense. Combs describes persons with adequate personality as those who: "(1) perceive themselves in essentially positive ways, (2) are capable of acceptance of self and others, and (3) perceive themselves as closely identified with others."[34]

The child who is developing an adequate personality has available a great store of positive perceptions of self which gives him the courage to function. He is not compelled to defend the self or to select experiences to fit faulty assumptions and perceptions. He is more open to total experience and more free to choose. He can assess himself more honestly and accurately, and hence his level of aspiration tends to be more realistic. He does not need an immediate solution to all of his problems and is free to take a problem-solving approach instead. This type of child is spontaneous, creative, original and is free of some of the forces which bear upon the child who feels inadequate. He trusts himself and is free to accept others without any negative anticipation that social interaction provides a bad experience.

In contrast, the child who is developing an inadequate personality does not feel equal to the problems of life. He tends to think of himself as unwanted, inferior to others, unacceptable, or incompetent. He has many negative definitions of self and lacks the courage to meet the demands of life's tasks. In the extreme, we find this in the delinquent and the emotionally disturbed who may be belligerent or aggressive as a cover-up protection from the revelation of what he considers to be his real self.

This child sees life as a constant threat, and, being threatened, he tends to overreact. He may try too hard, brag too much, or in countless ways

[34] Combs and Snygg, *Individual Behavior*, p. 248.

strive to prove that he is adequate. He generally produces a rather set and inflexible behavior pattern, and his view of life makes him generally unsuccessful in his relations with others.

The self concept is a most significant aspect of the individual. Considerable emphasis has been placed on knowing the child, usually by getting information about his background, intelligence, achievement, social relationships, emotional development, and in certain instances even his rate of growth. However, none of these directly identifies for us the child's concept of himself. This must come through more than cursory observation or attention to the various measurements typically obtained for an individual. One needs to know what the various traits mean to the child and what use he is making of them. How do they serve him in his interpersonal relationships?

The developing concept of self is important not only for the child's effectiveness as a learner, but also for his mental health. Therapists have come to recognize the importance of the self concept. Olson and Wattenberg stated:

> Mental health is dependent upon the strength of ego, the wholesomeness of the self concept. As psychoanalysts gain more experience with children as contrasted with adult neurotics, they have more and more stressed understanding of ego psychology. Meanwhile, the proponents of client-centered counseling, led by Carl Rogers, have found their work consisting largely of helping clients gain a self concept which leads to inner harmony.[35]

IMPLICATIONS

1. It is important for each adult, parent, and teacher to examine the significance of his role in the formulation of the child's self concept.
2. It might be well for each school to take a careful inventory of the way in which individual teachers affect the development of feelings of adequacy and the concept of self in children.
3. The classroom atmosphere seems to be significant in producing feelings about self, and should be under continual examination.
4. If children are to develop feelings of adequacy, they should be given opportunities to share in real responsibilities, not tasks created to provide busy work.
5. The teacher should continually examine ways in which she can get more information about the self. The variety of techniques suggested in Chapter III should be studied and examined in order to determine which produce the greatest amount of information for the individual teacher.

[35] W. Olson and W. Wattenberg, "The Role of the School in Mental Health," in *Mental Health in Modern Education,* 54th Yearbook of the National Society for the Study of Education (Chicago: University of Chicago Press, 1955), p. 105.

6. Since self-understanding is a crucial area, the development of programs like the one originated by Ojemann at the University of Iowa[36] or those recommended by Jersild[37] should be considered for each school district and classroom.

7. A continual child study program on an in-service basis through institute days and workshops can provide opportunities for the development of child study skills in teachers.

8. It seems pertinent to recognize that by the time the child enters school, a good part of his self concept has already been formulated. Perhaps schools would do well to devote time to preschool parent education.

9. The role of the teacher in the formulation of the concept of the adequate achiever needs continuing attention.

10. The testing programs of schools, which have been directed toward measures of intellectual achievement and interest, might well direct themselves toward more effective ways of acquiring access to an understanding of the self. Teachers and administrators should be encouraged to collect full and more effective anecdotal records.

11. Methods of developing feelings of adequacy in the child through encouragement, love, and guidance should be utilized at all levels, and particularly in the elementary school grades.

12. Parents should be helped to recognize that each child is unique and functions in terms of his self concept. Ways to create better relationships between parents and children should be devised so that true understanding is promoted.

13. Research by Thomas and his associates indicates that child-training practices have different behavioral results, depending on the nature of the child.[38] We must become more aware of the significance of the primary reactive characteristics of the child and recognize that behavior is not merely a direct result of parent or teacher management practices.

14. As the child matures, external stimuli are increasingly subordinated to the control of perception and the central processes and socioemotional adjustment. A consideration of the area of perceptual development is increasingly important for educators in order to affect significantly the child's development. His perceptions must be considered as fundamental to the educational process.

15. The child's productivity is affected by the manner in which he perceives the teacher's feelings about himself. Academic achievement and classroom behavior are enhanced when the child perceives these feelings as favorable.

[36] Ojemann, *A Teaching Program.*
[37] A. Jersild, *Self Understanding in Childhood and Adolescence.*
[38] Thomas, *et al., Behavioral Individuality.*

SUGGESTED READINGS

Articles

Davidson, H. and G. Lang, "Children's Perceptions of Their Teachers' Feelings Toward Them Related to Self-Perception, School Achievement, and Behavior," in *Readings in Educational Psychology,* eds. V. Noll and R. Noll, p. 388. New York: The Macmillan Company, 1962.

Haimowitz, M., "Criminals Are Made, Not Born," in *Human Development: Selected Readings,* eds. M. Haimowitz and N. Haimowitz, p. 359. New York: Thomas Y. Crowell Company, 1960.

Jersild, A., "Self-understanding in Childhood and Adolescence," in *Readings in Child Development,* eds. W. Martin and C. Stendler, p. 473. New York: Harcourt, Brace & World, Inc., 1954.

Reckless, W., S. Dinitz, and E. Murray, "Self-concept as an Insulator against Delinquency," in *The Child. A Book of Readings,* ed. J. Seidman, p. 219. New York: Holt, Rinehart & Winston, Inc., 1958.

Books

Perceiving, Behaving, Becoming, Yearbook. Washington, D.C.: Association for Supervision and Curriculum Development, 1962.

Ausubel, D., *Theory and Problems of Child Development.* New York: Grune & Stratton, Inc., 1958.

Jersild, A., *In Search of Self.* New York: Teachers College, Columbia University, 1952.

Snygg, D. and A. Combs, *Individual Behavior,* rev. ed. New York: Harper & Row, Publishers, Inc., 1959.

8 THE DEVELOPMENT OF INTELLIGENCE AND MENTAL PROCESSES

Intellectual development is, perhaps, one of the most misunderstood areas of child study. Although parents and teachers both use the term IQ (Intelligence Quotient) frequently, they usually exhibit an unawareness of fundamental concepts regarding intelligence. Some people, for example, equate high intelligence and the capacity to do school work. They often ask the question, "Why does Johnny who has a high IQ function poorly in school?" They assume that an intelligence test score is a complete predictor, encompassing motivational, emotional, and personality factors. A single score in a psychological study cannot tell us much about an individual; it is meaningful only in relationship to the total set of factors.

Miss Iverson, a young teacher, is talking with the principal about her class. Results of the fall intelligence tests have just been given to the teachers, and she is attempting to relate her classroom experiences with the test scores. First, she is concerned about Fred. On the intelligence test he produced one of the highest scores in the class. However, she sees little evidence of high ability in his classroom performance or the completion of homework assignments. She asks, "Is it possible to have such an IQ and not really succeed in school work, and if so, why?" This immediately reveals a fundamental lack of understanding of what the score can tell us about an individual.

She then looks at Susie's score, which is perhaps one of the lowest in the room, although still within the average range for Miss Iverson's class. Miss Iverson takes exception to this test score, saying, "Why, Susie is one of my best students. She always completes her homework assignments. She tries her hardest, and she gets good grades on most of the tests." How is Susie's comparatively low score on this test and her successful classroom performance explained? Can a child's IQ fluctuate? What would be revealed by a look at intelligence tests given to Susie in the past? Is it possible that Susie is in the category that is seldom mentioned with much concern, the overachiever?

Has she, by dint of effort, been able to establish a position within the class that is considerably beyond her indicated potential?

Mr. Delavan, the principal, says,

> Let's look at all the relationships that are involved. Yours is a sixth-grade class. We already have two other intelligence test scores on this group. Fred has always scored high in potential ability, and we have as yet to see any evidence of this capacity within the classroom. However, when we look at the home and family relationships and some of the physical factors related to his case, it becomes apparent that his IQ score is probably accurate and that we need to devise new methods of encouraging him to function. What are some of Fred's interests? Is there any way you can work these into the classroom setting?
>
> As to Susie, her two earlier IQ scores were considerably higher and placed her in a more favorable position within the group. Since the IQ tends to fluctuate, Susie's highest score would remain most representive of her ability. No child is ever able to score higher than his capacity and perhaps Susie was not functioning at her best on the day of the test and hence produced a low score. A minimum estimate of a child's capability is the child's highest IQ score.

---

1. Try to secure for analysis test results of a classroom group. You might volunteer to assist a teacher with the data on his pupils, whose names could be kept confidential. Compare the range in abilities and the variance between IQ, grades, and achievement scores. What other specific data would you need to explain paradoxes that appear?

All teachers need help in learning to analyze the meaning of test scores more effectively. There has been far too much unsophisticated utilization of both intelligence test and achievement test scores in the classroom. The scores can provide us with a measure of individual differences in performance in certain instances, but a single score should not be used to predict the potential of a given individual or to make permanent educational decisions. Perhaps a good policy for all teachers would be to recognize that test scores are most effectively utilized in the classroom in conjunction with other types of data. The teacher should also consider the child's personality, social development, physical makeup, concept of self as an achieving individual, and the way he has chosen to adjust to classroom expectations.

As we begin our study of intelligence, some questions might be posed. First, what do we mean when we talk about intelligence? Is there only one kind, or are there several kinds of intelligence? Is the IQ constant, or does it fluctuate? How much is the IQ influenced by heredity, how much by environment, and what can an individual do to improve the IQ scores of a given set of children? Are cultural factors present which prevent the child from scoring as well as he might? Does the "culture-free," "culture-fair" test really eliminate the factor of inequality of experience, and if we get a "culture-free" test, what kind of prediction does it give of functioning in schools that are closely tied to the culture? How is intelligence measured, and how often should it be measured in the schools? Is it possible for a child to raise his IQ through a change of environment, tutoring, intensive study, cramming, travel, and other types of experiences? How do emotions affect the intellect? Is it possible for emotional instability to affect the intelligence score?

CONCEPTS AND THEORIES OF INTELLIGENCE

All of us have some idea of what we mean when we say an individual is intelligent or lacks intelligence. Actual observations of behaviors are commonly used as indicators of intelligence. The speed and quality of an individual's response in a situation with intellectual components would certainly give us some idea of his intelligence.

The concept of intelligence has a variety of meanings, which are difficult to reduce to one simple definition. Intelligence has been defined as the ability to carry on abstract thinking, the ability to generalize, and the method of response to a problem situation.

Since Alfred Binet stimulated more psychological research studies on intelligence than any other single psychologist, perhaps we should begin with his definition of intelligence. Binet believed that intelligence was a combination of capacities that enabled the individual to adapt and be self-critical. In his general-factor theory, he included the abstract, mechanical, and social areas of behavior as part of intelligence. Binet was concerned originally with establishing an accurate diagnosis of the intelligence of the retarded. His task was to determine whether certain students were ready for school experiences. In his tests, Binet stressed the examination of all types of capacities in order to determine criteria for stating that a child lacks the capacity to do scholastic work. In his original tests, in France, in 1905, Binet emphasized the primary factors of reasoning, comprehension and judgment. He proposed to set up a scale of tests to measure the development of the mental processes. Among the processes he included memory, images, recall, and attention. He established an age-scale approach to intelligence and eventually began to include children at all levels of intelligence. Binet made a most significant contribution to the study of intelligence. The construction of the intelligence scale and the emphasis on individual differences made a lasting contribution to the measurement of intellect.

The Binet test is based on an age-scale performance formula. The normal child passes all items at age six when he is six. The normal eight year old has a mental age of eight, the normal ten year old a mental age of ten.

Terman at Stanford University revised these scales in 1916, 1937, and 1960. The scale at the six-year level investigates vocabulary, differences in the meaning of words, ability to pick out missing elements in a picture, number concepts, opposite analogies, and maze tracing.

Lewis Terman first translated, revised, and published in 1916 a Stanford revision of the Binet-Simon test to be used in English-speaking cultures.[1] In this work Terman defined intelligence as the ability to carry on abstract thinking and to utilize abstract symbols in the solution of problems. Terman's research seemed to indicate that vocabulary was the best single indicator of an individual's general intelligence. Terman's revision of the Binet was redone in 1937 and then again, posthumously, in 1960; it provided psychology with an extremely useful predictor of the capacity to utilize abstract symbols in a variety of cultural settings.

Not all psychologists have accepted Binet's and Terman's definitions of intelligence. Some have developed intelligence scales based on different assumptions, such as the Wechsler and Thurstone assumptions.[2, 3]

Charles E. Spearman began the transition from the general-factor theory to multiple-factor analysis, through his development of a two-factor theory of human capacity.[4] He called the two factors involved in the intellectual performance of a task "G" and "S." "G" underlies all mental functioning and is considered the common denominator in all sorts of mental performance. This factor varies from individual to individual but is consistent in all aspects of a given individual's mental functioning. Since mental functioning in unrelated situations calls for different types of mental accomplishments, a specific factor must also operate in each situation. The factor "S" varies not only from individual to individual, but also within the individual, i.e., intraindividual variability.

L. L. Thurstone was an important figure in the early development of factor analysis. He believed that a single intelligence index was inadequate for the purpose of describing mental capacities. He believed that a great many factors entered into specific skills in a variety of combinations. Multiple-factor analysis was designed to discover and isolate fundamental human traits, and Thurstone was able to isolate the following factors: ability to verbalize, word fluency, number facility, memory, visualizing or space thinking, perceptual speed, induction, and speed of judgment. The

[1] L. M. Terman, *The Measurement of Intelligence: an Explanation of and a Complete Guide for the Use of the Stanford Revision and Extension of the Binet-Simon Intelligence Scale* (Boston: Houghton Mifflin Company, 1916).

[2] D. Wechsler, *The Measurement and Appraisal of Adult Intelligence* (Baltimore, Md.: Williams and Wilkins, 1958).

[3] L. L. Thurstone, "The Differential Growth of Mental Ability" (Chapel Hill, N.C.: University of North Carolina, The Psychometric Laboratory, 1955).

[4] C. Spearman, *The Abilities of Man* (New York: The Macmillan Company, 1927).

results of Thurstone's Analysis of Intelligence appears in the Primary Abilities Test (PMA) published by Science Research Associates.

The 1963 edition of the PMA covers grades K–1, 2–4, 4–6, 6–9, and 9–12. The purpose of the test is to investigate primary mental abilities considered most significant in schoolwork. As defined in the manual, the five primary abilities measured by the test are:

> V—Verbal Meaning:
> The ability to understand ideas expressed in words. In the later school years this is the most important single index of a child's potential for handling academic tasks. At the lower levels it is tested by a vocabulary test in picture form; at the upper levels, by a verbal vocabulary test.
> N—Number Facility:
> The ability to work with numbers, to handle simple quantitative problems rapidly and accurately, and to understand and recognize quantitative differences. At the lower-grade levels, the N scores are determined by a pictorial test that requires no reading. Addition problems are also used. At the upper levels, arithmetical reasoning problems are included.
> R—Reasoning:
> The ability to solve logical problems. Separate measures of this ability are not provided in the batteries designed for grades K through 4. In the 4–6 battery it is measured by word-grouping and figure-grouping tests; at the upper levels, by word-grouping, letter-series, and number-series tests.
> P—Perceptual Speed:
> The ability to recognize likenesses and differences between objects or symbols quickly and accurately. This ability is important in acquiring reading skills but tends to plateau at a relatively early age. For this reason it is included only with the three batteries designed for the lower grades.
> S—Spatial Relations:
> The ability to visualize objects and figures rotated in space and the relations between them. The test measuring this ability appears in every level of the PMA and is important throughout the school years.[5]

Numerous psychologists have suggested that there are really different kinds of intelligence. Thorndike said intelligence might be divided into three areas—abstract intelligence, or the ability to deal with the symbolic, e.g., a word, a code, or a geometric figure; mechanical intelligence, or the ability to deal with concrete objects; and social intelligence, the use of psychological principles involving problems of human relationships.[6]

[5] SRA Examiner's Manual, *Primary Mental Abilities* for Grades 4–6 (Chicago: Science Research Associates, Inc., 1963), p. 5.
[6] E. L. Thorndike, *The Measurement of Intelligence* (New York: Teachers College, Columbia University, 1926).

2. As you observe people about you, are you able to determine differences in their ability to do abstract, mechanical, or social tasks? How would a view of intelligence—abstract, mechanical, and social—affect your role as a classroom teacher? How might you go about investigating mechanical and social intelligence? How would the discovery of these factors serve as an encouragement to children who may not abstract well?

A considerable amount of research has been based on factor analysis, and perhaps as many as fifty different intellectual factors may have been identified. J. P. Guilford has attempted through factor analysis to develop a unified theory of intelligence.[7] He defines a factor as a unique ability needed to do well in a particular class of tasks. Guilford devised a theoretical model of one hundred twenty cells, each of which represents a distinct ability. In his model, the factors are classified in three fundamental ways: processes, such as memory, cognition, divergent production, convergent production; contents or materials, such as symbolic, semantic and behavioral; and products, result of applying a particular operation to content, including units, relations, and systems.

Guilford speaks of several kinds of intelligence. Concrete intelligence enables one to use figural information; abstract intelligence affects abilities pertaining to both symbolic and semantic content; and, finally, social intelligence, which enables one to work effectively with people. Thus, Guilford presents us with a background which might eventually be used in understanding the development and the measurement of intelligence.

From the phenomenological point of view, intelligence is a function of interaction. Intelligence is seen as dependent upon the richness and variety of perceptions possible for the individual at a given moment. Psychologists like Combs have pointed out that in most individuals the quality of perception hinges on the experiences the individual has accumulated.[8] Combs believes that the quality of an individual's intelligence is affected by exposure to a wide variety of experiences that permit him to improve perception. Implicit in the perceptual approach is the belief that a person will not behave any more intelligently than he believes he can. A child who is convinced that he cannot do arithmetic and spelling or understand geography will act in accordance with his convictions. To enable him to utilize his capacities, his convictions must be changed. Intelligence then is considered as a product of the interaction of a person and his perceived psychological environment, and the intelligence test does not accurately measure the potential differentiations the individual can make, but his functional perceptions. The phenomenologist would, therefore, caution

[7] J. P. Guilford, "Three Faces of Intellect," *American Psychologist,* 14, August 1959.
[8] A. Combs, "Intelligence from a Perceptual Point of View," *Journal of Abnormal and Social Psychology,* 47, July 1952, 662–73.

users to recognize the factors that limit perception, such as physical conditions, opportunity, experiences, exposure to symbolic events, and the individual's own goals and values.

---

3. What does Combs add to our understanding of intelligence? How does Combs differ from Thorndike, Thurstone, and Guilford? What is the difference between a psychology of possession and a psychology of use?

MENTAL GROWTH

As a child develops, he makes increasingly complex adaptive responses to his physical and social environment. Mental development can be inferred from this behavior. While children differ widely in both rate and pattern of mental development, developmental progression can be observed and, to an extent, measured.

Mental growth curves have been developed for infants. In one of the earlier studies of mental development, a group of thirty-one male and thirty female infants were studied.[9] During the first two years of life yearly increases in point scores were noted, as shown in the accompanying graph. Scores indicate that the infants' mental development was rapid to about the ninth or tenth month, after which deceleration was evident. (Figure 8-1)

Since tasks required on an infant test are of a motor and perceptual nature, behavior growth in the early months of infant development has been demonstrated to have little predictive validity for the later tests of development of intelligence.

To understand individual mental development, it is necessary to study longitudinally the development of intelligence in individuals.

Curves derived from averages of the mental development of a group of children differ from repeated tests of individual children over a period of time.[10]

In any study of mental development, we should always be cautious about inferring the rate of development from mental test scores. These scores do not represent absolute measurements, the size of which are necessarily equivalent at each point on the scale. For example, the year's mental development, even in the case of an average child, may not be the same between any two successive years. The intellectual increment between the ages four and five is not necessarily the same size as the incre-

[9] N. Bayley, "Mental Growth During the First Three Years," *Genetic Psychology Monographs,* 14 (1933), 39.

[10] E. Cornell and C. Armstrong, "Forms of Mental Growth Patterns Revealed by Reanalysis of the Harvard Growth Data," *Child Development,* XXVI (1955), 169–204.

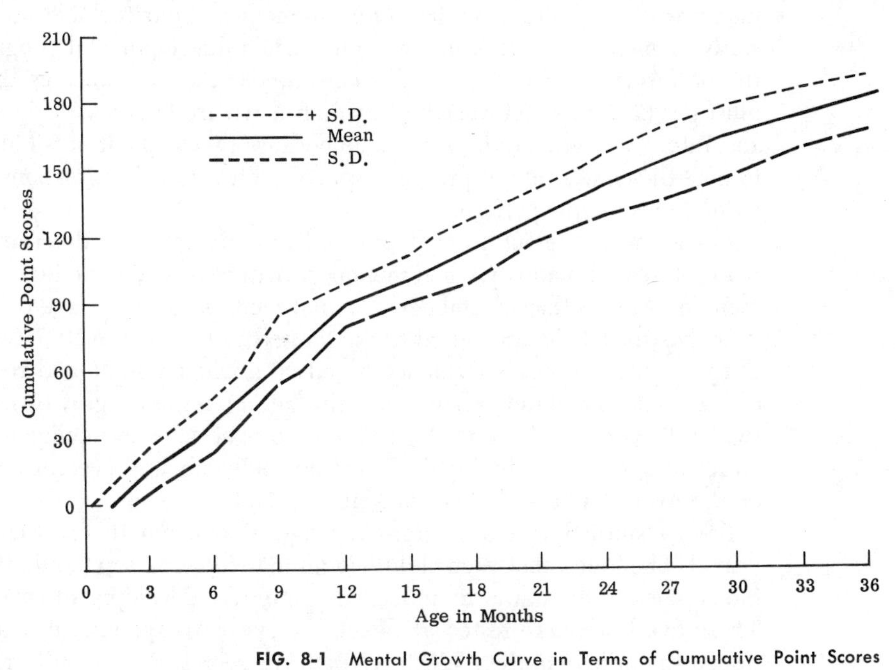

FIG. 8-1 Mental Growth Curve in Terms of Cumulative Point Scores

From N. Bayley, "Mental Growth During the First Three Years," in *Genetic Psychology Monographs*, Vol. 14 (1933), 39.

ments between eight and nine or twelve and thirteen. We do not have an absolute scale for measurement in the intellectual area.

Intelligence in young children is measured by functions considerably different from those used to measure older children. Thus, it is obvious that the scales are far from equivalent. On the Binet a four year old is asked to identify objects in a picture vocabulary, name objects from memory, discriminate between forms, draw opposite analogies, and do simple comprehension items. At age eleven he would be required to produce a design from memory, comprehend verbal absurdities, define abstract words, memorize a sentence, solve problems, and indicate how certain objects are similar. The abilities being measured at eleven are somewhat different and cannot be assumed to be merely an extension or expansion of four-year-old abilities.

Curves representing scores made on repeated administrations of tests may not reflect actual intellectual development. Courtis maintains that no single type of growth curve can adequately express the pattern of mental growth because of the nature of the items included on the typical intelligence test.[11] These curves lack stability, he believes, because they do not

[11] S. Courtis, "The Measurement of Growth," Detroit, Mich.: 9110 Dwight Ave., 1930.

measure a uniform function in a uniform manner. Courtis thinks adequate study of mental growth will come only when developmental progress in the performance of a single act is considered. Courtis indicates that we must get back to single-variable research if we are to study development accurately. Growth curves have value because they make it possible for us to note the child's rate of progress, spurts, plateaus, and regressions in relation to his unique pattern.

Researchers in mental development have attempted to determine the point of mental maturity when mental growth ceases. The finding of Terman and Merrill that mental age does not increase after the age of fifteen years has since been attributed to the limited ceiling on the 1937 Revision of the Stanford-Binet.[12] Evidence based on a wider sample and retesting of the same population shows that the age of terminal growth may be twenty-five or even beyond. There are reports of gains in intelligence test scores at age twenty-five on the Wechsler-Bellevue, and even at age fifty on the Army Alpha and Concept Maturity Test.

Bayley studied five boys from the age of one month to twenty-five years.[13] She found that each child had an individual pattern, and after the infancy period there was an underlying pattern of development constancy. These five boys were tested at twenty-five years of age and all had continued to improve in their Wechsler-Bellevue scores. Bayley indicates that the intellectual processes measured had not reached a ceiling, with fourteen out of fifteen participants continuing to show gains. Thus, the issue of terminal growth in development of a cognitive process varies considerably from individual to individual.

Research in mental development has pointed to some general trends. During infancy and the preschool period, the abilities measured by intelligence tests are generally perceptual and sensory-motor in nature. Following this early stage of development, the elementary school years use tests in which abstract intelligence tends to be most important. Abstract abilities are highly correlated. During preadolescence and later on, tests show a considerable differentiation of intellectual abilities. Thurstone demonstrated a differential growth rate for mental abilities. Perception, reasoning, and space abilities develop somewhat earlier than numerical and memory abilities, while verbal abilities develop more slowly.[14]

In its time, The Harvard Growth Study was probably one of the most comprehensive longitudinal studies in the field of physical and mental

[12] L. Terman and M. Merrill, *Measuring Intelligence: A Guide to the Administration of a New Revised Stanford-Binet Test of Intelligence* (Boston: Houghton Mifflin Company, 1937).

[13] N. Bayley, "On the Growth of Intelligence," *American Psychologist,* X (1955), 805–18.

[14] L. L. Thurstone, *The Differential Growth of Mental Abilities,* No. 14 (Chapel Hill: University of North Carolina Psychometric Laboratory, 1955).

growth. Some of the conclusions of Dearborn and Rothney are significant for our study of intellectual growth.

> 1. Physical and mental growth are essentially individual affairs. No two cases have been found to have exactly the same developmental history as indicated in terms of their deviation from the averages of groups of which they are members.
> 2. The relationship between physical measurements and mental measurements is so low that the knowledge of one does not enable us to predict the other.
> 3. The use of different mental tests over the years indicates that each test is characterized by its own single and peculiar differences with respect to the problems of practise effect and its relation to individual test problems.
> 4. The group mental tests used in this study yielded higher IQ's than the Stanford-Binet tests.
>
> 8. In general, children tend to remain throughout the period of their mental growth (to age sixteen) in the same classification as they were at age eight.
> 9. In general, individuals tend to perform at the same level on verbal and non-verbal material which appears in group mental tests.
> 10. Complete substitution of non-verbal for verbal material in mental tests, would result in handicapping as many children as does the use of tests using verbal material only.
> 11. Mental growth, as measured by the type of group mental tests used in this study, continues much beyond the age of adolescence, although with markedly decreased rate after the age of twenty.
> 12. The possibility of using the percentage of growth, based on the estimated maximum growth of the individual, or of an unselected group, in preference to the mental age technique, and the inadequacy of the commonly employed intelligence quotient, as an index of mental growth has been demonstrated.
> 13. The advantage of using individual growth curves constructed with the above described "growth unit" has been noted.
>
> 15. Performance on mental tests does not seem to be related in any way with pubescent growth spurt.[15]

In a more recent analysis of the Harvard Growth Study, Ethel Cornell and Charles Armstrong found general patterns of mental growth occurred in spurts.[16]

1. A single growth curve theoretically reaching maturity between the ages twenty-six and twenty-seven, maturity being indicated by a mean level of ability regarded as just above average.

2. Two growth curves—the earlier one terminating around age thirteen, the second one not becoming evident until age fifteen or sixteen, with ma-

[15] W. Dearborn and J. Rothney, *Predicting the Child's Development* (Cambridge, Mass.: Sci-Art Publishers, 1941), p. 341.
[16] Cornell and Armstrong, "Forms of Mental Growth Patterns."

turity theoretically indicated at about twenty-three to twenty-four years of age, at a level slightly above average. (Female)

3. Two growth curves—most rapid development from nine to thirteen, the later period one of slow increase with maturity theoretically reached at age twenty-eight to twenty-nine years, at the highest mean level of ability of all the patterns. (Male)

Individual differences in mental growth are observed in early infancy. When compared to a group, the mental growth of children seems to remain at a fairly fixed position, unless some serious changes in conditions of development occur. The child who fails to grow consistently cannot be predicted. The growth curve of intelligence can be generalized, but without certainty because of individual differences in both rate and maximum.

---

4. What are the implications of the nature of mental development for the instructional process? How much information regarding the mental development of a child do you feel is important for classroom planning?

Nancy Bayley pointed out some striking examples of variation in mental growth.[17] One child in her study, Mark, varied from his highest score when tested at one month, to group norm at one year, to the lowest one-fourth at two years; he remained at this position relative to the group until age seven, then rose steadily until he received the following IQ scores: at nine years 117; at ten years 122; at twelve years 130. Gerald, the brightest six month old, was consistently slow from then on, scoring 85 at nine, 84 at ten and 76 at eleven. Charles rose from the twenty-fifth percentile at age one year to average intelligence at four years and scored 146, 149, and 153 at nine, ten, and eleven years of age. These scores would place him in the ninety-ninth percentile of the Stanford-Binet scale.

In the Berkeley Guidance Study, one girl rose from the thirty-first percentile at twenty-one months to the ninety-ninth at six years. Another at the same age dropped from the fifty-fourth to the sixth percentile. These extreme variations are not the rule, but they do show the danger of trying to predict the IQ, particularly in the early years.

The age at which an individual ceases to grow in intellectual ability may range from adolescence to the twenties. Increases in ability after the age of twenty appear to be horizontal—in other words, an extension of knowledge.

Our study of mental growth curves indicates the necessity for a revised

[17] N. Bayley, "The Role of Intelligence" in *Mental Health in the Classroom,* ed. P. Witty, 13th Yearbook of the Department of Supervisors and Directors of Instruction of the National Education Association (Washington, D.C.: National Education Association, 1941), pp. 53–54.

conception of intelligence by the schools and teachers. It seems reasonable to suggest that the research presented should shake the belief of those who tend to think that a single intelligence test will predict a mental growth pattern.

To speak of the constancy of the IQ without considering the many factors which affect this score at different age levels is to disadvantage a great percentage of the children. The use, in the elementary school, of IQ scores for the development of homogeneous groups becomes a particularly naive concept. Constancy of the IQ can now be disputed, and teachers, administrators, and psychologists would do well to consider problems involved both in the measurement of intelligence and the mental growth curves before attempting any early classification of individuals.

---

5. If there is adequate evidence that the IQ is not constant at certain stages of development, what does this imply for the use of IQ's in the school? How much does a first-grade intelligence test result tell the fifth-grade teacher?
6. In Mr. Hurley's fifth-grade class Joan has an IQ of 115, Jack 117, Janet 115, and Bill 95. What does this information tell him about these children? What questions would you have about these scores?

FACTORS INFLUENCING INTELLIGENCE

Physical and Hereditary Factors

A natural endowment unfolds maturationally and sets limits on potential intellectual functions. This native intellectual endowment varies among individuals, and its maturation is hindered or assisted by the type of stimulation available in the environment during the early years. By comparing increments in mental and physical growth in curves of mental and physical development, Abernethy found that rates of physical and mental growth were essentially unrelated within the normal range of individual differences.[18] He believed that the entire period of development is involved in determining the small positive correlations typically found between physical and mental growth during childhood.

Olson and Hughes found a general correlation of all aspects of child growth when plotted according to derived age values.[19] Examples of this growth pattern for two children are presented in the figure 8-2.

[18] E. Abernethy, "Relationships Between Mental and Physical Growth," Monograph, Society for Research in Child Development, I, No. 7 (1936).
[19] W. Olson and B. Hughes, "Growth of a Child as a Whole," in *Child Behavior and Development*, ed. R. G. Barker (New York: McGraw-Hill Book Company, 1943), pp. 199–208.

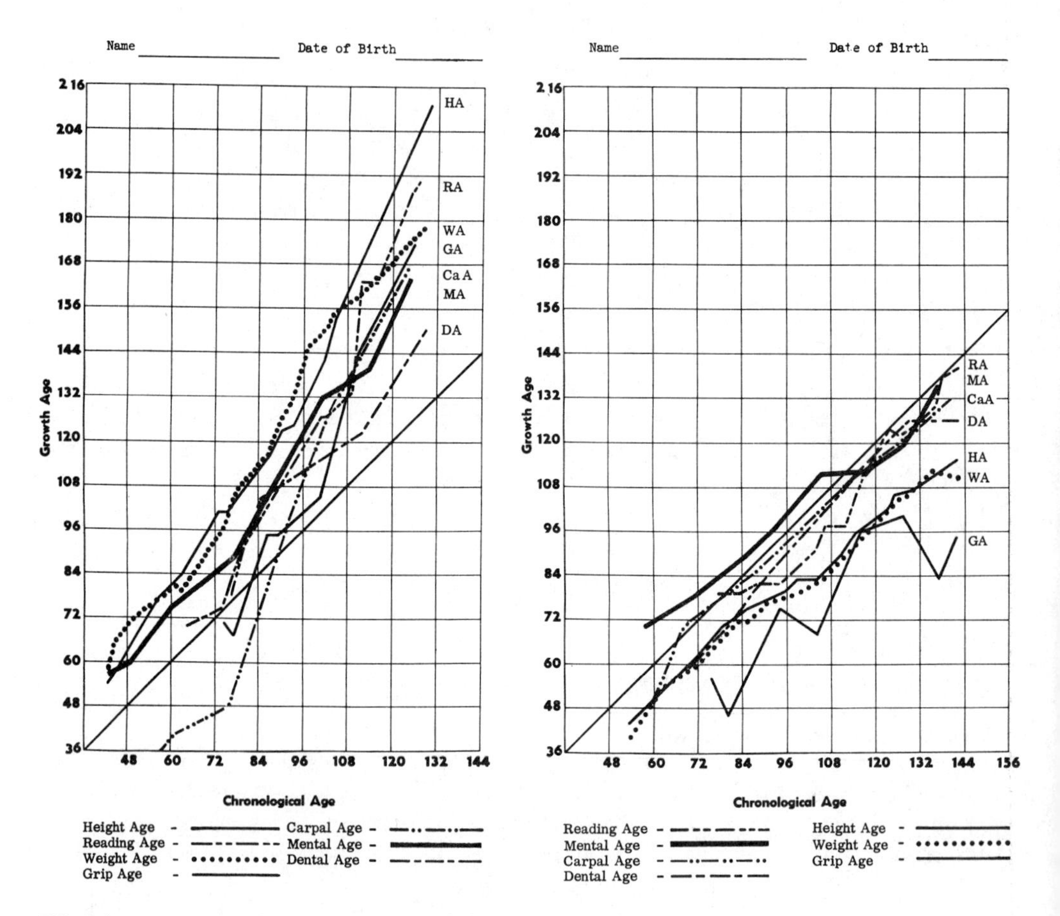

FIG. 8-2

The general "going-togetherness" of all aspects of child growth in two children (A and B) who are developing at different rates of growth. The separate curves represent height age (HA), reading age (RA), weight age (WA), grip age (GA), carpal age (CaA), mental age (MA), and dental age (DA). Note that the units along the ordinate are in terms of derived "growth ages."

By permission of W. C. Olson and B. O. Hughes, in *Child Behavior and Development,* eds. Barker, Kounin and Wright. Copyright 1943 by McGraw-Hill Book Company.

Shuttleworth, who worked with data from the Harvard Growth Study, also found that both boys and girls with early maximum-growth ages in standing height proved to be more intelligent than children with late maximum-growth ages.[20] His findings support the evidence of Abernethy, Olson, and Hughes that growth proceeds in patterned fashion.

Environmental and Cultural Factors

Investigations (conducted since the beginning of psychological research) tend to show that the higher the socioeconomic status, the higher the average intelligence of the children. The basic question is whether higher socioeconomic position helps to raise the level of intelligence or, more simply, whether intelligent people rise in the social scale? It has been demonstrated that the intellectual level of the underprivileged can be improved by raising their socioeconomic levels, especially if an early enough start is made. However, not every child gains and the degree of improvement varies greatly. The culturally rich home environment tends to lift the IQ, some believe as much as twenty points, while the home environment devoid of positive cultural influences, may lower the IQ as much as twenty points. More adequate research on this issue is still needed. Some problems obviously exist in failure of the tests to equate for cultural differences.

What does the upper socioeconomic group provide that results in a higher intelligence quotient? The most important factors appear to be nutrition, adequate medical attention, security (derived from freedom from economic deprivation), and exceptional educational advantages. A child, devoid of advantages in the area of food, clothing, physical and mental care, is frequently a culturally deprived child who scores low on the intelligence test. The most extensive documentation of the significance of experience in determining the growth of learning ability has been made by Hunt.[21]

During World War II, armed services tested the intelligence of people from all sections of the country. Scores were found to parallel the amount of money per pupil spent on public schools in the various states. Men from states with high educational expenditures had the highest average IQ scores.

Some argue that tests favor the upper socioeconomic group. This argu-

[20] F. Shuttleworth, "The Physical and Mental Growth of Girls and Boys Age Six to Nineteen in Relation to Age at Maximum Growth," Society for Research in Child Development Monograph, 1939, 4, No. 3.

[21] J. McV. Hunt, *Intelligence and Experience* (New York: The Ronald Press Company, 1960).

ment is made particularly by people interested in developing the culture-fair tests.[22]

The upper socioeconomic classes provide advantages, but psychologists believe that a "good psychological home" is more important than a home with just economic advantages, since every child has a unique set of nature and nurture experiences. The family atmosphere and family constellation for him are different from his brothers' and sisters'. The child has a distinct primary reactivity pattern and a capacity to use the nature and nurture factors in a distinct and unique manner.

The nature and nurture, or, hereditary and environment problem is not easily solved. Most research studies on this problem are inconclusive. The best conclusion to date is that the influences of heredity and environment are inextricably interwoven, and, hence, it cannot be demonstrated that one is a more significant factor than the other.

Emotional Factors

Richards studied the development of a disturbed boy, with an emphasis upon the relationship of intelligence-test performance at various ages to the child's life situation during the same period.[23] He produced two sets of data, test scores and a history of the individual's adjustment at the time of each testing. The intelligence testing showed the following results on the Stanford-Binet at various ages: the average IQ for all testing was 124, the individual IQ's fluctuating between 117 and 140. There are four trends in the curve he obtained for IQ's between the ages of three and ten. First, a rise of eleven IQ points from age three to four, then a drop of thirteen points from five to six, a rise again of twenty-five points from six to eight years, and finally a drop of eighteen points from eight to ten years. The boy, referred to as Bobbie Jones, was studied at the Fels Research Institute. The Fels Parent Behavior Scales were used several times throughout the years. Projectives tests such as the Rorschach and the Thematic Apperception Test were available. (Figure 8-3)

Bobbie's father, a college graduate with an IQ of 127, was a businessman in moderately good circumstances. The child's mother had some college training and had done secretarial work before marriage. During the first five years Bobbie seemed to lead a normal life, perhaps with a greater than usual attachment to the mother, although he was also close to his father. The father played with and read to the boy frequently. During the

[22] K. Eels, A. Davis, R. Havighurst, V. Herrick, and R. Tyler, *Intelligence and Cultural Differences: A Study of Cultural Learning and Problem Solving* (Chicago: University of Chicago Press, 1951).

[23] T. W. Richards, "Mental Test Performance as a Reflection of the Child's Current Life Situation, A Methodological Study," *Child Development*, XXII (1951), 221–33.

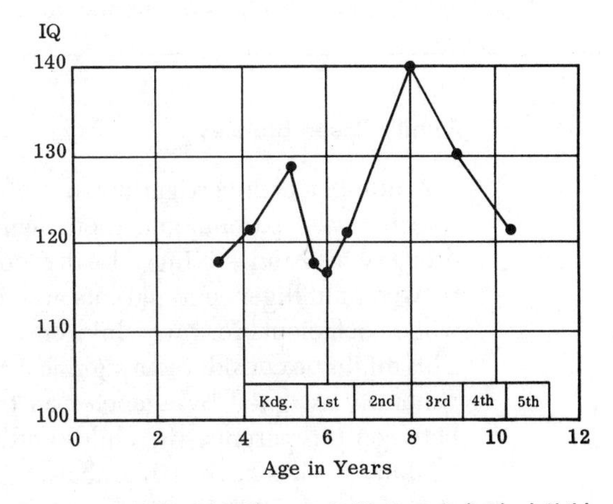

FIG. 8-3 Changes in IQ in an Individual Child

period from five to ten, immediately preceding the rise in IQ, the father, in addition to active business during the day, started a company which took most of his evenings. Bobbie saw less of him, but they continued to have a good relationship. In the period from age six to eight, when the IQ rose twenty-five points, during the middle of the second grade, he was switched from a stern disciplinarian to a more sympathetic teacher. He continued with her through the remaining year and a half. Thus, he spent a year and a half of the two years during the ages six to eight with this teacher. At the same time, his father gave up his night work and started spending considerable time with Bobbie. Whereas, the father had formerly been tense and nervous because of the two jobs, he became a new man, more thoughtful and easier to live with. The Fels Parent Behavior Scales applied to the home during this time showed that the home was always well-adjusted and democratic but that it now accentuated these characteristics. It was during this period that Bobbie's IQ was 140. Thereafter, in the later phase, the home atmosphere was more severe with less devotion, affection, and support of Bobbie.

During the last phase, ages eight to ten, when the IQ dropped eighteen points, Bobbie's "understanding" teacher became a tired and inactive teacher and eventually experienced a tumor operation. Bobbie himself was promoted to the fourth grade, where he had a severe teacher. In summarizing this history, Richard commented on the following points: the school situation, which fluctuated with the rise and fall in IQ; the role of the father, which fluctuated with the rise and fall in IQ; and the fact that the highest IQ was obtained during the period in which the child-centeredness of the home was at its highest.

7. Discuss the significant factors which affect the possession and use of intelligence. What can teachers or parents do about these factors?

Family Resemblances

A number of investigations on intelligence have explored the relationship between parents and their own children, parents and adopted children, twins, and siblings. Leahy noted that the coefficients correlation between intelligence in parents and adopted children correlated about .20 while coefficients for own children were generally found to be about .50.[24] This might be considered a significant difference since adopted children are generally assigned by agencies on the basis of a fairly high relationship between the parents, the child, and the educational setting of the home.

Many studies have shown that in general we can demonstrate a correlation of about .50 between the intelligence of fathers or mothers and their children. This same approximate correlation has been found between siblings, who live in somewhat the same environment.

Correlations between the intelligence of identical twins who have developed from the same fertilized ovum usually range between .70 and .90. Newman, Freeman, and Holzinger found that the IQ's of twins who experienced the same environmental opportunities and education were on the whole closer than the IQ's of twins whose environment and education differed considerably.[25] They also noted that identical twins who were reared apart were, as a group, more alike than siblings who were reared in the same home.

Honzik suggested that there is a significant relationship which changes with age between parental ability and the child's intelligence test scores.[26] For example, she found a shift from a coefficient correlation of about .05 between mother and child at age two to a coefficient as high as .35 at age five and thereafter. Data from Skodak in the same figure show similar relationships between the adopted child's IQ and the true mother's education. Honzik concluded that the parent-child correlations reflect individual differences which are largely determined genetically.

Shields did a study of forty-four monozygotic, or one-egg twins with exactly the same hereditary equipment. He found a correlation on intelligence of .76 when these twins were reared together, a correlation of .77 when reared apart, and a correlation of .51 in dizygotic twins where he-

[24] A. Leahy, "Nature-Nurture and Intelligence," *Genetic Psychology* Monograph 17, 1935.

[25] H. Newman, F. N. Freeman, and K. J. Holzinger, *1937 Twins, A Study of Heredity and Environment* (Chicago: University of Chicago Press), pp. 381–82.

[26] M. Honzik, "Developmental Studies of Parent-Child Resemblance in Intelligence," *Child Development,* 28 (1957) 215–28.

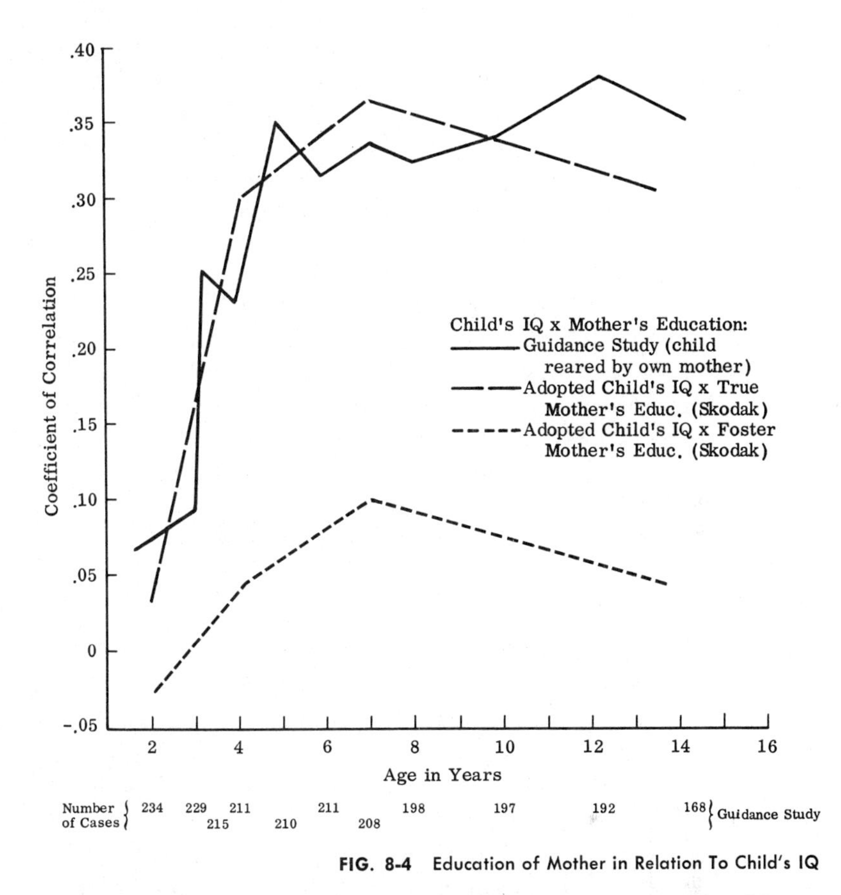

FIG. 8-4 Education of Mother in Relation To Child's IQ

Reproduced by permission of Marjorie P. Honzik, "Developmental Studies of Parent-Child Resemblance in Intelligence," *Child Development,* 28 (1957), 215–228. Courtesy of the Society for Research in Child Development.

reditary equipment is not identical.[27] This points to the strong influence of heredity.

School Factors

A basic question is the extent to which the child's intelligence is influenced by the type of schooling he receives and the time he receives it. There have been some investigations in connection with nursery school and the raising of a child's IQ. Olson and Hughes found that nursery school children from privileged backgrounds did not differ significantly in intel-

[27] J. Shields, *Monozygotic Twins: Brought up Apart and Brought up Together*" (New York: Oxford University Press, Inc., 1962).

lectual growth from nonnursery school children who also came from privileged backgrounds.[28] Remember that these children came from homes where nursery school experiences could add little to the nurture of the child's intellectual development. In this study, then, no special intellectual effects were attributed to nursery school and kindergarten attendance for children who experienced adequate nurture in their own homes.

Skodak and Skeels did a study in an orphanage, which provided a minimum amount of stimulation and opportunity and in which, as a result, were many deficient and deprived children available for research.[29] Two groups were used in this experiment—an experimental group and a control group. Both groups remained residents of the orphanage, but for several hours each day the experimental group attended a nursery school. Skodak and Skeels found the children who attended the nursery school over a period of twenty months showed on an average a gain of 4.6 points in IQ, with some individuals showing larger gains. During this period, the control children showed an average loss of 4.6 points. It was also demonstrated that gains in social and emotional areas were much more impressive than IQ gains.

PREDICTING INTELLECTUAL GROWTH, CONSTANCY AND RELIABILITY IN INTELLIGENCE TESTS

Tests are used not only to determine the present status of the individual but also to make predictions about his future growth and status. In order to make an effective educational decision, we need to have the best possible measures of intelligence available.

Anderson concluded that the prediction of later status from early test scores will be less accurate the younger the child is at the time of first testing or the longer the interval between tests.[30]

After the appearance of speech in the child, tests begin to have greater predictive value. In general, it could be concluded that indices for prediction of future development are quite ineffective until the age of six or seven. Some of this ineffectiveness is due to the fact that infant intelligence tests deal with functions that are quite different from those on tests used during the elementary school years and adolescence. There are many reservations about items on the Gesell Schedule for predicting intellectual status which are administered prior to age two or even age five.

[28] W. Olson and B. Hughes, "Subsequent Growth of Children with and without Nursery School Experience," National Society for the Study of Education, *Intelligence: Its Nature and Nurture,* 39th Yearbook, Part II (Bloomington, Ill.: Public School Publishing Co., 1940), pp. 237–44.

[29] M. Skodak and H. M. Skeels, "A Final Follow-up of One Hundred Adopted Children," *Journal of Genetic Psychology,* 75 (1949), 85–125.

[30] J. E. Anderson, "The Limitations of Infant and Pre-School Tests in the Measurement of Intelligence," *Journal of Psychology,* 8 (1939), 351–79.

Intelligence is a developing function and the stability of measured intelligence increases with age.[31] Bayley did a comprehensive study of the intellectual growth of forty children between ages one month and eighteen years of age, which showed wide differences in the growth patterns of individual children in the area of mental ability.[32] The shifts were almost unpredictable, occurring at all age levels and in a wide range of abilities. In an article in the *American Psychologist*, in 1955, Bayley presented some of the different patterns of intellectual growth between one

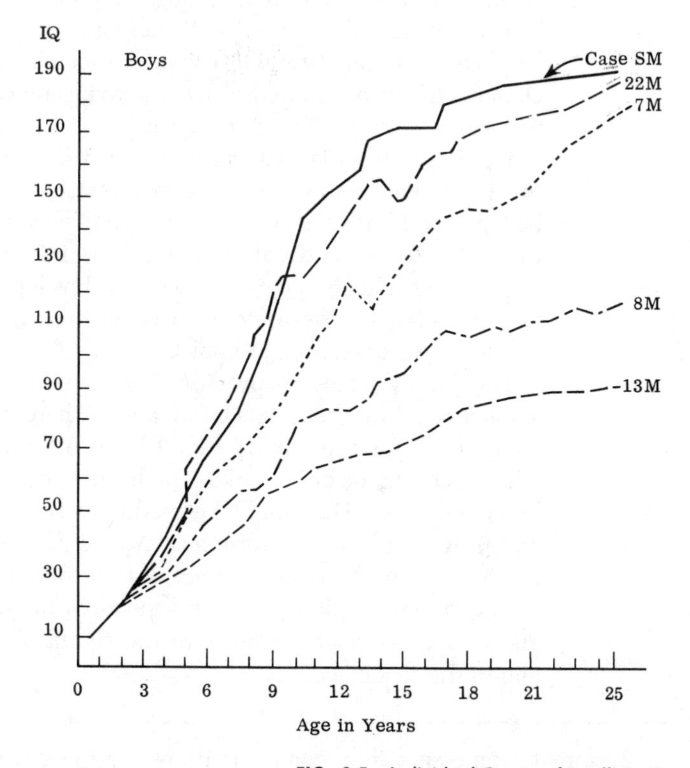

FIG. 8-5 Individual Curves of Intelligence

Individual curves of intelligence of five boys, from one month to 25 years. The scores on the ordinate have been converted into deviations from the 16-year-old mean, all in direct proportion to the 16-year-old standard deviation (here called 16-D scores).

From N. Bayley, "On the Growth of Intelligence," *American Psychologist*, 10 (1955), 814. By permission of the American Psychological Association.

[31] B. Bloom, *Stability and Change in Human Characteristics* (New York: John Wiley & Sons, Inc., 1964).
[32] N. Bayley, "Consistency and Variability in the Growth of Intelligence from Birth to Eighteen Years," *Journal of Genetic Psychology* (1949), pp. 165–96.

month and twenty-five years of age.[33] The data clearly illustrate differential periods of acceleration in individuals.

FOSTERING THE GROWTH OF INTELLIGENCE

Factors have been identified as beneficial to the growth and development of intelligence. The psychological climate that the child is raised in is one of the most significant. The child needs to feel accepted and valued as an individual. His ideas, thoughts, and even idiosyncracies should be listened to, accepted, and discussed in a mature fashion. He should not be laughed at as immature because he has an idea that is different. Instead, a climate should be created in which having unique ideas and making contributions to family living are rewarded.

The implication is that the child must be encouraged to make choices, solve problems, and become independent in his thinking. This type of behavior should always be reinforced and encouraged. It is also vital that the child be provided with materials and information which permit problem solving. He should be allowed to develop new uses for old tools, to see new relationships, to do creative writing, and to have access to a wide variety of experiences and books.

The family needs to provide a system for the regular recognition of achievement in the intellectual area. There should be an atmosphere which provides stimulation for all kinds of broad intellectual growth and which permits the child to work on his developmental problems and developmental tasks. He should be made aware of the alternatives and then encouraged to solve the problem. Adults need to have faith that children can learn from the consequences of their decisions.

The growth of intelligence is dependent upon a stimulating atmosphere and a creative relationship with the significant adults both in the home and in the school.

---

8. Formulate some specific recommendations for the promotion of intellectual development during the preschool, primary, intermediate, and junior high years. What are the respective roles of the child, parent, and teacher in these plans?

MEASUREMENT OF INTELLIGENCE

Schools and placement agencies have been interested in the subject of intelligence testing because of its implications for placement. Intelligence

[33] N. Bayley, "On the Growth of Intelligence."

tests attempt to predict the individual's capacity to function generally in tasks that require scholastic aptitude. They measure the individual's ability to cope with situations requiring the exercise of mental processes and try to measure the ability to comprehend the situation, apply past experiences, and solve the problem presented.

Tests are designed on the premise that intelligence can not be measured directly but is inferred by the observation or evaluation of behavior. Behavior has been grouped at various chronological age levels, and decisions have been made as to what is intelligent behavior for a given age level. The measurements are converted into norms for representative groups of a population, so that eventually individuals can be classified as having intelligence like a typical five year old or eight year old. Some tests, like the Kuhlmann-Anderson, used a median score in an attempt to avoid the averaging of scores in determining the norms.

Most tests of intelligence place a premium on the ability to do abstract thinking through the use of symbols. Vocabulary also is of great importance in measuring intelligence. Many psychologists believe that as a child matures his vocabulary is the best single indicator of intelligence as related to scholastic aptitude. This measurement of vocabulary can be made in an individual test, such as the Stanford-Binet or the Wechsler Intelligence Scale for Children, or in group testing.

For a long time, test makers have been concerned with the problem of avoiding measuring only differences in cultural opportunities or education. An effective test item combines a criterion of novelty and universality. It is novel in the sense that it has not been encountered before by individuals taking the test; it is universal to the extent that all, at a certain level, may have had some experience related to it.

The group intelligence test has frequently been shown to have a high relationship to the extent, level, and quality of the child's educational experience. When we speak of measuring intellectual potential or "native capacity," therefore, we need to be aware of the overlapping of hereditary and environmental factors.

The teacher and school administrator must be aware of some of the problems involved in the measurement of intelligence. We must not assume that tests with similar titles measure similar behaviors. We must always determine whether the group on which the norms for this test were based is comparable to the children we are testing. It is also pertinent to recognize that tests with dissimilar titles may actually measure the same thing. It is quite applicable in testing to ask, "What's in a name?" Intelligence testing with children must hold to a definite concept about what the test items are seeking to predict.

Psychologists engaged in test construction also need to recognize the cyclic nature of mental development. At certain times mental development proceeds more rapidly than at other times. Those who use intelligence tests in the schools should recognize that children with identical IQ's seldom function identically. One reason for this could very well be that they had acquired their mental-age points on different kinds of abilities and tasks.

Inhelder and Piaget also found differences in the modal age of children at a given stage on two different tasks.[34] The age level for attainment of a given stage appears to be specific to a task rather than general, so that the child can operate at stage two on one task and at stage one on another.

The first individual intelligence test was the Stanford-Binet. Originally devised for use in dealing with a specific problem in France, it was later revised by Terman and then Terman and Merrill, and has been used extensively in the United States. The test items in this scale have been arranged in the order of empirically determined difficulty from the age of two upward. Items are always scored on a pass or fail basis. There are six test items at each half-year level from age two to five and six items at each yearly age level thereafter until the age of fourteen. Thereafter, the test provides for average and superior adult levels. The items have been arranged so that the normal child of a given age is expected to perform at his chronological-age level. Retarded children perform below the level, gifted children above.

Another frequently used individual intelligence test is the Wechsler Intelligence Scale for Children (WISC), which the psychologist uses diagnostically to determine areas of strength and weakness. The Wechsler test, developed and originally copyrighted by David Wechsler in 1949, abandoned the concept of mental age originally introduced by Binet in 1908. The Wechsler test has instead worked on the basis of a deviation intelligence quotient. The IQ is obtained by comparing the child's test performance with the scores earned by individuals in a single age group, not with the composite age group. This was done in an attempt to keep the standard deviation of IQ's identical from year to year, so that a child's obtained IQ does not vary unless his actual test performance as compared with his peers varies. The Wechsler test also permits development of a verbal, performance, and total or full-scale intelligence quotient. The verbal factors include information, comprehension, arithmetic, similarities, vocabulary, and digit span. The performance factors include picture completion, picture arrangement, block design, object assembly, coding, and mazes.

Group intelligence tests are frequently used in the schools to make educational decisions. Close analysis reveals that many mental-ability tests being widely used are really strictly measures of classroom achievement, while others are quite independent of classroom instruction. The person

[34] B. Inhelder and J. Piaget, *The Growth of Logical Thinking from Childhood to Adolescence* (New York: Basic Books, Inc., 1958).

who selects or uses tests needs to know what the test actually measures. Individual deviations due to motivation, fatigue, distraction and the like may not be noted in a group-testing situation.

The following list includes some of the tests now being used in the public schools:

1. The California Test of Mental Maturity. Authors, E. T. Sullivan, W. W. Clark, and E. W. Tiegs. Publisher, California Test Bureau. Grades four to twelve.
2. Cattell Culture-fair Intelligence Test. Author, R. B. Cattell. Publisher, Bobbs-Merrill Co., Inc. School-learned skills not required. Grades three to twelve.
3. Differential Aptitude Tests. Authors, G. Bennett, H. Seashore, and A. Wesman. Publisher, Psychological Corporation. Items generally well-constructed and frequently used in grades eight to twelve to make educational and vocational decisions.
4. Lorge-Thorndike Intelligence Test. Authors, I. Lorge, R. L. Thorndike. Publisher, Houghton Mifflin Company. A promising instrument for predicting achievement in grade one. Series considered to be a well-constructed set of growth scales.
5. Science Research Associates Tests of General Ability (TOGA). Author, J. C. Flanagan. Publisher, Science Research Associates. Measures cultural understandings and reasoning with geometric forms.
6. Henmon-Nelson Tests of Mental Ability. Authors, T. A. Lanken, M. J. Nelson. Publisher, Houghton Mifflin Company. Places a great emphasis on reading; scores tend to correlate well with teacher grades. Grades three to twelve.
7. Otis Quick Scoring Mental Ability Tests. Author, A. S. Otis. Publisher, Harcourt, Brace & World, Inc. Grades four to twelve. Places a great emphasis on school skills.
8. School and College Ability Tests (SCAT). Author, Educational Testing Service Staff. Publisher, Educational Testing Service. Grades four to twelve. A new test, which provides both a verbal and a quantitative score. Considered to be a good measure of school-learned abilities.
9. Kuhlman-Anderson Intelligence Tests. Authors, F. Kuhlman and R. G. Anderson. Publisher, Personnel Press. Grades three to twelve. Well-constructed and considered to be one of the better measures of growth available. Emphasizes both reading and achievement skills.
10. S.R.A. Primary Ability Test. Grades four to twelve. Authors, L. L. Thurstone and T. G. Thurstone. Publisher, Science Research Associates. Grades four to twelve. Stresses reading, arithmetic and reasoning abilities.

Because the testing field is frequently under attack from critics of education, it is important that the teacher and the parent understand more adequately the school testing program and some of the significant concepts related to it. Robert Bauernfeind's *Building a School Testing Program* (Boston: Houghton Mifflin Company, 1963) is recommended to those interested in investigating testing problems further.

---

9. What are the crucial questions to ask in setting up a school testing program to measure intelligence and achievement? Plan an elementary school testing program to cover just these two areas. Defend your program and the instruments selected in terms of your school's educational objectives.

INTERPRETATION AND USE OF TEST RESULTS

Individual tests permit a more reliable measure of intelligence than a group test. The motivation and effort produced are more uniform when the child works under the supervision of an examiner in a one-to-one relationship, and the examiner can observe the individual to determine if there is sustained effort and attention.

You should always be aware of the standard error of measurement for any test you use. For example, an IQ of 90 should never be thought of as exactly 90, but rather between 80 and 100. The instruments used for measurement are not precise, and the scores should not be taken as exact measurements.

Test results should be considered in terms of the reliability of the instrument. Has it been demonstrated that the test yields approximately the same result when applied to a number of children of the type you are concerned about? Also, is the test valid in the sense that it has accurately predicted the kind of precise information that you need for the decision you have to make? Are the norms representative of the characteristics of the group that the child being tested has to compete with? Are the size of the norm population and the recency of the sampling adequate?

A reading disability frequently affects IQ test performance on paper and pencil tests. Some evidence indicates that where reading is accelerated, the IQ is equally accelerated, whereas the child who is slow or retarded in reading may produce an intelligence score lower than his potential. Such factors as those related to reading can be checked out through the use of the individual test. It is also possible to give nonverbal tests to clarify the effects of a reading disability. The culture of the individual, his background, and previous set of experiences should always be considered to see whether they are comparable both to the norm group and to the groups with which he is currently competing.

---

10. If you can get access to individual and group scores on intelligence tests, determine the amount of variation between the scores, and develop an explanation of the variation for these children.

In interpreting the results of tests, the culture and environmental opportunity of the child must be taken into consideration. The same score means one thing in a child from deprived circumstances and another in a child from a rich cultural environment. The teacher should remember that IQ's on group tests may measure abstract intelligence or scholastic aptitude and that this is only one type of ability. Group tests rarely measure the ability to work with things or with people, nor do they measure the ability to solve many concrete, practical problems. The child who scores low on group intelligence tests generally has trouble with academic work. However, he may have a good ability in mechanical, social, artistic, or other areas. Thus, tests may tell us not only what behavior is present and what is not present but may give us clues for other types of investigation.

---

11. How can the teacher get clues about the presence of mechanical, social, artistic, or creative abilities in a child without using tests?

Since tests can be interpreted in a variety of ways, those who use the tests must learn to recognize the meaning of the test score. The accompanying chart (Figure 8-6) gives a picture of the normal curve of distribution and the meaning of relative scores as expressed in percentages, standard deviations, cumulative percentages, and percentile equivalents.

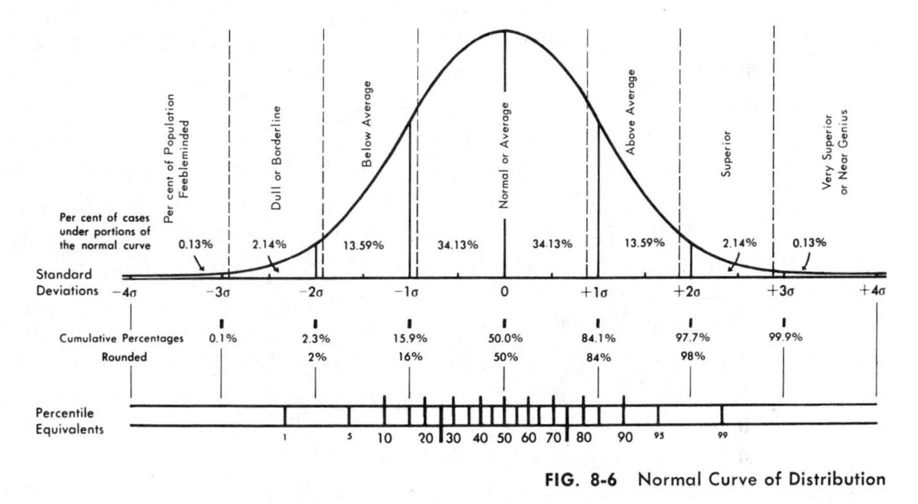

FIG. 8-6 Normal Curve of Distribution

From Test Service Bulletin, No. 48. New York: The Psychological Corporation. Distribution labels have been superimposed.

READINESS TESTING

A significant evaluation problem for the school is the widely varying capacities evident in the functioning of children as they enter kindergarten and first grade. An effective readiness test should provide the kind of information that makes it possible to adapt the educational program to the individual. It is quite evident that capacities develop at different rates in different children and that chronological age is an extremely poor measure to attempt to correlate with any given ability. Although we accept the fact that children do not begin to speak or walk or sit up at the same age, our schools seem to assume that children are ready to learn on the basis of chronological-age factors.

When accurate readiness information is available early enough, educational planning can be devised to create the most successful experience possible for the individual. In the past, readiness tests have generally been group tests of the paper and pencil variety. The Metropolitan Readiness Test is a good example. It attempts to determine readiness for learning by measuring a number of different skills which contribute to success in schoolwork. Group intelligence tests have also been used to measure the general mental maturity of the beginners. Tests used in this manner would include the California Test of Mental Maturity Pre-Primary Series, the Detroit Beginning First Grade Intelligence Test, Kuhlmann-Anderson Intelligence Tests, the SRA Primary Mental Abilities, and the Pintner Non-Language Primary Mental Tests by Rudolph Pintner of Teachers College, Columbia University, New York.

Individual tests of readiness have received increasing attention. The Brenner-Gestalt test is an example of an individual measure of school readiness. The test is comparatively brief, taking about 10 minutes to administer individually to each child, and measures whether the child is able to work with certain concrete number concepts. Does he recognize the number a set of dots represents; can he count the number of dots in a given set? He is also asked to reproduce a sentence and to reproduce a Gestalt figure. The final part of the Brenner-Gestalt Test requires him to draw a man. Dr. Anton Brenner of the Merrill-Palmer Institute, Detroit, Michigan, has set up a scoring system and a set of standards to evaluate readiness for school work based on these measures.

Another individual measure of school readiness is the battery of tests developed by Frances Ilg and Louise Bates Ames of the Gesell Institute of Child Development.[35] This test determines a developmental age by giving the child a battery of behavior tests, including an interview; writing of name, address, letters, numbers; copy forms; Gesell incomplete-man test; right and left test; Munroe visual one and visual three; naming animals; giving home and school preferences; Lowenfeld mosaic tests. Tables of norms for each test are also available. These tests are designed to be used at the entrance to both kindergarten and first grade. They are set up so as to project a total view of the child and his readiness for the varied tasks of school.

The revised Stanford-Binet has also been used frequently to determine readiness for school tasks. The Psychological Corporation has been interested in this problem and as a result has undertaken development of a

[35] F. Ilg and L. Ames, *School Readiness* (New York: Harper & Row, Publishers, Inc., 1964).

test to measure intellectual functioning in children age four through six and one-half years, the period just prior to formal schooling. In general, this new test is a downward revision of the WISC that operates as a distinct and separate scale. The Wechsler Preschool and Primary Scale of Intelligence consists of the following items: information, animal house, vocabulary, picture completion, arithmetic, mazes, sentences, geometric designs, block designs, similarities, and comprehension. This test was standardized during 1964.

---

12. If your instructor has access to individual readiness testing materials, contrast these materials with group measures of readiness, and make a practical recommendation for evaluating 250 kindergarten children for first-grade readiness.

THE GIFTED CHILD

For our purposes we shall consider the child who has consistently scored an IQ of 130 or more as gifted. We would also like to expand the concept to include any child who shows exceptional performance in any worthwhile function. Thus, giftedness might include not only the intellectually talented, but those with promise in mechanics, music, linguistics, social capacities, and artistic and physical areas, as well as the intellectually talented. Certainly it would include dramatics and creative writing.

DeHaan and Havighurst divided the intellectually gifted into two groups for educational purposes.[36] The highest 1 per cent they refer to as "first order or extremely gifted," and the remaining upper 10 per cent are the second-order gifted. They point out that the extremely gifted are very rare and probably deserve a different type of educational experience than the second-order gifted. The IQ may serve as a base instrument for the screening or pointing up of certain kinds of giftedness but at the same time, all teachers have the responsibility to attempt to determine the varieties of giftedness present in their classroom. Our plea is to use more than the IQ in the search for the gifted child.

The Handbook by Kough and DeHaan provides the teacher with a variety of observational techniques for discovering special abilities and disabilities.[37]

For the student especially interested in the gifted child, the following are recommended:

[36] R. DeHaan and R. Havighurst, *Educating Gifted Children* (Chicago: University of Chicago Press, 1957).

[37] J. Kough and R. DeHaan, *Teacher's Guidance Handbook I, Identifying Children Who Need Help* (Chicago: Science Research Associates, 1955).

Hollingsworth, L., *Children Above 180 I.Q.* New York: World Book Company, 1942.

Terman, L. M., *A Gifted Child Grows Up*. California: Stanford University Press, 1947.

Terman, L. M., et al., *Genetic Studies of Genius,* Vol. I. *Mental and Physical Traits of a Thousand Gifted Children.* California: Stanford University Press, 1925.

Witty, P., *A Genetic Study of Fifty Gifted Children,* Yearbook of the National Society for the Study of Education, 39 (II), 401–408.

In the past, gifted children have been more frequently found in racial groups offering superior economic, social, and educational opportunities, but exceptions have appeared, indicating that superior abilities can occur in any of the races or ethnic groups that compose the American population. Some studies have shown that puberty is reached somewhat earlier by the gifted than by the average child. Inadequacies of gifted children generally occur in subjects requiring motor coordination.

The gifted have presented special educational problems for the public schools. Since the number of gifted is always small in comparison to the total population, it has been difficult to devise an effective system to handle them. Early solutions were to accelerate the gifted by letting them enter school early and permitting them to proceed through school at a rapid rate, with early admission both to high school and college. Some school systems have provided special schools or special classes for these exceptional children. A more common plan is to enrich the gifted child's curriculum. He is given the opportunity to go into the material of the regular classroom at greater depth; he also broadens his horizon by being forced to evaluate and determine critically his own progress and to make creative contributions and reactions to the material he is studying.

SLOW-LEARNING CHILDREN

The slow-learning child is able to achieve extremely limited success in most school programs, which are geared to chronological age. Slow learners proceed through the schools with a continual set of limits on their capacities. Part of this group, referred to as the educable mentally retarded and the trainable mentally retarded, require special educational facilities. The goal for these children is to provide them with some minimum standards in the area of academic skills and maximum standards in caring for self and social adjustment.

The general IQ score used to denote the educable mentally handicapped is a rating between 50 and 80.

Mental maturation has been demonstrated to be a biological process which can seldom be forced through artificial means. Mentally retarded children, for instance, are rarely able to learn to read until their mental age has reached at least six years eight months to seven years.[38] It has been demonstrated that the mentally inadequate child not only has a slower process of intellectual development, but is also limited in his abilities to absorb and cope with a variety of situations. There is a definite limitation on both the qualitative and quantitative aspects of his capacity. Mental inadequacy, then, seems generally to be a biological restriction.

For educational purposes, the retarded have been divided into the following groups: those who can take regular classes and are considered to be dull-normal slow learners with IQ's perhaps between 75 and 85. The next group is the educable, who are marginally independent and have IQ's between 50 and 75. Trainable classes should be established for children whose IQ's are between 25 and 50. Children with IQ's below 25 need nursing care and are totally dependent.

CREATIVITY IN CHILDREN

Recent years have brought an increased interest in the subject of creativity. It is accepted that the traditional measures of intelligence measure at best only a few of man's abilities. If we are truly to seek out the creative child, we need to enlist a new set of measures. Torrance estimates that if we were to identify gifted children solely on the basis of intelligence tests, we would eliminate from consideration approximately 70 per cent of our most creative individuals.[39] The difference between creativity and high scores on intelligence tests is most clearly illuminated in Torrance's findings, in which the highly creative child was differentiated on the Minnesota Tests of Creative Thinking from the highly intelligent on the Stanford-Binet. In the group studied, the highly creative ranked in the upper 20 per cent on creative thinking, but not on intelligence, while the highly intelligent group ranked in the upper 20 per cent on intelligence but not on creativity. A very small overlapping group was high on both intelligence and creativity.

It has been suggested by leaders in the field, such as Torrance, that the guidance person in the schools might well play the role of sponsoring the creative child, providing an atmosphere for communication of the child's ideas and helping to see to it that the child's creative talent is recognized. Guidance personnel can assist parents and teachers to understand the child's divergence.

The creative child is one who is daring and courageous in his thinking. He is able to break away from conformity and is open to experiences. He

[38] C. Benda, "Psychopathology of Childhood" in *Manual of Child Psychology*, ed. L. Carmichael (New York: John Wiley & Sons, Inc., 1954), p. 1128.
[39] E. P. Torrance, *Guiding Creative Talent* (Englewood Cliffs, N.J.: Prentice-Hall, Inc., 1962).

is ready to have one thing lead to another. This child is curious, imaginative and inventive, an innovator. Traditional intelligence tests have placed a great stress on convergent thinking, where the individual who conforms is at an advantage. The Minnesota Tests of Creative Thinking and the tests by Getzels and Jackson place less stress on the traditional academic value system and a greater stress on divergent thinking.

Guilford has spent a considerable amount of time conceptualizing the creative-thinking ability and methods of assessment. The monograph by Guilford and Merrifield[40] summarized modifications of this theory. An examination of the factors now included in Guilford's conceptual framework is of interest. Sensitivity to problems is tested, for example, by asking the subject to suggest two improvements in a common appliance. In measuring word fluency, the individual is asked to write words that end with a specified suffix or words that begin with a specified prefix. For expressional fluency, the individual is asked to write a four-word sentence when the first letter of each word is given. For word arrangement, he is required to write sentences containing four specified words. For ideational fluency, he puts down as many ideas as possible or writes as many words as possible on a given topic. Evaluation of semantic, spontaneous flexibility occurs when the individual is asked to write a variety of uses for brick or to list peculiar uses for common objects. For originality, the child is asked to write clever titles for a story or to produce symbols to represent an activity or an object. This is only a small sample of the way in which Guilford has gone about conceptualizing and assessing creative thinking. However, it is apparent even from this small sample that if such tests were commonly used in the public schools we would be starting to differentiate a new type of exceptional child.

The Minnesota Tests of Creative Thinking have been divided into three categories—nonverbal tasks, verbal tasks using nonverbal stimuli, and verbal tasks using verbal stimuli. Torrance gives a detailed description of these tests.[41]

IMPLICATIONS

1. IQ differences between boys and girls are small enough to be considered unimportant.

2. Tests do not measure some aspects of mental activity. They must be considered as samples of behavior.

3. Grouping should not lull the teacher into believing that child study

[40] J. P. Guilford and P. R. Merrifield, *The Structure of Intellect Model: Its Uses and Implications,* Rep. Psychological Lab., No. 24 (Los Angeles: University of Southern California, 1960).

[41] Torrance, *Guiding Creative Talent.*

and individual needs have been taken care of through some superficial division of students.

4. A single intelligence test score does not predict a mental-growth pattern.

5. The great similarity between achievement and intelligence tests should serve as a caution when utilizing these measures to study "underachievement."

6. There are qualitative as well as quantitative differences in intelligence.

7. Instruction should be paced to the rate of mental growth. This implies that frequent measures be taken so that some knowledge of rate is given consideration.

8. Each classroom usually includes a large range in mental and intellectual ability.

9. There is evidence of various kinds of intelligence. Any adequate inventory of "intelligence" should take into account the existence of various types, and provision should be made for involving them all in the school setting.

10. Curves based on repeated tests of individuals over time vary from curves derived from averages of mental development. Individual graphing gives a more accurate picture of intellectual development.

11. Intelligence tests do not provide absolute measures in which points between measures on the scale are equivalent. We cannot consider growth in mental age from seven to eight to represent the same distance as mental age from nine to ten.

12. Tests at different age levels measure different functions. Caution should be used in making early predictions that have long-range implications for a child's placement.

13. The culturally rich home environment frequently has a favorable influence on intelligence test scores. Children who come from "culturally deprived homes" may need additional enrichment experiences to compete equally.

14. Intelligence is also subject to fluctuations related to the child's personal-social experiences and emotional life. Great fluctuations in scores should be studied in terms of factors influencing the fluctuation. The classroom teacher should be alert to her influence on these scores.

SUGGESTED READINGS

Articles

Bayley, N., "On the Growth of Intelligence," in *Human Learning in the School,* ed. J. DeCecco, p. 456. New York: Holt, Rinehart & Winston, Inc., 1963.

Combs, A., "Intelligence From a Perceptual Point of View," in *Educational Psychology,* ed. R. Loree, p. 122. New York: The Ronald Press Company, 1959.

Davis, A., "Social-Class Influences Upon Mental Problem-Solving," in *Readings in Child Development,* eds. W. Martin and C. Stendler, p. 104. New York: Harcourt, Brace & World, Inc., 1954.

Torrance, E., "Factors Affecting Creative Thinking in Children: An Interim Research Report," in *Readings in Educational Psychology,* eds. W. Morse and G. M. Wingo, p. 188. Chicago: Scott, Foresman & Company, 1962.

Books

DeHaan, R. and R. Havighurst, *Educating Gifted Children.* Chicago: University of Chicago Press, 1957.

Hunt, J. McV., *Intelligence and Experience.* New York: The Ronald Press Company, 1960.

Torrance, E., *Guiding Creative Talent.* Englewood Cliffs, N.J.: Prentice-Hall, Inc., 1962.

9 EMOTIONAL DEVELOPMENT

The complex study of emotions provides us with a view of the vital subjective influences in the child's life. We observe Johnny's temper tantrum and contemplate the cause or purpose. We note that Mary at one moment seems quite mature and secure and at another displays seemingly unrelated, immature crying behavior. One of the most difficult aspects of child life for the adult to comprehend is the area of emotional development. And it is in this area of the emotions that the parent or teacher is frequently ineffective because of his own emotions and feelings. The adult who is either overly sensitive or excessively controlled has difficulty in developing empathy with the child's fluctuating emotional life, and hence difficulty in his interactions with the child.

What, then, is emotional maturity? Is it reached at a specific point in time, or is emotional development subject to considerable intraindividual variability? The child who is apparently mature and balanced in his emotional life suddenly becomes easily upset, resorting to temperamental outbursts. Is emotional development cyclic, like other forms of development? What are the symptoms of emotional maladjustment? How serious is thumbsucking, nail biting, enuresis, and other tensional outlets? What is the criterion of emotional maturity? What can the teacher do to help the child become more mature emotionally?

Sometimes we think emotion should be curbed and controlled; is it not also true that emotion can add to the richness of living? Some believe the schools should work within the curriculum to achieve maximum emotional development for all children.

What can administrators and teachers do to establish a healthy emotional climate within the school setting? How does emotional development relate to methods of discipline, and how do we go about encouraging control from within?

Adults must deal with a variety of emotional problems which are frequently developmental in nature. They need to develop an understanding of the problems of children's fears, temper, anger, jealousy, and anxiety and an insight into the importance of acceptance and affection in the development of the human being.

An increasing amount of psychosomatic defense seems to be developing in children. Excessive anxiety, aggressiveness, and dependency associated with childhood reactions to illness may require psychological treatment. We need to be alert to the relationship between some illnesses and emotions.

Fred is a fifth grader of average mental capacity and physical assets. In his relationships with peers and the academic task, he frequently becomes excessively disturbed and emotionally disorganized. He comes to school on the bus and upon disembarking finds that he must stand in line to get in the building. The delay annoys him, and he begins to push and shove in an attempt to advance himself through the door. The patrol boys resist, and he is referred to the principal's office for his rebellious and disobedient behavior with the appointed peer authorities. His approach to the principal is sullen and angry. No amount of understanding and acceptance seems to change Fred's attitude that people always have it in for him and are against him; the world is unfair. Sent to the classroom, he begins the school day. When a paper in arithmetic is returned, he is quite upset. The teacher has indicated that several problems were incorrectly done and must be redone. He is argumentative and feels this, too, is unfair.

Here, in short, is a brief rundown on a child who presents an emotional problem to the school and the classroom teacher.

Betty is a third grader. She appears to like school when things are going well. She is overly concerned about getting her work in on time and completing all the assignments correctly. Classroom tests and additional assignments tend to create some unusual anxiety. At times she has headaches and stomach aches, and requires excuses from class. Other types of psychosomatic indicators are manifested by this child.

---

1. What kind of information would you need to have about Fred and Betty in order to understand their behavior? What stimuli seem to provoke emotional behavior? If emotions are purposive, what might be the purpose of their behavior? Suggest some methods by which we might begin to change Fred's or Betty's relationship with peers and the school task.

Any observation of children's behavior immediately reveals great individual differences in emotional reactions. The differences are as wide in range as differences in the physical and intellectual areas. Most important of all is the fact that children react differently to the same type of emotional stimulus. Their past experiences and concept of self tend to have a significant effect upon the meaning of the emotional situations that occur in their lives.

THE NATURE OF EMOTION

Although the term emotion is freely used, its precise definition is difficult to set forth. Emotions involve feelings, impulses toward action, and the subjective element of perception that produces the feelings and impulses.[1] For our purposes, expressions of feelings that exceed mildness and become intense will be considered as emotion. Emotions play a significant role in the development of the child. Some believe that emotion is prior to all experiences and is fundamental to them to the extent that all learning is acquired in emotional terms. We tend to act on the basis of how we have perceived the situation, and this state of feeling has a significant effect on our total perception and behavior. The total organism is involved in emotions, which have some physiological concomitants.

We should think of emotions positively as well as negatively. Emotions can be disorganizing or a source of motivational energy; they can give richness and vitality to the individual's actions. Feelings can be pleasant as often as they are unpleasant. The range of response in the emotional life of any given individual is great.

Emotions might be described in terms of the movement they inspire between people. Adler believed that emotions were accentuations of character traits and that like character traits they had a goal and a direction. From this point of view, emotions occur whenever they are appropriate to the given style of life and the behavior pattern of the individual. The purpose of emotions, then, is to modify to his benefit the situation of the individual in whom they occur.[2]

Emotions can be viewed as moving the individual toward people as well as against or away from people. Adler used the term disjunctive and conjunctive emotions. He described disjunctive emotions as those which tend to separate us from people. Anger and sadness would be examples of disjunctive emotions. Conjunctive emotions, such as joy, sympathy, and modesty, join us with people.

Jersild speaks of negative and positive emotions. Negative emotions—anxiety, fear, and anger—occur when the individual's self is threatened; positive emotions occur when the individual's goals are enhanced and he feels secure.

Study of emotions shows that reactions are highly individualized or personalized. From child to child different situations elicit humor, joy, fear, or anger. In each situation it is desirable to determine the reaction of other people to the child's emotional behavior. What is the effect of the emotion on peers, parents, and teachers? Sometimes merely by observing the con-

[1] A. Jersild, *Child Psychology*, 5th ed. (Englewood Cliffs, N.J.: Prentice-Hall, Inc., 1960).

[2] A. Adler, *Understanding Human Behavior* (New York: Harcourt, Brace & World, Inc., 1927), p. 265.

sequences of the emotion it is possible to determine, to an extent, the goal or direction of the emotion.

---

2. Observe children at free play, with parents or in the classroom. Note carefully the effect of the child's emotion on peers and adults. Can you determine the goal of some emotional behavior?

PHYSIOLOGICAL CHANGES DURING EMOTION

Changes, which can be readily identified, occur in the functioning of the physiological processes of the body during an emotional experience. The hypothalamus and the autonomic nervous system coordinate the expression of emotional reaction. As the child develops, the emerging process of differentiation affects the feelings and the methods of expression. The self concept and increasing cognitive capacities produce the differential interpretation of events which involve the self. A child may be able to control outward manifestations of anger, fear, or jealousy, but the physiological changes are to a great extent outside of his control. In the emergency fear pattern, for example, the circulatory system becomes more efficient owing to the rise in pulse rate and blood pressure. The individual has an increased amount of energy as a result of the secretion of adrenalin and glucose. The digestive and salivary processes of the body are inhibited, and hence make little demand on the body. These changes, sometimes referred to as the emergency pattern or adaptation pattern, prepare the body for combat or flight.

Great individual differences in the intensity of emotional and physiological responses that accompany emotional behavior can be observed among children. Research reveals that the major emotions are associated with distinct patterns of autonomic reactions.[3] While emotions are highly variable, variance within the individual is less than the range found among individuals in the total population.[4] Some children appear unruffled and undisturbed even in distress; others appear to be under emotional tension more often than not. These variations seem to be due to the physiological organism and the individual's past environmental and cultural situations. Some children seem to inherit a physiological system that is more sensitive. Even at birth great differences in temperament and emotional reaction can be noted. It has also been discovered that children who grow up in environments which they perceive to be secure, nonthreatening, and

[3] A. Ax, "The Physiological Differentiation between Fear and Anger in Humans," *Psychosomatic Medicine* 15 (1953), 433–42.
[4] J. Lacey and R. VanLehn, "Differential Emphasis in Somatic Response to Stress," *Psychosomatic Medicine* 14 (1952), 71–81.

accepting generally experience fewer instances of strong disintegrative emotion.

Certain factors associated with poor health, hunger, and fatigue, tend to predispose the child to emotionality. If the child has insufficient opportunity to rest or if his physiological food needs are not met, he is more predisposed to the disintegrative type of emotion.

---

3. How do you account for the relatively great range in temperament and emotional response in children? What do research findings say about these individual differences?

FUNDAMENTAL EMOTIONAL NEEDS

In understanding children it is important to recognize the significance of need theory. Fundamental needs are not only organic but include psychological needs which have developed during the process of socialization and the emergence of self. Individual needs of the child serve as the basis for his educational experience.

Needs arise from the interaction of the child with his total psychological field. They are individualized and are as unique as the numerous situations which the child experiences. Snygg and Combs have attempted to define needs from a phenomenological point of view. They hypothesize one basic need, which would encompass all of the varied human needs, "for the maintenance and enhancement of the self."[5]

In this sense psychological needs arise in connection with the protection and development of the self. In education the teacher helps each child to become aware of his own needs, and then utilizes them in the motivational process. Discovering and defining his own needs can serve as the child's basis for educational progress.

---

4. How can the teacher identify needs in the classroom? What processes are available to assist the child in developing a greater awareness of his needs?

Numerous lists of basic human or emotional needs have been developed. We shall discuss needs in terms of three primary areas—physiological or organic, social, and self.

Physiological needs are basic and include the need for air, food, water,

[5] A. Combs and D. Snygg, *Individual Behavior*, rev. ed. (New York: Harper & Row, Publishers, Inc., 1959), p. 58.

clothing, shelter, and adequate rhythm between activity and rest. The school must be aware of these needs in working effectively with the child. When a fundamental physiological need is ignored, the educational process is usually interfered with. In some instances, where children's basic physiological needs have not been met, the school and other social agencies may have to arrange for them in order for the child to function in an educational setting.

Social needs involve the interpersonal relationships it is essential for the child to establish with both peers and adults. These needs would include love, acceptance, and belonging.

Each child should be loved and accepted as he is, preferably within the home situation from parents and siblings. However, some children do not receive acceptance and love in the home, and, as a result, the teacher, in his relationship with the pupil, must compensate somewhat for this lack in the acceptance he shows the child. The student's knowledge that the teacher is concerned and interested in him as an individual is an integral part of the affectionate relationship. The student benefits from this good human relationship.

Belonging is another social need. The child needs to be a part of the group and to feel both acceptance and identification with others. Much psychological stability comes from membership in a group and the place held within it. Belonging is a basic human need with which the teacher must be concerned. The development of sociometric techniques makes it possible for each teacher to understand somewhat more effectively than previously the social relationships within the class and to assist in arranging relationships which do more to enhance and maximize the feeling of belonging in each child.

Self needs include the needs for independence, recognition, and self-direction. Each child needs to feel able to take responsibility. The child wants to feel that he can make some decisions for himself. The level of decision is not immediately as important as the provision of increasing opportunities to make decisions as he grows and matures.

The child also needs recognition. He requires success in some areas and recognition of his success by others, both peers and significant adults. Other children's acknowledgment of assets of an individual child helps him find his place within the social group. When the teacher points to the child's assets and strengths, a positive relationship is begun, increasing his feelings of security and relative freedom from threat.

Lawrence K. Frank is most frequently associated with the development of the fundamental needs theory in relationship to children. Among the important needs Frank would add for our consideration are protection from unnecessary deprivation, acceptance as a unique individual, freedom to grow at one's own rate, reassurance and affection during the early training and feeding experiences, assistance in accepting authority and external regulations, and warmth of mothering at home and in the school.[6] Frank saw these needs as basic for all children.

Needs are always considered within a specific culture and psychological setting. The man who most advanced the construct of needs in the sociocultural setting was Robert J. Havighurst. His concept of developmental tasks covers a combination of needs personally felt in the individual's society. For Havighurst, developmental tasks which rise out of the needs of the individual within his social environment serve as a criterion for satisfactory development in a specific culture. Success in developmental tasks leads to adjustment and success with later tasks; failure leads to disapproval by the social group, maladjustment, and difficulty with later tasks. The concept of developmental tasks provides us with a basis for the utilization of need theory. As we have already seen, they set up broad criteria for the measurement of educational goals relevant to the needs of children.

Meeting these basic needs is vital for the proper development of the individual. Security, belonging, recognition, approval, status, and independence all are basic to the mental health of the child. The child must have relationships in which he can be certain that he is understood and accepted for what he is. Such status and approval make him free to take on responsibility and move in the direction of self-realization. Sometimes this type of acceptance comes from the peer group outside of the school setting; other times it comes in the family relationships. When it is not supplied outside the school, however, acceptance in the school by the teacher and by the child's classmates becomes an especially important element in the child's emotional development. Both teacher and parent should be aware of basic needs in general and the specific basic needs of the individual child. Whenever a developmental problem arises, a good beginning is to determine whether the child has any unmet basic needs.

---

5. On the basis of several observations and your study of a school-age child, describe the way in which you feel his basic needs are met in the setting in which you have observed him. You might also infer from his behavior how you feel his basic needs in general are being met. Which developmental tasks for this child need particular attention?

A DEVELOPMENTAL THEORY OF EMOTIONS

Emotional development is a product of both maturation and learning. Gesell, in particular, emphasized the importance of the maturational elements in emotional development. Gesell believed that emotions could be fully understood only in relationship to the total developmental pattern

[6] L. K. Frank, "The Fundamental Needs of Children," *Mental Hygiene,* July 1938, pp. 353–79.

and the maturational effects. Since maturation was essential for the child's physiological and mental growth, it followed, he felt, that it was also a key to understanding emotional growth. Maturation, for instance, plays a significant role in influencing the development of intelligence in the child. It also affects his height, weight, strength, and motor coordination. All of these attributes have an effect on the child's self concept and his relationship with others.

Emotional development takes on a pattern as the child matures. Gesell developed a set of typical behavioral expectations and affective attitudes which accompany emotional maturing. While these descriptions were linked to specific chronological ages, they are best understood as portraying the sequences of development. The reader interested in such descriptions will find them presented in detail in the publication by Arnold Gesell and Frances Ilg.[7]

As the individual's growing capacities emerge, his emotional behavior may change as an accompaniment of the total growth effect. For example, as the child increases in physical strength and intelligence, he may be less afraid of things which previously brought a fear response; the same situations may evoke a more pleasant response.

Emotional development proceeds from the relatively undifferentiated emotional responses of the infant up through what has been termed as emotional maturity. Bridges developed the schematic approach to understanding emotional development that is illustrated on the following page.

Figure 9-1 illustrates how emotional development proceeds from relatively undifferentiated excitement at birth to the early differentiation between distress and delight by about three months of age and the eventual full complement at age two of fear, disgust, anger, jealousy, distress, excitement, delight, joy, elation, affection for adults, and affection for children. By age five we are able to distinguish the emotions of shame, anxiety, fear, disgust, disappointment, anger, envy, distress, jealousy, excitement, hope, delight, joy, elation, affection for children, and affection for adults.

---

6. How are growth gradients in emotional development of value to parents and teachers? How might they be misleading?

When the child reaches school age, he must adjust to a whole new environment. School frequently arouses mixed feelings about necessary adjustments to work tasks, a new significant adult, and a new set of peers. These emotional upsets decrease as the child learns to master his environ-

[7] A. Gesell and F. Ilg, *Child Development* (New York: Harper & Row, Publishers, Inc., 1949), pp. 289–91.

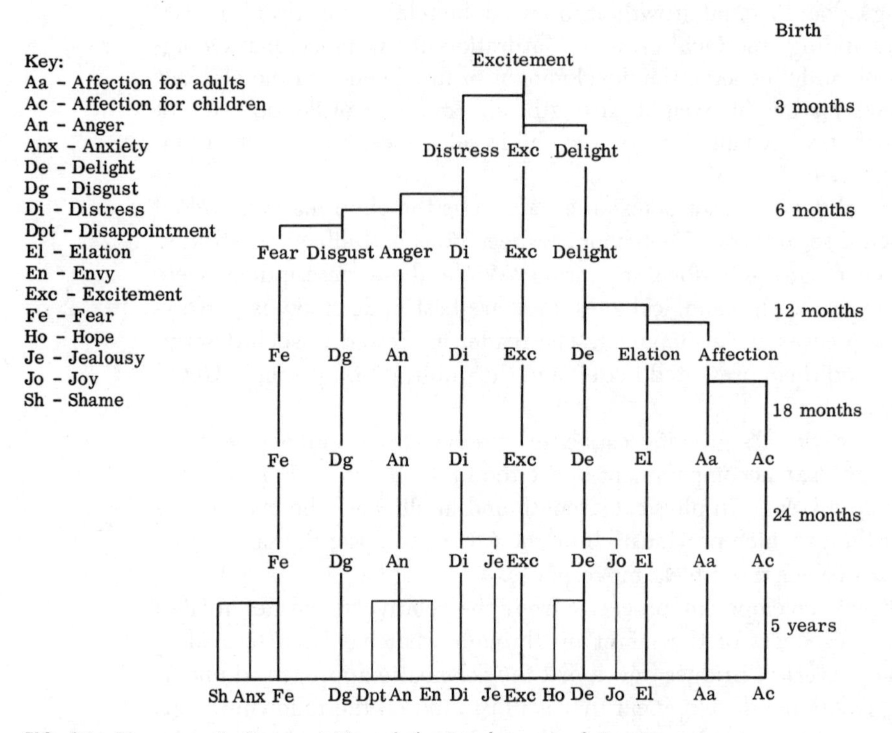

FIG. 9-1 Diagrammatic Representation of the Development of Emotion

Combined from two diagrams by K. M. B. Bridges, *Journal of Genetic Psychology,* 37 (1930), 524 and *Child Development,* 3 (1932), 340. From H. B. English, *Dynamics of Child Development,* p. 114. New York: Holt, Rinehart & Winston, Inc., 1961.

ment and begins to feel competent socially. Teachers of kindergarten and primary children need to be masters of understanding and empathy. At the same time, they must assist the children eventually to accept the new relationships and new expectations.

Emotional behavior at birth is quite diffuse and totally lacking in differentiation. Research has shown that no definite emotional patterns can be detected in the overt responses of infants to a variety of situations, such as the sudden loss of support, restraint, or delay in feeding. During the first weeks of life, the most common response is one of general agitation, without a specific relationship to the stimulus. However, the fact that some infants respond to provocation and others do not indicates a tremendous variety of individual differences in emotions already present at the time of birth.[8]

[8] F. Ilg and L. Ames, *Child Behavior* (New York: Harper & Row, Publishers, Inc., 1955), p. 157.

Gesell found that at the age of a month the child would give different discomfort cries for hunger or pain, and that delight or pleasure, characterized by a smile or a vocal expression began by the age of three months. However, some feel that emotional behavior in neonates is not truly patterned. About the time the child is six months of age, distress is frequently differentiated into anger, disgust, or fear. At this age the child withdraws from an unfamiliar person whom he might previously have accepted on the same terms as a close relative. About this time he also begins to distinguish facial expressions and verbal cues. He is quite aware of the friendly face or the threatening voice. From this period on, emotional responses become increasingly differentiated. By one year the child is elated in response to events or persons for which he feels delight; for example, he will show a pleased reaction to the stimulus of the bottle or to someone who is ready to play with him. By eighteen months, jealousy appears as a further differentiation of the child's distress. At this time his affection for adults becomes somewhat different from his affection for other children. The process of emotional development, then, moves from generalized excitement to differentiation and discrimination.

At a fairly early age, some believe by the age of three, the basic emotional behavior patterns have been well-established. Thereafter, most changes in basic emotional behavior patterns are a result of specific environmental changes.

The child's emotions differ from an adult's. They are simple and spontaneous. Typically, the young child's emotions last a short time and then end, perhaps even abruptly. The young child may be quite intense in showing elation or fear, much more intense than is common in a more mature individual. Children's participation in events generally has a more emotional basis than adults'. Children react subjectively to experiences, and their responses are frequently emotional. The child is not as able to conceal his true feelings and emotions as the adult. The child's feelings are more on the surface, and his emotions can be detected by his appearance, tension, or psychological movement.

FACTORS PREDISPOSING THE INDIVIDUAL TO EMOTIONALITY

Responsibility for the appearance of excessive disintegrated emotion rests with various factors, including physical condition and health, intelligence, social environment, and family relationships. The child who is affected by poor health and who is easily fatigued may exhibit excessive excitement or emotionality. Mothers frequently notice that when a child is off his usual eating or sleeping schedule he is more irritable.

Children who are more intelligent than the average tend to have a broader perception of the world, which enables them to perceive and comprehend the great variety of emotions from the serious to the ridiculous, the tragic to the humorous, and thus to participate in a wider range of emotions.[9] The child who comes from a continually tense social environment in which interpersonal pressures within the family and extreme disciplinary methods are utilized, tends to be more emotional.

The child who is spoiled, neglected, or overprotected in the family tends to display inappropriate emotional behavior.

The position in the family constellation has an obvious effect on the child's emotionality; dependent upon the psychological position the child has different challenges and expectations from other members of the family. Certain competition within the siblingship causes tension. The oldest child who is always expected to be responsible and stay ahead of the siblings may have more situations in which he is expected to prove himself.

---

7. Observe some children in a nursery or other preschool setting. Are there already great individual differences in emotionality? How do you attempt to account for these differences?

THE ROLE OF LOVE IN HUMAN DEVELOPMENT

In order for the child's emotional life to develop adequately, he must feel loved. The amount of affection given to the child during the early years of life seems to be related to the kinds of relationships which he can eventually form with other individuals. The security that the infant gets when his needs are met and the emotional relationship with the mother is satisfactory are vital during early infancy.

Research by Goldfarb and Spitz indicates that children institutionalized during infancy who do not experience consistent "mothering" become apathetic and socially unresponsive.[10] They point up the importance of relatively consistent gratification from some person.

Renee Spitz also tells of an experiment in a nursery and a foundling home. The nursery children were raised by their mothers; those in the foundling home were cared for by overworked personnel. Both institutions provided adequate food, medical attention, and housing. Results showed that the nursery children developed normally, but 37 per cent in

[9] F. Holmes, "An Experimental Study of the Fears of Young Children," eds. A. Jersild and F. Holmes, in *Children's Fears,* Child Development Monograph 20 (1935), 167–296.

[10] W. Goldfarb, "Psychological Deprivation in Infancy and Subsequent Adjustment," *American Journal of Orthopsychiatry,* 15 (1945), 247–55; and R. Spitz, "Hospitalism: An Inquiry into the Genesis of Psychiatric Conditions in Early Childhood," *Psychoanalytic Study of the Child,* I (1945), 53–74.

the foundling home died during the two-year observation. This condition has been titled "Marasmus," indicating that the child is completely starved for affective emotional interchange.[11]

Affection shown the child during his first years of life, then, is of extreme importance. One of the most important functions of the parent is to transmit a genuine feeling of love and concern. When the child feels a severe lack of affection, he is often prone to such destructive tendencies as suspiciousness, fear, and aggression.

The role of love and affection in the child's development is most significant. Being loved gives the child his basic security; being valued as he is becomes vital for complete acceptance. When the child feels loved he is more able to accept himself and others. He no longer needs to reassure himself of his worth but is free to extend himself to others. His social interest is cultivated.

Being loved permits the child to identify with peers, parents, and the culture.

The mature self feels love, acceptance, and belonging to the extent that it can extend love and acceptance to others. Love is manifested in happiness, satisfaction, affection, and a greater capacity to enjoy the experiences of life. The individual has a feeling of desiring to please, wanting to give and serve.

Love permits the individual to be more completely spontaneous, and to lower his guard. Love is a relationship comparatively free of striving. Self-actualized love is characterized to an extent by a reduction of the defenses and greater honesty. The accepting emotional climate frees one from the damaging effects of hostility and anxiety.

Maslow believes that psychological health comes from being loved.[12] The self-actualized individual has both the power to love and the ability to be loved.

The climate of feeling in the home provides the original source for the child's development of self and his feelings of adequacy. A climate of love enables the child to develop more adequate concepts of self, society, and the world.

EMOTIONAL MATURITY

Psychologists differ considerably in their emphasis on the role of maturation in the development of emotional behavior. Gesell believed that maturation is responsible for the gradual evolution of emotional expression in infants and children. He strongly disagreed with the view that emo-

[11] R. Spitz, "Motherless Infants," *Child Development*, 20 (1949), 145–55.
[12] A. Maslow, *Motivation and Personality* (New York: Harper & Row, Publishers, Inc., 1954).

tional development is largely a phenomenon of social stimulation. According to Gesell, maturation influences the expression of emotion through the development of capacities, rather than through the ripening of a specific, innate response pattern. Jones demonstrated that while visceral components of emotional response are not highly correlated with the vigor of vocal and motor components during the neonatal period, this correlation is increased in preschool children, indicating that the integration of various aspects of emotional development are dependent partially upon maturation.[13]

For Gesell, as the individual became more adequate physically, intellectually, and socially through the development of his capacities, there was a concomitant emotional growth. Outside control gradually disappears as the child's emotions mature, and ultimately the emotionally mature individual is able to function on the basis of inner controls. In our culture growing up requires that the child relate in a certain way, express his anger in a controlled manner, and learn a number of other culturally approved expressions of emotion. Thus, a considerable amount of our emotional behavior is learned and related to a specific culture.

Additional emotional development occurs within the educational process of the schools.

Emotional maturity is always relative. A five year old has emotional maturity if he is capable of the emotional behavior we judge fitting for a five year old. Emotional maturity, however, develops throughout life. It is also a form of maturity from which one can regress most quickly. The child becomes more emotionally mature as the parent permits him to accept responsibilities and become independent and self-sufficient.

Jersild presents one of the most comprehensive lists of the stages involved in the child's moving toward maturity in the emotional area.

"A change from being a creature who at first receives much, gives little, to one who is capable of giving as well as of receiving, and capable of learning to get enjoyment from giving.

Development of capacity to identify oneself with a larger social group, and the ability to participate emotionally in the fortunes of the larger group.

Development from the status of being the child of the family to the status, ultimately, of being able to have children of one's own and, along with this development, a capacity to exercise the feelings and attitudes involved in being a parent psychologically, whether or not one is a parent biologically.

Progressive sexual development and the capacity after puberty for enjoying mature sex experiences.

[13] H. E. Jones, "The Galvanic Skin Reflex as Related to Overt Emotional Expression," *American Journal of Psychology*, 47 (1935), 241–51.

An increased capacity for bearing the inevitable sufferings and pains connected with life and growth without feeling abused.

An increased capacity for sympathy and compassion as one assimilates the meaning for self and others of the joys and vicissitudes of life."[14]

Emotional maturity, then, is not a state in which all problems are solved but, instead, is a continual process of clarification and evaluation, an attempt to integrate feeling, thinking, and behavior.

---

8. Since emotional maturity is an important facet of development, how might we measure it? Are there any practical child-study techniques through which the school might assess whether the child is developing adequately in this area? What expectations of emotional maturity might the teacher have in grade two that would differ from expectations in grade six?

HELPING THE CHILD'S EMOTIONAL GROWTH

Emotional development is an individual matter. No two children ever react in exactly the same manner or make the same responses to the same environmental situation. They actually do not have the same experience. Their temperament, past experiences, primary reactivity pattern, and personalized reaction influence their responses. Whether a child will respond with fear, anger, joy, or delight to a given stimulus probably depends on his past experiences, his present psychological condition, and his feeling of security. The child must be known intimately and individually before we can help guide him in his emotional growth.

Individual social and emotional behavior patterns are quite apparent in almost any group of children. There is the happy, confident, spontaneous individual who reacts naturally to both children and adults. He is cheerful, emotionally stable, and feels loved and secure. He does not need to be first or the most in order to be a success. Another type is the aggressive bully, who is always challenging or terrorizing others. He is rude, loud, acting out, and aggressive. He is frequently bossy and boisterous. Inwardly, he is afraid and insecure, fearful that he is not accepted or wanted. This child is frequently the product of a broken home where he has no place. There is also the shy, withdrawn individual who feels unacceptable, different, and lacking in self-confidence. Believing himself to be inadequate and a failure, he withdraws to books and other activities which do not require social interaction. In some way or other the significant others in his life have failed to accept this child as he is.

[14] A. Jersild, "Emotional Development," in *Manual of Child Psychology*, ed. L. Carmichael (New York: John Wiley & Sons, Inc., 1954), pp. 861–62.

It is important, then, for all of us to recognize the general patterns observable in emotional development. At the same time, we need to see the individualized pattern and the manner in which a specific child is seeking to satisfy his needs. For emotional development to proceed adequately, there should be available sufficient love, encouragement, and guidance. It is not merely a matter of suppressing and inhibiting emotional reactions. Instead, we need to be concerned about ways to rechannel the emotions to make them most effective in the development of the child. When we note the child who is fearful, angry, or sullen, we might suspect that this behavior has been reinforced in his interpersonal relationships. We can assume, too, that the happy, confident, joyful, and secure child has been encouraged in his behavior.

We must provide experiences that enable children to satisfy their basic needs in a manner which is socially acceptable and which stimulates and produces emotional growth.

Children can be assisted toward emotional maturity when we keep the channels of communication open between them and the significant adults in their life. The child must feel free to talk openly with either parent or teacher. He must feel that when he has a concern, some adult who values him is also concerned and can provide him with an opportunity for self-expression and clarification.

We need also to become most sensitive to the feelings of the individual. This requires knowing the way in which a child feels about his position within the group and in relationship to his own successes and failures. Many children need a substantial amount of encouragement in order to feel adequate themselves. It is also necessary to find ways to work more effectively with children in the encouragement of emotional expression.

Children's play is a significant part of their life. They should have opportunities to explore and express their feelings through play activity.

The clarification of feelings can occur through planned group discussion, role playing, and group counseling. This affords the child the opportunity to grow and develop in self understanding.

---

9. What are some appropriate ways by which a community, parents, or the school might facilitate emotional development? Can you think of any hindrances to this development in communities you know?

SYMPTOMS OF UNSATISFACTORY EMOTIONAL DEVELOPMENT

How can the parent or teacher know when a specific child's emotional development is seriously retarded and needs special attention? The signs are not as definite and clear-cut as in the areas of physical and intellectual development; still sufficient cues are present to indicate that a child has special problems in regard to emotional maturity. Evidence is usually present when the child's emotional responses are out of context or away from reality of what one might expect in response to a given stimulus. Johnny is far too angry; Susie is much too fearful.

The teacher frequently is in a better position than the parent to detect emotional maladjustment. In the classroom he has a wide range of behavior available through the actions of the children in a given chronological age range. The child who is deviant usually stands out.

If you keep in mind the basic needs and the developmental tasks, a ready guide is available in terms of the lack of facility by which an individual child solves the tasks and meets his needs. When a child is not achieving satisfactorily the developmental tasks of his age level, we can expect to note some symptoms of emotional maladjustment. Recognizing that each child must accomplish the work tasks of life by taking on responsibility in the home and in the school and the social tasks of getting along with peers and significant adults provides a criterion for satisfactory emotional development.

Some of the more common symptoms of unsatisfactory emotional adjustment include resistance to learning, speech problems, excessive daydreaming, oversensitivity, extreme dependence on peers or adults, resistance to the requirements of the classroom or the group, temper tantrums, overaggressive behavior, excessive dishonesty, crying, nervous tics, and withdrawal from the group.

Teachers are exposed to children who show some of these symptoms in varying degrees. However, whenever symptoms become extreme, you may be certain that interpersonal adjustment requires attention. These children produce this behavior because they are not happy with themselves. Deviant behavior is really a sign that the child needs help.

---

10. Observe a given age level in a school setting for several weeks. Attempt to see the children functioning in a variety of tasks. What evidence of unsatisfactory emotional development do you detect? Is any of this evidence serious? Discuss how the teacher might become more aware of emotional deviates in the specific classroom setting.

THE MANAGEMENT OF EMOTIONAL PROBLEMS

Every teacher works with children whose emotional problems interfere with school progress and personal-social development. These are children who cannot accept their responsibilities, peers, or teachers. Some statistics indicate that one out of every ten children born will present some serious emotional difficulty during his lifetime. Our challenge, then, is in the preventive field.

One of the basic requirements is early identification of the problems so that first-aid measures can be utilized.

Maladjustment may present itself in aggressiveness or withdrawal. It can especially be noted in failure to function socially and academically or in an inability to fulfill other responsibilities or developmental tasks.

Teachers should learn to recognize the cues and symptoms of maladjustment and faulty emotional development that children frequently provide. Teachers are very alert to some of these signs because they interfere with the teacher's control of the group. These signs include uncooperativeness, bullying, rebellion, dishonesty, and destructiveness.

Other equally serious symptoms are not so disturbing to the typical teacher and hence are frequently unnoticed. These include shyness, fearfulness, anxiety, daydreaming, overconscientiousness, compulsiveness, easy discouragement, and extreme sensitivity.

Other symptoms with emotional significance include thumbsucking, stuttering, nail biting, truancy, extreme competitiveness, depression and fearfulness, dissatisfaction with school and self, or rejection by peers.

The teacher is frequently confronted with these emotional problems in the classroom. It is important that he understand the child's general background and the teacher's effect upon him, in order to manage the situation successfully. In every instance, the teacher must first seek the meaning of the behavior. What is the child trying to communicate to me, to the group, and to the significant adults concerned with his actions? The aggressive, quarreling child needs to have limits set. He must experience the natural or logical consequences of his misbehavior. He needs to discover that aggressive behavior does not accomplish his goal and that a more satisfactory method of interpersonal contact is necessary.

The fearful child may be the product of conflict in previous unhappy experiences. Some of his fear may come from association with similar situations and a generalization by him to all teachers, all classrooms, all reading situations, or all arithmetic problems. In the school-age child, there may be considerable fear of failure and resulting humiliation. Children are also sometimes responsive to the fears and concerns of their parents. You may anticipate that each of the ages and stages of development brings about characteristic fears.[15] At the same time, it is the teacher's role to attempt to understand causation and purpose. This is where the observable elements related to fears need to be examined. Certainly, a major educational task is to develop skills in dealing with these fears. With increased skill and confidence, the child has practical ways of dealing with the feared situation. Many times the opportunity to participate, under guidance in a feared situation, helps relieve the anxiety and concern.

Teachers and parents also have responsibility to avoid creating fears by

[15] Ilg and Ames, *Child Behavior*.

threats and punishment. The fear of failure and of humiliation, the setting of unrealistic levels of aspiration, all tend to produce an unnecessary amount of fear and concern in the child. Most children overcome their fears as they become better informed and learn to understand, at least in part, the causes of things which they had feared.

We should also be concerned about the child who withdraws, who tends frequently to play alone or stay by himself not only at school but also at home. He has few friends, limited interests, and participates in few activities. His major satisfactions appear to come from daydreaming and a make-believe world of his own. These children generally feel inadequate and incapable of functioning effectively within the group. They have a faulty concept of self. The teacher's most important role is to help meet their needs and stimulate their courage.

Nonlearning disabilities, ranging from being slightly behind the class to a serious deviation from the grade norm, are frequently emotionally related difficulties. In some children failure to learn permits them to remain weak and helpless and to continue receiving additional service from parents and teachers. They cannot see any advantage in becoming mature in these areas and, in contrast, find many secondary gains in lack of functioning. This may also be a method of revenge on their parents, of showing them that he cannot be forced to function. The child who does not want to learn cannot be made to learn. He can be assisted by clarifying his goal. Awareness of his goal is the basis for change. The child is helped as he is accepted and comes to realize his abilities and alternative methods of functioning.

Speech problems are also bound into the total personality and emotional development of the child. We can note the child's concept of self, from his manner of speaking. His very tone of voice conveys his feeling about self. We can quickly tell the discouraged child from the self-confident one. A stuttering child is frequently a passive, submissive individual. He seldom is independent or able to make decisions on his own. He is concerned about how his actions will affect others, and always awaits their decisions. Stuttering is a signal that the child may have a dependency and revenge relationship with the significant adults in his life. The child must be made to feel secure within his home and school environment in order to begin to function effectively in the speech area.

The temper tantrum is another emotional problem. This emotional display indicates that the child is out to show that he can do things his way and nobody can stop him. The child should never be allowed to accomplish his purpose through a temper tantrum. Observe closely what social and psychological movement is sought through the temper tantrum, and make sure it cannot be accomplished through a temperamental act.

Jealousy is another emotion that children need assistance with. It is usually composed of several feelings at once—love, anger, hate, fear, and failure. Jealousy among siblings and a competition for status in the family are frequently noticed. Sometimes the jealousy relates itself to possible or threatened loss of parental approval and affection. It is frequently noted in the classroom when the setup is so competitive that children are competing with each other to be superior or first.

The child who is overambitious will be continually beset with problems of jealousy. The most effective way to deal with jealousy is with preventive measures. If each child is treated as an individual and is not compared, some of the causal reasons for jealousy are removed. It is also important to recognize the assets of each child. Consistent discipline in an atmosphere of cooperation and mutual respect will go a long way in managing jealousy.

---

11. Talk with some parents or teachers, and determine what they consider to be the major developmental and emotional problems they have with their children. Plan a group discussion for the class to present methods for managing emotional problems.

THE CHILD USES EMOTIONS TO SERVE PURPOSES

Emotions are more than a force behind behavior. They can be used to serve the individual's purposes; they can have a definite direction and support the intention of the individual.

Emotions need to be considered beyond the mere surface behavior they produce. They should be observed in terms of the movement they create. What is the direction toward which the child is moving when he utilizes certain emotions? The goal directedness of emotions becomes more apparent when they are seen in their social context. The child may select certain emotions to provoke specific responses.

Emotions can be used in a variety of ways. They are frequently used to obtain power. Johnny has a temper tantrum and his mother gives in because she is socially embarrassed, confused, or unable to come up with an immediate solution. From this experience Johnny is encouraged and reinforced in the use of temper. Close observation reveals that temper tantrums are used exclusively when an audience is present. They are not repeated unless the child is assured that he can win through this method.

Anger is another method of obtaining control. The angry child can oppose or dominate. He obtains power as he forces people to respond to him. If other children or adults withdraw and become afraid when he is angry, he is encouraged to continue this behavior.

Sadness is a disjunctive emotion, which may make the child feel weak. He attempts to improve his position by capitalizing on his weakness. The child who is sad frequently finds his place made easier as a result of the display of sorrow. Special services and privileges are often accorded him.

There are many other ways in which the child can use emotions to serve his purposes. When we come to see emotion as social tools, we can observe the way in which they are used to manipulate people. The child quickly becomes aware of the mother's response to his cry, his anger, or any other emotionally toned act. The adult, then, can assist the child's maximal development by recognizing the purposiveness of emotional life and responding in a manner which assists the child to cooperate with people instead of seeking to control them.

---

12. Understanding emotions as forces and causes is quite different from seeing them as purposive and goal-directed. Identify the schools of thought in psychology which take contrasting positions. Take a stand on this issue, and defend your position.

UNDERSTANDING AND EVALUATING EMOTIONS

One of the most difficult areas for accurate measurement and research is the study of emotional development. Some attempts to investigate emotional behavior have been made through paper-and-pencil tests, such as the Children's Manifest Anxiety Scale; the Institute of Child Study Security Test, Toronto, Canada, and the Affectivity Interview Blank. Anecdotal records have also provided many insights into the development of emotions over time in a given individual. Projective tests, such as the Rorschach and varied children's apperception tests, are other ways of measuring, evaluating, and understanding the emotions.

A considerable amount of research has been conducted with the Children's Manifest Anxiety Scale, and extensive amounts of normative data are now available for it. The Scale has been used with elementary school children at all grade levels from second grade up. Scores on the CMAS have been found to be highly related to social inadequacy and dissatisfaction with self.[16] Generally, studies show that anxiety has an interfering effect on performance, although some studies indicated that under certain conditions anxiety facilitates performance on complex tasks. In children, anxiety is negatively related to scores on tests of creativity.

Fuller developed the Affectivity Interview Blank, which provides a quantitative measure of affective life.[17] She selected questions from a variety of published tests and developed an interview blank. Her findings seemed to indicate that generally the overt behavior of children as per-

[16] B. Phillips, F. King, and E. Jennings, "Influence of Intelligence on Anxiety and Perception of Self and Others," *Child Development,* 31 (1960), 41–46.
[17] E. Fuller, *Manual for the Affectivity Interview Blank* (Ann Arbor, Mich.: Ann Arbor Child Development Laboratories, University of Michigan, 1951).

ceived by teachers and observers has a definite relationship to the child's verbalized feelings about himself.

Projective methods, by attempting to get into the child's private world of feelings, have permitted us to understand his affective life. In a projective presentation, the stimulus itself does not have a definite meaning. The investigator is interested in what the stimulus means to the specific child. Through the projective technique, internalized feelings, private meanings and perceptions are given to the stimuli.

The teacher is not expected to become proficient in formal projective testing techniques, which are administered by people with special training, usually psychologists. The Rorschach is the most widely utilized projective technique. Others, which provide pictures that permit the child to associate and reveal his fantasy life about a situation, are also available.

Teachers utilize projective methods when they show children pictures of selected situations and ask them to write a story. The autobiography, completion of stories, sentence completion, and writing on a preselected theme also provide teachers with opportunities to use a modification of the projective technique.

Some teachers select cartoons or drawings of family or school situations and ask the child to develop a story about the picture. In this technique the child tells what happened before the picture, what is happening now, and how he feels the story will end. This permits the teacher through the theme of the story to see the way the child perceives life, and his general style of life.

THE SCHOOL'S ROLE IN EMOTIONAL DEVELOPMENT

There is a growing realization on the part of both national and state mental health groups that the schools must play a more active role in developing programs which stimulate positive mental health. The development of emotionally mature behavior is a goal of education. In arranging the total school program, school administrations must take into consideration the significance of the basic emotional needs. There is also an increased need for early recognition and identification of emotional disturbance. Each child needs to feel a sense of accomplishment and to be interested in some aspect of the school program.

The teacher is in continual interaction with the student. His words need to be carefully considered to provide the best effect. Sarcasm, physical violence, and ridicule are generally damaging to the emotional development of children. Teachers, too, need to understand when behavior is normal and when it is a symptom of something wrong. For example, crying by a five or six year old on the first day of school might be accepted as a normal phase of development. However, crying by an eight or ten year old over a minor physical hurt, or always bursting into anger over simple frustrations are definite cues that something is wrong. The cause for the emotional deviation should be sought, and when behavior is excessively immature, the services of a skilled guidance person should be obtained.

Whether or not teachers realize it, the emotional stability of children is to a considerable extent influenced by teacher behavior. The young child is sensitive to the teacher's attitude on a variety of school issues. A smile of approval or a few words of sincere praise and encouragement may provide the child with the feeling of adequacy which he needs. By the same token, the teacher's ridicule and criticism may lead to a sense of inferiority or anxiety. When the child cannot find satisfaction through active-constructive behavior, he frequently tries to solve his problem through utilization of the defense mechanisms. Some children adopt psychosomatic defects. Respiratory disorders, allergies, ulcers, skin reactions, and headaches are at times best understood in terms of psychological factors. Other children attempt to build up their own prestige by tearing down others. This is a definite sign of insecurity, and such a child needs to develop a sense of belonging or a feeling of achievement so that he no longer needs to attack others. Teachers should work to develop constructive means of seeing that each child's basic needs are met in the classroom.

The teacher is really in the key position for early identification of emotional disturbance. Bowers has presented some excellent suggestions to facilitate early identification.[18] In a research project in California, he found 10 per cent of a group of fourth-, fifth-, and sixth-grade children to be moderately to seriously handicapped emotionally. In order to insure a more adequate identification, Bowers developed a process for in-school screening by teachers. The method is based on teacher ratings, peer perceptions, and self-perception.

---

13. Obtain a copy of *A Process for In-school Screening of Children with Emotional Handicaps,* by E. Bower and N. Lambert, Educational Testing Service, Princeton, New Jersey. How practical do you feel this method is for the average teacher? Can you think of other methods of early identification?

Teachers need to recognize the place of emotion in the learning process. Mild emotion can serve as a tonic to the body, pep up the child's feelings, and should be utilized by the teacher. There should be real fun in the classroom. Learning should be an active and exciting experience. The

[18] E. M. Bowers, *Early Identification of Emotionally Disturbed Children in School* (Springfield, Ill.: Charles C Thomas, Publisher, 1960).

child should be emotionally involved in his work to the extent that he sees meaning in the tasks and derives some genuine joy from them.

The meaning of events between two individuals always depends on how things have been perceived. Meaning, then, is a function of the individual's perception of self in relation to the world, and his perception of his goals and potential for becoming. Emotions are not the result of stimuli, but of meanings that come from the cognitive process. The individual, as he comes to know himself and his world, sees by successive evaluation in his culture what the people he loves believe. He may internalize this into a value system and a set of goals.

If we understand emotions in these terms, we become more concerned about the way children feel and what meaning the classroom situation has for the individual. Of greatest concern to the school is the teacher who is neither interested in or capable of recognizing symptoms of emotional maladjustment. It is inexcusable when a teacher fails to comprehend serious personality maladjustments. The teacher whose personal maladjustment leads to conflicts and eventual amplification of undesirable behavior in children is another serious problem.

Obviously, there are no set rules on how to help children with their emotional problems. What works with one child is not successful with another. However, each teacher can at least contribute the ability and willingness to be empathic, to see things from the child's point of view. At the same time, the teacher needs to maintain a genuine interest in subject matter, the child, and the desire to help him. Finally, the teacher's fundamental respect for the child, no matter how inappropriate his present behavior, can serve as encouragement in the development of emotional growth.

The teacher's tasks in the area of emotional development involve the provision of a therapeutic atmosphere, or classroom climate. He must know what things to correct and what to ignore. The teacher is always involved as a group leader, and should integrate the whole class into a well-functioning unit. The goal is to develop an enthusiasm for the learning process. As a result, understanding of group dynamics and group discussions needs to be brought into play.

To facilitate the development of group discussions in the mental health area, Dr. Ralph Ojemann, University of Iowa, has developed a series of materials titled, *A Teaching Program in Human Behavior and Mental Health.*[19] These handbooks supply materials and suggestions to aid teachers in developing a curriculum in human behavior. The purpose of this material is to develop in children an understanding of the reasons for behavior.

[19] R. Ojemann, *A Teaching Program in Human Behavior and Mental Health* (Iowa City, Ia.: State University of Iowa, 1960).

Another pioneer in the field of bibliotherapy is Edmund Bullis, who developed a series of weekly lessons and discussion periods.[20]

In dealing with emotional development, the teacher must see the child in the setting of his emotional needs and developmental tasks and must differentiate immaturities and misbehaviors. He must attempt to understand the purpose of misbehavior. Once he has diagnosed the child's goals, he must be concerned about redirecting faulty goals and faulty convictions. In order to change a child's behavior, we must change the direction of his psychological movement. This can be accomplished most effectively by understanding the child's convictions about people, life, and work, and helping him develop alternative and more healthy convictions about human relationships. We must remember it is not the overt behavior we seek to change but the child's goals and purposes. This necessitates providing a consistent relationship of mutual trust and mutual respect to enhance development. This relationship provides the child with support. Confidence and faith in the individual must be shown and he must be encouraged to meet the tasks of life.

IMPLICATIONS

1. There is a wide range of individual differences in emotional behavior. The teacher must be able to differentiate problems that are developmental from problems which need early treatment.
2. The feeling state is fundamental to the understanding of an experience. Children more often respond to a feeling than to the objective stimulus.
3. Some illnesses in childhood have emotional overtones and may be related to a psychosomatic defense.
4. Although emotions are frequently considered in a negative sense, they also have positive attributes and should be utilized to energize the learning process.
5. Need theory can be more effectively utilized in the educational process if we assist the child to become aware of his needs and help him to work toward their fulfillment.
6. Every child needs to experience some relationship in which he is recognized and accepted for what he is, with no implication that it is necessary to conform, improve, or change to become acceptable.
7. The child's emotionality is frequently affected by health, social, and family factors which can be modified.
8. There is a basic need early in life for affective interchange between

[20] H. E. Bullis and E. O'Malley, *Human Relations in the Classroom* (Wilmington, Del.: Delaware State Society for Mental Hygiene, 1948).

the child and a mother figure. Lack of this emotional interchange can produce serious defects.

9. Emotional maturity fluctuates to a greater extent than other maturities. The schools need to develop more effective methods of appraising this type of maturity.

10. Adequate opportunity for self-expression in the home and school, permitting a child to reveal, explore, and clarify his feelings, is important for adequate emotional development.

11. Children give us many signs of faulty emotional development early in life. As we become more sensitive to understanding these signs and institute early preventive and remedial measures, the mental health problem of adults can be significantly reduced.

12. Significant adults in the child's life need to be aware of emotional problems they create through fear of failure, the setting of unrealistic levels of aspiration, and sarcasm and ridicule.

13. Many nonlearning disabilities are increasingly being recognized as emotionally involved disorders.

14. Emotions are not only caused, but purposive, and need to be understood in terms of their social effects.

15. The school must play a significant role in emotional development in terms of its total organization, objectives, attention to individual differences, and methods for early identification of emotional handicaps.

16. Research now points to the patterned nature of individual emotional development. The individual is predictable in emotional areas when we comprehend the pattern.

17. Emotional development is partially dependent upon maturation and cannot be forced.

SUGGESTED READINGS

Articles

Bower, E., "A Process for Identifying Disturbed Children," in *Readings in Educational Psychology,* eds. W. Morse and G. M. Wingo, p. 325. Chicago: Scott, Foresman & Company, 1962.

Frank, L., "The Fundamental Needs of the Child," in *Educational Psychology: A Book of Readings,* ed. A. Coladarci, p. 122. New York: The Dryden Press, 1955.

Raths, L., "Application to Education of the Needs Theory" in *Readings in Educational Psychology,* eds. W. Morse and G. M. Wingo, p. 67. Chicago: Scott, Foresman & Company, 1962.

Symonds, P., "Education and Psychotherapy," in *Readings in Educational Psychology,* eds. W. Morse and G. M. Wingo, p. 308. Chicago: Scott, Foresman & Company, 1962.

Books

Bettelheim, B., *Love Is Not Enough.* New York: Free Press of Glencoe, Inc., 1950.

———, *Truants from Life.* New York: Free Press of Glencoe, Inc., 1955.

Caplan, G., *Emotional Problems of Early Childhood.* New York: Basic Books, Inc., 1955.

Detjen, E. and M. Detjen, *Elementary School Guidance,* 2nd ed. New York: McGraw-Hill Book Company, 1963.

D'Evelyn, K., *Meeting Children's Emotional Needs.* Englewood Cliffs, N.J.: Prentice-Hall, Inc., 1957.

Jersild, A., *In Search of Self.* New York: Bureau of Publications, Columbia University, 1952.

———, *When Teachers Face Themselves.* New York: Teachers College, Columbia University, 1955.

Ojemann, R., *A Teaching Program on Human Behavior and Mental Health.* Iowa City, Ia.: State University of Iowa, 1960.

Prescott, D., *Emotion and the Educative Process.* Washington, D.C.: American Council on Education, 1938.

Wolf, A., *Helping Your Child's Emotional Growth.* New York: Doubleday & Company, Inc., 1954.

10 MOTIVATION AND DISCIPLINE IN CHILD DEVELOPMENT

Child study is basically directed toward answering the question, "Why does the child act as he does?" When you answer that question, you have the means to help the child make a satisfactory adjustment. An underlying element is motivation, which directs or channels behavior toward goals. Motivation includes incentives, which initiate and sustain goal-directed activity. Until you know specifically the individual's motives, you cannot work effectively with him.

The purposive nature of behavior has been established. Generally, the child does not work with real effort or enthusiasm unless an activity has a purpose for him. Conversely, purpose serves to create activity. Generally purposes are highly individualized. The individual may even be unaware of his purposes. To guide the child's development, however, we do need to determine purpose as far as possible.

Behavior is motivated; furthermore, it is influenced by biological, cultural, and situational determinants which exist in the total field. Much can be said about motivation in general, but the essential point to keep in mind in understanding behavior is the specific psychological field of the individual.

Bill, age six, is a problem for Mother at home. He does not get ready for bed at the time she sets. His table manners are poor, and he eats only the foods he prefers. Dressing is also a problem, and she usually ends up dressing him in order to get him off for required activities. These are but a few of the problems that Bill presents at home. In school, Bill responds to the teacher in a most apathetic manner. School problems are the teacher's problems, not his. He functions only in a limited set of activities that meet his particular interests. In many activities, he reports, "I can't do it."

An examination of Bill's behavior reveals some of the problems in understanding motives and purposes. Bill's characteristic approach to life apparently is to get other people to fit into his plans. He has obviously come to believe that when he does not function, others will function for him or excuse him from what is required. There has been much talk about what Bill should do, but he has seldom experienced the consequences of his failure to function effectively. Somebody always sees that he is awake early enough, adequately fed, and dressed in time. At school the teacher has so many other demands to meet that by default he is indulged in his role of inadequacy. As a result Bill has been permitted to establish not so much that he cannot function, but that he will not function.

Do not oversimplify Bill and his problems. He was chosen to illustrate some of the simple activities that are pertinent to an understanding of motivation and discipline. It is important to utilize theoretical knowledge about motivation in order to understand practical motivational problems both in the home and at school.

In dealing with the broad field of motivation, both causation and purposiveness must be explored. A good beginning might be to note the distinction between motivation and incentives. Incentives, unless intrinsic, are contrived from without and are much more limited in concept than motivation. Incentives may consist of a variety of extrinsic rewards. In parent-child contacts and interactions they most frequently assume the form of bargaining. "If you pick up the room, we can go to the movies," "If you help with the dishes I'll let you play ball," or some other, "If you do this, I will do that." This type of bargaining cannot develop long-range motives. It provides only temporary incentives, and is based on a system of rewards.

If you are interested in changing behavior, whether it be in the home or the school, you must seek to establish some link between the child's already existing motives and the goals of learning. You must align what he wants to do with what he is capable of doing. Too much present motivation has been directed toward extrinsic rewards. Before children are in school any length of time, they are directed toward working for grades and other types of external evaluations. It is interesting to observe a class of highly spontaneous, creative, and interested kindergarten or first-grade children and then observe that same class some five or six years later when they have been subjected to the "motivation" of grades and function mainly in response to external incentives. Ways must be found to utilize intrinsic motivation, performing for the enjoyment and satisfaction in the act, in contrast to extrinsic rewards.

When the child is directed by self-evaluation instead of external judgment, he becomes comparatively free to function. He is no longer limited by external standards.

---

1. Observe children in the beginning years of school and then in the upper grades. Do you notice any real difference in their motivation toward work? Observe ways in which parents in your neighborhood

motivate their children. A careful recording of anecdotes of parent-child interaction in relationship to mealtime, supervision of play, and bedtime will provide an interesting opportunity to study local motivational patterns. Propose some ways in which you might deal with these motivational problems of the school and the parents.

In attempting to understand motivation and the purposive nature of behavior, note that not all motives are conscious. People are unaware of some of their motives and unconsciously attempt to control impulses which would be painful if they were conscious. Developing insight into the nature of unconscious motivation aids in understanding the concealed problem. This is important because the repression of problems serves to increase tensions.

MOTIVATIONAL THEORY

Many early theories of motivation were almost exclusively mechanistic, tending to arise from a drive-reduction theory. A considerable amount of research work was done with animals. Such experiments are always subject to question since the nature of the animals used is generally quite different from the complexities of human beings. Learning in human beings does not generally occur under extreme drive conditions.

Some early motivational theory was related to the study of instincts and the work of McDougall. He credited motivation to specific tendencies, which he called instincts. Originally, many instincts were believed to be inherited. Today, however, most theorists believe that motivation is dependent on both physiological and psychological processes.

Maier has made a distinction between behavior that is goal-directed and behavior that is caused by frustration, and seemingly lacks a goal.[1] He states that frustration leads to abnormal forms of behavior that are not oriented directly toward goals, and that this should be distinguished from "motivated behavior." Maier itemizes three types of behavior: (1) behavior with goal orientation; (2) behavior resulting from frustration; and (3) reflexes and automatic behavior that are regulated mechanically by neural structures.

Harry F. Harlow's work with primates and learning is reported in an article titled, "Mice, Monkeys, Men, and Motives,"[2] in which he first presents an exhaustive study and critique of the drive-reduction theory. Har-

[1] N. Maier, *Frustration: The Study of Behavior Without a Goal* (New York: McGraw-Hill Book Company, 1949).

[2] H. Harlow, "Mice, Monkeys, Men, and Motives," *Psychological Review,* 60 (1953), 23–32.

low emphasized the importance of the child's curiosity and investigatory motives, and indicates that any study of children will show differences in inherent patterns of response and motivational forces. Harlow suggests that the variables of real importance cannot be constant from one learning problem to another and that they are tremendously differentiated as we pass from one animal order to another. Since a considerable amount of past motivational learning theory has been developed from animal research, it is important to consider the work and opinion of Harlow, who has done much work with animals. Lewin also found that curiosity induces purposive behavior leading either to satisfactions or tensions.[3]

Maslow has developed a theory of motivated behavior based on needs.[4] He has set up a hierarchy of human needs beginning at the basic organic or physiological needs and proceeding up the scale to self-actualization.

Increasingly the belief has developed that motives represent a particular kind of perceptual or cognitive organization in the individual and that a mechanical stimulus-response theory, like the behaviorists' cannot fully explain motivation. Any analysis of motivation is incomplete without including variables not usually considered by the behaviorists. Prentice in particular has suggested a look beyond the physiological into the wider dimensions of motivation, including such concepts as novelty, difficulty, and threat.[5]

Bindra and Young's broader view of motivation includes both energizing and regulatory functions.[6] They do not restrict motivation to goal-directed activities. They go beyond purposive sets or intentions in their search for the determinants of activity.

No report on the study of motivation would be complete without some reference to what we have termed dynamic psychology. While the work of Freud, Adler, and Jung has been subjected to experimental and scientific analysis only in recent years, their influence upon current thought has been widespread. Motivational theory in dynamic psychology has rested upon the insight of the originators, who propounded the concepts of unconscious motives, repression, compensation, purposiveness, sublimation, and the other defense mechanisms.

For Freud, the id was the pleasure level of personality and the source of instinctual energy and impulsive, primitive drives. The superego also played a force in motivation in so far as it set rules and defined limits. It

[3] K. Lewin, *A Dynamic Theory of Personality* (New York: McGraw-Hill Book Company, 1935).

[4] A. H. Maslow, *Motivation and Personality* (New York: Harper & Row, Publishers, Inc., 1954).

[5] W. Prentice, "Some Cognitive Aspects of Motivation," *The American Psychologist,* 16, August 1961, 503–11.

[6] D. Bindra, *Motivation: A Systematic Reinterpretation* (New York: The Ronald Press Company, 1959); and P. T. Young, *Motivation and Emotion* (New York: John Wiley & Sons, Inc., 1961).

assisted the individual to identify with certain social rules, mores, and values. In the Freudian motivational scheme, the ego was under constant pressure from id and superego forces; from the interplay of these forces the defense mechanisms were formed enabling the individual to act in accordance with his view of reality. The basic instinctual energy behind motivation is the libido, according to Freud. The libido is the sexual drive in the broadest sense. Behavior is viewed in terms of releasing energies and pressures. The libido is described developmentally, changing with maturation and going through the successive stages that have been described as oral, anal, and genital.

Karen Horney saw child development as a maturational process which led to the full realization of the individual's capabilities. She postulated a force toward growth which led to an unfolding of the individual's potentialities.[7] This is similar to the organismic force for growth described by Olson and Millard. For Horney, the interference which caused the most anxiety was a lack of love. Under this anxiety and pressure the child would react either by moving toward people, withdrawing from people, or perhaps acting against them.

Henry Murray developed a complicated theory, consisting of an integrated aggregate of needs and perceptual presses (the power to affect the well-being of an individual). Murray listed a large number of needs, both social and personal, which a person required to reduce his striving behavior.[8] The intensity of these needs in each individual determined his personality. The resulting behavior, motivated by the need-press situation, he called a thema. He believed that one could infer the nature of the individual's needs by analyzing his thematic tendencies. From this theory developed Murray's Thematic Apperception Test in which the individual is shown ambiguous pictures. In telling a story about the picture and placing himself in the situation he projects his own needs and provides an opportunity to analyze his psychological movement.

Adler rejected the strong sexual emphasis of the Freudians and believed that a considerable amount of motivation could be explained in the movement to compensate for a real or felt deficiency. He stressed the fact that from early infancy the child was placed in a situation which developed feelings of inferiority. As a result, he was motivated to better his situation, a process described as compensation. According to present Adlerians motivation can be understood best in terms of the purpose of behavior as it occurs in a social setting. For Adlerians belonging is the basic need. They would urge an acquaintance with the subjective view of the individual to

[7] K. Horney, *Neurosis and Human Growth* (New York: W. W. Norton & Company, Inc., 1950).

[8] H. A. Murray, *Explorations in Personality* (New York: Oxford University Press, Inc., 1938); and H. A. Murray and C. Kluckhohn, eds., *Personality in Nature, Society, and Culture* (New York: Alfred A. Knopf, Inc., 1948).

grasp his private logic, in the belief that his motives are clearly revealed by the way he makes choices or decisions. Extensive research by Schachter has demonstrated the significance and power of the social needs in human behavior.[9]

The child's sense of inferiority and his striving to be superior or "better" are inseparable and can lead to exaggerations, which develop into psychological disturbances. Adler offered as a crucial factor in evaluating normal development the criterion of the degree of social feeling shown by the individual. He suggested that parents should prepare children properly for life by stimulating their social feelings, their concern for others. The child's constructive activities which demonstrate cooperation should be commented on in contrast to always noting the destructive activities and the attempts to feel superior.

---

2. Make an attempt to utilize Adlerian theory by categorizing children's activities in terms of useful and useless behavior (constructive and destructive). Give specific illustrations of your observation of the purposes of children. Whenever possible, report these incidents in anecdotal form.

Adler believed that the child's goals and motives could be determined from his attitude toward three basic questions of life. How does he handle the social problem of making friends and getting along with people? How does he react to the work tasks presented at different developmental levels? Finally, what is his attitude toward the opposite sex, and how does he play his sexual role?

Much of the writing on motivational theory has spoken of drive reduction; anxiety reduction; needs and satisfaction; tension reduction. The discussion generally deals with movement from disequilibrium to equilibrium. In our approach to motivation we shall attempt to go beyond a study of the drive and tension theories, agreeing with Jersild that there is a positive striving which goes beyond equilibrium.[10] Described as the drive toward self-fulfillment, this more positive view of motivation synchronizes with developmental theory.

A DEVELOPMENTAL THEORY OF MOTIVATION

A developmental theory of motivation expounds a growth impetus which is a type of seeking and not merely a striving initiated by tension. Accord-

[9] S. Schachter, *Psychology of Affiliation: Experimental Studies of the Sources of Gregariousness* (Stanford, Calif.: Stanford University Press, 1959).
[10] A. Jersild, *Child Psychology*, 5th ed. (Englewood Cliffs, N.J.: Prentice-Hall, Inc., 1960).

ing to Maslow there is a positive direction toward self-actualization in growth motivation.[11] Maslow's theory takes into account the integrated wholeness of the organism. It rejects any set of physiological drives as being the center of all human motivation and stresses instead the ultimate or basic goal of the individual. Motivated behavior is the way in which basic needs are expressed. Needs, then, are not treated in isolation. Maslow would feel that a listing of drives is not conducive to an understanding of human motivation and child development and that the focus must be on goals instead of drives. In his theory the field, the situation, and the cultural determinants must be taken into account.

Maslow argues that human needs arrange themselves in a hierarchy. At the lowest level are the physiological needs, food, water, air, sex, etc., which are basic and urgent. When the physiological needs are gratified, there emerges a new set of needs, related to safety. The safety needs of the child are met in an orderly world in which he can feel safe and sure. The child needs to be free of bodily illness, danger, continually disrupted routines, etc. The effects of failure to satisfy the safety needs are seen in the neurotic or psychotic child. When the basic organic and safety needs are met, the child is free to experience the higher needs for love, affection, and belonging. The child needs the affection of individuals and groups. When the love factor is thwarted, maladjustment and eventually more severe psychopathology can be predicted. It is important to recognize that in each individual the love need involves the opportunity to give as well as receive love. Many children are as deprived in their opportunities to give love as they are in opportunities to receive love.

---

3. Give an illustration of how the lack of fulfillment of safety or love needs can result in the neurotic or psychotic child. How can a child be deprived of opportunities to give love?

Maslow's next set of needs are the esteem needs for competence, mastery, adequacy, achievement, recognition. When these needs are not met, the individual is discouraged. When they are met, however, a new type of motivating force emerges—the need to self-actualize, to become whatever the individual is capable of. This need varies from individual to individual, and is highly dependent upon satisfaction of the physiological, safety, love, and esteem needs.

In the establishment of his hierarchy of needs, Maslow has made a significant contribution to motivational theory. He points out that while needs are highly individualized, the hierarchial order remains so that satisfaction at one level of need opens the way to the next level, developing

[11] Maslow, *Motivation and Personality*.

a motivational cycle toward self-actualization. In growth motivation there is no final need gratification or climax; the force toward self-actualization is continuous.[12]

There are many similarities between Maslow's point of view and some of the postulates of Kurt Goldstein[13] and the work of Carl Rogers.[14] They are all in agreement on the striving to actualize and enhance the organism as the prime human motive. For further reading consult the article by Maslow titled "A Theory of Human Motivation."[15]

---

4. To demonstrate your understanding of Maslow's concept of the hierarchy of needs, take several children, and illustrate how they may be at different stages in the hierarchy. How do you explain their varied stages?

THE MOTIVATIONAL NEEDS

In a consideration of motivation, it soon becomes apparent that certain needs—purposes and goals—establish themselves in a hierarchy as Maslow has well described. These needs and purposes can be understood best within the framework of the child's learning situation and his total development. His motives must be seen in a developmental sense. Havighurst's outline of developmental tasks, presented in Chapter II offers a guide to some of the tasks the child is working toward.

Acknowledging that needs are also affected by the level of maturity points to the significance of early and late maturation in motivation. The fact that many problems disappear with maturity cannot explain all behavior, but can be utilized in understanding difficult developmental stages.

The strongest motives in the child's life are frequently those which have in the past been appealed to most effectively. Motivation is best understood in the framework of the life style and self concept in which the internal consistency of behavior is exposed.

The life experience of each child determines the motives which evolve in his particular life style. His behavior is most directly affected by his perception and evaluation of all the factors in his life. The resulting attitudes determine the life style. These attitudes are first held on a trial-and-error basis, but eventually the child uses them as guiding principles. In

[12] A. H. Maslow, "Deficiency, Motivation, and Growth Motivation," in *Nebraska Symposium on Motivation*, ed. M. R. Jones (Lincoln, Neb.: University of Nebraska Press, 1955).

[13] K. Goldstein, *The Organism, Holistic Approach to Biology* (New York: American Book Company, 1939).

[14] C. Rogers, *On Becoming a Person* (Boston: Houghton Mifflin Company, 1961).

[15] A. H. Maslow, "A Theory of Human Motivation," *Psychological Review*, 50:4, July 1943, 370–96.

this process the child may misinterpret his needs and motives as well as the needs and motives of others. However, he learns to function on the basis of his assumptions however faulty. It is important, therefore, to consider motivational needs early in life. As the child's anticipations are confirmed and his view of life becomes set, it is increasingly difficult to change his picture of the world.

The first environmental setting is the general family atmosphere. Here examples, social levels, expectancies, and standards are set for the child. Family patterns are not necessarily deterministic for children, some of whom reject family standards and behave in direct opposition. The child may reject the religious values the family holds or he may reject other aspects of the family's socioeconomic position.

The family constellation also has an effect on the development of the child's needs and motives. His position within the family often is crucial in the development of his point of view. Similarity of traits in siblings is usually an expression of family atmosphere. On the other hand, differences in the traits of siblings reflect the position of the child in the constellation and his response to competition among the siblings.

The culture is also influential. The child is affected by groups to which he belongs or would like to belong. As has been pointed out, needs are influenced by the maturity of the individual. The infant's small number of needs soon begins to grow so that by maturity the human being has a complex interlocking system of needs and motives. The developmental nature of needs is clearly revealed in any review of the needs of the infant, the elementary school child, and the adolescent.

---

5. In light of the developmental theory of needs and motives, observe children at various developmental stages. Describe the way in which developmental needs are influenced by maturity factors.

The parent can play an important role in motivation. The home atmosphere should be accepting and encouraging. Experiences that interest and challenge the child should be provided. Standards set for the child should relate to his ability; recognition should be given when the standards are met. Consistent attempts to encourage curiosity should be developed, and the parent should seek to create an environment in which questions are freely asked and answered. The child should be encouraged to utilize the problem-solving approach whenever possible. The parent should be available to assist, but the child should find his own solutions to his problems and experience his own success.

Many arrangements and classifications of needs appear in the literature, and we shall attempt to integrate them with the point of view we have expressed. Prescott has described behavior in terms of a six-point framework which we shall utilize and expand in our description of needs and motives.[16]

Physical Factors

A child is born with certain physical needs. He has a need to safeguard his physical being and hence to satisfy the stresses of hunger, thirst, temperature, fatigue, and pain. The child is aware of these ever recurring demands and is almost continuously active in his efforts to satisfy them. As the child matures, he learns to control these needs, and the body participates in this control through the process of homeostasis. Behavior, then, originally is motivated primarily by physical needs, and it is only after these needs are satisfied that the child is free to take the next step.

The child needs physical help and a proper balance between activity and rest. He must have opportunities to function physically, to participate in a manner appropriate to his structure and the maturity level of his body, and to develop skills in managing the body.

Although Harlow has demonstrated that the best learning does not occur under strong drives, they cannot be ignored; therefore, understanding motivation once again forces a reconsideration of the developmental tasks. At different times in his life the child has different developmental needs related to the specific physical motives.

The school must consider the effect of homework in relation to physical needs. Too much extra work after school prevents the child from participating in activities which satisfy some of his physical needs. Similarly the aware teacher knows the importance of such break periods as recess, noon hour, change of work pace, and occasional rescheduling of routines.

Some psychologists also consider in this area what they call the individual's need for activity. Good learning situations provide opportunities for activity and the utilization instead of suppression of physical motives. Activity for the child in and of itself is pleasurable; he likes to be doing things. We need to appreciate the significance of this childhood characteristic as a motivating influence. Schools formerly attempted to teach the child to sit quietly until directed, but now are attempting to utilize the child's energy for educational purposes.

---

6. How might the schools more effectively utilize physical needs and motives in planning the total program? How can the teacher use these motives in her classroom?

---

[16] D. Prescott, *The Child in the Educative Process* (New York: McGraw-Hill Book Company, 1957).

Love Factors

Every child needs emotional security, which is derived from the certainty that he is loved. When he feels valued, security can serve to facilitate many other activities. The insecure child generally has persistent adjustment problems and does not function effectively either in the home or at school. The child's well-being depends on his ability to evoke the love of other children. He needs to participate in both giving and receiving love. The desire to be accepted can become one of the strongest motivating factors in the child's life. A considerable amount of what he does or attempts to do is motivated by a desire to please some other significant person in his life. The child who seemingly functions only to please himself is exhibiting a major symptom of failure in social adjustment and a faulty view of life.

Each adult at home and in school must recognize the importance of developing a relationship in which the child feels that he is pleasing someone whose love and respect he desires. The child's love relationships develop first with the parents and subsequently include siblings and other relatives. Various sources of security must be used in meeting the love needs. The healthy child's feelings of being approved, loved, and valued give him security and the strength to function effectively. It has been demonstrated that approval is a more effective reinforcer with the individual who has been deprived of approval than with the individual who has been satiated.

Gerwitz and Baer devised a problem in which children dropped marbles into one of two holes; they reinforced one of the responses with verbal approval.[17] In the experiment some of the children spent twenty minutes alone, socially deprived, before being presented with the problem; controls went directly to the experiment; and another group was "satiated" on the way to the experiment by extremely approving reactions on the part of the experimenter. They concluded that social drives appear to be responsive to deprivation and satiation. The importance of perceptive use of approval is apparent. All adults need to find more effective ways of recognizing the child's assets and strengths, and frequent use of this diagnosis of assets is of great value in developmental psychology.

---

7. Love relationships are significant in motivating the child's work. Illustrate how the lack of love relationships may affect a specific child's learning. How may the teacher utilize the love relationships in the learning situation?

---

[17] J. Gerwitz and D. Baer, "Deprivation and Satiation of Social Reinforcers as Drive Conditions," *Journal of Abnormal and Social Psychology*, 57 (1958), 165–72.

Cultural and Socialization Factors

The influences of subcultures on needs and motives are internalized by the child. It is really from the culture that some needs develop. We can observe differences in culture-based needs among nations and also among the subcultures within our nation or within a large city. The child must internalize the appropriate way to play his sexual role in our culture. As he moves from the home to the neighborhood, the school, and various other groups, he experiences the effects of his culture and must make a continuing series of readjustments to the different cultural factors with which he comes into contact. They all have an influence upon his perception of self and society. His internalization of some cultural traits may cause him to face the prejudice of other individuals. In some instances cultural factors in motivation stand out most clearly in the school situation. The standards and demands set up within the school may be in severe conflict with some cultural needs. The school's values may be quite inappropriate to the cultural group of some children.

The success motive is strong in our particular culture, and the child is given an early orientation toward the importance of success. He often reveals his attitude in the interest he displays in mastering particular situations. The child who has experienced success in the past approaches a challenge with confidence. He has every reason to believe that he will succeed again. It is important to arrange situations that provide success experiences and also to utilize the past success experiences of the child in motivating him. Robert White has termed this approach the motivation for competence.[18]

---

8. Give examples of differences in needs related to culture. How can the teacher be aware of these needs? How do they affect the instructional process?

Peer Needs and Motives

Each child needs to belong to a peer group. Released from the domination of his physiological and safety needs, he can move on to the emergence of social goals. He must be able to make a contribution to the group. Many opportunities are available daily, both at home and at school, to use responsibility to develop the sense of belonging. The importance of the child's need to affiliate and be socially acceptable can be seen everywhere. Frequently, this need to extend respect and service to others in our society is much neglected. Organic, physical, and love needs are quickly

[18] R. White, "Motivation Reconsidered: The Concept of Competence," *Psychological Review,* 66 (1959), 297–333.

recognized, but the value to the individual's mental health developed through mutuality in human relations is seldom considered.

The child must accept social obligations in order to develop beyond the infant stage. He must learn almost at once to become both dependent and independent, to recognize his contributions within the total social framework. As he matures, he adjusts to increasingly complex social situations in which mutuality and the giving and getting of ego recognition become more essential. It is important that early in life the child be taught a sense of personal worth. He should develop the social skills necessary for acceptance. These are parental tasks that go beyond providing for security and acceptance within the family.

The importance of belonging as a basic need has already been outlined. Social contact is vital to the normal personality development of the child; total isolation is generally intolerable for adults even if physical needs are met. Schachter provides an extensive review of the importance of social contact.[19]

If the child cannot get positive approval, he may be forced to receive recognition and belonging by behaving inappropriately. For some children the negative reaction of others is of much greater value than merely being ignored. The teacher should encourage the group to develop a group spirit. The delegation of duties and responsibilities so that each child can function as a member of the class is a highly significant task of the teacher. When peer needs are not met effectively and the child does not develop a proper sense of social feeling, the obstruction of developmental tasks and social adjustment is quickly evidenced. One criterion of adjustment is the development of social feeling.

---

9. Observe children at various age levels, and report on their social feeling and concern for others. Are the maladjusted those with less social concern and social feeling?

Self-developmental Needs

Each child needs to accomplish goals and progress toward the achievement of values and aspirations. He needs to experience success. This necessitates the opportunity to plan, make decisions, and work out plans to suit his values and goals.

The child needs to assure himself that he has succeeded and can achieve. He should be told when he is making progress and when his work deserves approval.[20] If the individual believes that no matter how well he

[19] Schachter, *Psychology of Affiliation.*
[20] R. Barker, "Success and Failure in the Classroom," *Progressive Education,* 19 (1942), 221–24.

works no one will take the slightest recognition of his achievements, incentive to work may be reduced almost completely. Teachers should be particularly aware of the importance of recognition as a motivational goal.

A child can be stimulated to achieve best when he has already experienced accomplishment. Thus, success in the early tasks is crucial. From simple successes he can progress to successes of a more difficult nature. Developmental teaching, then, becomes important. The teacher who attempts to make the child advance too rapidly brings about discouragement and a sense of failure instead of achievement.

Success needs to be measured in terms of the child's view of self. Learning should be geared to stimulate growth. Success is always a relative term. Problems the child is exposed to should be relatively difficult, but they should be within the grasp of his interests, past experience, and ability. Recognize, too, that achievement as a motivational need can be used to overcompensate for the individual's anxiety about his capacity to accomplish the tasks demanded by his role. The child may receive all of his satisfactions from school work and use this area as compensation for inadequate functioning in other areas.

Self-developmental needs particularly can be enhanced through the utilization of such incentives as novelty. A unique approach to materials that stimulate the child's curiosity can be effective. Berlyne has done research to substantiate that complex and varied stimuli attract more attention than do simple, more regular or familiar ones.[21]

---

10. How can the adult determine if he is moving faster than the child's interests? How can the self-evaluation of success be used in a practical manner with a group of children?

Feelings About Self Related to Motives

The child's feelings of security, adequacy, and belonging should free him to work toward self-actualization. As he meets his goals, he can experience the continual process of self-actualization which permits the development of creativity. Here the motivational needs of curiosity and inquisitiveness are also able to come into play.

We can see, then, that needs and motives are in one sense in a constant state of flux. Although they can always be related to the guidelines and life style, they are constantly changing in intensity and degree. They may be influenced by changes in the psychological environment, interpersonal relationships, and general cognitive structure of the individual.

[21] D. Berlyne, "The Influence of Complexity and Novelty in Visual Figures or Orienting Responses," *Journal of Experimental Psychology,* 55 (1958), 289–96.

UNCONSCIOUS MOTIVATION

In many instances motives may have an adaptive function that is not obvious to the behaver. When the individual's pattern of behavior consistently achieves results of which he himself seems to be unaware, what psychoanalytic theory has called the unconscious motives is operative. The behavior is an attempt to satisfy impulses which would be painful to the individual if he were aware of them. The teacher who encounters such behavior is dealing with repressed material. Awareness of the possibility of unconscious motives helps alert adults to problems which the child may be concealing. In the realm of more complex social motives, individuals often produce behavior which appears to be purposive and goal-directed and strongly deny the inferred motive. Some motivation operates outside of awareness.

Substantiation of the unconscious has been developed primarily from hypnotic studies and clinical experience. Kubie has summarized the clinical evidence regarding the method by which the conscious process becomes unconscious.[22] Erickson has illustrated through hypnosis how the unconscious process operates.[23]

RECOGNIZING THE CHILD'S MOTIVES

Understanding needs and motives is not enough. The understanding must be applied. We must always recognize that our own values, feelings, and attitudes play a role in our evaluation of others. The interaction of the personalities of child and observer must be taken into account.

One of the first attempts to understand the child's motives can be made through objective observation, but you must know what to look for. The actions of the child provide an excellent opportunity to develop insight into his motives. However, motives can take on meaning only as they are seen in relationship to the framework in which we are working and the purposive nature of all behavior. The keeping of anecdotal records with adequate sampling provides many clues to the motivation of the child. In viewing every act of the child as an expression of his attitudes, goals, and expectations, you note the individual behavior pattern. Some children function only when they produce, or excel, or are first; without special recognition they do not function at all. The child who is uncooperative and seems

[22] L. Kubie, "Problems and Techniques of Psychoanalytic Validation and Progress" in *Psychoanalysis as Science,* ed. E. Pumpian Mindlin (Stanford, Calif.: Stanford University Press, 1952), pp. 46–124.

[23] M. Erickson, "Experimental Demonstrations of the Psychopathology of Everyday Life," *Psychoanalytic Quarterly,* 8 (1939), 338–53.

to believe that he cannot be liked may be finding his place specifically by being disliked.

---

11. Give some specific examples of ways in which the child's behavior reveals his attitudes.

Teachers must be trained to recognize the psychological movement and exposure of character traits in all the interactions of individuals. Then, eventually, after they have presented systematic anecdotal information, anecdotal records may indicate the child's purposes, goals, and attitudes. Dreikurs shows how teachers can recognize the motives of children within the typical boundaries of the classroom and the techniques available to them.[24] First, they can try to understand the meaning of the child's behavior or misbehavior. Is he seeking attention, showing his power, getting even, or perhaps displaying his inadequacy. Secondly, they can watch their own reactions to the child's behavior. Frequently what teachers are inclined to do spontaneously gives the clearest insight into the child's goals. As they check their first reaction, they may see the direction of the child's goal. Mild feelings of annoyance may indicate that the child is just seeking attention. However, when they feel challenged and feel inclined to prove to the child that they can make him do it, they may be sure that the child's goal is power. Feelings of hurt and resentment are indicative of the revenge goal. When they feel like saying, "I don't know what to do about this," it is usually indicative that the child has sought to impress the teacher with his inability so that he can be free to function as he chooses.

In the same way, response to correction discloses the child's motives. His response to the adult's efforts to control him reveals the goal. The child who wants attention stops his disturbance when he receives attention. When he is challenging authority, the teacher's desire to have him control his actions only brings about stronger resistance. The child who seeks to get even may become even more hostile and violent at the adult's attempts to stop his behavior. In other words, the child's reaction to corrective efforts provides clues about the purpose of his behavior.

GOALS OF MISBEHAVIOR

The teacher must be alert to the general pattern of the child's behavior. As he pursues his goals, he may use active or passive methods, constructive or destructive methods. The child who feels accepted is free to use

[24] R. Dreikurs, *Psychology in the Classroom* (New York: Harper & Row, Publishers, Inc., 1957).

constructive methods; the child who feels rejected generally turns to destructive methods. Four basic behavior patterns—(1) Active-constructive, (2) active-destructive, (3) passive-constructive, (4) passive-destructive—will serve as a guide in understanding behavior.

The first goal, in which the attention-getting mechanism is operating, can be found in many children. Frequently it is not even recognized as a behavior problem. The competition common in school and society often encourages this kind of behavior. The passive-constructive attention getter who is merely "charming" is also frequently overlooked. His charm and dependence frequently make him a teacher's favorite. It is only the mischief maker who is readily recognized because of his active-destructive acts.

The second goal is the struggle for superiority between child and adult. Any pressure results in the child's fighting back and showing extreme aggressiveness. Adults who deal with this type of child feel personally challenged and tend to react with the feeling that they will show the child that they can control him.

The goal of retaliation or revenge generally leaves the adult feeling deeply and personally hurt by behavior. Children who use revenge need to be convinced that they can be liked.

The final goal of disturbing behavior, as described by Dreikurs, is the display of real or imagined disability. The child impresses the adult with his incapacities and, as a result, the parent or teacher characteristically throws up his hands in complete despair and permits the child to function in the way in which he chooses. The factors in understanding misbehavior are best portrayed schematically in the diagram in Fig. 10-1.

Diminished Social Interest →

Social Discouragement ↓

USEFUL		USELESS		
Active Constructive	Passive Constructive	Active Destructive	Passive Destructive	
"Success"	"Charm"	"Nuisance"	"Laziness"	AGM
		"A Rebel"	"Stubborn"	Power
		"Vicious"	"Violent Passivity"	Revenge
			"Hopeless"	Assumed Disability

Fig. 10-1 Behavior Patterns

R. Dreikurs, *Psychology in the Classroom*. New York: Harper & Row, Publishers, 1957, p. 15.

EFFECTIVE PROCEDURES IN MOTIVATION

Child-Adult Relationship

The importance of a good relationship between the teacher and the pupil, between the adult and the child cannot be overestimated. In order to influence the child's motives, there must be mutual respect and a mutual alignment between the goals of the adult and those of the child. No one can be influenced without friendly relationship. Many poorly motivated children are really the products of poor relationships. Motivational studies of children in the classroom show that frequently the personal qualities of the teacher are crucial in developing the child's motivation. This relationship consists of valuing the child, of providing opportunities for recognition, approval, and acceptance. The relationship can be characterized by kindness and firmness. Kindness shows that the teacher has respect for the child, while the firmness illustrates just as adamantly her respect for herself.

Encouragement

The teacher must become familiar with methods of encouragement. Evidence of the teacher's faith enables the child to believe in himself. This type of relationship gives recognition for effort and takes into account the necessity of sequential and psychological pacing, which permits successes. It recognizes and focuses on strengths and assets. In the simplest way, it conveys to the child the feeling that he can perform and that it is safe to try. The acceptance and encouragement method has been described by Dinkmeyer and Dreikurs.[25]

Page investigated the effect of teachers' comments on student performances with seventy-four secondary school classes.[26] A test on the subject matter was graded in three randomly assigned groups—the "no comment" group, the "free comment" group, and the "specified comment" group. The "no comment" group received no mark except the grade. The "free comment" group received the comment considered appropriate for the child and test concerned. The "specified comment" group received uniform comment believed to be encouraging. On the next test the "free comment" group achieved higher scores than the other two groups, and the "specified comment" group received higher scores than the "no comment" group. Specific encouraging comments have an effect on the students' efforts.

[25] D. Dinkmeyer and R. Dreikurs, *Encouraging Children to Learn: The Encouragement Process* (Englewood Cliffs, N.J.: Prentice-Hall, Inc., 1963).
[26] E. Page, "Teacher Comments and Student Performance: A Seventy-Four Classroom Experiment in School Motivation," *Journal of Educational Psychology,* 49, August 1958, 173–181.

Interest

Effective motivation always takes into account the interest factor. It attempts to exploit interests already present. It recognizes that interest can be created and that changes in behavior as well as changes more directly related to academic learning can be influenced by the development and creation of interests.

Early Success

It is important to provide immediate goals along the way. It has been demonstrated that success generally leads to higher and more realistic goals. The provision of immediate goals tends to build a motivational bridge.

Individual Success

In any activity efforts should be taken to insure success for each individual. It has been demonstrated by research that after success the level of aspiration tends to be raised; after failure it is lowered.[27] Careful planning can insure success in the acquisition of behavioral traits, characteristics, and attitudes, just as well as in academic learning.

Intrinsic Motives

Intrinsic motives provide a broad base for understanding behavior. By determining and using specific factors which already motivate an individual toward his immediate goals, movement can be taken toward accomplishing long-range goals.

Developmental Levels

It is always important to consider the developmental level of a task in any attempt to establish effective procedures in motivation. Consideration of the developmental levels offers a broader base for evaluation. Fritz Redl has given some examples of developmental differences.[28] He discusses the period when, in his terms, even nice children behave badly, when the child may keep his worries, fears, and concerns hidden within himself. Much of his behavior is considered bad and improper by adults. His extreme physical restlessness, his occasional regression to infantile

[27] K. Lewin, *A Dynamic Theory of Personality.*
[28] F. Redl, "Pre-adolescents: What Makes Them Tick," *Child Study*, 21 (1944), 44–48, 58–59.

habits, his conflict with adults, all cause concern about modifying his behavior. Redl illustrates the way in which developmental levels may affect motivation.

Extrinsic Motives

Adults are prone to use punishment, reprimands, and ignoring as methods of dealing with children. Some of the ineffective aspects of motivational factors will be dealt with later. They need to be mentioned here merely as part of extrinsic motivation. A considerable amount of motivation has been arranged on the basis of external rewards, which, when they become part of the psychological field, can be effective in the sense that they aid belonging, approval, recognition, or other basic motivational needs. However, extrinsic rewards, such as stars, badges, and grades, should always be considered in terms of the long-range objectives of an activity. They tend to encourage the child to work more for the reward than for the acquisition of the particular trait, skill, or ability. There has been much misunderstanding and confusion in the use of praise and blame. Thompson and Hunnicutt have pointed out the importance of understanding the varied personalities in the classroom when using praise and blame.[29] They concluded that when repeated often enough, praise increases the work output of introverts but not extroverts, and that blame increases the work output of extroverts, until it is significantly higher than that of extroverts who are praised or introverts who are blamed.

Knowledge of Results

As has been mentioned in several contexts, knowledge of results is a most important procedure in motivation. Teacher recognition and the development of an individual progress chart or the production of some feedback on development can be most effective in motivation.

Self-selection

Self-selection can be a most effective procedure in motivation. An application of the pacing concept, it permits the child to choose material at his own interest and ability level. Research has produced much evidence that all forms of learning can be facilitated by self-selection.[30]

[29] G. Thompson and C. Hunnicutt, "The Effect of Repeated Praise or Blame on the Work Achievement of 'Introverts' and 'Extroverts,'" *Childhood Education*, 30, No. 5 (January 1954), 212–15.

[30] W. Olson, *Child Development* (Boston: D. C. Heath & Company, 1959).

INEFFECTIVE MOTIVATION

Whether a particular motivation is effective or not must always be judged on an individual basis. What works with Johnny might not work with Billy. Some methods of motivation are generally ineffective, however. An unhealthy emphasis on competition can be an ineffective motivational procedure. It may work for some children but it frequently works best for the child who needs it least. The child who wants to compete is usually interested in the competition because he can win. Any recognition of individual differences raises the question of how many children are competing equally in some of the competition schemes current within schools, clubs, and other groups.

Ridicule and public reproof are other ineffective methods of motivation. So, too, is bargaining in which the adult gets the child to do something in return for a favor. This tactic only teaches the child to drive a "good bargain," and he becomes more concerned with winning the best in the bargain than in functioning. Getting the child to behave primarily to please the adult is never effective if it must be mentioned. If the relationship is a good one to begin with, the child wants to function on this basis. If the relationship is not good merely mentioning that the child should do it for the adult's sake does little to strengthen the relationship. Finally, since good "discipline" implies self-control, it can be judged by the lack of necessity for external interference and controls.

SELF CONCEPT AND LEVEL OF ASPIRATION

It has been demonstrated in the work of Sears that an important factor in determining the level of achievement which a child proposes for himself is his previous experience in similar situations.[31] The child's failure to achieve his stated goals usually results in the development of unrealistic aspirations for succeeding performances. He either estimates his future performance at an impossibly high level, or so low that he can obtain the goal without effort.

When children achieve near the level which they expect of themselves, their future expectations of performance are quite realistic. This factor should be used in working toward the development of the individual child. Sears demonstrated that self-confident, successful children have similar reactions to a level of aspiration situation, whereas unsuccessful children lack confidence and may adopt one of a number of different behavior techniques in ensuing situations. Obviously, the level of aspiration concept is closely related to the maintenance of self-esteem and the

[31] P. Sears, "Levels of Aspiration in Academically Successful and Unsuccessful Children," *Journal of Abnormal and Social Psychology*, 35 (1940), 498–536.

development of self-actualization. The general effects of motivation on learning have been summarized cogently by Melton.[32] The functions are to *energize* and make the organism active, to *direct* the activity of the organism, and to *select* what it defines as the consequences of responses and hence the later performance of the individual.

DISCIPLINE

One of the products of a more precise understanding of motivation should be the ability to direct groups or individuals effectively in learning situations. Whenever parents or teachers get together, the topic of discipline is frequently discussed. Teaching cannot exist without effective discipline. Parental training devoid of effective disciplinary techniques ends in maladjustment for the child and confusion for the parents.

Although there are many definitions of discipline, the concern here is with the type of disciplinary relationship which produces self-control and enables the individual to discover orderliness and to develop a reasonable degree of socially acceptable behavior. He becomes aware of his responsibility not only to himself but also to the group. The disciplined individual is able to accept external controls for the good of the group, and at the same time is continually moving toward the development of internalized controls, self-discipline. This type of discipline enables the individual to fit into varied responsibilities in democratic life. Disciplinary procedures definitely reflect the adult's understanding of the child; they should also reflect the goals and objectives we have in mind for the child's development.

This type of discipline is far different from the basically punitive approach but, instead, is educative in conception. Its goal is to shift from the external controls of the adult, parent or teacher, to eventual self-control.

The educative approach works toward the child's understanding the natural results of his behavior so that he is able to function effectively on his own even when he is not protected or "looked out for." Such discipline in the family fosters the development of family councils wherein the child participates in the formulation of rules for himself at home. In the classroom, the class council and the school student council are also effective ways to assist in the development of long-term discipline. It is apparent, then, that the objectives of discipline are closely allied with the objectives of learning and education.

The study of discipline draws upon an understanding of the child as already developed in other areas. First the great individual differences in-

[32] A. Melton, "Motivation and Learning," in *Encyclopedia of Educational Research*, rev. ed., ed. W. Monroe (New York: The Macmillan Company, 1950), pp. 672–73.

volved in disciplinary actions must be recognized. Children cannot be disciplined merely by treating all equally, but must be disciplined in accordance with individual differences and the meaning that the specific situation has for each child. There are varying levels of readiness in disciplinary situations, and maturity and the varied ages and stages of growth and development must be considered. Oppositional, negativistic, and hostile behavior appears at certain stages. This does not mean that all such behavior must be tolerated; however, it does indicate that some misbehavior can be alleviated simply by ignoring it. This procedure is effective if the purpose is to get attention; but it does not deal with the underlying needs. All disciplinary action should be taken with an awareness of whether you are only managing the symptom and not the real motive and problem. Understanding of the motive and the social reward the child receives is crucial in forming new relationships.

The preventive aspects of discipline should also be considered. The time devoted to preparing for a situation or using preventive discipline is well-spent. It has been found that when teachers use group discussion to integrate the group and to seek out voluntary participation, fewer disciplinary problems develop. Utilization of interests already present and group discussion techniques can facilitate group integration. The situation takes on the spirit of self-discipline, and a give-and-take relationship is developed.

---

12. List some methods which you would consider preventive discipline. Try to observe some group discussions to note ways in which this can be effective or ineffective. Take several specific problems, and describe your approach. How would you deal with rebellion, active or passive resistance?

The feeling of identification with the group can be a real asset in discipline. The individual adopts the attitude, "We have a problem," and identifies himself with the problem. The next step is always, "And what are we going to do about our problem?" Regardless of the philosophy of discipline, a kind, definite, and firm attitude will do much to establish rapport and respect in the individual. In the same sense, a well-timed sense of humor can be an aid to the disciplinary process.

An awareness of what should be heeded and what should be overlooked is also important in developing an attitude toward discipline. If behavior has social meaning, the way in which the need for disciplinary action has developed in the social setting should be of concern. Is the child doing this in order to belong, to be part of the group, to get attention, or to show that he can do as he chooses? Such inquiries lead to a recognition of the purpose of events which fall under the control of discipline. Being aware of some of the goals of misbehavior, the teacher can watch the social interaction within the room. What is there about the children involved which has helped to bring about this social interaction? As he checks his own spontaneous reaction, he gets clues about the purpose of the child's behavior. Again the child's response to correction is another tool in developing insight into disciplinary acts. There is a great tendency for a teacher to revert to autocratic methods as soon as he has been challenged or "tried out." It would be well to remember the ways in which children can provoke adults to display the kind of behavior they anticipate. A firm belief in the advantages of a long-range disciplinary program which develops self-control and self-evaluation is necessary.

In discipline as in other aspects of child study, we would encourage developing awareness of the individual's perceptual field. Note how he sees things and why this particular type of misbehavior appeals to him. Always look upon misbehavior as a signal. Recognize that treating only symptoms cannot effect cures. The symptoms do not lead to answers; they merely remind the adult of the need for developing a better understanding of the child and ascertaining why particular symptoms have developed in this child.

Any understanding of discipline is based on an understanding of some of the steps in growth and development. Flexible schedules in the consideration of individual needs eliminate many disciplinary problems. Whether working with the individual or the group, an opportunity for planning and individual and group goal seeking is important. In the light of all that has been said about individual differences, it seems important to bear in mind that some disciplinary problems arise out of failure to provide for the great range in capacities, interests, and purposes which exist in any group. Acceptance of the uniqueness of the individual helps in dealing with disciplinary problems. Recognizing that growth is a gradual process and that the steps in emotional growth are not continuous but consist of progression and regression, aids an understanding of the individual child. If a child is to develop self-discipline, he needs certain experiences. An understanding of the varied age levels and the important developmental tasks related to them opens the way to an understanding of the role of discipline in child development. An interesting book, which takes this approach, is *Child Behavior* by Frances Ilg and Louise Ames.[33] James Hymes has also written from this point of view in *Understanding Your Child* and *Behavior and Misbehavior*.[34]

[33] F. Ilg and L. Ames, *Child Behavior* (New York: Harper & Row, Publishers, Inc., 1955).

[34] J. Hymes, *Understanding Your Child* (Englewood Cliffs, N.J.: Prentice-Hall, Inc., 1952); and J. Hymes, *Behavior and Misbehavior* (Englewood Cliffs, N.J.: Prentice-Hall, Inc., 1955).

SOME "DO'S" IN DISCIPLINE

It is evident that any good discipline is not based upon simple rules but, instead, upon a total understanding of the individual and the field in which he operates. However, some generally acceptable principles might be enumerated for consideration.

1. The relationship is crucial to effective discipline. There must be a feeling of mutual trust. Without good will and the mutual alignment of goals, effective discipline can rarely be obtained.

2. Good discipline is based upon the establishment of a routine. The child needs to know what to expect, whether at home or in school.

3. Consistency and logical consequences are crucial. The child needs to feel that he can anticipate certain kinds of effective action from the parent as a result of misbehavior; and that even though the adult treats each episode individually in an attempt to be fair, nevertheless consistency in the consequences must be maintained. To the extent that the adult is able to create an atmosphere of calm and control, disciplinary matters become routine. Consistency in discipline appears to be most important. Studies by Bandura and Walters and McCord, McCord, and Zola indicate that a high incidence of inconsistent discipline contributes to antisocial behavior.[35]

4. Discipline is both preventive and corrective. A person responsible for the disciplinary situation can do many things to prevent the occurrence of events which necessitate his external control. Some of this involves keeping children within guidelines, letting them know what is expected.

5. The establishment of limits is necessary for a disciplinary situation to function consistently and routinely. The child needs to know what will happen. Most children want discipline; they want to be controlled, to belong, to conform, and to be part of a group. Sometimes children misbehave in order to see where they will be stopped. They are also concerned whether you care enough to stop them. The studies by Bandura and Walters show that under lax-hostile conditions, where hostility is generated and no controls are demanded from the child, the greatest amount of aggressive, noncompliant behavior occurs.[36] It appears that a considerable amount of nonconformity is associated with both overly strict and overly permissive discipline.

6. Some disciplinary situations are best managed when we know what not to be concerned about or what not to interfere with. This type of "planned ignoring," as Redl has referred to it in *The Aggressive Child,* helps since it averts a continual negative interaction between the adult

[35] A. Bandura and R. Walters, *Adolescent Aggression* (New York: The Ronald Press Company, 1959); and W. McCord, J. McCord, and I. Zola, *Origins of Crime* (New York: Columbia University Press, 1959).
[36] Bandura and Walters, *Adolescent Aggression.*

and the child.[37] The disciplinary situation teaches a child to accept the results of order and sets up ways to avoid interpersonal conflict.

Good discipline, then, builds within the child the courage to function effectively. It encourages him to live effectively within the group. It helps him to see that he cannot always react impulsively and be acceptable. It should also point out some of his fallacious concepts of effective relations between people and provide experiences in cooperative human relationships.

The adult needs to look at his goals in taking disciplinary action. The purpose should be to assist each child to grow and develop in a manner that is personally satisfying and socially acceptable. In order to accomplish this, it is necessary to adopt definite policies in child training, whether in the home or school. In this connotation reward and punishment cannot be effective as long-run motives. The child who is rewarded soon comes to believe that rewards are his right. As a result, he demands a reward for every "good thing" he does. This same child would react to punishment by seeking retaliation so that a continual "getting even" goes on between the parent and the child. Punishment does not solve the basic problem. It merely eliminates undesirable behavior which frequently takes another direction as long as the basic problem remains. For some children, punishment provides a real challenge, and the opportunity to stand up against authority or to demonstrate counteraggressive hostility can be elicited by punishment procedures. Sears and colleagues demonstrated that punishment for aggression does not inhibit its expression.[38] In a study of nursery school children, boys demonstrated a positive relationship between punitiveness and overt aggression in school. Girls appear to have as strong aggressive reactions to maternal punitiveness as boys, but tend to inhibit its expression in the classroom.

The basic approach with the child, then, is characterized by a good relationship, mutual trust, encouragement, and the mutual alignment of goals. It recognizes that effective discipline is based upon action instead of talk. Many disciplinary situations are made impossible because the adult talks too much and the child becomes "deaf" in the sense of not hearing anything unless the voice is raised. Most children understand quite well what is expected of them, and conversations should be restricted to friendly interactions. Effective discipline bears no resemblance to impulsive reactions to disciplinary situations. It is, instead, based upon a belief in the importance of training and long-range goals.

This view of discipline believes in the establishment of order and the avoidance of conflict. It holds that the child learns best when he experi-

[37] F. Redl, *The Aggressive Child* (New York: Free Press of Glencoe, Inc., 1957).

[38] R. Sears, J. Whiting, U. Nowls, and P. Sears, "Some Childrearing Antecedents of Aggression and Dependency in Young Children," *Genetic Psychology Monograph*, 47 (1957) 135–234.

ences the consequences of his situation. Natural consequences are inherent in many situations and can impress the child with the disadvantage of disregarding order or failing to cooperate. While not all situations permit employment of natural consequences, there are many more opportunities to utilize consequences than most people recognize. The power of the consequence lies in the fact that it expresses the social order and control of the group, not just that of the individual parent or teacher. You act as the representative of order, and all are affected alike, enabling the child to learn that it is more satisfying to observe order than to violate it.

The trained and creative disciplinarian finds many opportunities to utilize natural consequences. He permits the child, for example, to make decisions. Does he want to stay in his seat, or does he constantly want to get out? If he chooses to get out, he is really choosing to stand, not to sit. In this way, the child may even choose to stand throughout the day and then make another choice on another day. At times the natural consequences may seem harsh, but they must also be evaluated in terms of effectiveness. It seems apparent that effective discipline does not necessitate repetition but takes care of the situation as permanently as possible.

---

13. Think of some ways in which classroom misbehavior can be dealt with on the basis of its own natural or logical consequences.

IMPLICATIONS

1. Since many of the child's motives are firmly established early in life, greater attention to parent education is needed. In some school districts parent education, with a concentration on the parents of preschoolers, would be the most effective preventive discipline step that could be taken.
2. While much can be said about motives and motivation in general, it eventually comes down to an analysis of the individual. This, again, points to the necessity of adequate and intensive child study via cumulative records.
3. There is a difference between what the child cannot do and what he will not do. With increased awareness of the role of the child's will and decisions, effective remediation of behavior can be instituted.
4. The adult must be careful to analyze whether he is dealing with the motive or merely with incentives in attempting to change behavior. Extrinsic rewards are limited, and do not produce long-range changes.
5. Self-evaluation is superior in that it focuses on the individual and can produce greater long-range results than judgment by external standards.
6. Motives are increasingly recognized as more than mere drives, but

are considered perceptual and cognitive events. It is unwise to always draw direct analogies between animal experiments and work with children.

7. An understanding of developmental tasks and methods of solving life tasks can serve as a guide to understanding behavior. The child's characteristic approach to the tasks reveals the style of life.

8. Maslow's hierarchy of needs theory serves as a basis for understanding levels of needs. As the basic needs are taken care of, it becomes possible for the child to work toward the higher needs and self-actualization.

9. The school needs to account for physical needs and motives in planning a total school program. Failure to do so handicaps the pupil-teacher interaction.

10. The relationship between child and adult is crucial to effective motivation. There must be opportunities for the child to give as well as receive love.

11. Since the success motive, the motivation for competence, is a strong factor in changing behavior, planning for success experiences is a basic motivational technique.

12. Mutuality and belonging can be utilized to change the child's capacity to function. An understanding of group dynamics offers many opportunities to change behavior.

13. Maturity factors must be considered in any understanding of the individual. Age characteristics and the maturity level enter into motivating specific children.

14. The family atmosphere, family constellation, and the culture are all influential in the formation of the child's style of life and preferred motives.

15. The child's goals and purposes are often revealed when the adult checks his first impulsive reaction to a particular situation.

16. Seeing behavior in terms of behavior patterns and goals of misbehavior can provide a framework to facilitate understanding, as long as this approach is not used mechanically.

17. The encouragement process can help the child change his view of self and his evaluation of society.

18. Ineffective procedures in motivation are too frequently practiced. Motivational processes can frequently be improved by merely cataloging and recalling what should not be done.

19. The mutual alignment of goals between the child and adult reduces the tension and changes behavior permanently.

20. Certain types of disciplinary procedures provoke a battle for power and recognition. The family council and classroom council can use the strength of group authority in discipline.

21. The curiosity motive has been demonstrated to induce purposive

behavior. Utilizing the child's curiosity can bring change by working with intrinsic motives which already exist in the child.

22. Social needs are potent in influencing human behavior. An understanding of group influence on the child's behavior provides both the context of the behavior and the setting for re-education.

23. Approval is effective in reinforcing behavior, but it must be used in a discriminating manner. The individual who has been satiated with general approval is not as responsive to approval. Specific encouraging comments have a positive effect on the student's efforts.

24. Some confusion in motivational techniques occurs because enough consideration is not given to the varied personalities to be motivated. The evidence indicates that motivation is only effective in terms of the specific personality toward which it is directed.

SUGGESTED READINGS

Articles

Bortner, D., "Pupil Motivation and Its Relationship to the Activity and Social Drives" in *Readings in Educational Psychology,* eds. W. Morse and G. M. Wingo, p. 258. Chicago: Scott, Foresman & Company, 1962.

Maslow, A., "A Theory of Human Motivation" in *Readings in the Psychology of Human Growth and Development,* ed. W. Baller, p. 255. New York: Holt, Rinehart & Winston, Inc., 1962.

Page, E., "Teacher Comments and Student Performance: A Seventy-Four Classroom Experiment in School Motivation" in *Readings in Educational Psychology,* eds. V. Noll and R. Noll, p. 264. New York: The Macmillan Company, 1962.

Sears, P., "Levels of Aspiration in Academically Successful and Unsuccessful Children" in *Readings in Child Development,* eds. W. Martin and C. Stendler, p. 437. New York: Harcourt, Brace & World, Inc., 1954.

Books

Dinkmeyer, D., and R. Dreikurs, *Encouraging Children to Learn: The Encouragement Process.* Englewood Cliffs, N.J.: Prentice-Hall, Inc., 1963.

Dreikurs, R., *Psychology in the Classroom.* New York: Harper & Row, Publishers, Inc., 1957.

———, *Children: The Challenge.* New York: Duell, Sloan & Pearce, Inc., 1964.

Hymes, J., *Behavior and Misbehavior.* Englewood Cliffs, N.J.: Prentice-Hall, Inc., 1954.

Maslow, A., *Motivation and Personality.* New York: Harper & Row, Publishers, Inc., 1954.

Redl, F., The Aggressive Child. New York: The Free Press of Glencoe, Inc., 1957.

———, *Understanding Children's Behavior*. New York: Bureau of Publications, Columbia University, 1949.

Redl, F. and W. Wattenberg, *Mental Hygiene in Teaching*, 2nd ed. New York: Harcourt, Brace & World, Inc., 1959.

Young, P., *Motivation and Emotion*. New York: John Wiley & Sons, Inc., 1961.

11 PERSONALITY DEVELOPMENT

The recess bell rang, and Miss Davis guided her third graders down the hall and out the door into the playground, pausing long enough to see that Miss Marsh was on yard duty. She went down the hall and turned in at a door marked, "School Psychologist, Mrs. J. Wilkes." Mrs. Wilkes looked up as Miss Davis entered and sat down. "What is troubling you, Norma?" she asked. "That Tommy Shepherd has the most contrary personality that I have ever seen, and little Jean Ann Sorenson seems to have no personality at all," was the answer. Miss Davis went on to describe in detail some of her problems with the two children.

When she was finished, Mrs. Wilkes laughed softly and said,

> And yet, Norma, if you were to have Tommy next year you might not feel he presented any problems at all. Tom is a slow-maturing child and this, combined with his competitiveness, leaves him feeling continually defeated. When we rearrange our groups he will be placed with boys more like himself and possibly he will be able to compete more equitably. With Jean Ann I believe we need to make a more definite effort to integrate her into the classroom group. She is new to our school and lacks a feeling of belonging. I will run a sociometric study with you and see if we can identify some children she would like to associate with. Then we can attempt some environmental changes to facilitate her social development.

The bell rang at that point, and Miss Davis had to return to her room. What Mrs. Wilkes had said stayed with her, and she began the kind of diagnostic thinking advisable for all teachers if they are to do their best to understand the children they are teaching.

Teachers and parents have responsibilities in the area of personality development. They are significant adults and have an important effect on the child's personality development. The mother has a major amount of interaction with the child during the preschool years and is a primary influence in shaping the development of the child's emerging traits.

Recent research findings indicate, however, that the school years, ages six to ten, have even a more significant effect on personality development than had been previously acknowledged.[1]

The teacher has the opportunity both to study and observe the child individually and to compare his development with that of many others in his age range. To function effectively in the area of personality development, a growing concern of the schools, each teacher needs access to at least two types of information. First, he needs general information about the developmental levels of all children. He should know what might be expected of the typical eight year old, ten year old, adolescent, etc. He should understand the sequential nature of development, viewing mental levels as ensuing sequences not bound by chronological ages. Secondly, he needs precise information on each child's specific developmental level.

Gesell suggests that even in the personality area, development tends to proceed on a sequential basis. However, the chronological age is not an effective measure of personality development. Individual differences must be understood in any assessment of development. Each child's cumulative folder should include information that assists in understanding his goals and personality.

Before beginning our study of personality, we might consider some of the fundamental questions to be discussed. First, what is meant by the word personality? How can personality be evaluated? Are there effective measures of personality? Is personality inherited, or is it the result of environment? Is the false dichotomy of inheritance or environment as the vital force in personality development now complicated by a third force, the self, and its effect on the development of personality? Is personality consistent, or is it readily subject to change? Some psychiatric conceptions have indicated that personality is formulated early in life, perhaps before the age of six, and does not experience any fundamental changes thereafter. What is the evidence concerning changes in personality and chronological age? What is the effect of the home on personality development? Does assuming responsibility assist in the development of character? Can the schools, through daily classroom experiences, assist in formulation of healthy personality development? Are there school activities which may serve as deterrents to the development of personality? These are some questions the student might consider as he begins a study of personality.

DEFINITION OF PERSONALITY

Personality includes the whole individual, his physique, temperament, skills, interests, hopes, appearance, feelings, habits, intelligence, and achievement. It includes both what he is today and what he hopes to be. In particular, it includes the way in which he relates himself to others and

[1] J. Kagan and H. Moss, *Birth to Maturity* (New York: John Wiley & Sons, Inc., 1962).

the reactions he encounters. Personality is subject, then, to the influence of the following major factors: (1) hereditary potential and primary characteristics of reactivity; (2) environmental situations, and (3) the personalized subjective meanings and interpretations the individual gives to his experiences.

Personality is not static, but rather a dynamic, constantly changing concept. The personality is obviously responsive to such factors as the parents' relationship to the child, peer contacts, teacher management, and many other factors in the child's total field. The child always has the ability to do more than respond to situations that occur about him. He also has the capacity to interpret and react to his experiences.

When we speak of personality, we shall stress in our definition the uniqueness of the individual. Personality really is what the child means when he refers to "I." Understanding the individual's personality means understanding the organization of his behavior as a totality. Personality is composed of all the feelings, attitudes, values, and behavior which make each person a unique individual.

THEORIES OF PERSONALITY

There are varied viewpoints relating to the nature, structure, and development of personality. The student of child development needs to be generally familiar with the various theories about personality. The advanced student can explore a particular theory more thoroughly than our cursory overview permits by referring to the suggested reading list at the end of the chapter.

Gesell developed a theory of the personality growth of children during the first sixteen years of life based on his biographical and clinical approach to child development. He offered a descriptive approach to the understanding of personality development. Prediction is based exclusively on the assumption that personality organization, like all other development, is also sequential. If you accept Gesell's sequences, you can anticipate each stage and make predictions about the development of the individual. In Gesell's books is a considerable amount of descriptive material about the characteristics of the average or typical child at certain ages.

Gesell's theory has both advantages and disadvantages for parents and teachers. It permits them to see that some behavior is developmental in nature and does not require unnecessary concern. At the same time, it may lead them to accept traits as developmental which may not be "normal" for the particular individual. The developmental approach to personality flows through a series of sequences. However, each individual's timing in going through the sequences is unique.

For the person who must deal with a large group of individuals, such as the teacher, it is helpful to know the general expectations for a given age group.

---

1. Gesell and Ilg, in *Child Development* (Harper, 1949), give a comprehensive description of child development from Gesell's point of view. Observe several children at an age level you select. Compare your findings. If there are differences, how do you account for them?

Kurt Lewin used a number of Gestalt and topological concepts in his theory of personality.[2] In his theory, Lewin was primarily interested in identifying and measuring the general variables that determine behavior at a given moment in time and in identifying the general laws that underlie individual differences in children.

Lewin believed that an understanding of the general laws of personality dynamics was basic to description and prediction of a given individual's behavior trends. Lewin believed that behavior was a function of the person and his environment, and he developed the equation $B = f\ (PE)$. In the equation, B, behavior, is f, a function of the simultaneous interaction of the person's individual differences and environmental influences. The equation indicates the comprehensiveness of his approach to understanding the total personality.

Lewin made us aware of the important constructs to consider in understanding an area so complex as personality. Although he recognized enduring characteristics in any individual's personality organization, he was pessimistic about the long-term prediction of future patterns of behavior.

The constitutional theory of personality is concerned with the various personality types. Sheldon, for example, worked out a classification of body types based on the concepts of endomorphy, mesomorphy, and ectomorphy.[3] For his typing, endomorphs have a relatively large presence of fatty tissue, mesomorphs have more muscle and bone tissue, and ectomorphs have relatively more tissue in the central nervous system. His research indicated that three temperaments in adult males correspond fairly well with the three physical types. Kretschmer also developed a theory of physique and body types.[4]

Sigmund Freud's approach is one of the most comprehensive of the theories of personality organization and has had significant influence on the thinking of psychiatrists and psychologists.

In Freudian theory, the human personality is analyzed in terms of the

[2] K. Lewin, *A Dynamic Theory of Personality* (New York: McGraw-Hill Book Company, 1935).
[3] W. Sheldon, *The Varieties of Temperament* (New York: Harper & Row, Publishers, 1942).
[4] E. Kretschmer, *Physique and Character* (New York: Harcourt, Brace & World, Inc., 1925).

intrapersonal interactions between the id, the ego, the superego, and the outside world. In the Freudian model, the id is the unconscious, unmoral, and illogical force. The id is dominated by the pleasure principle, and is the reservoir of psychic energy. The ego represents reason and logic, and is often referred to as the executive of personality. The ego integrates and organizes the mental processes involving id impulses, sanction from the superego, and demands of the outer world. Thus, the ego is involved in attempting to satisfy the three other forces and yet maintain a coherent organization. The ego controls. It is the self described in other theories of personality.

The superego's principal function is to criticize ego and demand conformity. Its function is similar to the general notion of the function of conscience, and it is responsible for man's socially conforming behavior.

For Freudians, the way in which the ego typically meets the conflicting demands of id, superego, and outer world eventually determines the individual personality. The ego meets the various demands by unconsciously employing defense mechanisms to maintain the self. Different egos employ defense mechanisms in different combinations, which accounts for the great variety of personality structures.

---

2. How might the Freudian theory explain faulty personality development? What are some guidelines in Freudian theory which parents and teachers might find useful when they consider their roles in personality development?

Murray's theory of personality draws on both psychoanalytic and Gestalt principles.[5] He views personality as a set of needs and perceptual presses and emphasizes the complexity and wholeness of the perceptual and learning processes in personality formation. Murray developed a list of twenty-eight social-psychogenic needs which the individual requires in order to reduce his striving behavior. In this theory the needs and presses are functionally related, and the environmental press is frequently interpreted on the basis of present needs. To utilize Murray's theory requires an understanding of the solution of a particular complex need-press, called a thema. In Murray's theory, the general nature of an individual's needs can be understood and perceived by analyzing a large variety of his tendencies. If an individual does not need to defend the self, Murray's thema is more readily observed. Murray developed the Thematic Apperception Test, a projective test which elicits the themas of individuals.

Adlerians view personality as an irreducible whole and see the indi-

[5] H. Murray, *Explorations in Personality: A Clinical Experimental Study of Fifty Men of College Age* (Oxford, England: Oxford University Press, 1938).

vidual as interacting primarily in a social environment. For each individual there is one basic motivation, the need to belong, and from this other motives are derived. The individual's motivation is goal-directed and the dominant direction of psychological movement is supplied by the goal. The Adlerian is concerned primarily with the direction of psychological movement. The fundamental principle of self-determinism underlies the individual's behavior and an inner directedness arises from the individual's subjective view of the environment.

When Adlerians consider basic motivations of the individual, they always examine the purposive nature of behavior and the social direction of the motives. In the child, the psychological movement is formulated largely by his degree of social interest and inferiority-superiority feelings in the early years of development. The basic interaction in the family atmosphere and among the family constellation and the child's subjective interpretations of these experiences determine the degree of inferiority feeling and the social interest in an individual child.

From birth the child is seeking to make sense out of his world. We best understand his actions when we recognize the goal he pursues. His early experiences and his interpretation of them help build a plan for his subsequent conduct. He learns how significant adults in his environment respond, and he turns this knowledge to his advantage. Frequently, what appears to be merely a reaction on the child's part, by close observation proves to be purposive activity with a definite goal. The child learns to predict the behavior of significant others in his environment and then has a basis for future actions. It is just this process that makes child management a difficult task. Each new situation evokes different responses from different children, depending upon the subjective manner in which the situation is interpreted and integrated. Disciplinary responses vary from child to child dependent upon the individual's self structure. Eventually, the scheme which the child has tried and trusted to his satisfaction becomes his permanent plan of conduct, his life style. Adlerians would be interested in the child's heredity and environment but they would be much more concerned with his use of his environment and his heredity. What the child does with his situation and how he interprets it is vital in understanding the development of personality.

---

3. Explain faulty personality development on the basis of Adlerian theory. Adlerians place a greater emphasis on the psychology of use than on the psychology of possession. Clarify the role of the psychology of use in relationship to variances in personality.

The self theorists have made some interesting formulations in regard to the development of personality. For those interested in the child's development as viewed by self theorists it is particularly interesting to consider the work of Earl Kelley, Carl Rogers, A. H. Maslow, and Arthur Combs.[6] The phenomenological approach believes that people select, even as children, what they perceive. From the child's experiences with significant others, he begins to understand human relationships. It is possible for the child either to develop a healthy personality or an unhealthy personality based on relationships he has had with the significant others in his environment. Self theorists discuss personality in terms of the fully functioning person, who thinks well of himself and of others, who is open to his experiences, and who sees himself as part of the world and involved in the process of becoming. The fully functioning personality recognizes the importance of his values. He also sees the place of mistakes. He recognizes that he is not perfect, but that he can still function, and as a result, his experiences become an asset instead of a hindrance. This individual, then, lives with courage and integrity.

Rogers has said that the fully functioning individual really trusts himself and others. Psychological growth is only possible when the individual is fundamentally loved, respected, and accepted, both by others and by himself. This is referred to as healthy growth and has been termed by various individuals as emotional maturity, self-actualization, or self-fulfillment. Self theorists believe that the inner nature of man is not evil, but either "good" or "neutral." It is the function of the adult to encourage and to bring out the best in the individual instead of attempting to suppress or repress the inner nature. Self theorists believe that the normal child, when given a truly free choice, most of the time chooses what is good for growth. He would do so because it feels right and gives him pleasure; it appears to be good. This approach espouses the principle of self-selection.

---

4. How are the self theorists different from Freudians and Adlerians in their approach to personality development?

In many ways self theorists are similar to Willard Olson insofar as they believe in the individual design for growing and the growth urge that occurs in each individual. Olson adds the dimension of the differences in developmental timing which occur from child to child. His organismic approach includes a consideration of maturity and rate of development factors.

[6] E. Kelley, *Education for What Is Real* (New York: Harper & Row, Publishers, 1947); C. Rogers, *On Becoming a Person* (Boston: Houghton Mifflin Company, 1961); A. Maslow, *Toward a Psychology of Being* (Princeton, N.J.: D. Van Nostrand Co., Inc., 1962); and A. Combs and D. Snygg, *Individual Behavior*, rev. ed. (New York: Harper & Row, Publishers, 1959).

RESEARCH IN PERSONALITY DEVELOPMENT

A fairly large amount of research has been concerned with the development of personality. Some of the most productive work has come out of the longitudinal approach to the study of personality.

In their summary of a thirty-year longitudinal study, Kagan and Moss point out: "The most dramatic and consistent finding of this study was that many of the behaviors exhibited by the child during the period 6 to 10 years of age, and a few during the age period 3 to 6, were moderately good predictors of theoretically related behaviors during early adulthood."[7] They feel that there is more than adequate evidence to support the generally accepted notion that adult personalities are formulated early in childhood.

They also indicate a high degree of relationship between personality and the traditional expectations of sex-role characteristics. For example, passive and dependent behavior is subject to cultural disapproval for boys while it is approved for girls. The child quickly receives this communication, and knowledge of early childhood behavior permits rather effective predictions on the basis of the individual's sex. Mussen indicated that the degree of adoption of traditional masculine or feminine sex-role interests among adolescent boys was stable over a fifteen-year period and had derivatives in adulthood.[8] He found that subjects with high feminine-interest scores as adolescents were found to score higher as men on scales of nonmasculine interests.

The research of Kagan and Moss shows that considerable continuity between childhood and adult behavior is already evident during the first four years of school. "The poorer predictive power of behavior during the preschool years suggests that developments during the age period 6 to 10 induce important changes in the child's behavioral organization. The primary events of this period include (a) identification with parents and the concomitant attempt to adopt the values and overt responses of the parent; (b) the realization that mastery of intellective skills is both a cultural requirement as well as a source of satisfaction; and (c) the encounter with the peer group. The latter experience forces the child to accommodate, to some degree, to the values and evaluations made by peers."[9] It seems evident that the first four years of school and the consequent peer environment in school (ages six to ten) formulate behavioral tendencies which are maintained throughout young adulthood. This has many implications for school and early identification of individual differences. There is a strong suggestion, for example, that children who display intense striving for

[7] Kagan and Moss, *Birth to Maturity,* p. 266.
[8] P. Mussen, "Some Antecedents and Consequents of Masculine Sex-Typing in Adolescent Boys," *Psychological Monographs,* Vol. 75, No. 2, 1961.
[9] Kagan and Moss, *Birth to Maturity,* p. 272.

mastery during the early years of school are likely to maintain this attitude toward the academic task. Thus, the value of early identification of elementary school students for purposes of special educational handling is indicated. Children not involved in the academic task at an early age might profit from attempts at early modification of this pattern.

It was also found that a tendency toward passivity during the first three years of life could be linked to adolescent or adult personality types. Boys who were extremely passive prior to age three were found to be nonaggressive, socially inhibited, and dependent as adolescents. Early passivity during the first five years seems to have a direct influence on the child's future development.

The University of Minnesota Institute of Child Welfare did a longitudinal study in Nobles County. They found consistent changes with age in cognitive skills and knowledge areas, but it was extremely difficult to find by their methods similar changes related to age in emotional or personality areas.[10]

---

5. What hypothesis do you offer to explain the lack of consistent changes with age in personality or emotional areas?

Honzik and MacFarlane in their study found considerable differences between first-born boys and others.[11] First-born boys showed more withdrawing and internalized patterns, while the non-first born were more overt, aggressive, and competitive in their patterns. Their study indicated different tensional ages for boys and girls, and they speculated that this was probably related to the differential cultural pressures brought upon males and females in our society.

Escalona and Heider attempted to predict the behavior of thirty-one preschool children, ages three through six years, from observations during the first eight months of life and from some knowledge of their parents.[12] Predictions were found to be most accurate for degree of adoption of sex-typed traits, motor development, and capacity for attention. Accuracy in prediction was poorest for behavior in unfamiliar situations or with unfamiliar people, competitiveness, and quality of the relationship with mother.

[10] Institute of Child Development and Welfare, *A Survey of Children's Adjustment Over Time,* A Report to the People of Nobles County (Minneapolis: University of Minnesota, 1959).

[11] J. Macfarlane, L. Allen, and M. Honzik. *A Developmental Study of the Behavior Problems of Normal Children between Twenty-One Months and Fourteen Years* (Los Angeles: University of California Press, 1954).

[12] S. Escalona and G. Heider, *Prediction and Outcome* (New York: Basic Books, Inc., 1959).

Tuddenham, in reporting research at the University of California Institute of Human Development on the stability of selected behavior from adolescence to adulthood, indicated that irritability and ease of anger arousal in adolescents predicted similar tendencies for men, but not for women.[13] Social anxiety was stable from adolescence to adulthood in women but not men.

The book, *Longitudinal Studies of Child Personality: Abstracts with Index* (Cambridge, Mass.: Harvard University Press, 1959), by Alan Stone and Gloria Ongue, presents a most comprehensive annotated bibliography of longitudinal studies.

FACTORS INFLUENCING PERSONALITY DEVELOPMENT

Personality development is not isolated; it results from both planned and incidental experiences. Personality growth is modified by the three major factors of heredity, environment, and self.

Any study of the way in which the individual becomes a unique and distinct personality must recognize that these factors cannot be isolated. There is a continuous interrelationship among the three major factors significant in the determination of personality.

Heredity

Some aspects in the development of personality are inherited, for example, glandular influences, physique, physical appearance, rate of maturation, and other genetic influences. Inheritance tends to set the boundaries or limits beyond which the individual usually does not develop, no matter how salutary the environment in which he lives.

In a consideration of hereditary factors, it is important to recognize the individualized manner in which each child uses his hereditary endowment. The same handicap, for instance, does not mean the same thing to each afflicted child. Some children with defective vision or crippled limbs almost use their handicap as an asset in their total development.

It is apparent that the individual's constitutional make-up influences the personality in a number of ways, even though indirectly. Studies show that even the newborn can be rather accurately classified as unusually active, fairly active, or quiet.[14] These differences are apparent almost immediately after birth and are attributable primarily to hereditary factors. Research also tends to point out that infant activity patterns tend to re-

[13] R. Tuddenham, "The Constancy of Personality Ratings Over Two Decades," *Genetic Psychology Monographs,* 60:3, August 1959.

[14] A. Thomas, H. Birch, S. Chess, M. Hertzig, and S. Korn, *Behavioral Individuality in Early Childhood* (New York: New York University Press, 1963).

main fairly stable throughout the early years. It is obvious, then, that the type of temperament with which the child enters the world has some effect on his total personality development.

Other factors of significance which may be attributed to heredity include physical appearance and physique. The child who is strong and of pleasing appearance has natural advantages in interaction with both his parents and peers in contrast to the child who lacks these advantages. Extensive studies of body build and personality by both Kretschmer and Sheldon indicate some relationships between physique and personality.[15] Physique certainly has an influence on early personality development of the child and perhaps has a sustaining influence throughout childhood. As already observed, there are considerable variations in the age at which children reach physical maturity. However, because many current criteria, both in school and in society in general, are based upon chronological age, children of the same chronological age, with considerable variation in actual maturity, are grouped together. A late-maturing child, therefore, is likely to be treated as immature and inadequate, while an early-maturing child is likely to be credited as being more grown-up physically, socially, and emotionally. In the area of motor skills, there are definite advantages to being an early-maturing child as these skills have an influence on perception of self and acceptance by others.

Research has been conducted to compare the personalities of the late- and the early-maturing child. Late maturers tend to reveal more personality difficulties than early maturers. The study by Mussen and Jones points to the fact that the late maturers make inadequate self-evaluations and are more dependent and more rebellious.[16] Early-maturing boys were found generally to feel adequate, accepted by others, self-confident, independent, and mature. It is apparent, then, that the early-maturing child generally has advantages.

---

6. What are the potential advantages to the child's personality in early maturation? Observe some children, and note personality differences which might appear to be related to hereditary potential or early maturation.

In a consideration of hereditary or biological factors in personality development, bodily structure and size, maturation and rate of development, physical features, endocrine development, early constitutional differences

[15] Kretschmer, *Physique and Character;* and Sheldon, *The Varieties of Temperament.*
[16] P. Mussen and M. C. Jones, "Self Conceptions, Motivations, and Interpersonal Attitudes of Late and Early Maturing Boys," *Child Development,* 28 (June 1957), 255.

such as generalized sensitivity, physical vigor, energy, and activity level, are all important determinants. Genetic forces which influence our physical health and development occur within the organism from conception throughout life. Some functions of our nervous system and endocrine glands play a significant role in determining patterns of action and outlook on life.

Environment

The next set of factors influencing personality derives from environment or culture. Obviously, the child or physical organism exists in a society and, as a result, must meet with sets of cultural demands. Hutt and Gibby found marked differences among cultures in respect to early patterns of infant-mother interactions.[17] In Indonesia the baby is frequently taken care of by the father while the mother works; their pattern of feeding would differ from the Hopi Indians, who are extremely indulgent in feeding. The Hopi infants are breast-fed by the mother whenever they show an inclination for nourishment. Hutt and Gibby concluded that behavior of the newborn child is considerably influenced by his early experiences and by his cultural heritage. However, they did not believe it was possible to predict resultants in personality development from individual, isolated, specific factors in the child's cultural experiences. The child's first acquaintance with cultural demands occurs within the family atmosphere. His first opportunity to observe how human beings live with one another is by observation of Mother's and Father's relationships.

The child also participates in the culture through family constellation. A growing amount of evidence indicates that the child's psychological position in the family constellation has an effect upon his personality development. The only child has experiences which influence his personality. In the same way, the eldest, the middle, and the youngest child have experiences which influence their development. Being the only boy or the only girl in a large family also has some psychological effects. The approach to life, then, is formulated out of these early experiences in the family atmosphere and the family constellation and through the continuing influences of his psychological position in the family.

---

7. Observe a group of children in a class, club, or large family. Obtain some data relative to their family atmosphere and family constellation. How has the family atmosphere and the family constellation affected the development of their unique personalities?

---

[17] M. Hutt and R. Gibby, *The Child: Development and Adjustment* (Boston: Allyn & Bacon, Inc., 1959), pp. 51–55.

It is apparent that the child's cultural group influences the development of his personality significantly in that it limits what he has an opportunity to learn. It sets up limits on the variety of experiences and situations which he is able to experience, and hence his development is partially conditioned by the culture into which he is born. Training factors and methods of child rearing differ from one culture to another, and obviously variations exist also in regard to one's social class.

In our society, we find great differences in attitudes toward child-rearing practices. Lower-class mothers permit behavior and attitudes which a middle-class mother would not tolerate. Children from various social classes exhibit differences in personality which can be related to the variations in methods of child management. Certainly the values, interests, and attitudes of our social classes vary, and as a result, children are encouraged or discouraged to develop specific personality traits.

---

8. Give specific examples of the effect of culture on personality in children. Give examples of how varied cultures on the American scene affect the development of personality.

Many early learnings in the family, which play an important part in the total socialization of the child, have a lasting influence upon the child's development. Goldfarb, for example, found striking differences among children who are markedly deprived of personal maternal care in the earliest years of life.[18] He found that children reared in an institution were retarded intellectually, had more frequent language and speech difficulties, and exhibited distinct differences in personality adjustment. He concluded that social and emotional maladjustment was permanently influenced by early severe deprivation.

Personality develops partially as a result of learning roles, which are influenced by family atmosphere, position in the family constellation, cultural background, and sociocultural patterns. The social environment of the neighborhood, community, and school, the customs, mores, and values of the people we live with also influence the roles we adopt. The culture establishes basic personality types. Interpersonal relations with all significant adults and peers have an influence upon the cultural factors in personality development.

Self

In the development of personality, the self, the ego, or the life style must be considered. We are an agent in our own development. Our

[18] W. Goldfarb, "Variations in Adolescent Adjustment of Institutionally Reared Children," *American Journal of Orthopsychiatry,* 17 (1947), 449–57.

unique frame of reference and our assumptions about self and the world in relation to self play an important part in all of our development. The unique life style encompasses a unique pattern of abilities, habits, interests, values, and concepts and on the basis of this style of life, many decisions about the utilization of hereditary, environmental, and cultural factors are made. Each individual plays a part in determining his values.

PRINCIPLES OF PERSONALITY DEVELOPMENT

Personality is best understood when seen as a developmental process. Inheritance plays a part in determining the range of development possible for an individual, but many other influences are significant in personality development. Children show considerable differences even in the first weeks of life. Eventually the child identifies with the personalities of those about him. Frequently parents note that the child is imitating their language and some behavioral characteristics.

The mature personality seems to be in the process of being shaped even before the child begins school. However, there are many significant influences upon personality development once the child comes into contact with forces outside of the family, such as neighborhood children and schoolmates. Those who take the developmental approach to the understanding of child growth see personality development as part of a total growth effect, not isolated from other aspects of growth. Personality is affected somewhat by the developmental stage of the individual, as illustrated by Gesell.

The Characteristics and Components of a Healthy Personality

Normal adjustment is a relative thing; each child experiences some anxiety and from time to time displays behavior which is not acceptable to others or to himself. However, children who function within the normal range of behavior are said to have a healthy personality. They are children with realistic goals, capable of satisfying their needs, and functioning within society in a socially acceptable manner.

A characteristic of the child with a healthy personality is social interest. He is concerned about others as well as himself. This is obviously a trait that emerges gradually with maturity. The child demonstrates some empathy or a capacity to understand how others feel and also how others feel about him. His behavior is characterized by a courageous approach to life. He feels competent and able to function and exudes self-confidence.

The child who is maturing in a healthy direction is the child who is becoming less dependent and more self-directed. He is better able to make responsible decisions and is oriented more toward reality than toward what Freud postulated as the pleasure principle. He is able to postpone his own gratification. The mature personality also moves from a major consideration of self to a concern for others and their needs.

The Mid-Century White House Conference on Children and Youth listed the following as components of a healthy personality:

1. A sense of trust. If, in the first year, the child's needs are met, it is likely he will develop a sense of trust.
2. A sense of autonomy. The child has a feeling of self-sufficiency and strength as a result of making choices.
3. A sense of initiative. He is able to plan and follow through on his ideas, to be creative.
4. A sense of duty and accomplishment. He recognizes the importance of cooperation and of work; enjoys the feeling that he is able.
5. A sense of identity. He knows who he is and what is his role.
6. A sense of intimacy. He knows he is with others and cares for others.
7. A parental sense. He has an interest in caring for children of his own.
8. A sense of integrity. He has the ability to accept life and the people involved in it.[19]

Witmer and Kotinsky in *Personality in the Making*[20] presented eight stages of development toward maturity which have been summarized by Coleman as follows:[21]

AGE PERIOD	CHARACTERISTIC TO BE ACHIEVED	MAJOR HAZARD TO ACHIEVEMENT
Birth–1 year	Sense of trust or security—derived from affection and gratification of needs.	Neglect, abuse, or deprivation of consistent and appropriate love in infancy; harsh or early weaning.
1–4 years	Sense of autonomy—child viewing himself as an individual in his own right, apart from parents although dependent on them.	Conditions which interfere with the child's achieving feeling of adequacy or his learning of skills such as walking.
4–5 years	Sense of initiative—period of vigorous reality testing, imagination and imitation of adult behavior.	Overly strict discipline, internalization of rigid ethical attitudes which interfere with the child's spontaneity and reality testing.

[19] Mid-Century White House Conference on Children and Youth, Fact Finding Report (Raleigh, N.C.: Health Publications Institute, 1951).
[20] H. Witmer and R. Kotinsky, *Personality in the Making* (New York: Harper & Row, Publishers, 1952).
[21] J. Coleman, *Abnormal Psychology and Modern Life* (Chicago: Scott, Foresman & Company, 1956), p. 70.

AGE PERIOD	CHARACTERISTIC TO BE ACHIEVED	MAJOR HAZARD TO ACHIEVEMENT
6–11 years	Sense of duty and accomplishment—laying aside of fantasy and play and undertaking real tasks, developing academic and social competencies.	Excessive competition, personal limitations, or other conditions which lead to experiences of failure, resulting in feelings of inferiority and poor work habits.
12–15 years	Sense of identity—clarification in adolescence of who one is and what one's role is.	Failure of society to provide clearly defined roles and standards; formation of cliques which provide clear but not always desirable roles and standards.
15 years–Adulthood	Sense of intimacy—ability to establish close personal relationships with members of both sexes.	Cultural and personal factors which lead to psychological isolation or to formal, rather than warm, personal relations.
Adulthood	Parental sense—productivity and creativity for others as well as self.	Failure to master developmental tasks, resulting in egocentric, nonproductive person.
Adulthood	Sense of integrity—acceptance of the dominant ideals of one's culture, sense of continuity of past, present, and future of the meaningfulness of life.	Lack of tradition, consistent values, and support from culture leaves much for the individual to work out for himself; thus many unable to find meaning in life and to accept its limitations.

Summary chart by J. C. Coleman in *Abnormal Psychology and Modern Life* (Chicago: Scott, Foresman & Company, 1956) based on Chap. 1 of *The Making of a Healthy Personality* by H. Witmer and R. Kotinsky (New York: Harper & Row, Publishers, 1952).

DEVELOPMENTAL TASKS AND PERSONALITY

Personality development can frequently be best understood when seen in the context of specific developmental tasks, relevant to the culture, which are demanded of the individual by maturation and social pressures. These tasks each child must master if he is to maintain a normal course of development. When the tasks are not mastered, the child invariably suffers from immaturities and incompetencies, which tend to handicap his future progress in subsequent developmental tasks.

The developmental tasks are sometimes seen more effectively when viewed in relationship to five stages of development with which the school is concerned. (See table on the following page.)

THE TASKS OF FIVE STAGES OF DEVELOPMENT IN TEN CATEGORIES OF BEHAVIOR

	INFANCY	EARLY CHILDHOOD	LATE CHILDHOOD	EARLY ADOLESCENCE	LATE ADOLESCENCE
I Achieving an appropriate dependence-independence pattern.	1. Establishing one's self as a very dependent being. 2. Beginning the establishment of self-awareness.	1. Adjusting to less private attention; becoming independent physically (while remaining strongly dependent emotionally).	1. Freeing one's self from primary identification with adults.	1. Establishing one's independence from adults in all areas of behavior.	1. Establishing one's self as an independent individual in an adult manner.
II Achieving an appropriate giving-receiving pattern of affection.	1. Developing a feeling for affection.	1. Developing the ability to give affection. 2. Learning to share affection.	1. Learning to give as much love as one receives; forming friendships with peers.	1. Accepting one's self as a worthwhile person, really worthy of love.	1. Building a strong mutual affectional bond with a (possible) marriage partner.
III Relating to changing social groups.	1. Becoming aware of the alive as against the inanimate, and the familiar against the unfamiliar. 2. Developing rudimentary social-interaction.	1. Beginning to develop the ability to interact with age-mates. 2. Adjusting in the family to expectations it has for the child as a member of the social unit.	1. Clarifying the adult world as over against the child's world. 2. Establishing peer groupness and learning to belong.	1. Behaving according to a shifting peer code.	1. Adopting an adult-patterned set of social values by learning a new peer code.

Adapted from "The Tasks of Five Stages of Development in Ten Categories of Behavior," pages 84–87, *Fostering Mental Health in Our Schools,* 1950 Yearbook. (Washington, D.C.: Association for Supervision and Curriculum Development, 1950.)

GUIDING CHARACTER DEVELOPMENT

An important role is played by both parents and teachers in the formation of character.

A boy, ten years old, refuses to cooperate with the requests of his parents. He also lacks responsibility in the school tasks. The parents wonder why this is happening to them.

In another family the parents find that most of their time is spent "refereeing" quarrels among their children. The spirit of harmony is rarely present. They ponder the cause of these poor interpersonal relations.

The family must reassume the responsibility for training the child. History shows that when parents fail in this responsibility a decadent culture evolves. Too many signs are already present in our culture to ask whether this analogy is applicable to our country.

Do we recognize appropriate roles in the family? Do we know how to raise children in a democratic atmosphere?

One of the most important tasks of parents is to guide the character development of their children. Happiness within the home, success in interpersonal relations, and eventual personal social maturity all stem from early foundations laid in the home.

Many parents are becoming increasingly aware of their responsibilities in forming character. However, they are sometimes confused about proper methods and the goals of training.

To influence character you must have a clear picture of what to expect. Character is not identical with ethical or moral behavior. Ethical behavior in an individual means unselfish love and a willingness to defend what he believes. Morality only implies the individual's willingness to conform to the existing standards of a group in a specific situation. Character is a more inclusive term, indicating the choices the individual makes when his actions affect the welfare of others. Character has often been defined simply as the way people behave away from home when they feel they are not being observed by anyone who matters. The person with character has values and standards which go beyond personal gratification. Character education must be comprehensive training applicable beyond either the school or home.

The most significant influences on character appear to be in the home. However, the school and the community, as represented in the values of people who hold social power, are also influential on character. The child observes closely to see the parents' reaction to the faulty value systems of people within the community. He also notes the parents' response to the individual who values money more than correct judgment or who seeks material things more than human values. The parent who either actively accepts or fails to oppose faulty values is teaching a more significant lesson through his actions than through his words.

The church is also an influence upon the emerging character of the child, although studies have indicated that it is not as significant a factor as might be expected.

Piaget's conception of the stages in the development of the child's moral judgment is: (1) nonrecognition of rules; (2) recognition of rules as absolute and morally correct, as given by authority; (3) recognition of the conventional, arbitrary character of rules; and (4) manipulation of and recognition of the changeability of rules.[22]

In an extensive study of character development, Robert Peck and Robert Havighurst attempted to answer the question, "What is character?" by conceiving of a series of successive stages in the psychosocial development of the individual which they labeled amoral, expedient, conforming, irrational-conscientious, and rational-altruistic.[23] These stages can be briefly defined as follows: The amoral individual disregards the effect his acts have on others. He is egocentric and out only for personal gratification. The psychologist refers to this individual as the psychopath or character disorder. The expedient individual's behavior is more controlled. He is considerate of others when it helps him accomplish his goals. The conforming individual learns a role and is able to make choices acceptable in his group. His behavior is entirely motivated by social approval. For him, a choice between his judgment and the group's desire is generally controlled by the group. The irrational, conscientious individual acts on the basis of values he holds emotionally, not rationally. He is dependent on rules and finds self-respect in following a code endorsed by authority. The rational altruistic individual understands standards and is able to make decisions about what is important in a situation. He is concerned about the welfare of others and is able to consider others because he also has a very deep self-acceptance.

Many individuals pass through all of the stages and sometimes they regress. However, the stages are not to be considered as sequential, nor is it mandatory that each individual pass through each stage.

The extensive research of Peck and Havighurst points to the prime significance of family influences on character development.[24] They found that moral stability was most significantly influenced by an atmosphere of mutual trust and consistency. The individual's feelings of adequacy which permit him to make decisions were also best developed in an atmosphere of trust and consistency. Mutual trust among family members was identified at a statistically significant level as important in character development. The child's character maturity appeared to be directly related to the degree of consistency, mutual trust, and mutual approval he experi-

[22] J. Piaget, *The Moral Judgment of the Child* (New York: Harcourt, Brace & World, Inc., 1932).

[23] R. Peck and R. Havighurst, *The Psychology of Character Development* (New York: John Wiley & Sons, Inc., 1960).

[24] R. Peck and R. Havighurst, *The Psychology of Character Development.*

enced within his family. If these same attitudes were operative in school relationships, character development would be facilitated. Sears found that the more the control of the child is love-oriented, contrasted with physical punishment, the more effective is parental control over desirable behavior, and the stronger the development of the child's guilt feelings for improper behavior.[25]

The importance of consistency, mutual trust, and mutual approval in the development of children was found in other societies also. Margaret Mead, in her anthropological studies, found that highly cooperative, friendly, warm, and considerate personalities were produced in a tribe, the Arapesh, who had formed a group with almost complete social equality.[26] In the Arapesh, neither age nor sex gave superior social status. The groups which showed the highest amount of mutual trust and mutual approval produced the most cooperative children, according to Mead.

The parent concerned about guiding the child's character formation can turn to specific guidelines for action. First, he can become more aware of the importance of the family atmosphere. Proper character formation comes when the child feels emotionally secure and accepted as he is. The parent is able to utilize the child's desire to be approved. This is different from endeavoring to make the child dissatisfied with his position or indicating you feel he can do better. When the child demonstrates a strong, healthy character trait, it should be reinforced and approved. The child should be taught always to seek ways of solving ethical problems with reason. The parent who desires the child to function ethically and with good character not only within his presence but also away from the influence of the family, provides the child with opportunities to deal with conflicts and gain experience in solving them. The child's experiences can then be translated into a philosophy of life.

The goal becomes one of developing in the individual a growing ability to make decisions based on a sound philosophy of life. In all of this the parent recognizes that each individual develops a unique pattern of central purposes, which serves as a criterion for him in making social decisions. The atmosphere may remain consistent but variations in management to account for individuality are necessary. The specific child is best understood when the parent can see what his purposes are and how he tends to interpret his experiences.

Certain principles emerge from the work done on character.

1. There is no age of discretion. The child does not suddenly exhibit good character because he has lived longer. Character is not directly related to aging.

[25] R. Sears, E. Maccoby, and H. Levin, *Patterns of Child Rearing* (New York: Harper & Row, Publishers, 1957).
[26] Margaret Mead, *Sex and Temperament in Three Primitive Societies* (New York: Mentor Books, 1950).

2. Early and continuous training in character development is essential. The child needs consistent experiences, beginning early in life, that help him make the right decisions.

3. Character and spiritual values are effective only when they become an integral part of feelings, thoughts, and convictions. The atmosphere should be such that the child feels this is the right way of life.

4. Character can be taught best within the family circle through example and by regular application.

5. The child learns the desired character response when he experiences satisfaction through ethical responses and annoyance through undesirable responses.

6. Reinforcement is most significant when used promptly. The consequences of an act should be apparent immediately if change of behavior is expected.

7. Punishment should be replaced by logical consequences. When we punish, we do not permit the child to learn from his controls, but only to defer to our controls. However, in using natural consequences, the child learns from the natural and logical disturbance of order. He has a choice and learns he is not disregarding the adult but the order of the specific community.

The parent interested in affecting the child's character development must be able to inspire the child to achieve what he is capable of. This would be done most effectively when the parents (1) value the child as he is; (2) show a faith in the child that enables him to have faith in himself; (3) give recognition for effort, not just for achievement; (4) recognize and utilize the child's interests, assets, and strengths.[27]

Regardless of the research examined, one factor appears consistently: children learn more from what we do than from what we say. Moralizing not backed by example is wasted. Character tends to be an accurate reflection of the way in which the individual has been treated or feels he has been treated. The parents' responsibility, then, is to provide the necessary conditions for facilitating character development within the home atmosphere.

DEFENSE MECHANISMS IN CHILDHOOD

It has been demonstrated that behavior patterns which are repeated over a period of time become fixed. A child's responses to the tasks of life may not, at first, be too patterned or discernible, but as time progresses and he continues to react in certain ways to certain situations, his pattern

[27] D. Dinkmeyer and R. Dreikurs, *Encouraging Children to Learn: The Encouragement Process* (Englewood Cliffs, N.J.: Prentice-Hall, Inc., 1963).

becomes apparent. The child, through his actions, reveals his goals, needs, and purposes. Adults need to understand how the child views life and to recognize that a considerable amount of his personality is formulated on the basis of how he perceives the world. Even though some of his perceptions may be based on faulty assumptions, they, nonetheless, determine his interaction with others.

How, then, does the child go about meeting psychological problems when his goals become difficult to reach? Regression is one of the mechanisms or dynamisms utilized. It implies that the child has given up and retreated to a past stage. This sometimes stems from a sense of failure, which prompts the child to retreat to a happier previous success. If the child can realize that he was once successful, he may then gain the courage to go on and repeat his success. Some children, however, become satisfied with the accomplishments of the past, and, convinced that they are not able to repeat their success, use regression as a solution. Regression sometimes takes the form of fairly complete social withdrawal from cooperation with people. The teacher and parent need to be alert in spotting regression, as children who use regression rarely bother adults. Nevertheless, adults should be concerned about them, because regression can be a significant behavior tendency in childhood.

Another indication of maladjustment is the child's tendency to blame others for his shortcomings. Some children convince themselves that the blame is never theirs, that things are out of their control, that others get them into trouble. The child who regularly uses this mechanism is headed toward a personality difficulty. He cannot really face himself honestly; he always explains his faults by saying that people do not like him, or the teacher does not understand him, or nobody cooperates with him.

Being suspicious of others is another unhealthy behavioral tendency, which can affect the child's adjustment to life. The child who is suspicious and introverted can eventually develop paranoid tendencies in which he comes to believe everybody is against him.

Young children often unconsciously project their ideas on other persons. Projection is a defense mechanism in which the child places the blame on someone else, saying, "My brother doesn't like you," or "My teacher won't permit me." This type of projection solves personality problems for the child. Some children repress their difficulties; are always "forgetting"; they cannot remember homework, parental expectations, or anything else which seems unpleasant to them.

You must always recognize that nearly everyone employs defense mechanisms. They are significant only when exaggerated. Each defense mechanism described you have probably observed in others and in yourself. The significant factor is the frequency and intensity of occurrence in solving problems in contrast to approaching the difficulty directly.

Children fall into the habit of utilizing undesirable tendencies because of faulty training. The child who has a good relationship with the significant adults in his life gains the courage to deal with all kinds of people and with his peers. Each child should actually be encouraged to develop self-assurance and an understanding of his problems and the problems of others. The child would not be engrossed only in his own problems, but would learn to show concern for others.

In studying the defense mechanisms and significant behavior tendencies in children, be alert to the severity of the use of such traits as hatred, cruelty, rationalization, fear, illness, daydreaming, and feelings of inferiority as methods of problem solving. Children in increasing numbers are exhibiting such psychosomatic disturbances as ulcers, asthma, fatigue, enuresis, etc. When there is no physical basis for the physiological disturbance these complaints may be taken as early evidence of faulty personality development.

---

9. Are the defense mechanisms described to be anticipated in all children as part of growing up? How would you manage specific mechanisms? What is the difference in the parents' and the teachers' role in dealing with the mechanisms?

CONSISTENCY AND CHANGE IN PERSONALITY

The central core of the child's personality is in the process of formation, so that it is possible for personality changes to occur. However, as the child continues to experience specific situations and come up with set interpretations of his experiences, an unfolding style of life or self concept develops.

Those who believe in the consistency of the individual's self concept point to the ego as functioning in such a manner as to maintain a consistent state of personality organization, which is quite comparable to the physiological functioning of the homeostasis mechanism. Some research in personality tends to substantiate this theoretical position held by psychiatrists and psychologists.

Lee Stott found that a tendency in most of his cases for the pattern which characterized the child when he entered nursery school at age two and one half persisted at least through the years of regular attendance at the Merrill-Palmer School.[28] This consistency has to an extent also been demonstrated in studies at the University of California Fels Research Institute and in other longitudinal studies.[29]

[28] L. Stott, "The Identification of Four Childhood Personality Traits as Expressed in the Social Interaction of Preschool Children," *Selected Papers,* Inter-Institutional Seminar in Child Development (Detroit, Mich.: Merrill-Palmer School, 1958).
[29] J. Kagan, "American Longitudinal Research on Psychological Development," *Child Development,* 35 (1964), 1–32.

An often quoted study in this area is one by Shirley, which concluded that personality differences can already be noted at the time of birth and that babies sampled showed a marked degree of consistency in personality as they grew older.[30] For example, the irritable baby remained relatively more irritable, even though irritability decreased with increasing age.

Neilon did a personality study of fifteen of Shirley's subjects at age seventeen.[31] He concluded that personality similarities in an individual persist over a fairly extensive period of life and that consistency is characteristic of development.

McKinnon did a longitudinal study of the personality development of sixteen children from ages three to eight or nine.[32] For his research purposes he divided the children into four groups, conformity of a constructive type, caution and lack of self-confidence, active and forceable approach, and withdrawal. McKinnon found a persistence in behavior to the extent that ten of the sixteen remained in the original grouping during the five- to six-year period of study. It was possible to demonstrate consistency in personality.

The most comprehensive longitudinal study of personality development has been done by Kagan and Moss.[33] They found "passive withdrawal from stressful situations, dependency on family, ease-of-anger arousal, involvement in intellectual mastery, social interaction, anxiety, sex-role identification, and pattern of sexual behavior in adulthood were each related to reasonably analogous behavioral dispositions during the early school years." The stability of these characteristics is closely related to appropriate roles for males and females in our culture.

---

10. Consistent findings point to the early setting of personality patterns which remain relatively fixed. What does this imply for the school curriculum, parent education, and school guidance programs?

THE SCHOOL AND PERSONALITY DEVELOPMENT

The school has a significant effect on personality development. Teachers cannot really say they are concerned only with intellectual development and not personality development. The child is a whole person, and the school needs to be aware of the teacher's effect as model, example, and

[30] M. Shirley, *The First Two Years: A Study of Twenty-Five Babies' Personality Manifestations* (Minneapolis, Minn.: University of Minnesota Press, 1933).
[31] P. Neilon, "Shirley's Babies After Fifteen Years: A Personality Study," *Journal of Genetic Psychology*, 73 (1948), 175–86.
[32] K. McKinnon, "Consistency and Change in Behavior Manifestations," *Child Development Monographs*, No. 30 (1942).
[33] Kagan and Moss, *Birth to Maturity*, p. 266.

guide. The teacher's behavior serves either to establish or change the child's conception of the world and people. Teachers in the early primary grades can have a significant effect on personality development. As the Fels Research Study indicated, the years from age six to ten are particularly crucial.

The elementary school teacher needs to be particularly aware of peer relationships and their effect upon individual development. Through sociometric and other child study techniques he can become more aware of relationships and their effect upon the personalities in the classroom. Lippitt and Gold found a correlation between various types of classroom socioemotional structures, the stratification of those who are looked up to or down on, and mental health.[34] Healthy personality development can also be facilitated through curriculum flexibility.

Interpersonal relationships in the school have a significant effect upon the child's feelings of status and self-confidence. Teachers need to be aware that they are dealing with children from various social classes, and that these social classes and their values have an effect upon the way in which the child adjusts both to the tasks of school work and achievement and the social tasks of getting along with adults and children. Wilson investigated the aspirations of boys with similar social origins who were attending schools characterized by different climates of aspiration. Among sons of both professional and manual workers, more of those attending middle-class schools than of those attending working-class schools wanted to go to college. Peer-group norms and the dominant class character have strong influence on aspirations.[35]

---

11. What are some specific steps the school administration concerned about healthy personality should take? What are some ways the school should be working with the problems of social-class influences?

THE EVALUATION AND ASSESSMENT OF PERSONALITY

An often neglected factor in studying the child in the school setting is the assessment of personality development. Personality is always available for assessment in that the child continually reflects his goals and purposes in all of his behavior. Assessment is not easy, however, and it might be wise to consider initially the problems involved in the measurement of personality.

One of the first problems is the elusive nature of personality. Personality

[34] R. Lippitt and M. Gold, "Classroom Social Structure as a Mental Health Problem," *Journal of Social Issues*, 15, No. 1 (1959), pp. 40–49.
[35] A. Wilson, "Residential Segregation of Social Classes and Aspirations of High School Boys," *American Sociological Review*, 24 (December 1959), pp. 836–45.

traits are not well-defined, and, as a result, it is often difficult to study personality functionally. Another problem in personality study is sampling. The extent to which certain traits are present in the child is important. If research had revealed the presence of consistent mutually exclusive personality traits, the problem of measurement would be relatively simple, but definite single variables in personality study are not yet easily identified.[36] Cattell at the University of Illinois has been involved in a long-term study of personality, which thus far corroborates the continued existence of this problem.

The entire personality of the child theoretically could be charted by stimulating him to reveal one or two specific expressions of each trait. However, personality is specific to a given situation and often varies depending on social situations. Therefore, the problem of adequate samples of personality is basic to any study and assessment.

Another measurement problem is reliability. If tests and measures are to be of value, responses elicited must be consistent. Comparable results should be secured when the measures or assessments are repeated after a lapse of time. However, personality factors, which encompass feelings and attitudes, are modified and changed in accordance with fluctuations in experience and the emerging self concept. Hence, a repetition of the same test might result in different results which actually reflected changes in personality and not a lack of reliability. Therefore, reliability takes on a different connotation when we are measuring personality change.

Validity is another problem in personality study. As for all tests, a personality test is considered valid when it actually measures what it claims to measure. Personality test items are usually determined to be valid on the basis of their diagnostic value in discriminating between various groups of children who possess the qualities being measured in high or low degree.

Personality tests are also made valid to the extent that items are disguised and the social desirability factor is controlled. The test should be adjusted to the child's reading level and test items should be selected with a consideration of the pupil's age level and general interests.

Methods of study in personality vary so greatly that consideration of some of the approaches might be worthwhile.

Some have studied personality on the basis of an individual's sociocultural membership, his status in the socioeconomic community. On this basis, personalities are classified in relationship to age, socioeconomic setting, social class, and other subgroup memberships. Other types of personality study have been done on the basis of collecting the personal documents of the individual. A considerable amount of information can

[36] R. B. Cattell, *Personality: A Systematic Theoretical and Factual Study* (New York: McGraw-Hill Book Company, 1950).

be obtained through autobiographies, diaries, essays and the like. Some personality study has been done by asking individuals to write short answers to the direct question, "Who are you?" This technique can be productive in getting at the child's perception of self in relation to the world.

Personality study is also done on the basis of samples of behavior. The child's behavior is time-sampled, and observations are made at different periods in the day, week, and month of the child's life. Other personality study is done with rating scales; teachers or psychologists are asked to rate the child on certain traits.

---

12. Discuss the advantages and disadvantages of the comparatively informal measures of personality.

For purposes of child study, we can probably divide the instruments for personality assessment into four major categories. First are the rating scales, paper-and-pencil devices for rating the individual on a scale of personal character. Personality inventories are standardized instruments in which the subject checks his reactions to a wide variety of specific questions. Projective methods examine the individual's internal personality organization and view of life on the basis of his interpretations of pictures, ink blots, incomplete sentence tests, or story-completion tests. The final method is direct observation, in which the subject's overt behavior is observed in both typical situations and situations involving desirable and undesirable behavior.

The value of the rating scale is always highly dependent upon the degree of training given to those who are asked to rate. Rating scales have the advantage of requiring observation of a child's behavior. They do not need to be inferential, but rather rely on actual observation. The personality inventory is another form of rating in which the child rates himself. Inventories have been designed to measure a number of traits or dimensions of adjustment. Although these tests are convenient and frequently get below the surface in tapping an individual's own personal experiences and feelings, they are limited by the individual's ability to understand himself and to give an accurate report. The subject must be motivated in his desire to cooperate, or the report will have little value. Frequently, item analysis of self-report ratings can be effective in helping the teacher or psychologist to understand the personality of the individual. Generally, though, personality tests for children are still in a primitive stage.

The projective test makes an attempt to probe into the unconscious life to get at the individual's goals, purposes, and themes. Methods of projective testing usable with children include the Rorschach Ink-Blot Test, various picture-theme projectives, word association, and play- or doll-therapy techniques. The basic assumption in this type of testing is that an indi-

TEST	AGE OR GRADE LEVEL	VARIABLES, FEATURES
1. California Test of Personality, California Test Bureau, Del Monte Research Park, Monterey, California	Grades Kdgn–3, 4–8, 7–10	Feelings about Self and Social-adjustment Components
2. IPAT Children's Personality Questionnaire, Institute for Personality and Ability Testing, 1602–04 Coronado Drive, Champaign, Ill.	Ages 8–12	14 Personality Dimensions
3. Institute of Child Study Security Test, Institute of Child Study, University of Toronto, Toronto, Ontario.	Grades 4–8	2 Scores: Consistency, Security, Tentative Norms.
4. Mental Health Analysis, California Test Bureau, Del Monte Research Park, Monterey, California.	Grades 4–8	Mental Health Assets and Liabilities
5. Science Research Associates, Junior Inventory, Science Research Associates, 259 East Erie Street, Chicago 11, Ill.	Grades 4–8	A Problem Checklist

PROJECTIVE	AGE LEVEL
1. House-Tree-Person Projective Technique, Western Psychological Services	5 and over
2. Machover Draw-A-Person Test, Karen Machover, Charles C Thomas, Publishers	2 and over
3. Make a Picture Story, Psychological Corp.	6 and over
4. The Michigan Picture Test, Science Research Associates	8–14
5. Revised Bender Gestalt, Max Hutt	7 and over
6. Rorschach, Grune and Stratton	3 and over
7. Thematic Apperception Test, Henry A. Murray, Harvard University Press	4 and over

vidual will project his needs, goals, and purposes under what appears to him at the time to be an irrevelant stimulus.

Work with the projectives supplies the data for the psychologist to make some conclusions about the child's perception of self and the world about him. Doll play is frequently interesting in providing some insight into the young child. Other forms of expressive behavior also help permit inferences about personality; children's drawings, the drawing of a house-tree-person, easel painting, incomplete stories, and incomplete sentences are other methods of measurement.

The Rorschach Ink-Blot Test is based on the assumption that general personality trends can be ascertained from the subject's interpretations of what he sees in a series of ink blots. This test, of course, is highly dependent upon the skill and experience of the administrator.

Another form of projective is the picture analysis test, in which the child is presented with a series of pictures and is asked to tell a story about them as to what is happening now, what happened before, and what will happen. It is assumed that the individual reveals his personality as he makes up the story about each picture, describing the events, the outcome, and the feelings and thoughts of the characters. Projective personality study when professionally done can give considerable insight into the personality of the individual.

Personality, then, is one of the most significant aspects of child study, and teachers need to know a considerable amount about it. We have seen that there are various theories about the way in which personality is organized. We have noted a number of factors that influence personality development. It is apparent that there is considerable interrelationship between the major factors—the organic or biological, environmental or cultural, and the personalized apperceptions of the individual. Although personality has been shown to be relatively consistent and predictable, we recognize that certain methods of child training help to produce a more effective, healthy personality than other methods of child training.

IMPLICATIONS

1. The school years, ages six to ten, have a most significant effect on long-range personality development. Guidance services, involving early identification and therapeutic change, should be an important part of the early elementary school years.

2. The teacher is in a particularly crucial position to observe and compare the child's personality development in relation to the peers. More emphasis should be placed on obtaining systematic observations, preferably anecdotal, from the teacher, and on encouraging teachers to record their observations.

3. There is need to become more sophisticated in understanding developmental "ages and stages." "Stages" must always be seen in terms of the individual's development and not as devices to explain all kinds of inadequate functioning; otherwise, stages can serve as a deterrent to investigating problem areas in the child's development.

4. Several personality theories point to the importance of the goal, theme, and the striving for self-actualization. Close observation of the direction of the child's psychological movement can help explain behavior.

5. Psychological growth is facilitated as the individual is loved, respected, and accepted both by others and himself. This focuses on the nature of the relationship necessary for growth and the importance of self-understanding. Teachers should work with pupils on self-understanding both incidentally and through planned instruction.

6. The child's approach to mastery of the academic and intellectual skills is not only a measure of intellect, but an indication of his ability to acquire satisfaction through his own development. The personality of the child with adequate potential who does not function should be studied.

7. Our culture makes certain expectations of the child based on sex-role characteristics. The child is held to certain sex roles regardless of differences in temperament and primary characteristics of reactivity.

8. Some late maturing children tend to have more personality difficulties than early maturers. They make more inadequate self-evaluations, and are more dependent and rebellious. If the school took into account variances in maturational rate in making educational plans, permitting the slow maturer more time to develop, this could have a beneficial effect on personality development.

9. The cultural group influences the development of personality. A wide exposure to varied cultures should help to broaden the child's personality and enable him to be more accepting of personality differences.

10. The child with a healthy personality has social interest; he is concerned about others as well as himself. Activities should be planned which foster and stimulate social interest.

11. The development of responsibility plays a major role in the development of personality. Regular opportunities to assume responsibility should be provided. Responsibility should not be held up as a reward, but used to help develop children's capacity to function and feel adequate.

12. Peck and Havighurst's stages in the psychosocial development of the individual provide a standard to evaluate character development. Teachers can use these stages to conceptualize more adequately their goals in the area of character development.

13. Havighurst and Peck found that stability is most significantly influenced by an atmosphere of mutual trust and consistency. These traits, long acclaimed by theorists, were demonstrated to be significant by research. They epitomize the desirable home and school atmosphere.

14. There is no age of discretion. Character development is a task requiring both incidental and planned educational experiences.

15. The child can learn most adequately by building his controls, not deferring to our controls. This necessitates permitting him to learn from natural and logical consequences.

16. Children learn more from example than from verbalizing. Character tends to be a reflection of the way the child feels he has been treated. The nature of the adult's example and his relationship with the child are the most powerful tools of instruction.

17. Defense mechanisms are found in all children and are only symptoms. They point to the difficulty, but should always be seen only as clues to the child's faulty perceptions.

18. The many studies which demonstrate early differences and consistency in personality point to the importance of parent education groups and the early utilization of counseling facilities, when indicated.

19. The culture plays an important role in the formation of personality traits. The teacher's awareness of the varied cultural expectations in the group related to school achievement and behavior can serve to explain the value systems of the children. Peer group norms and the character of the dominant class have a strong influence on level of aspiration.

SUGGESTED READINGS

Articles

Hartshorne, H., and M. May, "Studies in the Organization of Character," in *Psychological Studies of Human Development*, 2nd ed., eds. R. Kuhlen and G. Thompson, p. 432. New York: Appleton-Century-Crofts, 1963.

Kagan, J., and H. Moss, "Stability of Passive and Dependent Behavior from Childhood to Adulthood," in *Readings in Child Psychology*, 2nd ed., ed. W. Dennis, p. 486. Englewood Cliffs, N.J.: Prentice-Hall, Inc., 1963.

Stott, L., "Stability in Ascendance-Submission," in *Readings in Child Psychology*, 2nd ed., ed. W. Dennis, p. 501. Englewood Cliffs, N.J.: Prentice-Hall, Inc., 1963.

Books

Bloom, B., *Stability and Change in Human Characteristics*. New York: John Wiley & Sons, Inc., 1964.

Davis, A., and R. Havighurst, *How Your Child Gets His Personality*. Boston: Houghton Mifflin Company, 1947.

Kagan, J., and H. Moss, *Birth to Maturity*. New York: John Wiley & Sons, Inc., 1962.

Lewin, K., *A Dynamic Theory of Personality*. New York: McGraw-Hill Book Company, 1935.

Lundin, R. W., *Personality, an Experimental Approach*. New York: The Macmillan Company, 1961.

Peck, R., and R. Havighurst, *The Psychology of Character Development*. New York: John Wiley & Sons, Inc., 1960.

Thomas, A., H. Birch, S. Chess, M. Hertzig, and S. Korn, *Behavioral Individuality in Early Childhood*. New York: New York University Press, 1963.

Witmer, H., and R. Kotinsky, *Personality in the Making*. New York: Harper & Row, Publishers, 1952.

12 DEVELOPMENT AND EDUCATIONAL ACHIEVEMENT: ACADEMIC GROWTH

We have seen many ways in which the child grows and develops. Now we shall look at him in terms of his educational problems and academic growth. Let us begin by asking some of the questions we want to consider. Is it really possible to be an "overachiever"? What does "underachievement" mean? Is there any relationship between development and achievement? What can we do about the child who appears to be fast developing but is not achieving? Does the age of entrance to school have any effect upon educational achievement? Is there any demonstrated relationship between growth patterns and rates of development and academic achievement?

Those who accept organismic theory believe that the child's achievement is a result of internal and external forces, i.e., maturation, the environment, and the child's view of the achievement task. From this point of view, as indicated by some of the research findings of Willard Olson, achievement is highly related to development.[1]

THE RELEVANCE OF CHILD DEVELOPMENT FOR EDUCATIONAL PRACTICE

Awareness of some of the fundamental principles of child development is a basic requirement for educators. Schools in their organization, curriculum planning, and actual teaching experiences should reflect an understanding of child development.

The unique and constantly emerging pattern of growth for each child must be considered in educational planning. Sound educational decisions consider the interrelationships of pertinent developmental factors. For example, early maturers require

[1] Willard Olson, *Child Development*, 2nd ed. (Boston: D. C. Heath & Company, 1959).

different experiences than children who are characteristically late-maturing.

The great individuality of all growth demands that the teacher have some insight into the relationship between developmental factors and the learning process. The teacher must be more concerned with the individual's developmental age than with the chronological age, which is inadequate as a basis for educational decisions. Growth has been demonstrated to be sequential, as have many phases of development. In the development of skills a child generally talks before he is able to read and reads before he is proficient at spelling. Educators should take these sequences into account when planning the educational process. Research in programed instruction indicates that the learning process should be much more sequential than it has been.

The great difference in developmental rates points to obvious differences between boys and girls; however, these are differences in timing of development rather than differences of sex. Understanding the rate of development of each child is imperative. Rate in this sense is a description of the amount of increment in either function, i.e., words comprehended, or in structure, i.e., inches of height per unit of time during which measurements are available. There is some evidence that children inherit a family pattern in rate of development. Research by W. Olson at the University of Michigan has shown great similarities within the family in developmental rates, particularly between siblings,[2] Tanner states: "Identical twin sisters, with the same genes, reach menarche an average of two months apart. Non-identical twin sisters, with the same proportion of different genes as ordinary sisters, reach menarche an average of about ten months apart."[3]

Awareness of the significance of the individual rate of development leads to a better idea of the appropriate time to introduce educational tasks. This approach requires that the teacher attempt to comprehend the individual's rate and, in evaluating the child, compare development within the individual. Teachers would focus on individual increments, and not group percentiles.

The cyclic nature of growth suggests that the teacher focus on the individual and his particular cycle. It should also serve as a reminder to the teacher that patience in the learning situation is a necessity, not just a virtue. At every grade level teachers need to know which children have begun their growth spurt in which specific subjects and which children appear to be nearing the completion of a cycle. Curriculum planning does take into account characteristic traits of developmental stages, but consideration of the cyclic status of the individual is also needed.

[2] Olson, *Child Development,* p. 208.

[3] J. M. Tanner, *Education and Physical Growth* (London: University of London Press, 1961), p. 98.

Resistance to displacement, or the wisdom of the body principle, leads to recognition that the organism tends to maintain its pattern. Obviously, maturation and readiness must precede many types of learning if they are to be most effective. This internal ripening is a necessity. Reading forced ahead of maturity produces not only ineffective reading, but frequently personal-social-emotional disturbances. Much growth research indicates that pacing is a superior technique to forcing and pressure. Pacing implies, of course, a comprehensive knowledge and understanding of the individual and his particular pattern. The principles of development, therefore, continually return the focus to the individual learner.

There is no research evidence to indicate that progress can be forced or hastened and produce permanent gain, except in instances of environmental deprivation. Generally, forcing and pressure are detrimental influences on the learning process.

---

1. Give some examples where you believe forcing would be effective after educational deprivation.

An understanding of child development suggests that grouping is not an educational solution in itself because children do not learn as groups. Regardless of the group children are put in, they learn in accordance with their abilities, their rate of development, their purposes, and their capacities. An essential requirement is a supply of meaningful tasks at appropriate developmental levels presented in an encouraging manner to facilitate the development of self-confidence. Again, the implication is strong that there must be adequate and intensive child study by the classroom teacher.

Some research has shown a gradual, consistent, and statistically significant increase in the efficiency of the performance of simple learning tasks which follows an increase in age. When the same experiments were done to test the relationship between learning and intelligence, it was discovered that learning efficiency was not just a simple function of intelligence. Learning efficiency depends somewhat on the developmental maturation process.[4]

In each classroom are children of varying capacities, maturing at different rates, making both quantitative and qualitative changes. In any understanding of the child, his maximum potential and the rate at which he is traveling toward that maximum must always be considered. Some children have high potential but begin growth slowly. The onset of certain phases of their developmental design begins later than it does for the

[4] D. Akutagawa and E. P. Benoit, "The Effect of Age and Relative Brightness on Associative Learning in Children." *Child Development*, 30 (1959), 229–38.

early maturer. Teachers can observe fundamental differences in the timing of the cycle. Examples include children with the same mental ages who are growing at different rates toward the same maxima; two children with different mental ages who are going toward different maxima but at the same rate. Nature and nurture are complexly involved in the development of the individual, who tends to preserve a constant internal state, homeostasis, in spite of external changes. Several educational experiments illustrate this principle, which is also termed resistance to displacement. Children tend to maintain their rate of growth and developmental pattern over a period of time.[5]

---

2. Illustrate some educational problems which demonstrate the importance of understanding the timing of the child's growth design and his rate of maturation.

Millard and Rothney emphasize the significance of studying individually the development of children. Their case studies illustrate the way in which increases in rate of growth have an effect upon total development. Like Olson, they found an achievement-environment relationship. In their conclusions, they state: "It appears that the rises in the achievement curves are part and parcel of a total relationship between organism and environment."[6] It is significant to recognize that the child demonstrates growth even in the face of a declining status within the group or in comparison to some norm. Millard and Rothney pointed out that there was adequate documentation in all the cases reported to indicate that development was primarily a total organismic product. However, they did acknowledge that there are enough exceptions to please those who do not accept this assumption. They called for extensive experimentation on whether environment and culture can raise and affect the basic rhythm, timing, and degree of similarity of growth which they felt was the result of an organismic effort. They conclude: "In all cases the achievement patterns show an increase in growth rate at nearly the same time."[7]

---

3. What is the implication of the finding of a relationship between the total organism and achievement? How can a study of the achievement pattern of an individual be of value in educational planning?

---

[5] Olson, *Child Development,* p. 42.
[6] C. V. Millard and John Rothney, *The Elementary School Child: A Book of Cases* (New York: Holt, Rinehart & Winston, Inc., 1957), p. 633.
[7] Millard and Rothney, *The Elementary School Child,* p. 634.

To Millard and Rothney it seemed that the universality of this phenomenon gave strength to the validity of the organismic theory. The effective teacher must be concerned about the individual's maturity, his readiness, and his interests. Plans for curriculum must take into account the developmental tasks expected at the level of an individual with his particular growth factors. The child who is tall and well-developed may have problems in learning to get along with agemates that are different from those of the individual who is small but accelerated intellectually.

There has been some questioning of the organismic concept. It has been demonstrated that intellectually gifted children tend to be taller and heavier and become pubescent earlier.[8] However, a test of the organismic age concept in children at three grade levels showed no tendency for acceleration in mental age to be accompanied by similar acceleration in weight age, or dental age.[9] Klausmeier and associates have also questioned the organismic age concept.[10]

To this point, the significance of physical factors in the development of educational achievement has been stressed. They lay the foundation for achievement. Upon this foundation are placed nurture factors. The child does not grow properly without an adequate environment. He does not learn to read without experiences in reading. Achievement test results illustrate well that the child cannot do arithmetic problems when he is unfamiliar with the basic processes. The teacher is required to provide enriching experiences with meaningful material. Ideally, instruction should be flexible and provide for individual differences. As teachers become more fully aware of the wide range of abilities in any given room, they must take on guidance functions to aid instruction. The teacher truly aware of individual differences cannot write lesson plans in each subject for thirty children; neither can she write thirty lesson plans in each subject. The child must mature and take on increasing responsibility for his learning and academic progress.

---

4. We are discussing the two concepts of nature and nurture that affect academic growth. What is your view of their relative role in educational achievement?

---

[8] F. K. Shuttelworth, "The Physical and Mental Growth of Girls and Boys Age Six to Nineteen in Relation to Age at Maximum Growth," *Monograph of the Society for Research in Child Development*, 4, No. 3, 1939; and L. Terman, *Genetic Studies of Genius Vol. I Mental and Physical Traits of a Thousand Gifted Children* (Stanford, Calif.: Stanford University Press, 1939).

[9] P. Bloomers, M. Knief, and B. Stroud, "The Organismic Age Concept," *Journal of Educational Psychology*, 46 (1955), 142–150.

[10] H. Klausmeier, A. Beeman, and I. Lehmann, "Comparison of Organismic Age and Regression Equations in Predicting Achievements in Elementary School," *Journal of Educational Psychology*, 49 (1958), 182–186.

THE INTERRELATIONSHIP OF ACHIEVEMENT AND DEVELOPMENT

There is evidence of a general growth factor appearing throughout all development and influencing the rate of maturation. This growth tendency controls such factors as skeletal development, development of permanent teeth, physiological functioning, and development of intelligence. Rates of various structures and functions vary within the framework of the child's central growth tendency. The Harvard Growth Study showed that children who were physically advanced for their age scored higher in mental ability tests than those who were less mature but of the same chronological age.[11] The great effect that maturation has upon development must be recognized. Environmental factors may assist growth and modify it, but they do not generate development. "Growth is an impulsion and as a cycle of morphogenetic events is uniquely a character of the living organism. Neither physical nor cultural environment contains any architectonic arrangements like the mechanism of growth. Culture accumulates; it does not grow."[12]

Maturation is also influenced to some extent by the different environmental factors that the individual contacts.

Without nurture potential traits do not develop to their maximum, while with proper nurture development can be nearly complete. However, when an individual or a specific trait is limited in potentiality, no amount of effort will bring it up to the set standard. Limits are imposed on all learning tasks because of the unalterable growth processes that take place within the child.

In attempting to guide the individual to maximum development, the growth factors must be considered. Each child has a unique rate, even though the sequence of accomplishments in different children tends to be uniform. The educational process must consider variances in readiness and never overlook the fact that the educational achievement of any child is a product of growth forces within and of the experiences provided for him by the environment.

The effect of growth forces on the learning process is most readily seen in experiments like the Millard spelling experiment which has already been referred to in Chapter V, "Learning."

---

5. What would be some methods for assessing readiness in various areas and at varied levels of development?

---

[11] Shuttelworth, *Physical and Mental Growth.*

[12] A. Gesell, "The Ontogenesis of Infant Behavior" in *Manual of Child Psychology,* ed. L. Carmichael (New York: John Wiley & Sons, Inc., 1954), p. 358.

In a section titled, "Children Who Surprised Us,"[13] Olson reports on the record of a child who showed a severe delay in reading to almost age ten, combined with a steady rise in intelligence and achievement toward the close of his total development. He indicates that under the combined influence of added maturation and experience, this individual who appeared quite slow and retarded in the early elementary years, eventually graduated with honors from a leading university. Olson refers to these children as late maturers or "late bloomers." He encourages teachers to consider this example and to keep the door open for children who are traveling at a slower rate. He indicates that such children only take a longer period of time to travel the same road, but that it is vital for the schools to keep the road open.

As a child matures and comes into contact with various educational experiences, his concept of self as an achiever is being formulated. The late-maturing child has a greater possibility of becoming discouraged. It is hard for him to anticipate or expect success in the academic world through the customary channels. As teachers plan educational experiences, they need to keep in mind the effect of maturity factors on academic development and on the child's eventual concept of self as an achiever. This concept of education directs the establishment of educational plans which allow the child to experience success by moving at his own pace and places more emphasis on maturation than on mastery. Mastery would have only meaning in relationship to the child's specific rate and developmental level.

Wrightstone, in a summary of the research on nonpromotion and personality, indicates that nonpromotion reduces the child's self-respect and security, while increasing his feelings of inferiority.[14]

---

6. Specifically, contrast educational experiences that stress maturation in contrast to mastery. Which growth factors appear to be the significant ones for the teacher in an analysis of the learning process?

There is increasing evidence of the importance of the early school years in achievement. In summarizing some of his research, Bloom states "The absolute scale of vocabulary development and the longitudinal studies of educational achievement indicate that approximately 50% of general achievement at grade 12 (age 18) has been reached by the end of grade 3 (age 9)."[15]

Bloom notes that this points to the great importance of the preschool

[13] Olson, *Child Development*, p. 220.
[14] J. W. Wrightstone, "Class Organization for Instruction," *What Research Says to the Teacher*, No. 13 (Washington, D.C.: National Education Association, May 1957).
[15] B. Bloom, *Stability and Change in Human Characteristics* (New York: John Wiley & Sons, Inc., 1964), p. 127.

period and the first few years of school in the development of general achievement and learning patterns. It also suggests the need for highly effective school environments in the primary grades, while questioning the value of educational remedial measures at a later stage.

The interrelationship between achievement and development is obvious when the influences of one form of growth on another are studied. Certainly, a large boy with good coordination has advantages in physical activities. By the same token, these physical skills may make him more acceptable socially with other boys. The poorly coordinated child has more occasion to be emotionally upset and disappointed with self. We could go on to show a host of interrelationships among the developmental factors.

To summarize, the organismic approach requires that you do not teach so much as you provide opportunities for educational achievement. It postulates a basic growth urge which is significant in academic achievement and the dependence of development upon both maturation and learning.

INDIVIDUAL DIFFERENCES

Each child is a unique human being, different in rate of growth and development. Each, therefore, differs in achievement. Probably the most important element that we need to deal with in all of education is the element of individual differences. They seem to be omnipresent but at the same time are frequently either misunderstood or ignored.

The effective teacher accepts individual differences and learns to work with them effectively. He is aware that the classroom always presents children with great differences and that there is no way of homogenizing children so that individual differences are removed.

Each individual comes into the world with a unique inherited capacity; the various nurture forces have an influence upon his status, but it is always affected primarily by the basic inherited capacity. While heredity produces the tendency, the becoming is generally dependent upon environmental stimulation and opportunity. The teacher then can expect to find various levels of development for any behavior pattern. These variances occur among individuals at a specific chronological age level and also within the individual. The typical child has many ages. He has a mental age, achievement ages, a "social-emotional age," and various other developmental ages. Any curriculum designed for one of these "ages" alone falls short of ministering to the needs of the whole child. The graded system established in the American schools by about 1870 has produced a tendency to disregard in many ways the element of human variability.

---

7. Discuss some of the "ages" it is significant for the teacher to know in planning the learning situation.

Homogeneous grouping has rested on an assumption that traits are highly correlated within the individual, so that for example, a bright child is equally superior in all of his cognitive functions. The idea that intraindividual trait differences are negligible is not supported by research data. Burt found variability in reading and arithmetic in students at a given grade level, sectioned in regard to general intelligence, to be about 80 per cent of the range found for all children in that grade.[16]

Frequently these dimensions in individual differences are considered intellectual or academic. A close inspection of the differences among children reveals that children differ in a large variety of variables—talent in creative writing, musical and dramatic abilities, etc. Certainly their adjustment patterns are different. A look at another dimension shows great differences in speech, hearing, vision, and physical skills. Looking at physical factors uncovers differences in height, weight, general health, vitality, and dentition. A look, for example, at typical ten-year-olds reveals considerable variability, some of them being more like "eight" and others like "twelve."

There are also great differences in social adjustment, emotional reaction, utilization of defense mechanisms, and socioeconomic status. Children come to school with considerable variation in prior learning experience, family situation, and different peer relationships. As the teacher gets to know the child, he sees that each individual also possesses unique motives, goals, percepts of the world, and concepts of self. Any individual responsible for directing the learning process must recognize the great variety of significant individual differences which must be dealt with if the educational process is to be effective.

---

8. Take a specific class, and give a picture of the individual differences present. How would this affect the teaching and the learning situation?

THE ORIGIN OF INDIVIDUAL DIFFERENCES

Various factors operate in the development of the unique individual. These factors work within the total developmental pattern and its boundaries in producing uniqueness. One factor is the rate of development. Membership in a distinct family constellation which exists in a specific family atmosphere is also influential. Membership in specific social groups and subcultures has an effect on individual differences. The method of training utilized in the family has an effect upon individual differences. The role that the child plays within his peer group, the way in which he is

[16] Cyril Burt, "The Differentiation of Intellectual Ability," *British Journal of Educational Psychology*, 24 (1954), 76–90.

accepted, the method by which he searches for significance and status affect his development. The child's success and failure ratio has an effect upon the development of individual differences.

---

9. How does the child's success-failure ratio in his experiences affect the development of individual differences?

NORMS AND STANDARDS

Since a child is frequently compared with standards, it is important to recognize how standards are derived. The mean, median, or mode of a given group becomes the standard. However, if you look around the typical classroom and average the height, weight, or mental age of the children and divide by the total number present, you might find that very few, if any, children would fit this arbitrary standard. Frequently, some of the standards to which we hold the child have just as little meaning. The use of such standards, almost by the nature of the definition, relegates about half of the children to a position below average, if the average is considered to be the middle of the distribution.

Research related to the normal curve indicates that many distributions with human beings tend not to be normal. Dr. B. Hughes, a University of Michigan child development research specialist, found in his studies that 13 per cent of the group was the greatest number actually described by the norm.[17]

DeLong, in his research, found a number of grades in which no children fit the description of the average. He also found that only 25 per cent of other groups fit the description of the average when the average was interpreted broadly enough to include a range eight times the standard error of measurement.[18]

---

10. Secure some data relative to height, weight, or other scores on a group in a playground, social class, or classroom, and determine the mean, median, or modal score. How many children fit the standard? Secure the same data for your class; determine how many fit the mean, median, or modal score.

It appears rather confusing to apply a concept which assumes a normal curve as being descriptive of classrooms with children. If the normal curve

[17] B. Hughes, Address, Child Development Research Seminar, Walden Woods, Michigan, 1955.

[18] Arthur DeLong, Paper to Michigan Academy of Science Arts and Letters, February 1955.

were found, would it not be normal to find individuals both above and below the norm? This concept must be used most carefully, or you become trapped in an attempt to raise children to an elusive average. Some have suggested that each individual's pattern of development might be considered as a standard instead of the average of the group.

Olson and Hughes reported as early as 1944 that intensive study of fifty-six individual growth curves in reading did not enable them to find a single growth curve that would fit the description of the average value or norm.[19] They found that growth is a highly individualized matter and concluded that children differ in rate, level of growth, and pattern. The implication is that teachers must follow the readiness, seeking, and self-selection of the child. Olson and Hughes felt that the child would reject experiences for which he was not ready, implying the need for a broad curriculum and the child's participation in planning in order to maximize development. They recommended development of the concept of pacing in which the teacher insures an environment adequate to the needs of all children and adjusts the expectancies for each child according to the level and pattern of growth that he demonstrates. Since growth is so highly individualized, then, there would be no common expectancies for achievement.

---

11. Utilize the concepts of seeking behavior and pacing to show how they might be applied at a specific level in a school with a specific subject.

IDENTIFYING INDIVIDUAL DIFFERENCES

Readiness has been established as a significant concept. Therefore, the school must be organized carefully to identify individual differences and to determine when the child is ready. There is evidence that when the child is not ready, his ability to resist teaching and learning experiences is remarkable. When he is ready, he is interested, willing to spend time, ask questions, take suggestions, even ask for more. It is essential that teachers become more proficient at both thorough child study and the identification of individual differences. The teacher needs to have a detailed understanding of the child's capacity to function in the educational program.

---

12. Secure several evaluations of readiness such as the Metropolitan Readiness Test, the Brenner-Gestalt, and the School Readiness Test of the Gesell Institute. What is their rationale for readiness? How would you assess readiness in other areas?

---

[19] W. Olson and B. Hughes, "Concepts of Growth: Their Significance for Teachers," *Childhood Education*, 21 (1944), 53–63.

Prescott has suggested the need to know about factors in at least six areas—physical, love, social and cultural, peer, self-developmental, and self-adjustive—to determine the child's development and readiness.

In a comprehensive child study each teacher should collect information about the family atmosphere, the child's home, and the values in that home. He should have a clear picture of the family constellation; what is the child's ordinal position among the siblingship, and how does he view his place? It would be advisable to have available a developmental analysis which graphically shows the child's growth and the interrelationships between the varied developmental growths.

A thorough child study would include a picture of the child's social development. Sociometric devices could determine his place in the group, the way in which he is accepted, and ways in which he may not be acceptable to the group.

A child-study-centered school should be able to determine which developmental tasks the child has achieved and which he is still working at. The child study would clearly state the child's interests and aid in understanding his self concept, the nature and reasons for his psychological movement, his goals and percepts, and his most significant motivations. To determine these factors the teacher would need to keep adequate anecdotal records, including a record of the child's assets as well as his liabilities.

The teacher must be able to identify various intellectual traits. Does the child learn rapidly and easily? Does he use common sense? Can he see relationships? Does he reason? Is he aware of many things children at his age are not aware of? How is his vocabulary? Does he do things that indicate creativity? Are his reading capacity and interest in books above the general level of his class? What types of questions does he ask? In what ways does he demonstrate originality? Is he highly observant? Does he express himself clearly? Can he work in science and arithmetic beyond the level of his class? Is he willing to spend his time in experimentation in going into things which the ordinary student would not be challenged by? Does he have a cause-and-effect approach to learning? Is he interested in the reason for things? How much time will he spend on projects of his own? Is he able to develop stories from the beginning, to build up to an interesting conclusion, to give new twists and to show that he can organize his ideas? Does he choose descriptive words?

The teacher who can assess factors like these is moving beyond basing assignments on grade levels and specific subject matter. He is trying to assess specifically in what ways a child is different in his learning situation from other children. He notices the child's assets and liabilities. If the teacher is developmentally oriented, he is more concerned with growth than with comparisons. The teacher who looks closely finds some children who do not think effectively in the abstract area, who are unable to carry through directions, who do not understand complex game rules or directions, who cannot work independently, or who may be confused. The teacher should investigate what physical, organic factors which affect learning may affect exceptional children.

---

13. An effective project at this point would include making some detailed child studies. If this activity is not possible for practical reasons, study some cases presented by the instructor. The text, *The Elementary School Child: A Book of Cases* by C. Millard and J. Rothney (New York: Holt, Rinehart & Winston, Inc., 1957), or *In Pursuit of Self-Esteem: Case Studies of Eight Elementary School Children* by P. Sears and V. Sherman (Belmont, Calif.: Wadsworth Publishing Company, 1964), are other sources of child-study cases. Discuss the factors which seem to be most significant in a specific case.

THE RANGE OF INDIVIDUAL DIFFERENCES AS RELATED TO EDUCATIONAL ACHIEVEMENT

The range of individual differences is not likely to be reduced by the learning experiences typically provided for children in a system of mass education. No plan for grouping or any other administrative device can wipe out the range of differences. It is regularly noted that grouping plans only provide another method of looking at the range. Children at the various grade levels cannot be thought of as identical units; the range is a fact that must be considered, regardless of grouping.

Cook has pointed out that when a random group of six-year-olds enter first grade, 2 per cent will be below the average of four-year-olds in general mental ability and 2 per cent will be above the average of eight-year-olds. Disregarding the extremes at either end, a four-year range in general intelligence remains at the first-grade level. By the time this group reaches the age of twelve, sixth-grade level, the range has increased in just this one factor to almost eight years.[20] This gives some idea of the basic differences in mental ability found in a typical classroom.

E. Cornell did an interesting study which gives an insight into the range of achievement.[21] She found that a fair appraisal of several investigations placed the number of pupils who, in various school subjects, equal or exceed the modal achievements of the next grade above at almost one-third of the group. The percentage that falls at or below the modal achieve-

[20] W. Cook, "Individual Differences and Curriculum Practise," *Journal of Educational Psychology*, 39 (1948), 141.
[21] E. Cornell, *The Variability of Children of Different Ages and Its Relation to School Classification and Grouping*, Educational Research Studies, No. 1 (Albany, N.Y.: University State of New York, 1937).

ment of the next grade is only slightly less. Cornell's research showed that about 10 per cent deviate from the mode by as much as two full grades above or two full grades below. Among seven-year-old pupils, Cornell found the grade range in achievement to be from grade one to grade six. Her ten-year-old pupils range from a standard second grade to a standard ninth grade in achievement, with the middle 80 per cent spreading over three full grades. Cornell's study showed clearly the tremendous amount of grade overlapping in public school classrooms and the continual increase in this spread from grade to grade as children progress through the elementary school.

---

14. Secure data which illustrate the range of differences in a room, school, or district.

It becomes increasingly apparent that while the existence of significant differences in individual rates of learning is a firmly established psychological principle, it is also unaccepted in terms of daily classroom practice. Suppes conducted an intensive accelerated mathematics program with a group of gifted first graders.[22] He found a tremendous range in rate of learning so that at the end of the first four weeks the fastest child covered half again as much material as the slowest. This was in a group where all were preselected as gifted. His data from several studies indicate that the greatest improvement in actual subject-matter learning comes primarily from accommodation to individual differences.

Knowledge of these facts should increase awareness of the need to consider new methods and approaches in organization, administration, and curriculum. Some promising recent developments have occurred in development of nongraded schools and in the individualization of instruction.

SEX AND MATURITY DIFFERENCES IN ACHIEVEMENT

Research in the elementary school generally points to fairly consistent differences between boys and girls. On the average, girls perform better than boys in reading comprehension, vocabulary, and language skills, while boys tend to do better in arithmetic.[23]

Clark studied 69,354 pupils from 341 school systems in 48 states, using the California Mental Maturity Test and the California Achievement Test as a basis for determining ability and achievement.[24] He did not find dif-

[22] P. Suppes, "Modern Learning Theory and the Elementary School Curriculum," *American Educational Research Journal*, Vol. 1, No. 2 (March 1964).
[23] Cornell, *Variability of Children*.
[24] W. Clark, "Boys and Girls—Are There Significant Ability and Achievement Differences?" *Phi Delta Kappan* (November 1959), p. 73–76.

ferences in general intelligence between the sexes. In the area of language usage and spelling, the girls had a higher rate of achievement. The achievement of boys and girls in arithmetic and reading was the same.

It should be noted that while these differences can be shown between the averages, there is also a large amount of overlap between the sexes on any set of measurements at a given time. If the varied developmental rates are considered, it may well be that many of these differences are not so much sex differences as they are maturity differences. In practice, what happens is that schools often tend to retain boys in grades more often than girls, so that on the average a boy takes more time to complete eight grades of elementary school than girls. Many have speculated that possibly this difference is due to the fact that more boys than girls are immature when they enter kindergarten and first grade.

The school must recognize the real meaning of sex differences and adopt some methods of adjustment to individual growth patterns. At present, boys are generally penalized because of maturity differences. We might speculate that this could even have a long-range effect on their total development and attitude toward school.

Meyer and Thompson found a significant difference between boys and girls in classroom interaction with the teacher.[25] Boys receive more blame and disapproval from teachers. Due to basic biological and cultural differences, boys are more active and less conforming in the classroom. Teacher attempts to socialize or force male students to conform to classroom standards by means of dominating behavior, generate more aggression, withdrawal, nervousness, and loss of self-confidence.

Inez B. King did a longitudinal study of the children who entered first grade in the elementary schools of Oak Ridge, Tennessee, in 1940, and followed through until completion of sixth grade in 1946. The group was divided into two sections. The older group, upon entrance into first grade, had a mean age of six years and seven months, including a range from six years and five months to six years and eight months, with an intelligence quotient of 100.8. The younger group at the beginning of first grade had a mean age of five years and ten months including a range from five years and eight months to five years and eleven months. The mean intelligence quotient of the group was 102.04. At the completion of sixth grade, the group was given the Stanford Achievement Test. The younger group ranged from 9.6 to 3.8, with a group mean of 6.2. The older group ranged from 11.3 to 5.4 with a group mean of 7.68. During these six years the older group had only one retention, and the younger group had ten. The results of the study indicate that the slightly higher intelligence quotient

[25] W. Meyer and G. Thompson, "Teacher Interactions with Boys as Contrasted with Girls," in *Psychological Studies of Human Development*, eds. R. Kuhlen and G. Thompson. (New York: Appleton-Century-Crofts, 1963), p. 510.

of the younger group was not sufficient to offset the disadvantage of early entry into first grade.[26]

15. Observe a first- or second-grade class in a typical school. Are there any indications that either sex is more successful?

SIBLING AND FAMILY RESEMBLANCES

Research points to family resemblances in the ability to achieve in school. Olson states: "These resemblances appear early, are ubiquitous in every comparison, and give more predictive power than can commonly be found by differences among teachers, curriculum experiences, or details of methods."[27]

Sarah M. Schoonover made an investigation of resemblances in mental and educational ages of siblings. She found that resemblances in intelligence were somewhat greater than they were in achievement.[28]

THE ROLE OF THE TEACHER

The teacher who approaches the learning situation from a developmental point of view is concerned about fulfilling the fundamental needs of the child in order to assist his maximal development within society. To do this, the teacher must understand his particular needs and unique growth pattern. Assembly-line techniques have been successful in industry, but they lead to difficulties when applied to the classroom. Mass education which loses sight of the individual and his development is not effective in producing either academic growth or total development. In education, the goal is not to turn out a uniform product, but to accept the child as he is and bring him to the maximum level which can be expected for him. The teacher should be interested not only in how much the child learns, but in what attitudes are being formed toward the school, learning, and society.

One of the most exciting challenges that any teacher can face is that of understanding well each individual student in the classroom. As he comes to know their ability level, the curriculum for the individual can be formulated. The well-trained teacher always has some understanding of each individual's interests, purposes, assets, liabilities, and methods of seeking

[26] I. King, "Effect of Age Entrance into Grade I Upon Achievement in Elementary School," *Elementary School Journal,* 55 (February 1955), 331–36.
[27] Olson, *Child Development,* p. 154.
[28] S. Schoonover, "A Longitudinal Study of Sibling Resemblances in Intelligence and Achievement," *The Journal of Educational Psychology* (November 1956), pp. 436–42.

significance. Because the teacher is also the director of a group-learning experience, he must understand the way in which each child fits into the group and determine how the child seeks to belong.

It is basic to effective learning that the teacher understand the general range of capacities in the classroom and the range of learning experiences that are necessary if children of the same age are to achieve effectively in a specific field. Not all children learn in the same way, which requires adapting methodology to the individual differences of the classroom.

When the teacher truly individualizes his approach, it provides the opportunity to emphasize success instead of failure. Resultant encouragement should produce more sustained motivation. This approach necessitates taking a continuous inventory of the child's growth status and altering instructional techniques accordingly. One of the most urgent needs in education is the provision of time for teachers to learn about each individual child and assist in the development of fitting educational plans. This implies some teacher-pupil planning and mutual selection of goals from an early age. The educational task proceeds best when there is a mutual alignment of goals in contrast to a set of teacher-determined assignments and expectations.

The teacher might best assist achievement by recognizing the importance of some of the following tactics: (1) attempt to meet the child's specific needs and specific interests; (2) encourage the child to achieve at his maturity level and not in terms of group standards or norms; (3) assist the child to use new concepts and skills on a continual basis; (4) utilize the ego involvement of the individual to motivate and avoid threats and comparison.

The teacher with a developmental approach serves as a guide more than as an authoritarian. He is a student of children and a director of group dynamics, always ready to utilize either the individual or the group in making educational plans.

An emotionally healthy atmosphere in school is a positive factor influencing achievement. Spaulding gathered data from ten elementary schools in a California suburb, involving children in fourth through sixth grade.[29] He concluded that there was a significant positive correlation between height of self concept and the degree to which teachers were calm and acceptant in an atmosphere where there was a socially integrated learner-centered group. There was a negative correlation of height of self concept when the teacher was dominative and threatening. Achievement gains were positively correlated with the consistency, routine, and orderliness of the classroom teacher's behavior.

[29] R. Spaulding, "Achievement, Creativity, and Self-Concept Correlates of Teacher-Pupil Transactions in Elementary Schools," in *Readings in Child Behavior and Development,* 2nd ed., ed. C. Stendler (New York: Harcourt, Brace & World, Inc., 1964), p. 313.

When the teacher understands that the children in the classroom comprise a unique set of growth designs, his primary task is to understand the designs and to attempt to harmonize instruction with the design in contrast to teaching some mythical average. He becomes concerned about determining the pattern of individual development physically, psychologically, and academically. He recognizes that at first he may not understand the pattern of all children, but through continual child study he can eventually develop competency in child study and growth techniques to assist in accounting for the major share of individual patterns that must be dealt with in the typical classroom.

A study by Ojemann and Wilkinson indicated that when the teacher developed insight into the personalities of the children in the classroom, he became a more effective guide for learning and personality development.[30]

The teacher must recognize the variety of roles played in the course of contacts with children.[31] The teacher is primarily involved as a director of the learning process. Each student and the significant factors affecting readiness for learning must be understood. This involves responsibilities in evaluation of pupil progress and assisting students in developing self-evaluation. Teachers also serve as specialists in content areas, providing contact with the world of knowledge. Classes are groups, and hence the teacher is a group leader who must understand group dynamics.

CURRICULUM EXPERIENCES FOR GROWTH

The teacher must come with a diversity of expectations and anticipate a diversity of responses. His attitude about the management of individual differences is perhaps the most significant factor related to success in handling the differences. If he expects and accepts differences, he has a head start toward their management. This is in contrast to the complaint so frequently heard that Johnny and Jimmy do not learn the same way, or do not finish their lesson at the same time, or complete the same amount of homework.

This view of curriculum indicates that each child needs some experiences in which he can develop his talents to the optimum and in which he can experience some planned daily success in tasks he is interested in and considers worthwhile. This view holds that it is not necessary to plan for

[30] R. Ojemann and F. Wilkinson, "The Effect on Pupil Growth of an Increase in Teacher's Understanding of Pupil Behavior," *Journal of Experimental Education,* 8 (1939), 143–47.

[31] D. Dinkmeyer, "How Do You Think of Yourself as a Teacher?" *The Instructor,* Vol. 74, No. 1 (September 1964).

failure. Children have enough failure experiences without having the school construct them. Through the fixed curriculum, a number of children regularly experience failure situations which might be avoided. It is important for each child to be able to work and play with children who accept one another, to have opportunities to make constructive, creative contributions to a group project.

The teacher works on finding the assets of each child and encourages his total development. Aware that growth curves in academic and physical areas bear a resemblance to each other, the teacher is concerned about the total organism in the classroom. He attempts to learn as much as he can about developmental patterns in order to understand each child's specific maturity and readiness. Children are dealt with in terms of the interrelationship of their growth forces.

The modern curriculum always considers individual differences and the developmental tasks a specific child should be attempting. Only when the methods of teaching and the content are related to the needs of the specific organism and its maturity can the tasks the individual undertakes result in permanent growth. Other attempts to teach may result in rote learning and memorization, but do not necessarily produce permanent changes in behavior.

---

16. What are some criteria by which we could distinguish between permanent growth and memorization?

The curriculum planner faces a set of children with infinite variability. No two children are exactly alike in their various "ages," interests, abilities, experiential and cultural background, and social and emotional development. The concept of the normal or average child must give way to a new realization that each child is normal for himself, if he follows his own unique pattern of development. Trait variability within the individual has been discovered to be 80 per cent as great as individual variability within an age group.[32] Some individuals are twice as variable as others. For example, a child with a high IQ might be one of the best or one of the poorest readers in a group. This child might, however, be very proficient in arithmetic and uncoordinated in physical education. Studying the child's mental ability reveals that even intelligence is composed of varying factors, some abstract, some verbal, some dealing with number facility, others with word fluency, etc. Thus, teachers are increasingly becoming aware of the various ways in which a child grows and the various

[32] C. Burt, "The Differentiation of Intellectual Ability," *British Journal of Educational Psychology,* 24 (1954), 76–90.

kinds of ability within each child; they know it is their task to understand well these abilities in any curriculum planning.

Past attempts to improve the curriculum have been made through different plans of grouping. Since schools must group students on some basis, it has been assumed that grouping is a direct answer to individual differences. Grouping is not a solution to educational problems. Children may perform at the same general level on an achievement test but vary widely in all of the component abilities that make up the general score.[33] Some group homogeneity can be achieved on some interrelated variables, but considerable heterogeneity on other variables remains due to intraindividual variability.

However, the group setting appears to furnish a motivational influence. Banghart found significant differences in anxiety and problem-solving efficiency between cooperative and uncooperative groups when solving difficult problems, but not when solving easy problems.[34]

Barnlund found that group decisions based on cooperative deliberation were superior to decisions made in individual settings.[35] He believed there was increased effort and greater task orientation in the group setting.

However, grouping only lays the groundwork to enable one to work more effectively with individual differences. Individualization eventually becomes the key to effective learning. The individualization of instruction is based on a philosophy which produces a method. The crucial factor is the attention given to individual learning problems. The teacher who individualizes the curriculum believes that successful instruction must be paced to the individual pattern. This teacher recognizes that it is the total growth pattern of the child, not any specific factor which makes the child ready for learning.

Manning evaluated a program designed to serve individual needs.[36] He analyzed experimental and control groups in social studies, literature, and science in terms of relative achievement. The effects of individualization varies with pupils and subject-matter areas. The experimental group of sixth-grade pupils in science and literature with IQs of 120 and above made significant improvement; fifth-grade pupils in social studies of the same ability level made less progress than the control pupils.

Attempts have been made to do research in relation to varied individualization techniques. Marian Jenkins reports on self-selection in reading

[33] F. Tyler, "Intraindividual Variability" in *Individualizing Instruction,* National Society for the Study of Education, 61st Yearbook, Part I, Chapter 10 (Chicago: University of Chicago Press, 1962).

[34] F. Banghart, "Group Structure, Anxiety, and Problem Solving Efficiency," *Journal of Experimental Education,* 28 (December 1959), 171–74.

[35] D. Barnlund, "A Comparative Study of Individual, Majority and Group Judgment," *Journal of Abnormal and Social Psychology,* 58 (January 1959), 55–60.

[36] J. Manning, "Differentiating Instruction in the Content Subjects in the Intermediate Grades," *Journal of Education,* 142 (December 1959), 52–65.

with second-grade children.[37] In this study a total of eight classes were studied, with four utilized as controls. The control classes studied reading on the basis of a conventional basic reader and ability groupings. The experimental group of four classes utilized self-selection and individualized teaching. The 160 boys and girls in the classes were matched by mental age and socioeconomic background. The teachers were also matched in terms of educational training and experience. At the end of a full year of the experiment, the control group averaged 1.1 years of gain in total reading. The experimental group made a more impressive gain averaging 1.4 years in total reading. Forty-six per cent of the children in the experimental group scored gains of more than 1.6 years while only 25 per cent of the control group made this much gain. In comprehension of material read 59 per cent of the experimental group children gained more than two years in comprehension, while only 24 per cent of the control group made a similar gain. Even in vocabulary, the experimental group averaged almost a one-year gain over the control group.

One of the most carefully done research studies on individualization is reported by Jones, who sought to find out whether children would make greater progress in learning the common elementary skills when they were taught at their own level of achievement rather than when they were taught by the usual mass education procedures.[38] Her study involved 228 students in grade four. The students were placed in experimental and control groups. Both groups had the typical range of ability found in the typical classroom. In the experimental group, materials were used which ranged in difficulty from grades two to six, and the children were given materials and assignments appropriate to their achievement level. In the control group, instruction proceeded on the assumption that all students in the classes were ready for fourth-grade work—a common fallacy; all members of the class studied the same book, and common assignments were given. Some supplementary work was done but it was only incidental to the coverage of the regular texts. Measurement consisted of an achievement test in September and again in May. Jones reports consistent advantages to the experimental group. On the average, the experimental group showed development 2.5 months ahead of the control group. Individualization appeared to be more beneficial for students who were slow or just average than for the superior. This evidence contradicts the common belief that only the very superior or very slow need individual attention. Evidence from this study, because of the size of the sample and the experimental situation, should be given serious consideration when the

[37] Marian Jenkins, "Self-Selection in Reading," *The Reading Teacher,* 11, No. 2 (December 1957), pp. 84–90.

[38] Daisy Jones, "An Experiment in Adaptation to Individual Differences," *Journal of Educational Psychology,* 39 (1948), 257–72.

value of individualized instruction is weighed. This study was made in a public school system under typical public school conditions.

There are examples of attempts to study individual differences in areas other than reading. Weaver suggests that there are levels of learning, while the highest level may be the abstract, other levels below it can be dealt with effectively by graphic or concrete representations.[39] He suggests ways in which mathematical concepts may be dealt with by students at any level. In his plan, a given concept might be considered by an entire class, but students would work with it at different conceptual levels.

An encouraging factor on the educational scene is the continual development of materials which facilitate individual instruction. These materials are found in almost all fields of instruction. The interested teacher might consider some of the materials produced by Science Research Associates in the areas of reading, spelling, and arithmetic. Other publishers, such as the California Test Bureau, are also engaged in the production of materials for individualization. Other sources of material for the individualization of instruction can be found by encouraging wide use of the public school or library.

Olson has suggested that self-selection procedures in themselves when used systematically, are the most effective method for individualization. The provision of a wide variety of materials at varying levels of difficulty is basic to individualizing the instructional approach.

Children enter school with a wide range of abilities, and their achievement range continues to spread throughout the course of their elementary school experience. Good teaching does not reduce the range of individual differences, which really result in part from factors over which the teacher has no control. The differences develop because the children have different capacities, learning experiences, and interpretations of their experiences. The prime mistake in education comes when children in a grade are thought of as identical units. A uniform curriculum experience cannot and should not be provided for every child at a given age level. The concept of early and late maturation in regard to the reaching of maximum development before or after an average time, leads to a recognition of just one factor which may encourage individualization.

The concept of homogeneous groups of pupils receiving uniform instruction by mass educational techniques from a uniform textbook dies hard. Many fallacious assumptions support this approach. Some people believe that grade levels signify definite stages of educational achievement and that all pupils in a grade should be capable of coping successfully with the work outlined for that grade. They would suggest that pupils not be promoted to a grade until they are able to do the work set

[39] Fred Weaver, "Differentiating Instruction in Arithmetic—An Overview and a Promising Trend," *Education,* 74 (1954), 300–305.

up for that grade. These people even suggest that when relative homogeneity of a class does not prevail, it is a result of poor teaching or lax standards.

Some basic denial of trait variability both within the individual and within the group is expressed in this viewpoint. Under the most favorable circumstances, that is, when pupils are grouped on the basis of achievement test batteries heavily weighted in favor of reading and arithmetic, the reduction of reading and arithmetic variability is only about 20 per cent. Actually, the more effective the instruction, the more individual differences are provided for, and the more heterogeneous the instructional group becomes. Hence, the central problem remains—how best to meet the needs of individuals in groups of widely varying ability.

PERSONALITY FACTORS AND EDUCATIONAL ACHIEVEMENT

It is important to recognize the significance of the psychological structure of the child in relationship to achievement. Material in the preceding chapters relating to learning, social development, the self concept, intelligence, motivation, emotion, and personality have all treated aspects of the child's ability to achieve. Here we shall try to pull together and summarize the most significant factors.

Level of Aspiration

Successful pupils tend to hold aspirations close to their previous performance. Worell found that the more nearly students thought their work was up to their capacity, and the more their standing approached what they considered satisfactory, the higher their actual grades tended to be.[40]

Rosenfeld and Zander found that disapproval of inadequate performance had no effect on aspiration level, while disapproval of a performance the student felt was up to his capacity had negative effects on aspiration setting.[41] They found that indiscriminate reward reduced acceptance of a teacher's influence, while reward for adequate performance increased acceptance of the teacher's influence. In research studies it has been shown that when success and failure are manipulated, failure groups generally are unstable, at times setting unreasonably high goals and at other times goals below what they have already achieved. The success group usually set consistent goals slightly above their previous performance.[42]

[40] L. Worell, "Level of Aspiration and Academic Success," *Journal of Educational Psychology,* 50 (1959), 47–54.

[41] H. Rosenfeld and A. Zander, "The Influence of Teachers on Aspirations of Students," *Journal of Educational Psychology,* 52 (February 1961), 1–11.

[42] P. S. Sears, "Levels of Aspiration in Academically Successful and Unsuccessful Children," *Journal of Abnormal and Social Psychology,* 35 (1940), 498–536.

Anxiety

S. Sarason, in extensive research with elementary school children, found that some aspects of school studies favor the high-anxiety groups, while others favor the low-anxiety groups.[43] When students must decide quickly, the low-anxiety child has an advantage. In situations free of time pressure and where useful, cautious work is of value, the high-anxiety pupil has the advantage. Failure or the expectation of failure handicaps the test performance of children who test high in anxiety.

Reed reviewed the research on anxiety and concluded that both severe and very low levels of anxiety tend to reduce learning, while mild anxiety may function in a positive manner for some kinds of learning.[44]

I. Sarason reported that reassuring instructions facilitated the performance of high-anxious subjects and impaired the performance of low-anxious subjects on complex learning.[45]

Need for Achievement

McClelland and his associates found that their measure of need for achievement had a positive relationship to achievement under many, though not all, conditions.[46] They reported correlations as high as .50 between scores on the *n* achievement measure, and both grades and achievement test scores. It was also found that need for achievement is highly subject to situational influences, and is influenced by the interrelationship between varied motives.

Uhlinger and Stephens found some support for the hypothesis that high achievers have a greater need to achieve than low achievers.[47]

French and Thomas found that subjects with high need to achieve were more likely to reach a solution in a problem-solving task than were subjects with a low need to achieve.[48]

Roth investigated the effect of self attitudes on proficiency in school.[49]

[43] S. Sarason, K. Davidson, F. Lighthall, R. Waite, and B. Ruebush, *Anxiety in Elementary School Children* (New York: John Wiley & Sons, Inc., 1960).
[44] H. Reed, "Anxiety: The Ambivalent Variable," *Harvard Educational Review,* 30 (Spring 1960), 141–53.
[45] I. Sarason, "Effects on Verbal Learning of Anxiety, Reassurance, and Meaningfulness of Material," *Journal of Experimental Psychology,* 56 (December 1958), 472–77.
[46] D. McClelland, J. Atkinson, R. Clark, and E. Lowell, *The Achievement Motive* (New York: Appleton-Century-Crofts, 1953).
[47] C. Uhlinger and M. Stephens, "Relation of Achievement Motivation to Academic Achievement in Students of Superior Ability," *Journal of Educational Psychology,* 51 (October 1960), 259–66.
[48] E. French and F. Thomas, "The Relation of Achievement Motivation to Problem Solving Effectiveness," *Journal of Abnormal and Social Psychology,* 56 (January 1958), 45–48.
[49] R. Roth, "The Role of Self Concept in Achievement," *Journal of Experimental Education,* 27 (June 1959), 265–81.

He found that when demands for reading improvement are taken as a personal threat, the individual tends to defend and maintain his self concept. His nonimprovement groups were more defensive on measures of self than improvement groups.

While complete personality patterns cannot be broken up into anxiety, need for achievement, self attitudes, and level of aspiration, this division is a practical approach for research. The characteristics studied are subject to change and form part of a total style of life.

ORGANIZATION AND ADMINISTRATION POLICIES

Along with the teacher and the curriculum, the administrative policies of the school are crucial in facilitating a growth and development approach. These policies should make it possible for the teacher to know the student well enough to meet his needs. This necessitates requiring the teacher to engage in child study and providing time for him to do so.

The administrator must also provide instructional materials with a range of difficulty and interest appeal commensurate with the needs of the instructional group. Individualized instruction implies that the size of the class must remain within reason. No evidence has yet been produced about the most desirable size of class for individualization, but it is apparent that extremely large classes make the process difficult. This program necessitates a systematic testing that reveals growth as well as status. The permanent record folder and the cumulative record plan should chart the growth of each individual. The program also requires flexible grouping within class and the provision of a wealth of instructional materials.

IMPLICATIONS

1. Organismic theory directs us to look at maturational forces as well as environmental forces in academic development. Well-designed developmental records which portray the developmental status of each child should be kept.

2. The organization of the schools and the curriculum should reflect the developmental needs and developmental tasks of the child.

3. Early maturers and late maturers require different educational planning—they are not unfolding their design at the same rate or with the same timing.

4. There are appropriate times to introduce certain educational tasks; these times are often individualized and relate to specific maturities.

5. Focus should be placed more on the child's amount of growth and incremental change than on his status.

6. Forcing and pressure tend to have a detrimental influence on the learning process and academic growth.

7. Intensive child study by the teacher is crucial to individualization.

8. There is research evidence available that indicates rise in achievement is part of the total relationship between organism and environment. These relationships should be researched adequately to make more effective individual predictions.

9. Maturity factors have an influence on the concept of self as an achiever.

10. The typical child has many "ages," and the curriculum must take these into account.

11. Homogeneous groups operate on a fallacy that traits are highly correlated within the individual. Great intraindividual variability suggests homogeneous grouping is an impossibility and ineffective.

12. The utilization of averages as standards for children may provide a most inaccurate measuring stick for evaluation of individual growth.

13. Children at grade levels are not identical units, a range of abilities is always present, and it is mandatory to understand and deal with this range. Grouping is not a solution to educational problems.

14. Variability in the classroom is not only interindividual but intraindividual. In understanding this the complexities of any large-scale homogeneous grouping becomes apparent.

15. Basic biological and cultural differences which find boys less conforming in the classroom should be recognized by teachers. The use of dominative behavior by teachers is strongly advised against. Both sexes function more effectively and feel more adequate when there is less domination and the group is learner-centered.

16. It is important that students be enabled to work up to their capacity and experience success; this serves as a positive influence on their level of aspiration and actual accomplishment. Teachers must become more aware of the negative effects of disapproving performances that students feel are up to their capacity.

17. Awareness of the effects of anxiety level on learning should assist the teacher to structure the learning situation so as to generally reduce anxiety.

18. Nonpromotion reduces the child's self-respect and security and increases feelings of inferiority, usually resulting in reduced academic achievement. Schools need to implement the nongraded concept which implies proceeding in terms of the individual rate of development.

19. Bloom's research indicated that approximately 50 per cent of general achievement at grade 12 has been reached by the end of grade 3. Preschool and primary school experiences take on added significance and require careful planning. The school should make available its best resources in teachers, facilities, guidance, and other services at this point in the educational experience.

20. The individual range in rate of learning within all possible group-

ings is a significant factor in planning the education of children. Accommodation to these specific differences in rates of learning must occur in daily classroom practices.

21. There is evidence that an emotionally healthy atmosphere in the school not only affects personality development, but appears to be a positive factor influencing achievement. Even the teacher whose goal appears to be primarily gain in academic achievement should recognize that this can be accomplished more readily through the socially integrated learner-centered group.

SUGGESTED READINGS

Articles

Goodlad, J., "To Promote or Not To Promote?" in *Readings in Educational Psychology,* eds. V. Noll and R. Noll, p. 239. New York: The Macmillan Company, 1962.

Meyer, W., and G. Thompson, "Teacher Interactions with Boys as Contrasted with Girls," in *Psychological Studies of Human Development,* 2nd ed., eds. R. Kuhlen and G. Thompson, p. 510. New York: Appleton-Century-Crofts, 1963.

Torrance, E., "Creative Thinking through the Language Arts," in *Readings in Human Learning,* eds. L. Crow and A. Crow, p. 436. New York: David McKay Co., Inc., 1963.

Books

Goodlad, J, and R. Anderson, *The Non-graded Elementary School,* rev. ed. New York: Harcourt, Brace & World, Inc., 1963.

Millard, C., *Child Growth and Development.* Boston: D. C. Heath & Company, 1958.

————, *The Elementary School Child–A Book of Cases.* New York: Holt, Rinehart & Winston, Inc., 1957.

National Society for the Study of Education, *Individualizing Instruction,* 61st Yearbook, Part 1. Chicago: University of Chicago Press, 1962.

Olson, W., *Child Development,* 2nd ed. Boston: D. C. Heath & Company, 1959.

Tanner, J., *Education and Physical Growth.* London: University of London Press, Ltd., 1961.

13 THE CHILD IN THE FAMILY

Albert, age nine, always seems to forget, according to Mother. On rainy days he goes off to school without his galoshes; on cold days his scarf is left at home; he frequently forgets his homework. Mother is always very concerned and runs after Albert to remind him. If he is out of hailing distance by the time she discovers his "memory lapse," she hurries to school to supply the missing item. Despite her continual reminders, scoldings, and assorted punishments, the situation does not improve.

The Smiths moved to a new house so that Billy, age eleven, could have his own room, separate from the younger sisters. Unfortunately, but as one might suspect, Billy moved his old habits to the new setting. The bed remains unmade, toys are on the floor and not in the storage boxes provided, and clothing is assigned randomly to all areas but the clothes closet or clothes hamper. Mother's many appeals to pride or love for her result only in occasional slight improvement, and then a reversal to well-established habits.

The brief behavioral incidents described are not atypical of family life. For those in regular contact with children in the home, they are probably an all too painful reminder of the incapacity of parents to get children to assume responsibility and to carry out simple tasks of daily living.

---

1. Is the situation of Albert and Billy just part of growing up? Is it a stage of development all children experience? If it is a stage, when does the stage end? What would you advise the parents to do to change this behavior and these continual irritants to pleasant living within the family? Make specific suggestions for dealing with Albert and Billy.

THE ROLE OF THE FAMILY IN THE CHILD'S DEVELOPMENT

Psychologists, educators, and sociologists all agree that the family is the most significant single influence on the development of the child. The family is the major environmental influence and remains throughout life the most pervasive of all influences. It is in the family that the child either learns to trust people or to be fearful and uncertain of others.

The child can learn that Mother cares, responds to his call, and provides him with good food and protection from the elements. Some children, unfortunately, learn that Mother is inconsistent, unpredictable, and not always to be trusted. This can have a serious influence on their development.

It is in the home that the child first experiences the meaning of love. It is here that he comes to experience the give-and-take of family life. Does he know how to get along with his siblings? The child who cannot get along with his siblings may eventually have difficulty in getting along with other peers. One of the advantages of family life is the opportunity to learn the responsibilities of caring for others. In the family the child has the opportunity to take on responsibilities.

The family has a most significant role to play in the development of personality. The customs and beliefs of our society are first handed down within the family. Here, the child first observes and then internalizes the values of the parents. Social, political, and religious beliefs and customs are transmitted via the family.

Witmer and Kotinsky point out clearly the significance of the family in personality.[1]

> It is in and through the family that the main components of a child's personality develop. The struggle between feelings of trust and mistrust is first worked out in relation to the parents, and it is by family members that the autonomy and initiative characteristic of our society are encouraged or denied. The family members play an important part in relation to later personality components also.

It is in the family that the child first struggles with developing a feeling of adequacy. It is here that he is put to the test to show what he can produce or achieve. The family gives him his first objects for identification, and provides the situation for the eventual development of an ego identity. Kagan indicates that the significant motive for the identification process is the desire to possess desirable characteristics of the model.[2] The child wishes to possess adult qualities such as power, competence, strength, and receipt of affection. The integrity displayed in family relationships also is a model for the child in developing his own sense of integrity. The family usually teaches well what is punished and what is encouraged, what is

[1] H. Witmer and R. Kotinsky, *Personality in the Making* (New York: Harper & Row, Publishers, 1952), p. 174.

[2] J. Kagan, "The Concept of Identification," *Psychological Review,* 65 (September 1958), 296–305.

valued and what is ignored; and regardless of what parents say, the child is quite astute in observing what is actually adhered to.

---

2. What are some values the family teaches? Describe specific examples of incidental instruction which occurs in the family setting.

The family sets the stage for the development of many important personality characteristics, providing experiences both within and outside of the home.

The parents serve as the first socializing agents. Within the family atmosphere and the family constellation the child learns what he is and what it is that his parents and siblings expect of him.

The way in which learning proceeds and the large amount of time that the child spends in the preschool years with his family testify to the important role of the family as teacher in the crucial areas of attiudes, convictions, and beliefs which eventually determine actions. The family process of instruction is sometimes planned and other times incidental, but either way, the goals of transmitting the family culture are accomplished.

Some methods of teaching within the family are quite subtle. Teachers classify them as pure forms of indoctrination, in which the child is held up against the standards of the group. He is told, "We don't behave that way"; "people in our family never," etc. The child also observes and imitates the behavior of the significant adults in his life. He notices their interactions with one another; since these are the only models he has available for observation in the process of becoming a human being, they become his models for imitation.

Sometimes the child's behavior is directly encouraged or discouraged. The child who never puts his bike away and who is always reminded that Father put it away for him is learning that it is not so important to respond to what parents tell you to do as it is to note that even though they scold, they accomplish the task themselves. Some children are willing to experience parental discipline in order to obtain the complete attention of the parents to their problems.

---

3. What are some ways in which children pick up exactly the opposite attitude to that of the parents? Do you believe direct or indirect instruction is most effective in teaching attitudes?

In recent years it has been questioned whether the family plays as significant a role as it did in the past century. Some feel that the family no longer plays a major role in the education of individuals, in providing recreation, or in nurturing the child toward a specific vocation. However, anthropological studies reveal that the family is still carrying on major functions which are not in the province of any other social institution. Witmer and Kotinsky point out the following: "Three such essential functions have been identified: (1) to produce children and provide them with a setting of supporting affection; (2) to induct them, from infancy on, into the ways and values of the society; (3) to give them their initial identity within the community."[3]

The importance of affection in the emotional development of children has been demonstrated. The most natural place for this affection to be experienced is within the family setting where the child usually develops his closest personal relationships to parents, siblings, and relatives. It is truly within the family that the child is cared for because of himself, and not for what he can achieve. Many feel that being valued in this way gives one the courage to function and develop a healthy personality.

The educational function of the family, while perhaps not as comprehensive as in the past, is still an important element. The child learns within the family to make decisions and choices and experience the consequences of these decisions. Most of early social learning is experienced within the family.

Finally, the family provides the child with his initial identity. Here he is recognized as relating to a specific family and that family's attributes.

---

4. Describe the educational function of the family. In observing a group of young children, estimate the relative effectiveness of their families in performing educational roles. See if you can determine the family factors which account for the differences in the children.

THE PARENTS' ROLE

Parents are often placed in the position of continually seeing the discrepancy between their hopes and goals and actual accomplishments in child management. Many parents set high standards in terms of the performance they expect from their child in living within the family, with his peers, and at school. However, they frequently find the child falling far short of their expectations. Often, setting high goals brings about discouragement both in the child and in the parents. When goals are beyond normal expectations, the situation is constructed so that continual discouragement is inevitable. Bronfenbrenner found that children from

[3] Witmer and Kotinsky, *Personality in the Making*, p. 177.

achievement-oriented homes excel in planning and performance, but they are also more tense, domineering, aggressive, and cruel.[4]

Parents really must manage the basic education of the child in emotional, personal, and social matters. At the same time, parents seldom have adequate training and experiences to enable them to conduct this education efficiently. We require training for a great variety of professions, businesses, and trades, from the barber to the bricklayer, but at present anyone can become a parent. The result is a large number of adults who are playing highly significant roles in the development of the next generation and who are often quite unequipped to manage these roles adequately.

A growing struggle is taking place between the generations. Many parents were raised in comparatively autocratic situations. Respect was demanded, and questioning of authority was not tolerated. However, as the social and political climate of our democratic pattern of life has spread throughout the world, the autocratic home has become less acceptable and less efficient. The child actually does not see anywhere in his life a model for the autocratic relationship. If political leaders always go against the wishes of the citizenry, they are usually removed by the vote. In communities, social groups, and political organizations, leaders change, and the leader must have the cooperation of the group members if he is to maintain his position.

Schools are increasingly organized on a democratic basis, and the child observes that the teacher includes them in some planning. When the parent attempts to use a completely authoritarian approach in managing the child, he encounters resistance. Of necessity parents must learn new methods of managing children in a democratic era.

---

5. Make an analysis of leadership methods—autocratic, democratic, laissez-faire—employed by various people who have responsibility for child management. How does the variance or consistency in methods affect his attitudes?

The effective mother attempts to provide the best type of environment in which her child can grow and then watches him do so. This implies that she believes children can learn more from experience than from instruction and that she is convinced of the efficiency of learning from the consequence. This is not parental neglect, but a studied concern for the best environment in which to promote the total development of the child.

[4] U. Bronfenbrenner, "The Changing American Child—A Speculative Analysis," *The Journal of Social Issues,* Vol. 17, No. 1 (1961).

Emmerich, in controlled questioning of children, found that both boys and girls perceived the mother as more nurturing than the father.[5]

One of the most important attributes in parental management is consistency. Studies of child training practices usually indicate that they are effective only when used consistently. When a family is studied to determine which practices have the greatest impact on the child, it has been demonstrated that only those which seem to pervade the total family life are significant in distinguishing the development of children of one family from those of another.

Many parents are concerned because of the trend away from an adult-centered to a child-centered philosophy of raising children. They frequently confuse permissiveness and democracy and continually bounce from extreme authoritarian strictness to guilt feelings about overcontrol. The result is extreme permissiveness which is damaging to the development of the child. Apparently whether the parent is strict or permissive is not as important as the children's understanding of the purpose motivating the parent's attitude. The parent who truly loves the child and is concerned about his present and future development conveys this spirit to the child. It is more important to show the child that you are firm, because you respect yourself, and kind, because you love him, than to convince him of your authoritarian or overpermissive attitude. Children understand well the attitudes of adults toward them. If they live in a family where there is a wholesome concern for the child, the child's sense of security grows out of his recognition of the parents' love and concern.

When no limits are set for the child on being in at night, bedtime, use of the car, and other details, the child often feels insecure, in the belief that no one really cares what he does.

---

6. We frequently neglect to recognize the value of limits in providing security. Indicate some limits which are beneficial in producing security and limits which discourage.

Dr. Martha Wolfenstein did an interesting study of so-called "official" child-rearing culture in the United States.[6] She studied the first nine editions of *Infant Care,* which is published by the U.S. Children's Bureau and which first appeared in 1914. In the nine editions which covered the period from 1914 to 1951, Dr. Wolfenstein explored the management of five specific problems: thumbsucking, weaning, masturbation, bowel train-

[5] W. Emmerich, "Parental Identification in Young Children," *Genetic Psychology Monographs,* 60 (November 1959), 257–308.

[6] M. Wolfenstein, "Trends in Infant Care," *American Journal of Orthopsychiatry,* 33 (1953), 120–30.

ing, and bladder training. She was able to demonstrate that in the roughly forty-year span there have been substantial changes in the type of training methods recommended by the authors of *Infant Care.* For example, in 1914, masturbation and thumbsucking were both considered serious problems to be dealt with severely. Some extreme practices were recommended to handle masturbation, and various restraints were suggested for thumbsucking. The intervening period shows an almost continuous decline in the severity of recommendations made for these two problems. By 1951, it was almost suggested that both problems are really nuisance behaviors which might just as well be ignored as subjected to specific management.

The other problems experienced similar histories, although the rate of change varied. Recommendations for rather careful and severe weaning continued until about 1938. Bowel training had a similar history, with the trend to permissiveness beginning a little earlier. The early editions of *Infant Care,* called for quite severe management of bladder training, but again decrease in the severity of the recommendations has been continual since 1921.

Dr. Wolfenstein's study examines some of the "official" positions in the United States literature. It cannot be assumed, however, that they are necessarily representative of the actual patterns of child rearing. Within the United States are many subcultures. Within metropolitan areas like New York, Chicago, Los Angeles, or San Francisco, a large number of subcultures can be identified. It has been well-demonstrated that different cultures and socioeconomic classes foster and develop different sets of beliefs, practices, and values.

Bronfenbrenner found that the major changes in parental behavior over a twenty-five-year period indicated a move toward greater permissiveness, freer expression of affection, increased reliance on reasoning, or appeals to guilt in contrast to punishment, a narrowing of the gap between social classes in their patterns of child rearing, and an increasingly important position of the father as a more affectionate and less authoritarian agent of discipline.[7]

THE ROLE OF LOVE IN CHILD DEVELOPMENT

It has been commonly accepted that an affectionate and nurturing mother is essential for the most complete development of the child. While the assumption is generally made that almost every child receives this type of love, there is considerable evidence of rejecting mothers and mothers whose love is so possessive that it actually smothers the development of the individual. The type of love we shall set as a model is nonpossessive

[7] Bronfenbrenner, "The Changing American Child."

in nature. It respects the loved one to the extent that it does not make excessive demands; it develops mutual respect and mutual concern.

Many assumptions have been made about the effects of deprivation of mother love upon the child. Goldfarb has investigated extensively the effects of growing up without consistent mother figures.[8] Goldfarb found that institution children were less secure, more passive or apathetic, and more frequently retarded in speech, school, and mental proficiency. Goldfarb suggested, on the basis of his study, that foster children had better contact with society, were readier to enter into both work and social experiences, and were superior in every way to the institutionalized children.

Spitz, a physician, has published a series of papers on the effects of mother-infant separation.[9] Spitz found that the mothering provided by various nursery attendants proved to be disastrous for both the psychological growth and the general mental and physical health of the infants he studied. The children displayed marked differences or deficiencies in motor and social development and also failed to make expected progress in the physical growth areas. Spitz called this infant response to mother separation anaclitic, or dependency-related, depression. He pointed out the importance of the infant's strong need for a significant human relationship during the early phase of his development.

Bowlby's summary of studies indicated that the essential factor is the child's experience of an intimate and continuous relationship with a mother figure which is satisfying and enjoyable to both members of the relationship.[10] When this relationship existed, his findings indicated, anxiety and guilt developed in only a moderate and organized manner, while complete deprivation seemed to produce far-reaching effects on character development.

There has been considerable criticism of Bowlby's conclusions, which is perhaps best summarized by O'Connor, who indicates that on the basis of reexamination of the evidence, Bowlby's hypothesis regarding maternal deprivation is still only a hypothesis.[11]

Casler did an extensive critical review of the literature regarding maternal deprivation.[12] He contends that the terms "mothering" and "ma-

[8] W. Goldfarb, "Effects of Psychological Deprivation in Infancy and Subsequent Stimulation," *American Journal of Psychiatry,* 102 (1945), 18–33.

[9] R. Spitz, "Hospitalism: An Inquiry into the Genesis of Psychiatric Conditions in Early Childhood," *Psychoanalytic Study of the Child,* 1 (1945), 53–74; R. Spitz, "Hospitalism: A Follow-Up Report," *Psychoanalytic Studies of Children,* 2 (1946), 113–17; and R. Spitz, "Anaclitic Depression," *Psychoanalytic Studies of the Child,* 2 (1946), 313–42.

[10] J. Bowlby, *Maternal Care and Mental Health,* World Health Organization Monograph Series, 1952, pp. 16–155.

[11] N. O'Connor, "The Evidence for the Permanently Disturbing Effects of Mother-Child Separation," *Acta Psychologia,* 12 (1956), 174–191.

[12] L. Casler, "Maternal Deprivation: A Critical Review of the Literature," *Monographs of the Society for Research in Child Development,* Vol. 26, No. 2 (1961).

ternal love" have not been well-defined and suggests that some of the significant critical variables are seldom accounted for, such as the age at which separation occurred. Separation after the age of six months may only present the problem of breaking the existing bond with the mother. In a definitive study, he points out, the institution must be described adequately and the reason for specific separation listed. Investigation of Bowlby's summary of studies on institutionalization reveals that the majority of the studies did not consider the three variables of age of separation, reason for separation, and description of institution.

Casler's study caused him to argue:

> (a) the emotional, intellectual and physical deficits or decrements found in maternally deprived children cannot be rightly attributed to the deprivation itself; and (b) there are many accounts of deprived children who have not suffered harmful consequences. The next step, logically, is to learn why deprivation so frequently *is* followed by ill effects. The age variable has already been mentioned, as has the possibility of hereditary defect. The environmental variable is now to be considered, and it is—in this author's opinion—the most important of all.[13]

A number of investigators have sought to clarify the specific deprivation that exists. Montagu indicated that tactile stimulation during early infancy is vital for the subsequent development of the person.[14] Fischer reported on an investigation of three-month-old institutionalized children and concluded that some failure to function may be influenced by the child's lack of tactile stimulation and experience in being moved about in a pleasurable manner.[15]

Dennis and Najarian, in a thorough examination of a Beirut institution, indicated that failure to function on test items was related to lack of a normal amount of relevant experience.[16]

Casler related the various studies in a summary statement:

> In the psychologically unhealthy institutions studied by Spitz, Dennis and Najarian, and others, all of the important sensory modalities were understimulated. It may be appropriate, therefore, to refer the disturbances found among institutionalized children (at least in those cases when separation from the mother occurred before the age of six months) to "perceptual deprivation," including tactile and kinesthetic, rather than using the too-broad and yet too-specific term, "maternal deprivation."[17]

[13] *Ibid.*, p. 14.

[14] M. Montagu, "The Sensory Influence of the Skin," *Texas Reports on Biology and Medicine*, 11 (1953), 291–391.

[15] L. Fischer, "The Significance of Atypical Postural and Grasping Behavior during the First Year of Life," *American Journal of Orthopsychiatry*, 28 (1958), 368–75.

[16] W. Dennis and P. Najarian, "Infant Development Under Environmental Handicap," *Psychological Monograph*, 71, No. 7 (1957).

[17] Casler, *Maternal Deprivation*, p. 18.

The review of the literature by Casler is comprehensive and questions the concept of deprivation of maternal love. It indicates that deprivation of maternal love can have ill effects only after specific emotional responsiveness has been developed by the child. He indicates that ill effects found in children believed to be maternally deprived before this age probably have some other cause. This cause is identified as perceptual deprivation—the absolute or relative absence of tactile, vestibular, and other forms of stimulation. He believes that forms of social stimulation necessary for proper language development can be provided within an institutional setting.

A love relationship is important because it builds the feeling of self-respect and confidence referred to as the sense of security. It gives the individual the courage to meet whatever occurs in the give-and-take of life and permits him to utilize his experiences constructively.

The child develops his security from close relationships which provide love and affection. They give him a sense of support, acceptance, comfort, and value, which permits the child the freedom to develop his capacities and enables him to move from dependence toward independence. It is important that the significant adults in the child's life provide guidance which helps him recognize limits and at the same time fosters and encourages development of self-control.

Kluckhohn, in a comprehensive anthropological study, points to the importance of the emotional tone used by the parents.[18] He says that inferences cannot be drawn directly from an objective description of cultural patterns for child training to specific consequences in personality formation. There is evidence that almost identical systems produce contrasting results in relationship to the characteristic emotional tone in which they are administered and the meanings which the acts acquire for children in varied cultures.

Bronfenbrenner's research has even speculated that the "love-oriented" socialization techniques may have some negative as well as constructive aspects.[19] These techniques may undermine the capacity for independence and initiative in boys. The democratic family might even produce individuals who do not take initiative but look to others for decision.

THE CHILD'S SITUATION AND POSITION

Few parents recognize how consistently the child is searching for limits, seeking to find the boundary line between acceptable and unacceptable

[18] C. Kluckhorn, "Anthropological Studies of Human Relations," Unpublished paper presented to the Conference on Research in Human Relations, Rockefeller Foundation, February–March 1953.

[19] Bronfenbrenner, "The Changing American Child."

behavior. Parents should provide children with behavior choices which permit them to function on the useful side of life. They should not create situations in which undesirable behavior appears to be more attractive than cooperation. The child who disturbs but only receives parental admonitions, and the child who continually provokes the siblings are examples of ways in which children can involve the parents.

The child first learns the importance of property rights within the family. He wants people to respect his property, and he must learn to respect the toys and possessions of others. He should learn within the family atmosphere that one does not get without giving. Only through experiencing small difficulties can the child become prepared to experience more serious difficulties later on. The child who is always spared the consequences of his actions is being deprived of the opportunity to mature.

---

7. Give some examples of ways in which parents deprive the child of the opportunity to learn from consequences. What are some consequences which might be too extreme? Consider consequences which might be very beneficial for the child.

Parents should be aware of the tyranny which the child can exercise over them. They must refuse to meet infantile demands. Otherwise, they are only encouraging the child to be more obnoxious in his behavior. The child soon learns to turn the parents' attitudes to his advantage. Children are good observers, and as they note weaknesses in the parental system they respond to their advantage. The child should not be considered as a passive object of adult plans. Instead, we should be aware that he can and does utilize his ability to make subjective interpretations of events. In this manner a child can frequently turn defeat into a conquest. We must be cautious to avoid confusing antecedents with causality, and assume that a preceding event causes a personality trait. Ausubel indicates that the young infant's perceptual and cognitive immaturity tends to insulate him from the influence of parent attitudes.[20] Until the child can actually perceive the parents' attitudes, therefore, they influence immediate behavior more than personality development. Constitutional differences between children affect the way the child perceives the parents' attitude. Differences in child reaction either modify or stabilize the parents' attitude.

A considerable body of research has been related to ordinal position within the family and personality traits. Ausubel summarizes the research when he says: "Birth rank tends to be consistently related to certain per-

[20] D. Ausubel, *Theory and Problems of Child Development* (New York: Grune & Stratton, Inc., 1958).

sonality traits within a given culture."[21] Schachter concluded that first-born children in our society are generally more anxious, more dependent on others in anxious situations, and more inclined to go along with the group than other children.[22]

Helen Koch did an extensive study of sibling relationships and personality.[23] She found that the first-born child was generally judged to recover less readily from emotional upsets and anger. The middle child was more suggestible and social, while the youngest child seemed to be concerned about establishing his individuality within the family. Wile and Davis reported that the only child and the youngest child received an excess amount of attention and supervision and frequently displayed the most infantile home relationships.[24] The youngest child was most often spoiled, got the most, and exhibited most frequently the attention-getting mechanism.

In analyzing the child's position within the siblingship, you must always remember to look for the spacing of years, the ages and the difference in the sexes of the siblings, as well as the ordinal positions.

PARENT-CHILD RELATIONSHIPS

A significant study in the area of parent-child relationship was an analysis of the reports of 379 American mothers in regard to child-rearing practices from birth to kindergarten age.[25] Interviews were conducted with the mothers as part of a research project of the Harvard University Laboratory of Human Development. Parental attitudes were rated in terms of permissiveness, strictness, warmth, approach to child training, and punishment for aggressiveness. The findings indicated that the most pervasive quality was the warmth of the mother's feelings for her child; this seemed to have been an underlying factor in a number of the scales.

Maternal coldness was associated with the development of feeding problems and persistent bedwetting and also contributed to excessive aggression. It was demonstrated in this study that punishment was not effective as a long-term technique for controlling behavior. They found that

[21] *Ibid.*
[22] S. Schachter, *Psychology of Affiliation: Experimental Studies of the Sources of Gregariousness* (Stanford, Calif.: Stanford University Press, 1959).
[23] H. Koch, "Children's Work Attitudes and Sibling Characteristics," *Child Development,* 27 (1956), 289–310; and H. Koch, "Some Emotional Attitudes of the Young Child in Relation to Characteristics of His Sibling," *Child Development,* 27 (1956), 393–426.
[24] I. S. Wile and R. Davis, "The Relation of Birth to Behavior," *American Journal of Orthopsychiatry,* 11 (1941), 320–34.
[25] R. Sears, E. Maccoby, and H. Levin, *Patterns of Child Rearing* (New York: Harper & Row, Publishers, 1957).

the mother who rewarded and guided the child had a much better relationship and also was more frequently obeyed. In other words, warmth, guidance, and rewards served to produce effective discipline.

Miller and Swanson also did a comprehensive study of child-rearing practices in metropolitan areas.[26] This study was done in the Detroit area with 600 parents and their children. The study actually observed and recorded parental behavior and made an attempt to determine the effect of such behavior on the personality of the child. They found it extremely difficult to relate directly the personality of the parent and the personality of the child. As we might expect, each child perceives his family environment in an individual manner, and the interactions that he engages in must be recognized in this light. However, they frequently found a fairly significant relationship between child-rearing practices and the personality pattern of the child. The general traits they found helpful are similar to those of other studies, suggesting that although values vary from culture to culture, in general, parents should express warmth and respect for the child as an individual, value him, and provide effective ways of relating with him.

Miller and Swanson noted that each generation of parents has a new set of world, national, and local problems to deal with; hence the experience of previous generations is to an extent invalidated. The culture and environment are in a state of flux, and parents must be continually alert to the need for education in performing their role.

It is interesting to speculate on how parents develop their attitudes about child training. Many attitudes, of course, arise out of the broad culture and the subcultures. Others come from the parent's experience in childhood and within his own family unit. Finally, some experiences are modified by his own personality.

The parent who attempts to do a good job in the field of child management is beset by confusing advice. He can observe other parents in the neighborhood and immediately observe differences. The church he belongs to may express certain suggestions about raising the child. The school and the parents association may have suggestions. The mother who does much reading has available newspaper columnists and magazine stories regarding child management. If children are raised in proximity to the grandparents, another source of suggestion and control over the parents' thinking about child management is introduced. As a result, the variety and confusion of influences working on the parents' philosophy of child rearing become readily apparent. Naturally, most parents train their children in a way that accords with their own personality. It may be either a

[26] D. Miller and G. Swanson, *The Changing American Parent* (New York: John Wiley & Sons, Inc., 1958).

complete acceptance of the training conducted by their own parents, a complete rejection of these practices, or somewhere in between.

---

8. Interview several parents regarding their child training practices, and try to determine how they acquired their most significant attitudes. What influences would you be most controlled by as a parent?

The coming of the "modern" or "new" approach to child rearing has made considerable impact upon middle-class homes, in which reading material on child management is likely to be found. In these homes there is more communication between parents and child, with a greater acceptance of a questioning attitude on the child's part. Greater emphasis is placed on the development of reasoning and self-control in contrast to external controls by the parents.

In studying the data related to patterns of child rearing it is important to recognize that the underlying basic attitudes of the parents toward the child are perhaps more significant than any individual practice or set of practices. The child is quick to perceive if the parents really care and are concerned, and his perception may have a greater impact upon the relationship than any set grouping of practices. There are highly significant positive consequences to the child's personality from being accepted and loved.

Many well-intentioned parents frequently force their children to accept the parents' value system. They force children into activities representative of the parents' interests, whether they be intellectual, musical, or athletic. By rewarding these efforts, they are requiring of children the characteristics that the parents value. All of this, of course, is usually done out of the best of motivations, but in a most subtle fashion it communicates to the child that he is not acceptable as he is and that he needs to align his value system with that of the parents.

The Sears study showed that the mothers' permissiveness and punitiveness about aggression influence the amount of aggression the child displays in the home.[27] Their study indicated that in order to get a child to establish new habits, the old must be eliminated and suggested that maternal control might be more effective through the manipulation of the child's needs. Instead of punishment, she might establish a set of pleasurable activities related to the educational goals of the home.

The Sears studies indicated that mothers are more effective with children when they find ample time to play with the child, permit much affectionate interaction with the baby, and accept the child's dependency needs. Effective mothers praised frequently the child's production of a

[27] Sears, et al., *Patterns of Child Rearing.*

correct response. They also used reasoning more frequently than other mothers as a method of training.

Becker and his associates interviewed parents of normal and disturbed children and found that authoritarian and arbitrary maternal attitudes were correlated with the presence of conduct problems in children.[28] Excessively shy and timid children were associated with frustration of the child's autonomy.

It is interesting to note the following statement from *Patterns of Child Rearing:* "Our evaluation of punishment is that it is ineffectual over the long term as a technique for eliminating the kind of behavior toward which it is directed."[29] If just this simple sentence were completely understood and accepted by parents, it would probably have a significant effect upon child management practices in the United States.

---

9. Despite statements which question the value of punishment, it is a commonly used technique. What do you suggest as practical methods to demonstrate its ineffectiveness? Is there evidence that lack of punishment and control is harmful to development?

THE RELATIONSHIP BETWEEN INFANT DISCIPLINE AND PERSONALITY DEVELOPMENT

Sears and his colleagues showed that the mothers' child-rearing practices were significantly related to the dependency and aggressiveness in the young child.[30]

Radke did a study of parental attitudes and practices with the preschool-age child.[31] She found that children from homes which had been classified as autocratic were rated by their preschool teacher as being unpopular with associates, more unstable emotionally, more sensitive to praise and blame, more quarrelsome, and less considerate of others than children from the "democratic" homes. Radke did an excellent job of summarizing the types of child behavior most commonly associated with different types of homes in the following chart:[32]

[28] W. Becker, et al., "Factors in Parental Behavior and Personality as Related to Problem Behavior in Children," *Journal of Consulting Psychology,* 23 (April 1959), 107–87.
[29] Sears, et al., *Patterns of Child Rearing,* p. 484.
[30] R. Sears, J. Whiting, D. Nowlis, and P. Sears, "Some Child Rearing Antecedents of Aggression and Dependency in Young Children," *Genetic Psychology Monograph,* 47 (1953), 135–236.
[31] M. Radke, *The Relation of Parental Authority to Children's Behavior and Attitudes,* University of Minnesota Child Welfare Monograph, No. 22 (1946).
[32] *Ibid.*

TYPE OF HOME	TYPE OF CHILD BEHAVIOR ASSOCIATED WITH IT
Rejective	Submissive, aggressive, adjustment difficulties, feelings of insecurity, nervous, sadistic, shy, stubborn, noncompliant.
Overprotective, "babying"	Submissive, infantile, jealous, nervous, aggressive, feelings of insecurity.
Dominating parent	Dependable, shy, submissive, polite, self-conscious, tense, quarrelsome, disinterested, uncooperative, bold.
Inharmonious	Aggressive, neurotic, jealous, delinquent.
Defective discipline	Poor adjustment, aggressive, rebellious, jealous, neurotic, delinquent.
Harmonious, well-adjusted, calm, happy, compatible	Good adjustment, cooperative, independent, superior adjustment, submissive.
Logical, scientific approach	Self-reliant, cooperative, responsible.
Child accepted	Socially acceptable, faces future confidently.
Parents play with child	Security feelings, self-reliant.
Consistent, strict discipline	Good adjustment.

The Relationship of Home Atmospheres and Children's Behavior Drawn from Many Different Investigations. Adapted from M. J. Radke, *The Relation of Parental Authority to Children's Behavior and Attitudes.* University of Minnesota Child Welfare Monograph, 1946, No. 22 (c) 1946 by University of Minnesota.

However, it is important to recognize that clear evidence of the effect of child-rearing practices on personality is limited. Radke-Yarrow and Yarrow indicated in a comprehensive survey of the literature that there is still no unequivocal evidence of the exact nature of the processes by which conditions in early life are related to later development.[33]

Sewell and Mussen studied infant training practices with approximately 165 six-year-old children.[34] They interviewed the mother in regard to her child-training practices and also obtained ratings of adjustment from teachers. Under study were the following practices: breast versus bottle fed, self-demand versus regularly scheduled feedings, and gradual versus abrupt weaning. They found no direct relationship between the various methods of feeding gratification and later adjustment.

In a later study of Sewell, Mussen and Harris little relationship was found between the mother's permissiveness and one phase of socialization

[33] M. Radke-Yarrow and L. Yarrow, "Child Psychology," *Annual Review of Psychology*, 6 (1955), 1–28.
[34] W. Sewell and P. Mussen, "The Effect of Feeding, Weaning, and Scheduling Procedures on Childhood Adjustment and the Formation of Oral Symptoms," *Child Development* 23 (1952), 185–91.

such as feeding and later phases such as toilet training.[35] It becomes obvious, then, that we must look to all the attitudes and the total pattern of the parent's child-management practices.

THE REASON FOR MISBEHAVIOR

In dealing with children, it is important to have available some assumptions about the reasons for the direction children take in their relationships with parents, siblings, and peers. A very sound assumption to begin with is the recognition that whatever children do they usually do for excellent reasons. In other words, behavior makes sense to the behaver.

We already know from our study of the child that some of the reasons may be related to growth factors. Physical factors play an important role in determining behavior. Some of the misbehavior of children is eliminated as they mature and grow out of certain stages. However, it would be unwise to make the assumption that all behavior is merely due to a stage of development which will always pass. Many facets of behavior are not influenced merely by developmental changes.

Much of behavior is also a result of the present environment. The child is influenced by his setting and by the people about him. If misbehavior strikes him as the most effective way to develop a peer relationship, he may produce what parents call misbehavior. Some misbehavior is also influenced by the cultural setting. In certain groups it is acceptable to steal if you are hungry or to take coal if you are cold. All of our social classes permit moral deviations that are more related to the subculture than to any general moral rules.

A look at the basic needs again provides a better understanding of misbehavior by revealing whether a need is unmet. An unmet need is frequently the cue for misbehavior. Some children have a psychological hunger within which causes them to move toward a particular action.

Sometimes misbehavior is also merely the result of faulty relationships. The child sees his present behavior as the only possible way to function effectively with the people involved.

Other misbehavior stems from a lack of knowledge. The child does not know any better response than the present response. Misbehavior must also be understood in terms of its consequences. If the adult notes his reaction to the child's misbehavior, he may be able to determine its purpose. Does it merely annoy him, or does it make him feel challenged? This clue alone may indicate the difference between misbehavior to seek attention and misbehavior to show power. Sometimes misbehavior causes

[35] W. Sewell, P. Mussen, and C. Harris, "Relationship Among Child Training Practices," *American Sociological Review*, 20 (1955), 137–48.

the adult to feel that he, too, would like to get even. At other times the misbehavior or failure to function is so discouraging to the adult that he feels like giving up. These, too, can be helpful clues in diagnosing the goals of revenge or demonstrating inadequacy.

---

10. Utilize observation opportunities in schools, at recreation centers, and in homes to record examples of misbehavior. How do you account for the misbehavior? What would be your preventive steps to eliminate recurrence of the misbehavior?

THE METHODS OF TRAINING AND EDUCATING CHILDREN BY PARENTS

The parents' purpose should be to assist each child to grow and develop in a manner which is both personally satisfying to the child and socially acceptable. In order to accomplish this purpose, the parents must establish some policy of child training. High ideals and goals are seldom accomplished without planning. We have already seen the importance of consistency in any interaction with the child. If our goal is the development of the fully functioning individual who takes responsibility for his actions, then our decisions are dictated in the direction of developing a relationship which helps the child become more mature and more responsible.

One of the problems in parental childhood training is the lack of a consistent plan of action. Numerous specific problems occur in connection with eating, sleeping, toilet training, bedwetting, dressing, and the like; the key issue is not how to solve the individual's specific situations so much as it is the development of a consistent philosophy and approach to the child's development which encompass all types of situations.

The parent must learn quickly that each child is an individual who has distinct and unique assets, liabilities, and purposes. Frequently, a second child is confusing to the parent because he does not respond in the same manner as the first child. We need to learn that experiences with the first child in some instances may actually be a handicap to effective relationships with the second child. No two children perceive methods of training or their situation in the family in the same manner.

Basic to understanding children is the recognition of the importance of physical readiness. It is impossible to speed the development of gross motor abilities. Walking, crawling, and climbing, for example, are under physical maturational controls. You cannot force these learnings; you must follow their timetable. Practice is most effective with children when the child is sufficiently ready; earlier practice is not only ineffective but may serve as a deterrent to adequate development.

In working with children, the parent needs to be more aware of the purposes of the child's actions. What does the child get from this behavior? Frequently as the adult observes his own attitudes about the misbehaving child, he finds some answers to the purpose of the behavior.

It is always important to be aware of the effects of discouragement. When the child feels inadequate or inferior, he is actually incapacitated for effective functioning.

In all understanding of behavior, adults need to recognize increasingly that at the instant of action this behavior is the most effective way the individual knows how to behave. The behavior provides a knowledge of the child's level of development and goals. An increasing amount of evidence indicates that reward and punishment are not only ineffectual but also outdated. A child who is rewarded comes to consider it as his right; when he is not rewarded, he fails to function. Reward may thus become a method of extortion. On the other hand, the child who is punished winds up feeling that he has the right to punish others. Those who have observed children closely recognize that retaliation by the child is frequently more effective than punishment by the adult.

What, then, can we suggest in the development of a more effective philosophy and psychology of child training? First, let us begin with a commitment on the part of parents to develop a philosophy of human relationships within the family. This should not be haphazard and sporadic, but something that the parents need to think about and work at. The child must be convinced that there is a family policy and that the parents really mean it. This sets the stage for the development of an effective relationship, which is one of mutual respect and cooperation. In such a family, there is fun in sharing and fun in working together.

The parent who adopts this philosophy recognizes that children are great imitators, and that it is important to set the proper example. With this approach he must be interested in guiding the child toward proper activities. Of necessity then, the parent must provide the child with choices and options. The guidance approach to child training does not assume that the parents have all the answers, but instead it works toward eventually developing the greatest utilization of the child's ability to choose properly.

In any approach with children, however, it is good to recognize that things do not always work out well. When they do not, it is important to permit the child to learn from the consequences of his misbehavior. Unnecessary intervention to protect the child actually prevents his fullest development.

Natural consequences imply that the parent utilizes the reality of the situation rather than his personal power. Children learn best when they find out that order is in their favor.

We have talked frequently about the importance of need theory. The parent who recognizes the basic needs of children sees them as an effective instrument in the development of satisfactory behavior.

A basic method with children is one which encourages the child, values the child as he is, and works toward building each child's faith in himself. The encouragement approach, then, implies a recognition of effort and a focus on strengths and assets.

Crandall, Preston, and Rabson evaluated achievement by observations in the nursery school and at home.[36] They found a positive correlation between maternal reward of the child's seeking of approval for completion of a task and the child's striving for achievement, both in the nursery school and home settings.

Perhaps one of the most significant things that the parent can learn is to act instead of talk. Talking between parents and children frequently degenerates into a type of warfare, which only trains the child to become parent "deaf." The children act only when the parent's raised voice implies some impending serious action. Response is only under extreme pressure. Probably a fundamental rule would be never to explain to a child something he already knows or has heard repeatedly. This would eliminate a considerable amount of unnecessary parent-child interaction that is negative.

Sometimes children do not function well because they do not understand the situation and its requirements. It is essential to take time to teach children the skills and habits expected of them. Training time should not be at the moment of conflict. However, it is wise to recognize that if time is not spent in working with a child, an unnecessarily large amount of time will be spent in correcting him or providing remedial work.

SPECIFIC TRAINING SITUATIONS

As indicated, it is more important for parents to have a proper relationship with their children than to develop specific techniques to handle specific situations. A fundamental understanding of the child and the development of an affectionate, accepting attitude are more significant in solving specific training situations than any given set of rules. The purpose here, then, is not to discuss in detail a number of specific training situations, but instead to indicate briefly how the general methods might be applied to a specific situation.

Feeding practices, which have changed considerably even during the past forty years, frequently remain a problem for parents. The mother who is well-meaning and who attempts in a relaxed fashion to do what she

[36] V. Crandall, A. Preston, and A. Rabson, "Maternal Reactions and the Development of Independence and Achievement Behavior in Young Children," *Child Development,* 31 (June 1960), 243–51.

honestly believes is best, would probably be most effective in managing the feeding problems of her children. There are subtle cultural differences in feeding practices, but when a mother keeps in mind the purpose of foods—the nourishment of the body—then feeding does not become an area of warfare. If the child senses that the mother is particularly concerned about his feeding, the issue of what he eats becomes the battleground and an area on which he can "take a stand." Feeding disturbances when closely examined are frequently related to the general adjustment of the parent to the child. When irregularities in the feeding area become serious, it is most often evidence of a poor general relationship between the child and the parents. The parent who relaxes and refuses to reveal her concern to the child, is usually most effective.

Generally, in the American economy, it is impossible for a child with all the food available not to select a diet which, in the long run, would be balanced and suitable for his development.

Toilet training is another area that frequently provokes anxiety on the part of the parents. Although pediatricians generally encourage parents to delay bowel training until sometime during the second year for reasons of physiological readiness, it has been demonstrated that parents tend to train earlier than the recommended starting time. Data in the Sears, Maccoby, and Levin study indicate that mothers began bowel training at eleven months and that on the average it was completed at eighteen months.[37] It is interesting to speculate whether this training would have required seven months if the parents had begun the training at eighteen months. The Sears study indicated that mothers who are severe in toilet training put pressure in other areas. In other words, severity in toilet training was not an isolated attitude; these mothers also had expectations in regard to orderliness, table manners, and doing what is right. Sears showed a correlation of .47 between the severity of training and the children's emotional upsets, one of the highest correlations obtained in the entire study.[38]

It is most important that toilet training be conducted in a casual manner without pressures from the parents. Toilet training that is extremely severe or rigid is another way the mother indicates that the child is not doing what he is supposed to, with obvious concomitant effects upon his feelings of adequacy and security.

Parents frequently have problems in getting the child to dress himself. This is an area in which the child sometimes likes to hold on to his dependence. He wants to show that he cannot do it and that he is still a little child. If the parent takes special pains to dress the child or derives pleasure from the dressing act, the child sees no reason for doing so himself. A child needs to be encouraged and recognized for the things that he does

[37] Sears, et al., *Patterns of Child Rearing.*
[38] *Ibid.*

well in dressing, for this is another way in which the child matures by taking on his own responsibilities.

Most often parents become concerned about methods of dealing with aggression in the child. They want to know how you cope with the child who has extreme temper tantrums, who gets angry easily, or who wants to quarrel. The Sears study throws some light here by indicating that the pattern of child rearing that produced the most aggressive children was one in which the parents disapproved of aggression to the extent that they always punished with physical aggression of their own or physical threats to the child. This form of counteraggression seemed to generate the most hostility on the part of the child. Since all children produce some aggressive and hostile feelings, it is important that parents learn to handle them effectively. Sometimes the child can be diverted from his aggressiveness, or, in the case of inappropriate aggression, he can come to understand the reason why it is not permissible. In other instances, aggression may be transferred into competitive outlets or opportunities to engage in activities which reward aggressiveness within a socially acceptable pattern.

There are many areas of concern in child training—development of speech, weaning, play habits, washing and cleanliness, the beginning of school, and sibling strife and others. Instead of developing a fragmentary set of rules, however, the parent must bear in mind the fundamental principles of understanding and working with human behavior.

PARENT-TEACHER CONFERENCES

The practice of regularly scheduled parent-teacher conferences continues on the increase in the elementary school. They are not scheduled to meet an emergency, but to set aside prearranged time for planning, sharing, and discussion. It should, preferably, be conducted in the school setting and, if possible, at a time when both parents can attend. The purpose of the conference is to develop mutual understanding about the objectives of the school and the value system of the parents. Teachers should not approach these conferences in a condescending, fault-finding, or judgmental manner. If the parents feel that they are there to defend the child, the broader purposes of the meeting cannot be accomplished.

Parent-teacher conferences should provide an opportunity for exploration. The parents should feel accepted and understood, and should recognize that the teacher's main function is to work with the parents in maximizing the development of the child. In order for this to happen, the relationship that develops between parents and teacher must be one of mutual trust. A teacher once stated this in a most accurate manner to parents of kindergarten and first-grade children when she said, "We all know the children come to school with many stories about what happens at home, and certainly I recognize they bring some stories home that are exaggerated; so let's have an agreement, I'll promise not to believe all that I hear about you if you'll promise not to believe everything you hear about me." In essence, in a humorous manner, she was pointing out that children frequently dramatize both the home and the school setting. If parents feel that the teacher is empathic, understands their view, and attempts to assist them in the proper development of the child, they are then more open to suggestions and more likely to learn from their own experiences.

The first conference in the school year, perhaps in October, might be designed to give the teacher an understanding of the child's home situation and the culture and value system of the parents. At the same time, it should permit the parents some insight into the way in which the child is coping with the curriculum.

Sometimes school visits are most effective if the parent has had an opportunity first to hear the teacher discuss in a room meeting, with all parents in attendance, the general objectives of the curriculum at the particular grade level. An opportunity might also be given the parents to come and visit for several hours during a school day. In the school visit, parents would have an opportunity to see their child in relationship to a comparatively large number of children of approximately the same chronological age. This meeting might provide an opportunity to understand the ways in which the child usually approaches his problems. In observation, the parents could note if the child is independent or if he seems to depend on other children for direction. They could also grasp the interest level of the child in the subject matter being presented. The opportunity is also present to note if the child is an active participant and if he is cooperative and willing to share with others. They can sense both by his behavior at home and observation of him in the classroom if he really feels that school is fun.

Many other things might be observed when the parent visits the school, but these would certainly provide a wealth of information for parent-teacher discussions.

It would probably be well for the parent-teacher conference to be preceded with some type of printed introduction which indicates the amount of time available and the kinds of things the teacher will be presenting and which also has a space available for the parents to list specific questions they may have in regard to the school program.

Some schools have found that when parent-teacher conferences have been effective, they can be expanded to a three-way conference in which the parent, teacher, and child are present, possibly to discuss the child's progress in various subjects. Obviously, the objective here is to develop self-understanding on the part of the pupil and acceptance of the child's efforts on the part of the parents. There are still many opportunities in this area to develop more effective means of communication. However, with the assumption that education is really the problem of the child, the three-way conference furnishes the greatest opportunity to convey to all concerned that the child's education is the primary concern and that both parent and teacher are available to assist in maximum development.

IMPLICATIONS

1. The family is the most significant single influence on the development of the child. The school needs to develop methods to communicate more effectively with the family both to understand the subcultural factors the child interacts with and to attempt to influence the child.
2. The child's basic attitudes are formed in the family; hence parent education must be given more attention.
3. A major role of the family is to provide the child with a setting of supporting affection which nurtures development.
4. One of the most significant roles of the family is accepting and valuing the child as he is. Genuine acceptance and valuing produce self-confidence.
5. Parental training is not made effective merely by the setting of high standards. Standards may actually serve as a hindrance to development.
6. One of the most important tasks of the parent is to provide an environment which encourages proper growth and then to permit the child to learn through experience.
7. Consistency is considered to be a vital attribute for efficiency in child-training practices.
8. The setting of limits can give the child a feeling of security. Over-permissiveness communicates a lack of concern.
9. A nonpossessive love based on mutual respect has the most positive effect on children.
10. It has been demonstrated that birth rank is rather regularly related to personality traits. Since information on the family constellation is generally available in the schools, these data might be more effectively utilized in understanding feelings, attitudes, and convictions.
11. Studies of child-training practices continually place an emphasis on the role of warmth, mutual respect, and guidance.
12. The underlying attitudes of genuine care, valuing, and concern are more important than any set of practices.
13. New habits might be established more effectively by encouraging and recognizing them and making their performance pleasurable, rather than by pointing out the "don'ts."
14. Praise and reasoning have been demonstrated to be effective in raising children.
15. Punishment is not effective as a technique for eliminating misbehavior over the long term.

16. Children frequently learn best from natural consequences, and not from the parents' intervention.

17. The broad term "maternal deprivation" has now been identified more specifically in terms of perceptual deprivation, which includes tactile and kinesthetic deprivation. This provides a specific task for mothers and institutions to consider in contrast to a broad, general term.

18. The characteristic emotional tone of the parents in training the child affects the meanings which the children acquire. Specific personality traits always relate to the meanings given acts which appear to be identical on the surface.

19. Birth rank and psychological position in the family constellation seem to be consistently related to specific personality traits in a given culture. The perceptive parent and teacher consider the influence of the family constellation on the child's development and attempt to provide experiences which modify the emerging style of life and assumptions about self.

20. The child's striving for achievement is positively affected by maternal reward of the child's seeking for approval. Adult figures must be alert to recognize completion of a task by the child.

21. Authoritarian and arbitrary maternal attitudes in child management have been associated with both shy and timid children and the presence of behavior problems in children.

SUGGESTED READINGS

Articles

Bronfenbrenner, U., "The Changing American Child—A Speculative Analysis," in *Readings in Educational Psychology*, eds. W. Morse and G. M. Wingo, p. 83. Chicago: Scott, Foresman & Company, 1962.

Langdon, G. and I. Stout, "Backgrounds of Well-Adjusted Children," in *Readings in Educational Psychology*, eds. W. Morse and G. M. Wingo, p. 70. Chicago: Scott, Foresman & Company, 1962.

Maccoby, E., "Methods of Child Rearing in Two Social Classes," in *Readings in Child Development*, eds. W. Martin and C. Stendler, p. 380. New York: Harcourt, Brace & World, Inc., 1954.

Books

Beecher, W., *Parents on the Run*. New York: Julian Press, Inc., 1955.

Dreikurs, R., *Challenge of Parenthood*, rev. ed. New York: Duell, Sloan & Pearce, Inc., 1956.

Dreikurs, R., and Vicki Soltz, *Children: The Challenge*. New York: Duell, Sloan & Pearce, Inc., 1964.

Grams, A., *Children and Their Parents*. Minneapolis, Minn.: T. S. Denison & Co., Inc., 1963.

Gruenberg, S., *Parents' Questions*. New York: Harper & Row, Publishers, 1947.

———, *The Encyclopedia of Child Care and Guidance*, rev. New York: Doubleday & Company, Inc., 1963.

Ilg, F., and L. Ames, *Parents Ask*. New York: Harper & Row, Publishers, 1962.

Miller, D., and G. Swanson, *The Changing American Parent*. New York: John Wiley & Sons, Inc., 1958.

Sears, R., *Patterns of Child Rearing*. New York: Harper & Row, Publishers, 1957.

Symonds, P., *Psychology of Parent-Child Relationships*. New York: Bureau of Publications, Columbia University, 1949.

READINGS IN CHILD DEVELOPMENT

(B) Baller, Warren R., *Readings in the Psychology of Human Growth and Development.* New York: Holt, Rinehart & Winston, Inc., 1962.

(C) Coladarci, Arthur P., *Educational Psychology: A Book of Readings.* New York: Holt, Rinehart & Winston, Inc., 1955.

(C&C) Crow, Lester D., and Alice Crow, *Readings in Child and Adolescent Psychology.* New York: Longmans, Green & Co., Inc., 1961.

(C&C-RHL) Crow, Lester D., and Alice Crow, *Readings in Human Learning.* New York: David McKay Co., Inc., 1963.

(DeC) DeCecco, John P., *Human Learning in the School.* New York: Holt, Rinehart & Winston, Inc., 1963.

(D) Dennis, Wayne, *Readings in Child Psychology* (2nd ed.). Englewood Cliffs, N.J.: Prentice-Hall, Inc., 1963.

(H) Haimowitz, Morris L., and Natalie Haimowitz, *Human Development: Selected Readings.* New York: Thomas Y. Crowell Company, 1960.

(K&T) Kuhlen, Raymond G., and George G. Thompson, *Psychological Studies of Human Development* (2nd ed.). New York: Appleton-Century-Crofts, 1963.

(L) Loree, M. Ray, *Educational Psychology.* New York: The Ronald Press Company, 1959.

(M&S) Martin, William E., and Celia Stendler, *Readings in Child Development.* New York: Harcourt, Brace & World, Inc., 1954.

(M&W) Morse, William G., and G. Max Wingo, *Readings in Educational Psychology.* Chicago: Scott, Foresman & Company, 1962.

(MCK) Mussen, Paul, John Conger, and Jerome Kagan, *Readings in Child Development and Personality.* New York: Harper & Row, Publishers, Inc., 1965.

(N) Noll, Victor H., and Rachel P. Noll, *Readings in Educational Psychology.* New York: The Macmillan Company, 1962.

(P) Page, Ellis Batten, *Readings for Educational Psychology.* New York: Harcourt, Brace & World, Inc., 1964.

(R&A) Rosenblith, Judy, and Wesley Allinsmith, *The Causes of Behavior: Readings in Child Development and Educational Psychology.* Boston: Allyn and Bacon, Inc., 1962.

(R&R) Remmers, H. H., Harry Rivlin, David Ryans, and Einar

Ryden, *Growth, Teaching and Learning.* New York: Harper & Row, Publishers, Inc., 1957.

(S) Seidman, Jerome, *The Child—A Book of Readings.* New York: Holt, Rinehart & Winston, Inc., 1958.

(St) Stendler, Celia Burns, *Readings in Child Behavior and Development* (2nd ed.). New York: Harcourt, Brace & World, Inc., 1964.

II. Theories on Child Development

(B) "Implications of Recent Advances in Prediction and Control of Behavior" by C. Rogers, p. 16.

(DeC) "Walden II" by B. F. Skinner, p. 10. In (M&W) p. 100.

(L) "Developmental Tasks and Education" by R. Havighurst, p. 52.

(M&S) "Continuities and Discontinuities in Cultural Conditioning" by R. Benedict, p. 142.
"Age Patterning in Personality Development" by M. Mead, p. 170.
"Some Aspects of Navaho Infancy and Early Childhood" by C. Kluckhohn, p. 177.
"Psychoanalytic Characterology and Its Application to the Understanding of Culture" by E. Fromm, p. 207.
"Eight Stages of Man" by E. Erikson, p. 213. In (St) p. 243.
"Survey of Objective Studies of Psychoanalytic Concepts" by R. Sears, p. 221.
"An Inquiry into the Concept of Identification" by S. Stoke, p. 227.

(M&W) "Developmental Levels of Character: A Theory" by R. Peck and R. Havighurst, p. 122.

(R&A) "Youth: The Gesell Institute and Its Latest Study" by L. Stolz, p. 52.
"Incentives to Development and Means of Early Education" by L. Peller, p. 140.
"Competence and Psychosexual Stages of Development" by R. White, p. 213.

(S) "The Developmental Tasks of Children and Young People" by S. Corey and V. Herrick, p. 31.

(St) "Maturation and Infant Behavior Pattern" by A. Gesell, p. 25.
"Freudian Theories of Identification and Their Derivatives" by U. Bronfenbrenner, p. 102.

III. Child Study Techniques

(B) "The Educational Psychology of Persons" by H. Jones, p. 28.
"Basic Assumptions in Child Study" by D. Prescott, p. 45.
"A Dynamic Study of Children" by H. English, p. 52.
"Appraising Developmental Status" by L. Stott, p. 91.
"How Well Do Elementary School Teachers Understand Child Behavior?" by C. Stendler, p. 640.

(C&C) "Commonly Used Study Approaches" by L. Crow and A. Crow, p. 1.
"Current Methods of Studying Children and Adolescents" by W. Cruze, p. 4.
"The Formal Case Study" by A. Schwartz and S. Tiedeman, p. 13.

(H) "A Dynamic Study of Children" by H. English, p. 234.

(N) "A Study of the Effects of Teacher Knowledge of Pupil Characteristics on Pupil Achievement and Attitudes Towards Classwork" by K. Hoyt, p. 255.

(S) "Studying an Individual Child" by L. Shaffer and E. J. Shoben, Jr., p. 508.

IV. Principles of Development

(B) "The Miracle of Growth" by A. Gesell, p. 68.
"How Do Cells Differentiate?" by C. H. Waddington, p. 151.
"Influences on Growth: Heredity" by M. E. Breckenridge and E. L. Vincent, p. 175.
"The Developmental Tasks of Children and Young People" by S. M. Corey and V. E. Herrick, p. 329.
"Why Physical Growth is Studied" by H. Meredith, p. 361.
"Self-conceptions, Motivations, and Interpersonal Attitudes of Late- and Early-Maturing Boys" by P. Mussen and M. Jones, p. 377. In (R&A) p. 43, (P) p. 70, and (MCK) p. 419.

(C) "Concepts of Growth: Their Significance for Teachers" by W. Olson and B. Hughes, p. 65.

(C&C) "Hereditary Transmission" by P. Mussen & J. Conger, p. 37.
"Biological Inheritance, Environmental Influence, and Cultural Heritage" by L. Crow & H. Crow, p. 41.
"Approximate Timetable of Prenatal Development" by R. Watson, p. 69.

(D) "The Motor Sequence" by M. Shirley, p. 72.
"Environmental Influences Upon Motor Development" by W. Dennis, p. 83.
"Resemblances Between Identical Twins Reared Apart" by R. Woodworth, p. 394.
"Physical Maturity of Boys as Related to Behavior" by M. C. Jones & N. Bayley, p. 407.
"Shirley's Babies After Fifteen Years" by P. Neilen, p. 475.

(H) "Constitutional and Prenatal Factors in Infant and Child Health" by M. F. Montagu, p. 124.
"What Are Some of the Laws Which Govern Growth?" by M. E. Breckenridge and E. Lee Vincent, p. 144.
"Guiding the Development of the Preadolescent" by A. W. Blair and W. H. Burton, p. 652.
"The Later Careers of Boys Who Were Early- or Late-Maturing" by M. C. Jones, p. 708.

(K&T) "Heredity, Environment, and the Question 'How?'" by A. Anastasi, p. 111. (R&A) p. 20, and (MCK) p. 5.
"Twin Studies on Senescence" by F. Kallmann and G. Sander, p. 124.
"Physical Maturing Among Boys as Related to Behavior in Adolescence and Adult Years" by M. C. Jones and N. Bayley, p. 139.

(M&S) "Constitutional and Prenatal Factors in Infant and Child Health" by M. F. Montagu, p. 15.
"The Rationale of Assessing the Developmental Status of Children from Roentgenograms of the Hand and Wrist" by W. Greulich, p. 42.

"Physical Maturing Among Boys as Related to Behavior" by M. C. Jones and N. Bayley, p. 48.
"Results of the Self-Selection of Diets by Young Children" by C. Davis, p. 69.

(M&W) "What Psychology Can We Feel Sure About?" by G. Watson, p. 3.

(N) "Child Development and the Growth Process" by J. Anderson, p. 30.

(R&A) "New Directions in the Genetic Study of Personality and Intelligence" by J. P. Scott, p. 29.
"Physical Maturing Among Boys as Related to Behavior" by M. Jones and N. Bayley, p. 41.

(S) "A Proposed Reorientation in the Heredity-Environment Controversy" by A. Anastasi and J. Foley, Jr., p. 2.
"What Are Some of the Laws Which Govern Growth?" by M. Breckenridge and E. Vincent, p. 15.
"Development as a Product of Learning and Growth" by A. Jersild, p. 25.
"The Development Tasks of Children and Young People" by S. Corey and V. Herrick, p. 31.
"Some Environmental Factors Which May Influence Prenatal Development" by F. Montagu, p. 42.
"Sequence of Motor Development" by M. Shirley, p. 79.

(St) "Causes of Retardation Among Institutional Children: Iran" by W. Dennis, p. 93.
"The Regulation of Human Growth" by T. Tanner, p. 479.

V. Learning

(C&C) "A Cross-Cultural Study of the Reinforcement of Child Behavior" by W. Dennis, p. 52.

(C&C-RHL) "Basic Principles in a Good Teaching-Learning Situation" by Wm. Burton, p. 7.
"Learning: A Process of Change" by E. Haggard, p. 19.
"The Science of Learning and the Art of Teaching" by B. F. Skinner, p. 28. (P) p. 242, (L) p. 196, (R&A) p. 76, and (H) p. 578.
"Seven Principles of Learning" by S. Clement, p. 54.
"Conditions for Effective Learning" by R. Tyler, p. 66.
"Significant Learning: In Therapy and in Education" by C. R. Rogers, p. 79.
"Learning: I. Understanding, Transfer, and Retention" by R. C. Craig, p. 92.
"Teaching Machines and Programmed Learning: What Support from the Psychology of Learning?" by E. Hilgard, p. 448.

(DeC) "A Review of Factors in Learning Efficiency" by R. Gagne and R. Bolles, p. 30.
"The Teacher and the Improvement of Educational Practice" by F. McDonald, p. 52.
"Teaching Machines" by B. F. Skinner, p. 164. In (N) p. 313; (M&W) p. 144.
"The Rationale of Intrinsic Programming" by N. Crowder, p. 183.
"Recent Research on Human Problem Solving" by C. Duncan, p. 212.

(K&T) "Probability Learning in Children" by H. Stevenson and E. Zigler, p. 185.

(M&S) "A Primary Social Science Law" by C. Hull, p. 291.

(M&W) "Teacher Behavior Liked and Disliked by Pupils" by C. Leeds, p. 12.
"More Opportunity for Learning—or Less?" by A. Frazier, p. 151.
"Self-Selection as a Principle of Curriculum and Method" by W. Olson, p. 155.
"The Functions of Teaching" by J. Bruner, p. 162.
"Learning Theory in School Situations" by E. Swenson, G. Anderson, and C. Stacey, p. 174.
"Repetition and Learning" by I. Rock, p. 210.
"The Experimental Background of the Problems of Learning" by A. Rapp, p. 215.
"The Problem of Transfer—Then and Now" by Wm. Trow, p. 222.

(N) "Educational Theory and the Psychology of Learning" by G. Buswell, p. 198.

(P) "Learning: An Integration of Theories" by A. Frandsen, p. 50.
"Readiness for Learning" by J. Bruner, p. 206.
"Transfer of Training in General Education" by L. Humphreys, p. 217.
"The Difficulty Reduction Tendency in Perception and Problem Solving" by G. Hildreth, p. 234.
"Programmed Materials Today: Critique and Proposal" by H. Thelen, p. 253.

(R&A) "Theories of Learning and Behavior" by J. Whiting, p. 62.
"Reinforcement Today" by B. Skinner, p. 65.
"Learning and Thinking" by J. Bruner, p. 446.
"Transfer of Training" by T. Andrews and L. Cronbach, p. 451.
"Introduction to Learning Theory in School Situations" by T. McConnell, p. 467.

(R&R) "Are Theories of Learning Helpful?" by S. Kramer, p. 99.
"When Are Children Ready to Learn?" by W. Trow, p. 107.
"Motivation in Learning" by D. Ryans, p. 122.
"Ambiguous Is the Word for Transfer" by H. Tuttle, p. 172.

(S) "Development as a Product of Learning and Growth" by A. Jersild, p. 25.
"Investigation and Treatment of a Reading Disability in a Dull Child with Severe Psychiatric Disturbances" by D. Bartlet and M. Shapiro, p. 532.
"A. Nondirective Play Therapy With Retarded Readers" by R. Bills, p. 547.
"B. Play Therapy with Well-Adjusted Retarded Readers" by R. Bills, p. 561.

VI. Social Development

(B) "The Peer Culture of Youth and the School" by T. Bienenstok, p. 490.

(C) "Relationship Between Sociometric Status of Pupils and Teacher's Preference for Having Them in Class" by N. E. Gronlund, p. 206.

(C&C) "Sociometric Aids" by M. R. Routh, p. 11.

(DeC) "Groupness of the Group" by I. Lorge, p. 530.
"Student-Centered vs. Instructor-Centered Instruction" by W. McKeachie, p. 550.
"Measurement in Relation to the Educational Process" by D. Adkins, p. 575.

(D) "The Effects of Social Climates" by K. Lewin, p. 468.

(H) "An Experimental Study of Leadership and Group Life" by R. Lippitt and R. White, p. 312.

(K&T) "Critical Periods in Socialization" by C. Stendler, p. 81.
"Social-Cultural Background and Competitive Behavior" by J. McKee and F. Leader, p. 252.
"Social Perceptions and Attitudes of Children" by M. Radke-Yarrow, H. Trager, and H. Davis, p. 418.
"Friendship Fluctuations During Childhood" by J. Horrocks and M. Buker, p. 447.
"Anxiety in Children and Social Status" by B. McCandless, A. Castaneda, and D. Palermo, p. 462.
"Comparative Social Adjustments of Elementary School Pupils With and Without Preschool Training" by M. Bonney and E. Nicholson, p. 496.

(M&S) "An Investigation of Behavioral Contagion in Groups" by N. Polansky, R. Lippitt, and F. Redl, p. 493.

(M&W) "The Impact of Beginning First Grade" by C. Stendler and N. Young, p. 115.
"The Stages of Maturation in Socialized Thinking and in the Ego Development of Two Groups of Children" by A. Bobroff, p. 315.
"Group Discussion as Educational Process" by R. Dreikurs, p. 336.
"Group Life Space Interviewing in a Therapeutic Camp" by W. Morse and E. Small, p. 343.

(N) "The Effect of Teacher-Pupil Contacts Involving Praise on the Sociometric Choices of Students" by N. Flanders and S. Havumaki, p. 435.
"Peer Acceptance of Highly Gifted Children in Elementary School" by J. Gallagher, p. 454.

(P) "Social-Class Variations in the Teacher-Pupil Relationship" by H. Becker, p. 96.
"Social Learning Through Imitation" by A. Bandura, p. 274.

(R&A) "Social Behavior of Young Children in the Kibbutz" by H. Faigin, p. 160.
"Psychology of Group Behavior: The Class as a Group" by W. Trow, A. Zander, W. Morse, and D. Jenkins, p. 327.
"Classroom Social Structure as a Mental Health Problem" by R. Lippitt and M. Gold, p. 334.

(S) "Investigation of Areas of Disagreement in Sociometric Measurement of Preschool Children" by M. Dunnington, p. 205.
"The Social-Sex Development of Children" by E. Campbell, p. 214.

(St) "Relation of Early Socialization Experiences to Aggression in Middle Childhood" by R. Sears, p. 195.
"Methods of Child Rearing in Two Social Classes" by E. Maccoby, p. 272.

"Singularity and Stability of Profiles of Social Behavior" by W. Martin, p. 448.

VII. Development of the Self Concept

(B) "Value and Need as Organizing Factors in Perception" by J. S. Bruner and C. C. Goodman, p. 216.
"The Infant's Perception of the World and the Beginning of Self-Awareness" by L. Stone and J. Church, p. 228.
"Children's Attitudes Toward Peers and Parents as Revealed by Sentence Completions" by D. B. Harris and S. C. Tseng, p. 531.

(C&C-RHL) "Perceptual Development: Some Tentative Hypotheses" by G. Murphy & J. Hochberg, p. 207.
"Influence of Intelligence on Anxiety and Perception of Self and Others" by B. Phillips, E. Hindsman, and E. Jennings, p. 304.

(H) "The Case of Peter" by E. Erickson, p. 355.
"Criminals Are Made, Not Born" by M. Haimowitz, p. 359.
"Children Who Hate" by F. Redl, p. 375.

(M&S) "Value and Need as Organizing Factors in Perception" by J. Bruner and C. Goodman, p. 310.
"Self-Understanding in Childhood and Adolescence" by A. Jersild, p. 473.

(M&W) "They Learn What They Live" by H. Trager and M. Yarrow, p. 198.

(N) "Children's Perceptions of Their Teachers' Feelings Toward Them Related to Self-Perception, School Achievement, and Behavior" by H. Davidson and G. Lang, p. 388.

(S) "Self-Concept as an Insulator Against Delinquency" by W. Reckless, S. Dinitz, E. Murray, p. 219.

(St) "Self-Conceptions, Motivations, and Interpersonal Attitudes of Late- and Early-Maturing Boys" by P. Mussen and M. Jones, p. 419.

VIII. The Development of Intelligence and Mental Processes

(B) "Three Faces of Intellect" by J. P. Guilford, p. 397.
"Mental Growth and Personality Development: A Longitudinal Study" by L. W. Sontag, C. T. Baker, and V. L. Nelson, p. 418.

(C&C-RHL) "Intelligence: Its Nature and Measurement" by R. Harsh, p. 251.
"The Four IQ's" by E. Doll, p. 267.
"Three Faces of Intellect" by J. Guilford, p. 270. In (DeC) p. 435.
"The Act of Discovery" by J. Bruner, p. 423. In (DeC) p. 254.

(DeC) "Pace of Presentation, Number of Trials, and Amount of Practice as Determiners of Learning" by F. Kopstein, p. 311.
"The Meaning and Assessment of Intelligence" by Sir C. Burt, p. 419.
"On the Growth of Intelligence" by N. Bayley, p. 456.

(D) "Binet's Method of Measuring Intelligence" by L. Terman, p. 215.
"The Stability of Mental Test Performance Between Two and Eighteen Years" by M. P. Honzik, T. W. MacFarlane, and L. Allen, p. 223. In (N) p. 63; (St) p. 467 and (K&T) p. 311.
"The Development of Parent-Child Resemblance in Intelligence" by M. Honzik, p. 233.

"A Thirty-five Year Follow-Up of Intellectually Superior Children" by L. M. Terman and M. Oden, p. 516.

(H) "The Social and Emotional Problems of the Epileptic Child and His Family" by W. Lennox, p. 458.
"The Discovery and Encouragement of Exceptional Talent" by L. Terman, p. 595.
"Some Characteristics of Very Superior Children" by W. D. Lewis, p. 609.

(K&T) "Criteria of the Stages of Mental Development" by B. Inhelder, p. 28.
"The Inheritance of Mental Ability" by C. Burt, p. 285.
"The Adult Status of Persons Earlier Judged Mentally Deficient" by D. Charles, p. 343.
"The Development and Adult Status of Gifted Children" by L. Terman and M. Oden, p. 351.
"Language Growth and Intellectual Status" by M. Rigg, p. 406.

(L) "Intelligence From a Perceptual Point of View" by A. Combs, p. 122.
"Mental Test Performance as a Reflection of the Child's Current Life Situation: A Methodological Study" by T. W. Richards, p. 110.

(M&S) "The Limitations of Infant and Preschool Tests in the Measurement of Intelligence" by J. Anderson, p. 75.
"The Use of Infant Tests for Predictive Purposes" by S. Escalona, p. 95.
"Social-Class Influences Upon Mental Problem-Solving" by A. Davis, p. 104.

(M&W) "Factors Affecting Creative Thinking in Children: An Interim Research Report" by E. Torrance, p. 188.

(MCK) "Developmental Studies of Parent-Child Resemblance in Intelligence" by M. Honzik, p. 21.
"How Children form Mathematical Concepts" by J. Piaget, p. 304.
"Information Processing in the Child" by J. Kagan, p. 313.

(R&A) "Training and a Logical Operation by Children" by S. Ervin, p. 229.
"Upon the Necessity of Establishing a Scientific Diagnosis of Inferior States of Intelligence" by A. Binet and T. Simon, p. 283.
"Testing Intelligence and Aptitudes" by L. Thurstone, p. 291.
"Personality and I.Q. Change" by J. Kagan and L. Sontag, p. 297. In (K&T) p. 329.
"The Development of the Binet-Simon Scale" by A. Binet and T. Simon, p. 286.
"The Discovery and Encouragement of Exceptional Talent" by L. Terman, p. 303. In (R&R) p. 63.
"Should a Bright Child Start to School Before He's Five?" by R. McCandless, p. 313.
"Early Education of the Mentally Retarded" by S. Kirk, p. 317.

(R&R) "Measurement of Mental Systems—Can Intelligence Be Measured?" by W. Davis and R. Havighurst, p. 77.
"Kinds of Intelligence Differ, Too" by E. Weisskopf-Joelson, p. 97.

(S) "On the Growth of Intelligence" by N. Bayley, p. 250.
"Effects of Glutamic Acid and Social Stimulation in Mental Deficiency" by G. Chambers and R. Zabarenko, p. 267.
"The Discovery and Encouragement of Exceptional Talent" by L. Terman, p. 594.

(St) "Intellectual Processes in Children" by C. Stendler, p. 319.
"A Follow-Up Study of Inhelder and Piaget's *The Growth of Logical Thinking*" by K. Lovell, p. 361.
"The Development of Scientific Concepts in Childhood" by L. Vygotsky, p. 372.

IX. Emotional Development

(B) "Emotional Development in Early Infancy" by K. M. B. Bridges, p. 290.
"Some Psychosomatic Aspects of Childhood" by L. W. Sontag, p. 367.

(C) "Teacher Growth in Attitudes Toward Behavior Problems of Children" by M. Schrupp and C. M. Gjerde, p. 173. In (R&R) p. 246 and in (K&T) p. 503.
"The Fundamental Needs of the Child" by L. K. Frank, p. 122. In (R&R) p. 281.

(C&C) "How to Deal With Your Tensions" by G. S. Stevenson and H. Milt, p. 579.
"Projective Techniques" by L. Crow and A. Crow, p. 8.

(D) "Development After Noncontinuous Mothering" by D. B. Gardner, G. R. Hawkes, and L. Burchinal, p. 332.

(H) "A Laboratory Study of Fear: The Case of Peter" by M. C. Jones, p. 566.
"Child Care and the Growth of Love" by J. Bowlby, p. 155.
"Motherless Infants" by R. Spitz, p. 166.
"The Nature of Love" by H. Harlow, p. 190.
"Interpretation of Projective Devices" by C. Buhler, p. 265.

(K&T) "The Long-Term Prediction of Children's Adjustment" by J. Anderson, p. 559.
"Delinquency as a Mode of Adjustment" by W. Healy and A. Bronner, p. 574.

(L) "The Emotional Maturation Process" by I. Josselyn, p. 146.

(M&S) "The Inheritance of Emotionality" by C. Hall, p. 59.
"Studies of Fear as an Acquired Drive: 1. Fear as Motivation and Fear-Reduction as Reinforcement in the Learning of New Responses" by N. Miller, p. 252.

(M&W) "Emotional Development in Infancy" by R. Spitz, p. 46.
"The Infantile Disorders of Hospitalism and Anaclitic Depression" by S. Pinneau, p. 51.
"A Critique of Studies of Infant Isolation" by J. Stone, p. 58.
"An Application to Education of the Needs Theory" by L. Raths, p. 67.
"Our Troubles with Defiant Youth" by F. Redl, p. 135.
"Education and Psychotherapy" by P. Symonds, p. 308.
"A Process for Identifying Disturbed Children" by E. Bower, p. 325.
"Basic Approaches to Mental Health: The Human Relations Program at the State University of Iowa" by R. Ojemann, p. 330.

(MCK) "Separation Anxiety" by J. Bowlby, p. 140.

(N) "The Teacher and Mental Health" by N.I.M.H., p. 354.

"Teachers' and Clinicians' Attitudes Toward the Behavior Problems of Children: A Reappraisal" by H. Beilen, p. 361, and in (R&A) p. 434.

"The Emotionally Disturbed" and F. Redl and S. Jacobson, p. 463.

(P) "Case Study of an Authoritarian Family and Child" by E. Frenkel-Brunswik, p. 108.

"Diagnostic Thinking in the Classroom" by F. Redl and W. Wattenberg, p. 358.

(R&A) "The Elimination of Tantrum Behavior by Extinction Procedures" by C. Williams, p. 71.

"A Healthy Personality for Every Child" by E. Erikson, p. 202.

(R&R) "Behavior Problems of Children as Viewed by Teachers and Mental Hygienists" by A. Stouffer, p. 256.

"Early Behavior Problems as Signposts to Later Maladjustment" by L. Kanner, p. 318.

"Emotional Deprivation in Infants" by H. Bakwin, p. 326.

"Significant Symptoms in the Behavior of Young Children: A Check List for Teachers" by L. Peller, p. 336.

(S) "The Children's Form of the Manifest Anxiety Scale" by A. Castaneda, B. McCandless, and D. Palermo, p. 494. (H) p. 468.

"The Relation of the Children's Manifest Anxiety Scale to the Concept of Anxiety as Used in the Clinic" by R. Wirt and W. Broen, Jr., p. 501.

"Treatment of a Withdrawn Girl" by J. Kahn, p. 517.

X. Motivation and Discipline in Child Development

(B) "A Theory of Human Motivation" by A. H. Maslow, p. 255. In (R&R) p. 300 and in (S) p. 417.

(C&C-RHL) "Some Cognitive Aspects of Motivation" by W. Prentice, p. 356.

(DeC) "Mice, Monkeys, Men, and Motives" by H. Harlow, p. 85.

(D) "Desires Expressed in Children's Dreams" by S. Freud, p. 261.

(H) "Pre-Adolescents—What Makes Them Tick?" by F. Redl, p. 640. In (S) p. 609.

(K&T) "Origins of Achievement Motivation" by D. McClelland, J. Atkinson, R. Clark, and E. Lowell, p. 217.

(M&S) "Levels of Aspiration in Academically Successful and Unsuccessful Children" by P. Sears, p. 437.

(M&W) "Pupil Motivation and Its Relationship to the Activity and Social Drives" by D. Bortner, p. 258.

"Explorations in Classroom Management" by J. Kounin, P. Gump, and J. Ryan, p. 296.

(N) "The Effect of Repeated Praise or Blame on the Work Achievement of 'Introverts' and 'Extroverts' " by G. Thompson and C. Hunnicutt, p. 245.

"Teacher Comments and Student Performance: A Seventy-four Classroom Experiment in School Motivation" by E. Page, p. 264.

(P) "Classroom Discipline" by P. Symonds, p. 290.

(R&A) "Experience and the Development of Motivation: Some Reinterpretations" by J. McV. Hunt, p. 353.
"Success and Failure in the Classroom" by P. Barker, p. 370.

(St) "Children's Reactions to Novelty: An Experimental Study of 'Curiosity Motivation'" by C. Smock and B. Holt, p. 155.
"Motivation Reconsidered: The Concept of Competence" by R. White, p. 164.

XI. Personality Development

(B) "Cultural Factors in Personality" by C. Kluckhohn, p. 319.
"Origins of Personality" by P. M. Symonds, p. 595.
"Shirley's Babies After Fifteen Years: A Personality Study" by P. Neilon, p. 610; in (S) p. 584; in (St) p. 429.

(C&C) "Culture and Personality" by M. Hutt and R. Gibby, p. 47.

(D) "Personality Organization in Children" by J. Anderson, p. 303.
"Stability of Passive and Dependent Behavior from Childhood to Adulthood" by J. Kagan and H. Moss, p. 486. In (St) p. 437 and (MCK) p. 327.
"Predictions of Later Behavior from Childhood Evaluations" by E. Werner and E. Gallistel, p. 495.
"Stability in Ascendance-Submission" by L. Stott, p. 501.

(H) "Similarity in Teacher and Pupil Personality" by M. Amatora, p. 306.
"The Parental Attitudes of Mothers of Schizophrenics" by M. Zuckerman, M. Oltean, and I. Monashkin, p. 426.
"Non-directive Play Therapy" by V. Axline, p. 525.
"Group Interviewing in a Camp for Disturbed Boys" by W. Morse and D. Wineman, p. 584.

(K&T) "Personality Characteristics of Responsible Children" by D. Harris, A. Rose, K. Clark, and F. Valasek, p. 411.
"Moral Development in Childhood" by G. Medinnus, p. 426.
"Studies in the Organization of Character" by H. Hartshorne and M. May, p. 432.

(M&S) "Homeostasis as a Unifying Concept in Personality Theory" by R. Stagner, p. 3.
"Personality Profiles of Adolescents" by R. Havighurst and H. Taba, p. 460.
"Children's Textbooks and Personality Development: An Exploration in the Social Psychology of Education" by I. Child, E. Potter, and E. M. Levine, p. 479.

(M&W) "Youth and the Life Cycle" by E. Erikson, p. 38.

(MCK) "Personality and IQ Change" by J. Kagan, L. Sontag, C. Baker, and V. Nelson, p. 284.

(R&A) "A Theoretical Framework for Personality and Social Behavior" by R. Sears, p. 85.
"Conscience and Conflict: The Moral Force in Personality" by W. Allinsmith, p. 380.
"Intellectual Malfunctioning and Personality" by E. Weisskopf, p. 385.

(S) "Some Psychosomatic Aspects of Childhood" by L. Sontag, p. 466.
"Negativism as a Phase of Ego Development" by D. Ausubel, p. 475.

"Self-Acceptance and Adjustment" by C. Taylor and A. Combs, p. 502.
"Social and Personal Changes Following Nondirective Group Play Therapy" by L. Fleming and W. Snyder, p. 567.
(St) "Psychological Privation in Infancy and Subsequent Adjustment" by W. Goldfarb, p. 79.

XII. Development and Educational Achievement: Academic Growth

(C) "Questioning Some Assumptions Underlying Current Achievement Testing" by V. Sims, p. 580. In (R&A) p. 471.
"Individual Differences and Curriculum Practice" by W. Cook, p. 330. In (R&R) p. 194.
"Concepts of Growth: Their Significance for Teachers" by W. Olson and B. Hughes, p. 65.
(C&C) "Boys and Girls—Are There Significant Ability and Achievement Differences?" by W. Clark, p. 247.
"The Relationship of Intelligence and Achievement to Birth Order, Sex of Sibling, and Age Interval" by S. Schoonover, p. 250.
(C&C-RHL) "Creative Thinking Through the Language Arts" by E. Torrance, p. 436.
(DeC) "Viewpoints from Related Disciplines: Human Growth and Development" by D. Ausubel, p. 67.
"A Dispute About Reading" by R. Brown, p. 338.
"Education and the Psychology of Individual Differences" by P. Vernon, p. 482. In (M&W) p. 233.
"A Comparative Study of Achieving and Underachieving High School Boys of High Intellectual Ability" by E. Frankel, p. 501. In (N) p. 164.
(H) "Identity and Interpersonal Competence" by N. Foote and L. Cottrell, p. 55.
"Cases Illustrating Psychoanalytic Contributions to the Problems of Reading Disabilities" by P. Blanchard, p. 503.
(K&T) "Teacher Interactions with Boys as Contrasted with Girls" by W. Meyer and G. Thompson, p. 510.
"Age of Onset of Academic Underachievement in Bright Children" by M. Shaw and J. McCuen, p. 519.
"Some Generalizations Regarding Vocational Development" by D. Super, *et al.*, p. 527.
(M&W) "The Effect of Promotion Policy on Academic Achievement" by G. Kowitz and C. Armstrong, p. 369.
(N) "Effect of Age of Entrance into Grade I Upon Achievement in Elementary School" by I. King, p. 74.
"When Should Children Begin to Read?" by M. Morphett and C. Washburne, p. 83.
"The Discovery and Encouragement of Exceptional Talent" by L. Terman, p. 128.
"To Promote or Not to Promote?" by J. Goodlad, p. 239.
"The Effectiveness of an Approach to the Problem of Varying Abilities in Teaching Reading" by R. Hart, p. 298.
"Evaluation—More Than Testing" by H. Heffernan, p. 497.

"What Does Research Say About Self-Evaluation?" by D. Russell, p. 509.

(R&A) "Compulsivity, Anxiety, and School Achievement" by J. Grimes and W. Allinsmith, p. 420.

(R&R) "Theories of Behavior and Some Curriculum Issues" by G. Anderson, p. 188.

(S) "How Well Do Elementary School Teachers Understand Child Behavior?" by C. Stendler, p. 162.

"Sex Differences in the Distribution of Teacher Approval and Disapproval Among Sixth Grade Children" by W. Meyer and G. Thompson, p. 169.

"The Effect on Pupil Growth of an Increase in Teacher's Understanding of Pupil Behavior" by R. Ojemann and F. Wilkinson, p. 178.

"Concept Formation in Children of School Ages" by W. Vinacke, p. 294.

"Developing an Understanding of Human Behavior at the Elementary School Level" by F. Stiles, p. 383.

(St) "Achievement, Creativity, and Self-Concept Correlates of Teacher-Pupil Transactions in Elementary Schools" by R. Spaulding, p. 313.

XIII. The Child in the Family

(B) "A Study of Child Rearing" by R. Sears, E. Maccoby, H. Levin, p. 547.

(D) "Aggression in Doll Play" by H. Levin and R. Sears, p. 286.

(H) "Patterns of Child Rearing" by R. Sears, E. Maccoby, and H. Levin, p. 222.

(K&T) "The Child Rearing Process" by R. Sears, E. Maccoby, and H. Levin, p. 244.

(M&S) "The Effect of Home Environment on Nursery School Behavior" by A. Baldwin, p. 337.

"Methods of Child-Rearing in Two Social Classes" by E. Maccoby, p. 380.

(M&W) "Backgrounds of Well-Adjusted Children" by G. Langdon and I. Stout, p. 70.

"The Changing American Child—A Speculative Analysis" by U. Bronfenbrenner, p. 83.

(MCK) "Parent-Child Relations and Parental Personality in Relation to Young Children's Sex-Role Preferences" by P. Mussen and E. Rutherford, p. 225.

"Social Class and Parental Values" by M. Kohn, p. 345.

"Relationships between Dependence on Adults and Social Acceptance by Peers" by H. Marshall and B. McCandless, p. 367.

"Parents' Attitudes and Behaviors and Grade School Children's Academic Achievements" by V. Crandall, R. Dewey, W. Katkovsky, and A. Preston, p. 400.

(S) "Personality Development in the Family" by R. Sears, p. 117.

"The Child's Perception of the Parent" by J. Kagan, p. 138.

"The Assertive Behavior of Children as Related to Parent Behavior" by C. Meyer, p. 141.

(St) "The Later Effects of an Experimental Modification of Mothering" by H. Rheingold and N. Bayley, p. 86.
"Nurturance and Nurturance-Withdrawal in Relation to the Dependency Behavior of Preschool Children" by W. Hartup, p. 224.

Additional References:

Annual Review of Psychology (Stanford, California: Standard Reviews).
Child Development (Chicago: University of Chicago Press).
Child Development Abstracts and Bibliography (Chicago: University of Chicago Press).
Child Psychology, ed. Harold Stevenson, 62nd Yearbook of the National Society for the Study of Education, Part I (Chicago: University of Chicago Press), 1963.
Encyclopedia of Educational Research, ed. Chester Harris, 3rd ed. (New York: The Macmillan Company), 1960.
Handbook of Research on Teaching, ed. N. L. Gage (Chicago: Rand McNally & Co.), 1963.
Human Development, Readings in Research, by Ira J. Gordon (Chicago: Scott, Foresman and Company), 1965.
Manual of Child Psychology, ed. L. Carmichael (New York: John Wiley & Sons, Inc.), 1954.
Psychological Abstracts (Washington, D.C.: American Psychological Association).
Review of Child Development Research, eds. Martin Hoffman and Lois Hoffman (New York: Russell Sage Foundation), 1964.
Review of Educational Research (Washington, D.C.: American Educational Research Association).

INSTITUTES OF CHILD DEVELOPMENT AND CHILD STUDY

Child Development Laboratories, University of Michigan, Ann Arbor, Michigan

Child Research Council, Study in Human Development, University of Colorado Medical School, 4200 E. 9th Ave., Denver 20, Colorado

The Child Study Center, Yale University, 333 Cedar St., New Haven 11, Connecticut

Fels Research Institute for the Study of Human Development, Antioch College, Yellow Springs, Ohio

Gesell Institute of Child Development, 310 Prospect St., New Haven, Connecticut

Horace-Mann Lincoln Institute of School Experimentation, Teachers College, Columbia University, New York 27, New York

Institute of Child Development, Department of Psychology, University of Washington, Seattle 5, Washington

Institute of Child Development and Welfare, University of Minnesota, Minneapolis 14, Minnesota

Institute for Child Study, University of Maryland, College Park, Maryland

Institute of Child Study, University of Toronto, Toronto, Ontario

Institute of Human Development, University of California, Berkeley, California

Institute for Juvenile Research, 907 S. Wolcott, Chicago 12, Illinois

Iowa Child Welfare Research Station, State University of Iowa, Iowa City, Iowa

Menninger Foundation, Topeka, Kansas

Merrill-Palmer, 71 E. Ferry Ave., Detroit, Michigan

National Institute of Mental Health, Sec. Child Development, Bethesda, Maryland

Philadelphia Center for Research in Child Growth, 1701 Fitzwater St., Philadelphia 46, Pa.

Study of Behavioral Development, School of Medicine, New York University, New York

APPENDICES

PUPIL'S INTEREST RECORD

Name ______________________ Date __________ Grade ______

1. Names of siblings (list, beginning with oldest child) ______________

____

2. When you have time to do just as you please, what do you like best to do?

____

3. What are the names of your three best friends? ______________

4. Do you take special lessons outside of school? ____ Do you like them? ____

5. Is there some other kind of special lesson you would like to take? ______

6. Do you listen to the radio at home? _____ How much? _____ When? _____

   Favorite program: 1 ___________ 2 ___________ 3 ___________

7. Do you watch television at home? _____ How much? ___________

   Favorite program: 1 ___________ 2 ___________ 3 ___________

8. If you were going to be in a show/play, what kind of person would you like to pretend to be? Why?

9. If you were going to pretend to be an animal, what animal would you like to be? Why?

10. Which of these places would you like best to go: 1. Farm _____ 2. Circus __

    3. Zoo ____ 4. Museum ____ 5. Concert ____ 6. Stage play ____ 7. Ball game __

11. What would you like to be when you grow up? Why? ______________

12. Do you have a hobby? _____ Do you collect anything? ___________

13. What subject do you like best in school? ______________

    What subject do you like least in school? ______________

14. If you could have three wishes that could come true, what would you wish?

    ____

    Have you ever told these wishes to anyone else? To Whom?

    ____

    Have any of your wishes ever come true?

    ____

15. Most children sometimes feel afraid--what are some of the things that make you

    feel afraid? ______________________________

16. Do you like to read? _____ Does someone read to you? _____ What are the names of some books you have read or that have been read to you?

    ____

SENTENCE COMPLETION

1. Nothing makes me more angry than
2. What people like most about me is
3. I feel bad when
4. I'd like to have my picture taken when
5. People think of me as
6. What gets me in trouble is
7. I think of myself as
8. People who tell you what to do
9. I am happiest when
10. I can't
11. I am nervous when
12. I feel afraid when
13. I like
14. I wish
15. My greatest worry
16. I think my future
17. My ambition
18. The kind of animal I would most like to be
19. The two most beautiful things I've seen
20. I'd like to know

I AM A PERSON WHO

I AM A PERSON WHO	VERY MUCH LIKE ME	A LITTLE LIKE ME	NOT LIKE ME
1s. HAS MANY FRIENDS.			
2d. NEEDS A LOT OF HELP.			
3L. HAS TROUBLE GOING TO SLEEP AT NIGHT.			
4a. USUALLY DOES WELL IN SCHOOL.			
5s. LIKES TO PLAY ALONE RATHER THAN WITH OTHER CHILDREN.			
6a. SHOWS I AM BOTHERED WHEN I LOSE A GAME.			
7n. IS SICK A LOT.			
8a. ALWAYS GETS MY WAY.			
9L. FEELS I HAVE TO FIGURE OUT MY OWN PROBLEMS.			
10a. IS OFTEN TIRED DURING THE DAY.			
11a. IS GOOD AT A LOT OF THINGS.			
12s. ALWAYS LIKES TO DECIDE WHAT TO DO WHEN WE PLAY.			
13L. HAS A MOTHER AND FATHER WHO ARE AS NICE AS THE PARENTS OF MY FRIENDS.			
14n. USUALLY FEELS WELL.			
15s. LIKES TO SIT AND DAYDREAM.			
16a. CAN'T DO ANYTHING VERY WELL.			
17s. ALWAYS LIKES TO LET OTHER PEOPLE DECIDE WHAT TO PLAY.			
18s. THINKS THAT MOST PEOPLE TREAT ME FAIRLY.			
19n. FEELS THAT SOMETHING BAD WILL HAPPEN.			
20a. DOESN'T CRY MUCH.			
21L. IS PUNISHED A LOT FOR LITTLE THINGS.			

Page 2

I AM A PERSON WHO	VERY MUCH LIKE ME	A LITTLE LIKE ME	NOT LIKE ME
22a. IS USUALLY FULL OF PEP AND ENERGY DURING THE DAY.			
23L. OFTEN GETS MY FEELINGS HURT.			
24a. USUALLY HAS A LOT OF FUN.			
25L. WOULD LIKE TO DO MORE THINGS WITH MY FAMILY INSTEAD OF WITH FRIENDS.			
26s. FEELS THAT PEOPLE LIKE ME AS WELL AS THEY SHOULD.			
27d. LIKES TO WORK BY MYSELF.			
28s. THINKS THAT OTHER PEOPLE ARE HARD TO GET GET ALONG WITH.			
29L. WOULD LIKE TO DO MORE THINGS WITH FRIENDS INSTEAD OF WITH MY FAMILY.			
30L. FEELS THAT MY PARENTS THINK I AM ALL RIGHT.			
31s. FINDS THAT OTHER PEOPLE ARE USUALLY FRIENDLY.			
32s. LIKES TO BE BUSY DOING THINGS.			
33L. HAS PARENTS WHO DON'T UNDERSTAND ME.			
34s. GETS ALONG BEST WHEN I PAY ATTENTION TO OTHER PEOPLE'S FEELINGS.			
35a. SELDOM DOES WELL IN SCHOOL.			
36a. GETS ANGRY EASILY.			
37d. FINDS IT EASY TO PLAY BY MYSELF WHEN I HAVE TO.			
38s. DOESN'T PAY MUCH ATTENTION TO THE FEELINGS OF OTHER PEOPLE.			
39a. DOESN'T GET ANGRY VERY OFTEN.			
40d. FEELS I HAVE TROUBLE BECAUSE OTHER PEOPLE DON'T HELP ME.			

HEIGHT AGES FOR GIRLS

Height in Inches	Height Age	Height in Inches	Height Age	Height in Inches	Height Age	Height in Inches	Height Age
33.0	24	42.9	69	52.3	114	60.3	159
33.3	25	43.2	70	52.5	115	60.4	160
33.7	26	43.4	71	52.7	116	60.6	161
34.1	27	43.7	72	52.9	117	60.7	162
34.4	28	43.9	73	53.1	118	60.9	163
34.6	29	44.1	74	53.3	119	61.0	164
34.9	30	44.3	75	53.6	120	61.2	165
35.2	31	44.6	76	53.8	121	61.4	166
35.5	32	44.9	77	53.9	122	61.6	167
35.7	33	45.3	78	54.1	123	61.8	168
35.9	34	45.7	79	54.2	124	61.9	169
36.2	35	46.0	80	54.3	125	62.0	170
36.4	36	46.4	81	54.5	126	62.1	171
36.7	37	46.7	82	54.7	127	62.3	172
36.9	38	47.0	83	54.9	128	62.4	173
37.1	39	47.4	84	55.0	129	62.5	174
37.3	40	47.6	85	55.2	130	62.6	175
37.5	41	47.7	86	55.3	131	62.7	176
37.8	42	47.9	87	55.5	132	62.8	177
38.0	43	48.0	88	55.6	133	62.9	178
38.3	44	48.2	89	55.8	134	63.0	179
38.5	45	48.3	90	56.0	135	63.1	180
38.7	46	48.5	91	56.1	136	63.3	183
39.0	47	48.6	92	56.3	137	63.4	186
39.3	48	48.7	93	56.4	138	63.6	189
39.5	49	48.8	94	56.6	139	63.7	192
39.6	50	49.0	95	56.8	140	63.8	204
39.8	51	49.1	96	57.0	141		
40.0	52	49.2	97	57.2	142		
40.2	53	49.4	98	57.3	143		
40.4	54	49.5	99	57.5	144		
40.7	55	49.7	100	57.6	145		
41.0	56	49.8	101	57.8	146		
41.2	57	50.0	102	58.0	147		
41.3	58	50.1	103	58.2	148		
41.5	59	50.3	104	58.4	149		
41.7	60	50.5	105	58.6	150		
41.9	61	50.6	106	58.8	151		
42.0	62	50.8	107	59.0	152		
42.2	63	51.0	108	59.2	153		
42.3	64	51.3	109	59.4	154		
42.4	65	51.5	11C	59.6	155		
42.5	66	51.7	111	59.8	156		
42.6	67	51.9	112	60.0	157		
42.8	68	52.1	113	60.1	158		

The charts on this and the following five pages are from Willard C. Olson and Byron O. Hughes, *Manual for the Description of Growth in Age Units.* Ann Arbor: University Elementary School, University of Michigan, 1950.

WEIGHT AGES FOR GIRLS

Weight in Pounds	Weight Age	Weight in Pounds	Weight Age	Weight in Pounds	Weight Age	Weight in Pounds	Weight Age
24.6	24	38.9	69	65.1	114	98.7	159
25.0	25	39.4	70	65.7	115	99.5	160
25.4	26	39.8	71	66.4	116	100.3	161
25.8	27	40.3	72	67.1	117	101.1	162
26.1	28	41.2	73	67.8	118	101.9	163
26.5	29	42.0	74	68.5	119	102.7	164
26.9	30	42.8	75	69.2	120	103.5	165
27.2	31	43.6	76	69.7	121	104.3	166
27.6	32	44.5	77	70.3	122	105.1	167
27.9	33	45.3	78	70.8	123	106.0	168
28.2	34	46.1	79	71.4	124	107.0	169
28.5	35	46.9	80	71.9	125	108.0	170
28.8	36	47.7	81	72.5	126	109.0	171
29.3	37	48.5	82	73.0	127	110.0	172
29.7	38	49.3	83	73.6	128	111.0	173
30.2	39	50.2	84	74.1	129	112.0	174
30.5	40	50.5	85	74.7	130	113.0	175
30.8	41	50.8	86	75.2	131	114.0	176
31.0	42	51.1	87	75.8	132	115.0	177
31.2	43	51.4	88	76.5	133	116.0	178
31.3	44	51.7	89	77.1	134	117.0	179
31.5	45	52.0	90	77.8	135	118.0	180
31.7	46	52.3	91	78.4	136	119.5	183
32.0	47	52.6	92	79.0	137	121.0	186
32.2	48	52.9	93	79.6	138	122.0	189
32.6	49	53.2	94	80.3	139	123.0	192
33.1	50	53.5	95	81.0	140	124.0	195
33.6	51	53.8	96	81.7	141	125.0	200
33.7	52	54.5	97	82.4	142	126.0	204
33.9	53	55.1	98	83.0	143		
34.0	54	55.7	99	83.7	144		
34.5	55	56.3	100	84.7	145		
35.0	56	56.9	101	85.8	146		
35.4	57	57.6	102	86.8	147		
35.6	58	58.2	103	87.9	148		
35.8	59	58.8	104	88.9	149		
36.1	60	59.4	105	90.0	150		
36.3	61	60.0	106	91.0	151		
36.6	62	60.6	107	92.1	152		
36.8	63	61.2	108	93.1	153		
37.1	64	61.8	109	94.2	154		
37.3	65	62.5	110	95.2	155		
37.6	66	63.1	111	96.3	156		
38.0	67	63.8	112	97.1	157		
38.5	68	64.4	113	97.9	158		

AGE EQUIVALENTS FOR GIRLS FOR THE ERUPTION OF PERMANENT TEETH AND FOR THE STRENGTH OF GRIP

TEETH

Number of Teeth	Dental Age
1	69
2	71
3	73
4	74
5	77
6	80
7	83
8	86
9	89
10	92
11	97
12	103
13	108
14	112
15	116
16	118
17	121
18	123
19	126
20	128
21	130
22	133
23	136
24	138
25	141
26	145
27	152
28	153

GRIP

Kilograms	Grip Age	Kilograms	Grip Age
1.5	28.0	19.5	128
2.0	30.5	20.0	132
2.5	33.0	20.5	135
3.0	35.5	21.0	138
3.5	38	21.5	141
4.0	40	22.0	144
4.5	42	22.5	146
5.0	45	23.0	148
5.5	48	23.5	150
6.0	50	24.0	152
6.5	52	24.5	154
7.0	55	25.0	156
7.5	57	25.5	158
8.0	60	26.0	160
8.5	63	26.5	162
9.0	67	27.0	164
9.5	71	27.5	166
10.0	75	28.0	168
10.5	79	28.5	170
11.0	83	29.0	172
11.5	86	29.5	174
12.0	89	30.0	176
12.5	92	30.5	178
13.0	95	31.0	180
13.5	98	31.5	183
14.0	100	32.0	186
14.5	102	32.5	189
15.0	104	33.0	192
15.5	106	33.5	195
16.0	108	34.0	198
16.5	111	34.5	201
17.0	113	35.0	204
17.5	116		
18.0	118		
18.5	121		
19.0	124		

HEIGHT AGES FOR BOYS

Height in Inches	Height Age	Height in Inches	Height Age	Height in Inches	Height Age	Height in Inches	Height Age
33.8	24	45.8	74	54.1	124	63.1	174
34.1	25	46.0	75	54.2	125	63.5	175
34.4	26	46.2	76	54.3	126	63.7	176
34.6	27	46.4	77	54.4	127	63.9	177
34.8	28	46.6	78	54.5	128	64.1	178
35.0	29	46.8	79	54.7	129	64.2	179
35.2	30	47.0	80	54.8	130	64.3	180
35.5	31	47.2	81	55.0	131	64.5	181
35.9	32	47.4	82	55.2	132	64.7	182
36.2	33	47.6	83	55.3	133	64.9	183
36.4	34	47.9	84	55.4	134	65.1	184
36.6	35	48.0	85	55.6	135	65.3	185
36.9	36	48.2	86	55.7	136	65.5	186
37.2	37	48.3	87	55.9	137	65.7	187
37.4	38	48.5	88	56.1	138	65.9	188
37.6	39	48.6	89	56.3	139	66.1	189
37.9	40	48.8	90	56.4	140	66.3	190
38.2	41	48.9	91	56.5	141	66.5	191
38.4	42	49.1	92	56.6	142	66.8	192
38.6	43	49.2	93	56.8	143	66.9	193
38.9	44	49.4	94	57.0	144	67.0	194
39.1	45	49.5	95	57.2	145	67.1	195
39.2	46	49.7	96	57.4	146	67.2	196
39.3	47	49.8	97	57.6	147	67.3	197
39.4	48	49.9	98	57.8	148	67.4	198
39.5	49	50.1	99	58.0	149	67.5	199
39.8	50	50.2	100	58.3	150	67.6	200
40.1	51	50.3	101	58.5	151	67.7	201
40.3	52	50.5	102	58.7	152	67.8	202
40.5	53	50.6	103	58.9	153	67.9	203
40.7	54	50.7	104	59.2	154	68.0	204
41.0	55	50.9	105	59.4	155	68.1	205
41.3	56	51.0	106	59.6	156	68.2	206
41.6	57	51.2	107	59.8	157	68.3	207
41.7	58	51.3	108	60.0	158	68.4	208
41.8	59	51.4	109	60.1	159	68.5	209
42.0	60	51.6	110	60.3	160	68.6	210
42.1	61	51.8	111	60.5	161	68.7	211
42.2	62	52.0	112	60.7	162	68.8	212
42.3	63	52.2	113	60.9	163	68.9	213
42.6	64	52.4	114	61.1	164	69.0	214
43.0	65	52.6	115	61.3	165	69.1	215
43.3	66	52.8	116	61.5	166	69.2	216
43.5	67	52.9	117	61.7	167		
43.7	68	53.1	118	61.9	168		
44.0	69	53.3	119	62.1	169		
44.5	70	53.5	120	62.3	170		
45.0	71	53.6	121	62.5	171		
45.4	72	53.8	122	62.7	172		
45.6	73	53.9	123	62.9	173		

WEIGHT AGES FOR BOYS

Weight in Pounds	Weight Age	Weight in Pounds	Weight Age	Weight in Pounds	Weight Age	Weight in Pounds	Weight Age
26.3	24	44.1	74	67.8	124	104.0	174
26.6	25	44.8	75	68.3	125	105.0	175
26.9	26	45.5	76	68.8	126	106.0	176
27.2	27	46.1	77	69.3	127	107.0	177
27.6	28	46.7	78	69.8	128	108.0	178
28.0	29	47.3	79	70.3	129	109.0	179
28.4	30	48.0	80	70.8	130	110.0	180
28.8	31	48.6	81	71.4	131	111.0	181
29.2	32	49.2	82	71.9	132	112.0	182
29.6	33	49.8	83	72.5	133	112.8	183
30.0	34	50.4	84	73.0	134	113.6	184
30.4	35	50.8	85	73.5	135	114.4	185
30.8	36	51.1	86	74.0	136	115.2	186
31.1	37	51.4	87	74.6	137	116.2	187
31.4	38	51.7	88	75.1	138	117.2	188
31.6	39	52.1	89	75.6	139	118.2	189
32.0	40	52.4	90	76.1	140	119.2	190
32.4	41	52.7	91	76.7	141	120.2	191
32.9	42	53.0	92	77.3	142	121.2	192
33.4	43	53.4	93	77.8	143	122.0	193
33.6	44	53.7	94	78.3	144	122.8	194
34.0	45	54.1	95	79.1	145	123.6	195
34.3	46	54.4	96	80.0	146	124.4	196
34.6	47	54.9	97	80.8	147	125.2	197
34.9	48	55.4	98	81.7	148	126.0	198
35.0	49	55.9	99	82.5	149	126.8	199
35.1	50	56.5	100	83.3	150	127.6	200
35.2	51	57.0	101	84.1	151	128.4	201
35.4	52	57.5	102	84.9	152	129.2	202
35.6	53	58.0	103	85.8	153	130.0	203
35.8	54	58.5	104	86.6	154	130.5	204
36.2	55	59.0	105	87.5	155	131.3	205
36.7	56	59.5	106	88.3	156	132.1	206
37.1	57	60.1	107	89.1	157	132.9	207
37.4	58	60.6	108	89.9	158	133.7	208
37.7	59	61.0	109	90.7	159	134.5	209
37.9	60	61.5	110	91.5	160	135.3	210
38.0	61	62.0	111	92.3	161	136.1	211
38.2	62	62.4	112	93.1	162	136.9	212
38.4	63	62.8	113	94.0	163	137.7	213
38.8	64	63.3	114	94.8	164	138.4	214
39.5	65	63.8	115	95.6	165	139.2	215
40.2	66	64.2	116	96.4	166	140.0	216
40.5	67	64.6	117	97.2	167		
40.7	68	65.0	118	98.1	168		
41.0	69	65.4	119	99.0	169		
41.6	70	65.9	120	100.0	170		
42.3	71	66.4	121	101.0	171		
42.9	72	66.9	122	102.0	172		
43.5	73	67.3	123	103.0	173		

AGE EQUIVALENTS FOR BOYS FOR THE ERUPTION OF PERMANENT TEETH AND FOR THE STRENGTH OF GRIP

TEETH		GRIP					
Number of Teeth	Dental Age	Kilograms	Grip Age	Kilograms	Grip Age	Kilograms	Grip Age
1	70	2.5	28	20.0	121	37.5	195
2	73	3.0	30	20.5	124	38.0	196
3	76	3.5	33	21.0	127	38.5	197
4	78	4.0	35	21.5	130	39.0	199
5	81	4.5	37	22.0	133	39.5	200
6	83	5.0	39	22.5	136	40.0	201
7	85	5.5	41	23.0	139	40.5	203
8	88	6.0	44	23.5	142	41.0	205
9	92	6.5	46	24.0	144	41.5	206
10	96	7.0	48	24.5	146	42.0	207
11	101	7.5	51	25.0	148	42.5	209
12	107	8.0	53	25.5	149	43.0	210
13	113	8.5	55	26.0	151	43.5	211
14	118	9.0	57	26.5	152	44.0	213
15	122	9.5	59	27.0	154	44.5	214
16	125	10.0	63	27.5	155	45.0	216
17	127	10.5	67	28.0	157	45.5	217
18	131	11.0	71	28.5	159	46.0	219
19	134	11.5	75	29.0	162	46.5	220
20	136	12.0	79	29.5	164	47.0	221
21	138	12.5	83	30.0	167	47.5	223
22	139	13.0	86	30.5	169	48.0	225
23	143	13.5	89	31.0	172	48.5	226
24	144	14.0	92	31.5	175	49.0	229
25	146	14.5	95	32.0	177		
26	150	15.0	97	32.5	180		
27	156	15.5	99	33.0	182		
28	159	16.0	101	33.5	183		
		16.5	103	34.0	184		
		17.0	105	34.5	186		
		17.5	107	35.0	187		
		18.0	110	35.5	189		
		18.5	112	36.0	190		
		19.0	115	36.5	191		
		19.5	118	37.0	193		

FORM FOR PRELIMINARY RECORDING OF PHYSICAL DATA

NAME	BIRTH DATE	Age	Hgt.	H.A.	Wgt.	W.A.	Grip	G.A.	Age	Hgt.	H.A.	Wgt.	W.A.	Age	Hgt.	H.A.	Wgt.	W.A.	Grip	G.A.

INDIVIDUAL GROWTH RECORD CHART

NAME____________________ DATE OF BIRTH____________________ SEX__________

Grade — Year —	C. A.	H. A.	W. A.	G. A.	C. A.	D. A.	C. A.	M. A.	I. Q.	C. A.	Individual Tests

ACHIEVEMENT

Grade Year Date	P. M.	W. M.	Av. R.	Sp.	A. R.	A. C.	Av. A.	B. M.
Age Equivalent								
Grade Equivalent								
Grade Year Date								
Age Equivalent								
Grade Equivalent								
Grade Year Date								
Age Equivalent								
Grade Equivalent								
Grade Year Date								
Age Equivalent								
Grade Equivalent								

Grade Year Date	P. M.	W. M.	Av. R.	Sp.	A. R.	A. C.	Av. A.	B. M.
Age Equivalent								
Grade Equivalent								
Grade Year Date								
Age Equivalent								
Grade Equivalent								
Grade Year Date								
Age Equivalent								
Grade Equivalent								
Grade Year Date								
Age Equivalent								
Grade Equivalent								

CHILD STUDY OUTLINE

Name____ Grade________________
(last) (first)

Age____________ Date of Birth________________ Birthplace______________________

Sex_________ Church Membership____

Parents' Name________________________ Address___________________________

Parents' Occupation____________________ Socio-economic status________________

Parents' Attitude: cooperative, indifferent, actively uncooperative, belligerent

Family Atmosphere:

Family Constellation (List siblings chronologically):

Reason for Referral:

A General Statement of Problem:

Duration of Symptoms:

Health— General Physical Condition:____
Physician___________________________________

Previous Clinical Record:

Summary of Preschool Developmental History and Present Status:

School Progress and Attendance:
1. Reasons given by teachers for unusual achievement
2. Child's greatest asset
3. Child's best work
4. Child's poorest work

School Test Data:
1. Mental, intellectual
2. Achievement
3. Personal-social

Evaluation of Child's Academic Growth, Grades, Teacher Evaluations:

Child Study Techniques Utilized:
Autobiography
Interest Record
S.R.A. Jr. Inventory
Developmental History

Child Study Techniques Utilized (continued):
- Sentence Completion
- Life Style Guide
- Early Recollections
- Sociometric

Developmental Factors—provide anecdotal evidence:
1. Physical, organismic quotient
2. Love relationships
3. Cultural
4. Peer relation
5. Self-concept
6. Adjustment mechanisms

Values, Purposes, Faulty Assumptions:

Developmental Tasks Level:

Management of Life Tasks by the Child:
- Social—
  - Peers
  - Adults
- Work—
  - School
  - Outside of school
- Sex Role—
  - Values
  - Purposes, goals
  - Faulty assumptions

Corrective Actions Utilized:

Specific Encouragement Factors:
- Home
- School
- Recommendations

INDEX

V

W

Y

Z